Samuel Fuller

The Revelation of Saint John the Divine Self-Interpreted

Samuel Fuller

The Revelation of Saint John the Divine Self-Interpreted

ISBN/EAN: 9783337780012

Printed in Europe, USA, Canada, Australia, Japan

Cover: Foto ©Lupo / pixelio.de

More available books at **www.hansebooks.com**

THE REVELATION

OF

ST. JOHN THE DIVINE

SELF-INTERPRETED.

A COMMENTARY FOR ENGLISH READERS.

BY

THE REV. SAMUEL FULLER, D.D.,

PROFESSOR OF THE LITERATURE AND INTERPRETATION OF THE HOLY
SCRIPTURES IN THE BERKELEY DIVINITY SCHOOL,
MIDDLETOWN, CONN.

NEW YORK:
THOMAS WHITTAKER,
2 AND 3 BIBLE HOUSE.
1885.

Dedication.

TO HIS WIFE,

CHARLOTTE KINGMAN GREENLEAF,

FOR FIFTY-FIVE YEARS

THE PARTNER AND HELPER OF HIS LABORS AND STUDIES,

THE PAST AND PRESENT LIGHT, JOY, AND

LIFE OF HIS STUDY AND HOME,

This Volume is most fitly inscribed by the Author;

EVER PRAYING,

MAY WE BECOME POSSESSORS TOGETHER OF THE

GRACE OF ETERNAL LIFE IN THE

NEW JERUSALEM.

PREFACE.

AFTER centuries of virtual exclusion from the calendar, the Apocalypse of St. John is now inserted in the Tables of Lessons of Holy Scripture in the Book of Common Prayer. The last legacy of Christ to his church is beginning to be duly appreciated. Christians perceive that the inspired book, so long misunderstood and neglected, provides them with the most efficient armor in their incessant warfare with error and sin. They need courage and hopefulness: the Apocalypse abounds in these essential treasures.

The new position now occupied by the precious volume demands new recognition, and requires, on account of the enriching truths everywhere pervading its pages, familiar explanations in order to render its obscurities intelligible to all classes of readers.

We are painfully aware that many Christian people think the Book of Revelation a sealed depository. But our Lord himself does not fasten the arsenal with a seal. He ends each of his Epistles to the seven churches with this urgent exhortation: "He that hath an ear, let him hear what the Spirit saith unto the churches." He ends his parables with the same inviting encouragement. He evidently supposes his "unlearned and ignorant" first disciples can readily understand these figurative discourses. "How then will ye know *all* parables?" (Mark iv. 13.) Plainly, in Christ's judgment, the Book of Revelation is quite as intelligible as are his parables.

The book itself presumes that the first Christians comprehended its utterances. Without this presumption, the words which now follow are mockeries: "Blessed is he that readeth, and they that hear the words of this prophecy, and keep those things which are written therein" (Rev. i. 3). "Testify unto every man that heareth the words of the prophecy" (xxii. 18).

Since Christ made the Apocalypse to be understood, and since its first readers understood it, the book can be understood now. Christians of the nineteenth century can so far take the place of the first readers of the book as to "see with their eyes, and hear with their ears, and understand with their heart" (Isa. vi. 10). Whenever this possible internal substitution occurs, the discoveries and riches will be "pearls of great price" (Matt. xiii. 46).

The Apocalypse contains largely within itself the means of its own explanation. The very first voice St. John hears — "What thou seest, write in a book, and send it unto the seven churches which are in Asia" (i. 11) — reveals Jesus Christ as their *Judge;* since in the book he himself there utters both approvals and condemnations.

At this very spot does the Apocalypse itself open wide its own door of explanation. No reader is denied full and free entrance. Thus, Christ is *Supreme Judge* in the very first vision he grants us, and also throughout his seven Epistles.

In the second division of the Apocalypse (chapters iv.-xx. 1-10), *the Lamb is co-partner* with his Father in *the throne* of *judgment* erected at the beginning of the division (iv. 2), and sustained throughout the division. On this judgment-throne the Lamb is ever the same heart-searching Judge, deciding in this world the destinies of all men, and acting as Supreme Judge invisibly, and yet absolutely, so long as time itself shall last.

In chapter xx.11-13, the Son of God, even Christ (verse 6), is the *final* Judge of all the risen dead, both "small and great," whether buried on the unmeasured surfaces of the land, or in the unfathomable depths of the sea.

A throne of judgment does not exist without a court and its different actors. In the second division of the book, where Christ is the enthroned Judge, the plaintiff before the bar of his judgment-seat is his Church, ever living by succession, ever suffering, and ever pleading his vengeance (vi. 9, 10) against all her enemies in the present life, both heathen and nominally Christian.

The Judgeship of Christ is, therefore, one of the strong keys which render the opening of the many locks in this peculiar book ready and easy. Of this pervading subject of Christ's supreme Judgeship, the other portions of the volume are illustrations and confirmations.

Every person who reads the Apocalypse with this key the book itself provides, need not longer think its pages sealed and locked away from his knowledge. His progress may prompt him to exclaim, with St. Paul, "We are come unto Mount Sion, and unto the city of the living God, the heavenly Jerusalem, and to an innumerable company of angels, to the general assembly and church of the firstborn, which are written in heaven, and to God the Judge of all, and to the spirits of just men made perfect, and to Jesus the mediator of the new covenant, and to the blood of sprinkling, that speaketh better things than that of Abel" (Heb. xii. 22-24).

References to the principles of the original language of the Apocalypse could not be wholly avoided. Greek scholars will appreciate the necessity. The swell of the sea is always quickly felt by the experienced navigator. An actual voyage on the ocean sharpens practised eyes to discern, not only the underlying quicksands, but also the profound depths no line can fathom.

The Greek text of Westcott & Hort is used in this volume.

CONTENTS.

FIRST DIVISION.

	PAGE
CHAPTER I.	3
CHAPTER II.	21
CHAPTER III.	53

SECOND DIVISION. PART I.

CHAPTER IV.	95
CHAPTER V.	102
CHAPTER VI.	110
CHAPTER VII.	124
CHAPTER VIII.	133
CHAPTER IX.	143

SECOND DIVISION. PART II.

CHAPTER X.	157
CHAPTER XI.	165
CHAPTER XII.	189
CHAPTER XIII.	203
CHAPTER XIV.	235
CHAPTER XV.	249
CHAPTER XVI.	260
CHAPTER XVII.	279
CHAPTER XVIII.	294
CHAPTER XIX.	309
CHAPTER XX.	324

THIRD DIVISION.

CHAPTER XX. — *continued*	350
CHAPTER XXI.	356
CHAPTER XXII.	374

DIVISIONS.

The Book of Revelation separates itself into three divisions (chapter i. 4–7).

FIRST DIVISION.

The epistles to the seven churches (chapters i.–iii.).

SECOND DIVISION.

The symbolic history of the Church of Christ *before* his second advent (chapters iv.–xx. 10); namely, the various conflicts and triumphs of the Church.

The second division of the Apocalypse has two parts:—

1. The judgments of God on the heathen world (chapters iv.–ix.).

2. His judgments upon his apostate Church (chapters x.–xx. 10).

THIRD DIVISION.

The Church and the world of mankind *after* the second advent of our Lord, and the universal judgment (chapters xx. 11–xxii.).

The last judgment and its consequences (chapter xxii. 6–20 is a summary of the second division).

THE REVELATION OF ST. JOHN THE DIVINE.

FIRST DIVISION (Chapters i.–iii.).

CHAPTER I.

THE PREFACE (Verses 1–3).

1. THE Revelation of Jesus Christ, which God gave him, to shew in vision to his servants the events which must shortly come to pass: so in symbols he signified them by sending through his angel to his servant John.

The Revelation of Jesus Christ: the revelation of which he is the Author. The revelation he "shewed and signified" (verse 1).
God: the Father (see verse 6). "The times and seasons the Father hath put in his own power" (Acts i. 7).
To shew in vision: all things that he *saw* (verse 2).
His servants: Christ's people; *my* servants (ii. 20).
The events which: the antecedent (implied in "which") is embodied in the verb below, "come to pass."
Must: the Greek verb denotes *objective* necessity, created by God's purposes. On the contrary, "ought" (St. John xiii. 14) expresses the duty on its *subjective* side.
Shortly: a portion of the events predicted in the Apocalypse began to be fulfilled immediately. The complete fulfilment is even now still in the future.
So: the Greek particle has this meaning (xvii. 3): "so he carried me away."

He: Christ. "I Jesus have sent mine angel" (xxii. 16).

In symbols he signified them: the Greek verb has this signification. St. John xii. 33, "signifying what death he should die;" xxi. 19, "signifying by what death he should glorify God."

By sending: the Greek participle, because *following* its verb, describes *manner*. "So making peace" (Eph. ii. 15) is an instance.

Angel: Christ's interpreting angel (xxii. 6, 16).

Servant: Christ's prophetic servant (xxii. 9).

John: the apostle and evangelist, who, besides the Book of Revelation, wrote the fourth Gospel and three Epistles bearing his name.

2. Who testifies of the word of God, even of the testimony of Jesus Christ; that is, of all the visions he saw.

Testifies: in this book. The narrative aorist tense has the force of the present.

Who testifies: no other New-Testament writer but St. John applies this title of testifier to himself. Whenever, therefore, the title appears in any writing, it designates him as the author of the writing. He gives himself this title (John xix. 35, and 1 John i. 2). Its appearance here (Rev. i. 2) identifies him with John the apostle and evangelist, and thus proves that the author of the fourth Gospel and of the three Epistles of St. John is also the author of the Apocalypse.

Even: in the expression, "the word of their testimony" (xii. 11) (with this sense, the word *containing* their testimony), the testimony *explains* the preceding phrase, — the word. Since "testimony" is explanatory in xii. 11, "testimony" is explanatory in i. 1; and *even* is the meaning of the Greek conjunction between the two phrases, "the word of God," and "the testimony of Jesus Christ."

The testimony of Jesus Christ: the testimony he himself gives. He is "the faithful and true witness" (iii. 14).

That is: the clause, "all the visions he saw," is in apposition with the expression, "the testimony of Jesus Christ;" that is, expresses this apposition.

The visions he saw: only *in vision* ("I saw in vision," ix. 17) did St. John see the objects he describes in this book.

3. Blessed is he that readeth, and blessed are they that obey, the words of this prophecy, and keep the writings in it; for the time is at hand.

Obey: this sense of the Greek verb is warranted by iii. 20, "hear [obey] my voice." "He that readeth," and "they that obey," constitute but *one class of persons*. This is St. John's own usage in the Apocalypse, and in a beatitude example: "Blessed is *he that hath* [every one that hath, all that have] part in the first resurrection: on *such* [Greek, *these*] the second death hath no power, but *they* shall be priests of God" (xx. 6).

This usage, in xx. 6, forbids the explanation (Bible Commentary, vol. iv. p. 499) which, in i. 3, finds two classes, — the public reader of the Apocalypse in the days of St. John, and the public hearers of this reader.

Keep: observe (xii. 17).

Writings: the Greek participle signifies engraved, pictured, as well as written. The seven scrolls "written" (v. 1.) are covered with pictured emblems (vi. 1-8, etc.).

In it: in this prophecy, in this prophetical book.

For: gives the reason for reading, obeying, and holding fast the new revelations; namely, the time of their fulfilment is fast approaching; obedience will soon be rewarded; negligence will soon be punished.

The time: when the prophecies of the Apocalypse will begin to be fulfilled (1 Pet. iv. 17).

At hand: is coming near. The first time Christ appears in the Apocalypse, he appears as a judge (i. 10-18). With his appearance, then, his rewards and punishments in this life also begin to appear, and continue to appear throughout the second division of this book.

THE PROLOGUE (Verses 4-8).

This portion summarizes the contents of the entire book, by the following threefold division : —

(1) The seven churches, which represent the church universal (verse 4, first clause).

(2) The love of Christ, in the Apocalypse (verses 4-6).

(3) The justice of Christ, in the Apocalypse (verses 7, 8). The mention of Christ's love here *precedes* the mention of his justice, to assure us that "mercy rejoiceth against judgment" (Jas. ii. 13).

The prologue is to be explained, so far as possible, by the Apocalypse itself.

---

4. John to the seven churches which are in Asia : Grace be unto you, and peace, from him who is, and who was, and

who is to come; and from the seven Spirits which are before his throne.

(1) **Seven**: Ephesus (ii. 1), Smyrna (8), Pergamos (12), Thyatira (18), Sardis (iii. 1), Philadelphia (7), Laodicea (14; i. 11).

Besides the seven churches enumerated (i. 11), there were certainly, in Asia, three others: Colosse (Col. i. 1), Miletus (Acts xx. 17), Hierapolis (Col. iv. 13).

As seven is a complete number (Gen. vii. 2), the seven churches of Asia are representative, in their circumstances and character, of the "church universal," called "the churches" (Rev. ii. 7, 17, 29; iii. 6, 13, 22; xxii. 16).

Asia: Proconsular Asia (of which Ephesus was the capital), comprehending the western provinces of Mysia, Lydia, Caria, and part of Phrygia.

(2) **Grace**: the divine love manifesting itself to man.

Peace: the state resulting from the reception of this love.

Who is: the Self-existent (Exod. iii. 14). Here, God the Father.

Who was: the Eternal in the past, "from everlasting" (xi. 15, 17; Ps. xciii. 2).

Who is to come: to judgment. This is the explanation given by verse 7, "He comes *with clouds*" (xxii. 7, 12, 20).

Who is coming continually in this world, both to reward and to punish. He is thus exhibited in the first and second divisions of the Apocalypse, as the *present* Judge and Ruler of the world of mankind.

In verse 5, the Son of God is associated with the Father and Holy Spirit.

The seven Spirits: since the seven Spirits are the equivalent of the personal Holy Spirit (ii. 7, etc.), they must denote the Holy Spirit *in his various manifestations*.

Thus, St. John invokes grace and peace from the three Persons of the adorable Godhead.

Before the throne: in verse 6, the seven Spirits are "sent forth into all the earth;" they are therefore "before the throne," because they are *in readiness* to be sent into the hearts of all men.

5. And from Jesus Christ, the faithful witness, the firstborn from the dead, and the ruler of the kings of the earth. Unto him who loves us, and washes us thoroughly from our sins by his own blood.

Faithful: trustworthy (1 John i. 9).

The firstborn from the dead: St. Paul explains this appellation of Christ when he calls him "the firstfruits" (1 Cor. xv. 20) "of them that are now sleeping in Jesus" (1 Thess. iv. 14).

Of all human beings, our risen and ascended Messiah is the only one who as yet hath *bodily* immortality (1 Tim. vi. 16). That "immortality" in this place is only *bodily*, is certain from 1 Cor. xv. 53, 54, where "immortality" must be solely *bodily*, because contrasted with "mortal" and "corruptible," and with *bodily* "death" (verses 55, 56).

"Immortality" (Rom. ii. 7) has the same meaning. Bodily immortality is the special object of St. Paul's constant desire (Phil. iii. 11).

The Ruler: Jesus Christ is the Supreme Ruler of all kings and nations (Matt. xxviii. 18; 1 Tim. vi. 15). No pope can be this ruler.

The present love of Christ is his perpetual legacy and gift to his Church, and its unceasing fruition and enrichment (John xiii. 1).

Loves us, and washes us thoroughly from our sins: the Greek tenses here describe *present* actions. The Revision, 1881, has "loosed us." But *nowhere* in Bible Greek is "loosed" used with sins. "Wash" is repeatedly so connected (John xiii. 10; 1 John i. 7; Heb. x. 22). Usage is often of greater authority than manuscripts, and must be here. The Vulgate has *lavit*, "washes" (Gnomic "perfect").

Thoroughly: out of, is the meaning of the Greek preposition.

By: the Greek preposition is instrumental; required by Heb. x. 22, "washed *with*."

Blood: *shed* blood. "My blood *shed*" (Matt. xxvi. 28).

6. And makes us a kingdom, priests unto God, even his Father. To him the glory and the power due, for ever and ever. Amen.

Makes: "loves" (verse 4) imparts its own present time to "makes;" makes us, forms us into.

A kingdom: a *spiritual* kingdom (John xviii. 36).

Priests: *even* priests. In verse 10, the Greek demands this translation: "Unto our God a kingdom, even priests." Both in i. 6, and v. 10, the word "priests" is explanatory. "A kingdom of priests" (Exod. xix. 6); that is, devoted to God's service.

St. Peter defines the nature of this priesthood, making it *spiritual*, like the kingdom; "a holy priesthood, to offer up *spiritual* sacrifices" (1 Pet. ii. 5). Neither the kingdom nor the priesthood, in Rev. i. 5, is *external*. St. John does not here create and authorize laymen and lay-women to be literal priests in the church of Christ.

Unto God, even his Father: Granville Sharp, 1790, thus describes the usage, when, in the New Testament the conjunction *and*, becomes *even:*—

"When two or more personal nouns of the same gender, number, and case are connected by the copulative *and*, if the first has the definite article, and the second, third, etc., have not, *they both relate to the same person*."— AYRE, *Introduction Old Testament*, p. 216.

"God, *even* the Father of our Lord Jesus Christ" (Rom. xv. 6; also 2 Cor. i. 3; Eph. i. 3, Greek).

The English Version thus recognizes the usage, and anticipates Granville Sharp's rule by more than one hundred and fifty years.

Amen: St. John's affirmation and prayer. So be it.

7. Behold, he cometh with the clouds, and every eye shall see him; even all they who are piercing him: and all the tribes of the earth shall wail because of him. Yea, Amen.

(3) **Behold**: let every hearer consider the present subject with personal interest.

He: who loves us (verse 5).

Cometh: quickly (ii. 5, 16; iii. 11; xxii. 7, 12, 20), to administer justice. The reference here is not to the last and universal judgment-day, at Christ's second and final advent.

With the clouds: of punishment (xiv. 14–16). The imagery is from a thunder-storm, and describes Christ's present judgments. From thunder-clouds God "scatters and discomfits," in King David's time (Ps. xviii. 10–14).

"The Lord rideth upon a swift cloud, and shall come into Egypt. The Lord shall *smite* Egypt" (Isa. xix. 1, 22).

Into Egypt Jehovah came with a *single* cloud of punishment. In Rev. i. 7, the Lord Jesus Christ is in this world continually coming with *many* punitive clouds. The plural here denotes an indefinite number.

Every eye: eye for the person who sees. "No eye [no person] pities him" (Ezek. xvi. 5). Every person; that is, all persons.

Shall see: shall perceive *with the mind:*—

(*a*) by faith. "Seeing him who is invisible" (Heb. xi. 27).

(*b*) by the judgment. "I perceive that thou art in the gall of bitterness" (Acts viii. 23). "Ye see that a man is justified" Jas. ii. 24.

(*c*) by consciousness. "I see another law in my members" (Rom. vii. 23.

Rev. vi. 15, 16, afford an illustration of mental seeing, and a fulfilment of the prediction, "Every eye shall see him."

Him: Christ, *as Judge*. "In righteousness doth he *judge*" (xix. 11).

Even they who are piercing him: this clause explains the clause immediately preceding. Even they who are piercing Christ shall see their guilt and danger.

All they who: the Greek of Acts x. 41, 47, requires this translation.

Are piercing: this verb first occurs in Zech. xii. 10, where it is, according to John xix. 37, a prediction of the piercing of our Lord's hands and feet (Ps. xxii. 16) when he was nailed to the cross, and was thus crucified and cursed for our sins (Gal. iii. 13). Only his hands and feet were pierced in his crucifixion. The Roman soldier did not pierce his side. The Greek verb translated "pierced" (John xix. 34) appears in Bible Greek in only one other place (Ecclus. xxii. 19), where it describes a prick in a man's eye, and this so slight that it does not bring blood, but merely "tears." A spear-stroke of this mildness could not have *entered*, much less "pierced," our Saviour's dead and stiffened side.

St. Paul explains the nature of the piercing of which St. John speaks (Rev. i. 7). "They crucify to themselves the Son of God *afresh*" (Heb. vi. 6). A "fresh crucifixion" can be only in the spirit and intention of the crucifier. This "fresh crucifixion" is such hatred of Christ as would lead its possessor, could the mad scene be repeated, to shout with the Jewish rabble, "Crucify him, crucify him!" (Mark xv. 13, 14.)

Very many are always thus piercing Christ, and "putting him to an open shame," in every period of the world's history, and in every place where he is now preached as the only Saviour of lost men.

All the tribes of the earth: in contrast with the "twelve tribes of the children of Israel" (vii. 4), the representatives of the Christian Church; and therefore "all the tribes of the earth" is another name for "the world lying in wickedness" (1 John v. 19).

"The earth" is often, in the Bible, the synonyme of depravity and wickedness. "He that is of *the earth* is *earthly*" (John iii. 31).

Shall wail: shall beat themselves through grief; shall mourn most bitterly. "In that day shall there be a great mourning in Jerusalem, as the mourning of Hadadrimmon in the valley of Megiddon" (Zech. xii. 11), when the good king Josiah was killed in battle (2 Chron. xxxv. 20-25).

Because of him: from regard for Christ:—

(*a*) regard for his love (verses 5, 6). "We love him because he first loved us" (1 John iv. 19). "The love of Christ constraineth us" (2 Cor. v. 14).

(b) regard for his justice. "The great day of his wrath is come, and who shall be able to stand?" (Rev. vi. 17.)

Yea, Amen: in St. John's double affirmation and prayer, "Yea" translates a Greek affirmation; "Amen" translates a Hebrew affirmation.

The language of this verse 7 predicts the great success of the gospel of Christ in this world. His lifting-up draws all men to him (John xii. 32). He designs his judgments for our reformation. He chastens us "for our profit" (Heb. xii. 10). This declaration is confirmed by experience. "Before I was afflicted I went astray, but now have I kept thy word" (Ps. cxix. 67).

8. I myself am the Alpha and the Omega, saith the Lord God, who is, and who was, and who is to come, the Almighty.

The Alpha and the Omega: the first and last letters of the Greek alphabet are (verse 11) explained as meaning "the first and the last," and are therefore designations of eternity. In verse 11, "Alpha" and "Omega" are appellations of the *Son of God*. In verse 17, "the first and the last" are also appellations of the Son.

Alpha and Omega occur elsewhere in the Apocalypse only xxi. 6, and xxii. 13.

In xxi. 6, "I am Alpha and Omega, the beginning and the end," the promise, in the same verse, "I will give unto him that is athirst of the fountain of the water of life freely," connects this verse with vii. 17, "The Lamb shall lead them unto living fountains of waters;" and thus decides that the Alpha and the Omega of xxi. 6 is no other than the Lamb.

Equally certain is it that Alpha and Omega (xxii. 13) designates the Son of God. The immediate context establishes this certainty: "I come quickly," verse 12 ; "I am Alpha and Omega," verse 13.

Thus complete is the proof that the appellation Alpha and Omega (Rev. i. 8) designates *the Son of God*, and not the Father. Four times only does the appellation occur in the Apocalypse. Three times the appellation designates the Son of God. As these places *follow* Rev. i. 8, they are not only all the places which can possibly define this verse 8, but they are the explanations and definitions St. John himself creates and authorizes.

The Lord God: Lord means Supreme Ruler. God is thus defined by St. John: "God is light, and in him is no darkness at all" (1 John i. 5).

Almighty; all-powerful. "All power is given me" (Matt. xxviii. 18).

The several divine appellations — all of which are ascribed to the *Son of God* — magnify his Deity, and render it absolute.

THE FIRST VISION ST. JOHN HAS OF JESUS CHRIST
(i. 9–iii. 22).

The vision consists of —

(1) The manifestation of Jesus Christ to St. John (i. 9–20).

(2) The epistles to the seven churches of Asia (chapters ii., iii.).

9. I John, myself, your brother and joint partaker in the tribulation and kingdom and patience in Jesus, was for a time in the island which is called Patmos, for the word of God, even the testimony concerning Jesus.

John myself: the very John to whom Jesus Christ gave the revelation (verse 1). He is about to describe the circumstances of the revelation, and the prophetic commission he received from Christ with it.

Your brother: St. John and the members of the seven churches form a Christian brotherhood, because they are all animated by the same spiritual life Christ gives all his people.

Joint partaker: in the tribulation Christians are now enduring. It is a time of persecution by the Roman government (ii. 13); and St. John, banished to Patmos because he is a Christian, is a fellow-sufferer.

The tribulation: because the article *the* unites the three nouns — "tribulation" and "kingdom" and "patience" — in one group, they constitute the common allotment of Christians at the time.

And kingdom: because himself a spiritual king, St. John is enduring the distress inherent in Christ's kingdom. "In the world ye shall have tribulation" (John xvi. 33).

And patience: tribulation not only demands, but also works out, patience (Rom. v. 3). Patience itself inherits God's promises (Heb. vi. 12).

In Jesus: in the fellowship of Jesus (1 Cor. i. 9). The participation of the life of Christ involves the participation of his sufferings (John xv. 20; 1 Pet. iv. 13).

Was for a time: the Greek verb sometimes describes *temporary* being.

The time was about A.D. 95.

Patmos: a rocky island in the Ægean Sea, about thirty miles in circumference, and about forty miles from the mainland, and the mouth of the river Meander and the city Miletus.

The Apostle John was banished to this island by the Emperor Domitian, A.D. 81-96. The Emperor Nerva restored him to Ephesus, A.D. 96.

Even: see i. 2.

10. I was in the Spirit on the Lord's day, and I heard behind me a great voice as of a trumpet.

Was in the Spirit: was entranced by the Spirit (Acts xxii. 17). In a trance saw a vision (xi. 5).

The Lord's day:

(1) Our Lord rose from the dead on the first day of the week (Matt. xxviii. 1).

(2) The first Christians celebrated the Lord's Supper on the first day of the week (Acts xx. 7).

(3) Chrysostom testifies that this first day — mentioned Acts xx. 7 — is the Lord's day. — WORDSWORTH, *in loco*.

(4) "The Son of man is Lord of the sabbath" (Mark ii. 28).

(5) The word "Lord," in the expression "Lord's day," is, in the Greek, an adjective, and denotes *proprietorship*. The first day of the week is the Lord's day, because it belongs to him. *He made the day what it now is. He changed the sabbath from the seventh day of the week to the first day.*

There are intimations in the Bible why the manifestation of the Son of man to St. John occurred on the Lord's day: —

(1) He thus recognizes and honors his own day.

(2) The sabbath is an institution of blessing (Exod. xx. 11).

(3) To the Jews, the seventh day was a season of instruction and illumination from God. "Moses of old time hath in every city them that preach him, *being read* in the synagogues *every sabbath day*" (Acts xv. 21).

(4) On the sabbath day our Lord revealed himself to the Jews as God's anointed messenger (Luke iv. 18).

(5) In his manifestation to St. John, our Lord is a Revelator.

(6) In selecting his own day as the time of his manifestation, our Lord not only recognizes and honors the day, but also perpetuates the purpose of the sabbath as a season of blessing, and repeats the

illumination he grants the Nazarenes in their synagogue, by new revelations to his servant John.

Behind me: the terrors of the vision are presented gradually (Ezek. iii. 12). Were the trumpet-voice *in front* of St. John, his sight, as well as hearing, would be addressed, and produce an effect beyond all endurance.

Trumpet: heralds the infliction of judgments (viii. 13). With trumpet-voice God spake terrors from Mount Sinai (Exod. xix. 19).

11. Saying, The sight thou art seeing write in a book, and send it by the hand of messengers to the seven churches which are in Asia ; to Ephesus, and to Smyrna, and to Pergamos, and to Thyatira, and to Sardis, and to Philadelphia, and to Laodicea.

Art seeing: in the vision now beginning, and in the visions following.

Book: volume; a book was, in the time of St. John, a rolled scroll (Luke iv. 17).

By the hand of messengers: this is implied from Isa. xxxvii. 14. A separate scroll was sent to each of the churches.

12. And I turned to see the voice which was speaking to me, and when I turned I saw seven golden lamp-stands.

Voice: for the speaker (iv. 1). "There came *a voice* to him, Rise, Peter; kill and eat. But Peter said, Not so, *Lord*" (Acts x. 13, 14).

Lamp-stands: each lamp-stand was like the original golden candlestick, with its seven bowls or lamps on seven branches from the main stem (Exod. xxv. 31, 32; Zech. iv. 2). The lamp holding the oil was somewhat like a flattened bottle, with the wick issuing from the neck.

In this verse the seven lamp-stands are symbols of the seven churches of Asia. Each church is a lamp-stand lighted by Christ to shed abroad his revealed light (Matt. v. 14; Phil. ii. 16).

VISION OF THE SON OF MAN (Verses 13-16).

The shining constellations in the sky at night guided the ancient mariners safely in their devious and perilous voyages. The bright and illuminating symbols, with which the Holy Spirit by St. John fills the Apocalyptic heaven of prophecy, are our beckoning constellations on the dangerous voyage of our present inquiries. These prophetic symbols will surely conduct us to the calm and blissful "haven where we would be," on these two practicable conditions: (*a*) Find the position and design of each enlightening star; (*b*) Follow the radiant path the sparkling gem traces for our footsteps.

---

13. And in the midst of the lamp-stands a Person, like the Son of man, clothed with a garment falling to the feet, and girded close to the breasts with a golden girdle.

In the midst: the seven golden lamp-stands encircle the likeness of the Son of man. All are under the searching glance of his eyes of fire.

Like: the person in the vision seen by St. John is merely *like* the Son of man. The Son of man is not actually present. The symbolic description of the Son of man, chapter i., does not exhibit his person as he really now exists. His head is not actually white, neither his eyes nor his feet are real lightning-flashes; his tongue is not a real sword; his voice is not actually like the deafening roar of the restless ocean.

The *non-reality* of symbols must be our constant guide in the interpretation of this book of visions.

Likeness (not sameness, identity) is the characteristic of all the exhibitions in the Apocalypse. The neglect of this fact is the cause of very many of the erroneous interpretations of the book. The observance of the fact will insure correct explanations.

Son of man: (1) this expression, though without the article in the Greek, is not *a* Son of man, but is *the* Son of man; for the person here called in Greek, Son of man, is in ii. 18 "*the* Son of God." Son of man (i. 13) and the Son of God (ii. 18) are the *same* person. Because he is the Son of God, (*a*) he is not *a* Son of man, but *the* Son of man: (*b*) he is not *human*, but is *divine*.

(2) Greek words indicating *likeness* omit the article from the words which follow, and yet the article must be *expressed* in English. In i. 15, "as *the* voice of many waters" is in Greek thus: "as voice of many waters." This usage of comparative words requires us to translate the exact Greek, "like Son of man," "like *the* Son of man." No Greek would here translate, "*a* Son of man."

Clothed with a garment falling to the feet: in the following description, each member of the person of our Lord exhibits a different attribute of his divine nature, or performs a different action of almighty power.

Clothed: *self*-clothed. This is the peculiar sense of the Greek verb.

The Greek here identifies the imagery with Ezek. ix. 2, "Six men came, every man a slaughter weapon in his hand; one man among them *clothed with linen*, with a writer's inkhorn by his side."

In Lev. xvi. 4, the "linen coat" worn by Aaron is the *inner* tunic, because it is the *first* garment put upon him. The garment, therefore, seen by St. John on the person of our Lord, is referable to the *inner* tunic worn by the Aaronic high priest, and is a *sacerdotal* dress. It is, however, a *robe*, either priestly or royal.

The nature of the garment worn here by our Lord indicates his purpose. He appears, not for the display of kingly power, but, like Ezekiel's clerical scribe with an inkhorn at his side and a slaughter weapon in his hand, *to record sins, and to execute judgments.*

Girded close to the breasts with a golden girdle: the dative case in the Greek, indicating the closeness of the girdle to the breasts shows both the width and the strength of the girdle, and also the strength and power of our Lord the wearer.

14. And his head, even his hairs were white as it were white wool, as snow, and his sight swift as lightning.

White: *shining* white.

The whiteness denotes great age. "The *Ancient* of days" (Dan. vii. 9). The imagery in this verse is taken from the prophet Daniel; and not from Matt. xvii. 2, Mark ix. 3, as there our Lord's *head* is not mentioned. The whiteness, by being threefold (white, white wool, snow), is greatly intensified, and denotes unlimited age, even eternity.

"The eyes" here is another expression for sight (Mark xii. 11). Flame of fire is lightning (Ps. civ. 4).

15. And his feet, as on fire in a furnace, swift like the flashing lightning; and his voice as the voice of many waters.

"Fire" and "burned" (English Version) are synonymes. For this reason, the last clause of verse 14 and the first clause of verse 15 form a *synonymous* parallelism. Since a flame of fire (verse 14) is swift lightning; swift lightning, resembling "fine brass," that is, "polished [flashing] brass" (Dan. x. 6), is also intended (verse 15), because the two clauses are synonymous.

Rev. x. 1 confirms the explanation of "fine brass" we have just given. The mighty angel (x. 1), who is a symbol of Christ, has feet which are "as pillars of fire;" that is, are like the straight and brilliant white lines of flashing lightning on a thunder-cloud. These lightning-figures represent the feet as moving with inconceivable swiftness.

"Fine," refined; as silver and gold in the fire (Zech. xiii. 9).

The voice of mighty waters: the roar of the waves of the ocean (Ezek. xliii. 2; Rev. xiv. 2, xix. 6).

In Rev. xix. 6, "many" is the equivalent of "mighty." The substitution of "mighty" for "many" (English Version) is thus justified. St. John's images here are surpassingly sublime.

16. And holding in his right hand seven stars; and out of his mouth a sharp two-edged sword coming forth; and his appearance, as [when] the sun shineth in his strength.

In his right hand: the position at the right hand is most honorable (Matt. xxii. 44).

Seven stars: these stars may have been the gems of the signet-rings on the right hand of the Person now manifesting himself: —

(1) In the time of St. John, a man of high rank wore several signet-rings upon his right hand.

(2) This signet-ring was ornamented with precious stones.

(3) The gems of the signet-ring were sometimes called stars.[1]

The Son of man is about to send epistles to the seven churches of Asia. Some of the epistles contain severe and threatening reproofs. The seven stars — tokens of affection (Jer. xxii. 24) — assure the churches, that although he finds in them faults, and threatens to punish, they still have his love. The seven stars, as tokens of his affection, give emphasis to this declaration of his, "*As many as I love, I rebuke and chasten*" (Rev. iii. 19).

In their design, the seven stars on the right hand of the Son of man resemble the "rainbow round about the throne" of judgment (Rev. iv. 3). Both stars and rainbow symbolize the lesson, so welcome at all times to suffering hearts: in wrath God remembers mercy (Hab. iii. 2).

Out of his mouth: opened in anger. "His lips are full of indignation" (Isa. xxx. 27).

A sharp two-edged sword: this is the heavy broadsword of Thrace. The Grecian sword was shorter and lighter. Christ's sword in the Apocalypse is the Thracian blade, and is always the emblem of judgment and death (ii. 12, 16; xix. 15, 21).

---

[1] Liddell & Scott, Greek Lexicon.

Going forth: the sword is incessant in its action. His justice is an unceasing power.

His appearance, as [when] the sun shineth in his strength: the appearance of his whole person shone like the brightness of the meridian sun. In the Apocalypse, St. John for "face" invariably uses a different Greek noun from the one he employs here, which (John vii. 24) means "appearance."

Christ calls himself "the light of the world" (John viii. 12). As with the light of the meridian sun, he is now to illumine the future history of his Church and the world.

17. And when I saw him, I fell at his feet as dead. And he laid his right hand upon me, saying, Fear not; I myself am the First and the Last.

As dead: the unearthly splendors of the vision deprive St. John of all strength (Dan. x. 8).

Laid his right hand: a sign of favor (Matt. ix. 18).

The First and the Last: I am eternal. The eternity of Christ is the foundation and pledge of his unchanging love, both for St. John and for the Church (Deut. xxxiii. 27).

18. Even He who is living. And yet I was dead for a time; and yet, behold, I am living for ever and ever; and so I hold the keys of death and of hades.

Even: explains the preceding assertion, "I myself am the First and the Last."

He who is living: explains the First and the Last.

And yet: contrasting his life and death. The Greek verb here describes a *temporary* action.

For ever and ever: in contrast with the short time he was dead.

And so: the consequence of his possession of life eternal.

The keys: the power over (iii. 7). Hades is represented (Matt. xvi. 18, and here) as having "gates," to be opened by "keys."

Death: the separation of soul and body.

Hades: the invisible world, into which the soul enters at the death of the body. Fear not (verse 17). Nothing can harm you. Death cannot kill your soul. Hades cannot receive you until I open the door for your departure from this life. "Because I live, ye shall live also" (John xiv. 19).

19. Accordingly, write the visions which thou art seeing, —

both visions which are now, and the visions which are certainly to appear after these present visions.

Accordingly: looks back to the vision of Christ's Person (verses 11–16).

The visions thou art seeing: namely, in the Isle of Patmos, beginning with the vision of Christ's Person, and ending with the completion of the entire Book of Revelation.

The visions which are now: the visions described in chapters ii. and iii.

"The visions which are now, and the visions which are certainly to appear," divide the Apocalypse into two parts, — the present and the future. The present visions occupy chapters ii. and iii. The future visions fill the remaining chapters of the book.

20. The mystery of the seven stars which thou sawest on my right hand, and of the seven golden lamp-stands. [This is the explanation.] The stars are the angels of the seven churches, and the seven lamp-stands are the seven churches.

Are: that is, *represent*. Thus, Rev. iv. 5; Matt. xiii. 37–39, xxvi. 26.

The stars may be signet-gems (verse 16), and emblems of Christ's affection for the angels who represent the churches. The stars represent the angels. The angels represent the churches. Through this twofold representation, Christ exhibits and demonstrates his love for the seven churches. Since merely *representations*, the angels cannot be *proved* real Christian bishops. That they are, *must be assumed*.

Who are the seven angels of this verse?

The imagery of the seven angels is, we may conclude, derived from the prophet Zechariah, and therefore from no other source.

1. St. John employs elsewhere imagery taken from this very prophet.

(*a*) The "book written within and on the backside" (Rev. v. 1) is taken from Zech. v. 2, 3.

(*b*) "The two olive-trees and the two candlesticks" (Rev. xi. 4) must be referred to Zech. iv. 11.

Thus referring to Zechariah in these places, St. John may have previously referred to this prophet in Rev. i. 20, and in chapters ii. and iii.

2. Each angel in Rev. ii. and iii. represents a Christian church, and communicates to it divine revelations.

There is precisely *the same kind* of representation and of communication in the prophet Zechariah: —

(*a*) In Zech. i. 12, and elsewhere, whenever the angel appears, he acts *in behalf of the city Jerusalem, the old church of God;*

(*b*) And declares to it his revealed purposes (Zech. i. 13, etc., iii. 6, etc., iv. 14, v. 3, vi. 5).

The symbolic character of the Apocalypse deprives the seven angels of all *literalness,* and of all *literal* ministerial office, either as presbyters or primates. The seven angels are *symbols,* and not *actual* servants of the gospel. Since the angels in Zechariah, *the originals* of the angels in Rev. i. 20, ii. 1, 8, 12, 18, iii. 1, 7, 14, are not church officers, the angels in Rev. ii. and iii. are not church officers.

Prelacy in parity, in opposition to presbyterianism on the one hand, and to popery on the other, has, by the records of the New Testament and of early Church history, an impregnable position in the Christian Church, quite apart from the assumption that the angels of the seven churches are bishops.

The Bible recognizes only two kinds of sacred ministry, — the Jewish and the Christian; but no man, either in the one or in the other, is, in the Bible, ever called an angel. Consequently the theory that the angels of the seven churches are Christian bishops, is contrary to Bible usage, and must be pronounced an assumption.

There are no exceptions to the assertion that neither a Jewish nor a Christian minister is by the Bible ever called an angel.

1. "Messenger" (angel) (Matt. xi. 10; Mark i. 2; Luke vii. 27, repeated from Matt. iii. 1) is no exception, as the ministry of John the Baptist is itself exceptional.

2. The same is true of Luke vii. 24, since the messengers (angels) of John the Baptist are in no sense ministers.

3. The messengers (angels) mentioned in Luke ix. 52 are also without ministerial character.

4. No one will claim "the messenger [angel] of Satan" (2 Cor. xii. 7) as a minister, either Jewish or Christian.

5. The messengers (angels) Rahab receives (Jas. ii. 25) are "spies" (Josh. ii. 1), without any sacerdotal commission.

These five places are all the instances the Bible contains where the word "messenger" translates the Greek word meaning "angel."

So utterly are the Bible proofs wanting, that a minister of God, whether Jew or Christian, bears the name of angel. Since he does not, it is wholly assumption to regard the angels of the seven churches as Christian bishops.

THE RELATIONS OF THE SEVEN EPISTLES OF THE APOCALYPSE TO THE REST OF THE BOOK.

The seven epistles, occupying the second and third chapters of the Apocalypse, are *intermediate*, not only in their position between the first and fourth chapters, but likewise in their nature and office. Their intermediateness is characteristic.

(1) Of the brilliant and majestic appearance of the Son of man (i. 13–16), the seven epistles are both the design and the result. His manifestation occasions the epistles. Every feature of the manifestation is repeated in the epistles.

(2) In reference to the positions annexed to the third chapter, the seven epistles provide the requisite ingots, out of which are drawn the golden threads forming much of the shining and attractive tissue of the unexampled narrative.

From the epistolary section of the book are also taken the brightest gems of its abounding ornamentation, illustration, and instruction.

The seven epistles are, therefore, not, as they may seem at first sight, a detached and isolated intrusion into the Book of Revelation, but are essential contributions to the harmonious adaptation of its parts to each other, to its symmetrical structure, and to its full explanation. The epistles are indispensable *preparations* for the rest of the incomparable book.

CHAPTER II.

THE FIRST EPISTLE: THE EPISTLE TO THE CHURCH OF EPHESUS (Verses 1-7).

PRINCIPAL SUBJECT, BROTHERLY LOVE.

1. To the angel of the church in Ephesus write: These things saith he who holds the seven stars in his right hand, who is walking in the midst of the seven golden lamp-stands.

Saith he: the phrase is very often in the Book of Amos (i. 3, 6, etc.). The figurative style of this prophet is strongly reflected in the Apocalypse of St. John.

Holds: holds firmly. Christ holds firmly in his possession each one of the seven churches. His firm hand even now clasps to his loving heart every church, however small and however unnoticed by worldly men. He thus fulfils his cheering promise, "My sheep shall never perish. No one shall pluck them out of my hand" (John x. 28).

The seven stars: the seven signet-gems, as tokens of Christ's affection for the members of the Ephesian church, and for all church-members. The stars sparkle with this message: I write this epistle because I love you.

The reference of the seven stars is to i. 16, where is the same expression. It is the *first reference* in chapter ii. to chapter i. The reference is the beginning of a *series of seven recapitulations*, in chapters ii. and iii., of previous descriptions of the Son of man in chapter i.

The fact of *recapitulation* in the Apocalypse discloses the peculiar structure of the entire book, and also unfolds to us *its own method of self-interpretation*.

Walking in the midst of the seven lamp-stands: second part of the first reference and recapitulation. The place referred to is i. 13.

Walking: to supply the lamps with oil (Lev. xxiv. 2-4), and to preserve the union between the churches and himself (xxvi. 12).

In the midst: of the churches, as their official centre and spiritual head.

Christ, in his watchful love and present grace, now thus walks and thus provides, in the midst of all his churches, the wide world over.

2. I know thy works, even thy labor and patience, that thou canst not endure evil men, and thou art testing them who say they themselves are apostles (and yet they are not), and thou findest them false.

I know thy works: these words Christ addresses to each one of the seven churches. The words express these truths: (*a*) the omniscience of Christ; (*b*) the occupation of each church is Christian work.

A large portion of this work is the same as that Christ imposed upon Saul of Tarsus at the time of his conversion, — "to bear my name before the Gentiles, and the children of Israel" (Acts ix. 15). Each of the seven churches is, by its creation, a *missionary church;* and its mission work is *the conversion of both Gentiles and Jews.*

In his epistle to the church in Thyatira, Christ gives prominence to its mission work among the Gentiles. "He that overcometh, and keepeth my works unto the end, to him will I give power over *the nations* [Gentiles]" (Rev. ii. 26).

That "the nations" are the Gentiles, is proved by St. John himself, who, in the ten places in the Apocalypse where he uses the expression, by it distinguishes the Gentiles from the Jews.

The mission work for the conversion of the Gentiles, which Christ assigns to the church in Thyatira, he also assigns to each of the other six churches. Christ by his Spirit addresses his commands in this book to all churches. "He that hath an ear, let him hear what the Spirit saith unto *the churches*" (ii. 7, 11, 17, 29, iii. 6, 13, 22). As this command follows each epistle, all the churches are thus addressed by every one of the epistles; and, consequently, CHRIST, AT THE PRESENT TIME, CONSTITUTES ALL CHURCHES, EVERYWHERE, MISSIONARY CHURCHES.

Thy: Christ is addressing the church as a corporate body.

Works: in my behalf; "for my name" (verse 3).

Even thy labor: literally, beating; labor with stripes; toil accompanied with suffering; severe labor.

Patience: brave patience, endurance. Both labor and patience were necessary in the "stir" in Ephesus (Acts xix. 23-40).

Thy: in the Greek, the position of "thy" renders labor and patience *one* expression.

This power of *thy*, in Rev. i. 2, is possessed by the genitive "apostles" (Acts ii. 42), where not only the "doctrine," but also the "fellowship" and the "breaking of bread" and the "prayers," *belong exclusively to the apostles*.

Thus Acts ii. 42 furnishes the *model of the original Church of Jesus Christ*. By his inspiration and direction, the apostles gave the Church its "doctrine;" were the centres of church "fellowship;" themselves (not the laity) administered the Supper of the Lord; and composed and offered the "prayers" of the Christian assemblies.

Evil men: (Acts xx. 29, 30) "grievous wolves, not sparing the flock; men speaking perverse things, to draw away disciples after them."

Testing: "examining, proving" (2 Cor. xiii. 5).

Apostles: appointed by Christ. The impostors in the church of Ephesus claim his appointment. St. Paul encountered similar "false apostles" (2 Cor. xi. 13–15).

Christ, however, by pronouncing these self-made apostles "false," rejects their claims.

3. And so thou art retaining patience, and art enduring [them] for my name, and art not becoming weary.

Them: the evil men (verse 2).

For my name: for myself as made known to men. On account of thy regard and affection for me.

4. Yet I have this against thee: Thou art leaving thy first love.

First love: only in one other place in the Apocalypse does the word "love" occur, — ii. 19, where, from its connection with "service" ("ministering to the saints," 2 Cor. ix. 1), it must denote *the love Christians bear each other* (1 John v. 1; John xiii. 34).

At their first association as a church, the Christians in Ephesus "loved one another with a pure heart fervently" (1 Pet. i. 22). But now they are leaving their first love. Their mutual love is growing less, and is becoming cold.

They are, by this alienation from each other, defeating the great purpose for which the Son of God became incarnate, died to redeem them from guilt, and created them anew in his own image of love for others. This great purpose is the formation, in this hating world, of a *spiritual brotherhood* of renewed hearts, fervently loving each other because first fervently loving Christ their Redeemer and Sanctifier.

Christ assures the Ephesian Christians that their loss of mutual love is "against" them. St. John elsewhere shows us the frightful extent to which the injury goes. "He that loveth not his brother abideth in death. Whosoever hateth his brother is a murderer; and ye know that no murderer hath eternal life abiding in him" (1 John iii. 14, 15).

5. Accordingly, remember whence thou art falling, and repent, and do thy first works. But if thou dost not repent, and dost not do the first works, I am coming against thee, and I will move thy lamp-stand from its place, unless thou repent.

Accordingly: in view of thy relapse and fall.

Remember: in private. Each member of the Ephesian church is here thus addressed: Bring thy fallen and ruinous condition, occasioned by the loss of love for thy brethren, home to thy recollection and conscience.

Whence thou art falling: at the present moment. The perfect tense in Greek has the force of the present.

Whence: from what high elevation. Once thy place was a spiritual height.

(*a*) Christ and all truly loving souls stand on this lofty height. They form a peculiar and rare company. So unlike are they to the hating, quarrelling, harmful, tormenting, and tormented multitude below them, that we must call them good and loving angels incarnate.

(*b*) Supreme peace reigns on the summit where loving hearts are standing. There no lightnings flash; there no thunders roll. Christ's loving people hear the storm of angry voices, fighting hands, and hating hearts, in the world beneath; but the mad tempest does not rise high enough to touch them. It does not jar their abiding peace. Their day is unclouded sunshine. The soft winds of paradise cheer them, for they are close to its opening gate.

This is the spiritual height from which

Thou art falling: falling from a temple pinnacle, as the Devil urged our Saviour to fall; falling as wandering stars fall; falling as Satan fell in the sight of Christ.

Why art thou thus falling? Not because Christ thrusts thee down; not because loving Christians drop thee from their high standing-point. But thou art falling for the reason Sir Isaac Newton's apples fall, — *the earth draws them down;* for the reason wandering stars fall, — because *they leave their orbits;* for the reason the devils fell from heaven, — *they had not the dispositions fitting them to stay there.*

Falling from the love for Christ's people he demands of us, is often caused by our substituting for the motives he creates, the motives we derive from earthly considerations. The peculiar relation Christians bear to the incarnate Son of God, arising from their redemption by his blood, and from their endowment with his life and holiness, is the highest and strongest motive to inspire us with enduring love for all the redeemed and sanctified. But when we cease to "remember" this divine and most influential constraint, and exchange it for *their personal qualities*, the lower motive proves the weaker, and fails to preserve and continue the ardent feeling we once cherished. Thus the earthly and personal motive, because the feebler, so benumbs our affections, that we leave and lose the love we may have once entertained for our brethren in Christ.

Even then, however, our condition is not hopeless. We can be recovered from our deep falling. Christ himself points out the way. The way he prescribes is *repentance*, and return to our "first love."

Repent: repentance is an *after-view*. It is a change of mind and heart. It is a return of the whole soul, animated and reformed by the Spirit of Christ, to the love it may have formerly cherished for its brethren in Christ.

First works: the works prompted by love for Christ (John xiv. 15), and performed for the conversion, edification, comfort, and salvation of both Gentiles and Jews.

Am coming against thee: with special and personal judgments.

Move thy lamp-stand: remove the lamp, take away its oil, withdraw my grace from thy heart, leave thy declining spiritual life to die from exhaustion.

In interpreting Christ's words here, the *symbolical* nature of his language must be preserved fully and in every portion.

Unless thou repent: Christ repeats his exhortation to repentance to show its *remedial efficacy*, as well as its great and imperative necessity. With every duty he creates, he gives sufficient grace for its performance.

6. **But this thou hast in thy favor: Thou hatest the works of the Nicolaitanes, which works I myself also hate.**

Hatest: the Greek verb means to *feel* hatred. "Hateful" (Tit. iii. 3), on the contrary, means, from its verb, to *show* hatred.

Christ's life in us causes us to feel the same dislikes he feels. If, then, we hate and shun sin, his life and holiness are abiding in us, and we are his spiritual children.

The works of the Nicolaitanes:

The attempts to explain this passage *historically* have proved unsuccessful. Possibly the context may disclose the true explanation.

1. Our Lord himself, in the context, distinguishes between *old and new names* (ii. 17, iii. 12).
2. The "new name" is *figurative* ("Mystery," xvii. 5); "his name is *Death*" (vi. 8); "Wormwood" (viii. 11).
3. Our Lord uses the name "Jezebel" (ii. 20) in a *figurative sense*. He may, therefore, use other proper names in figurative senses, as Nicolaites (ii. 6) and Balaam (ii. 14).
4. Our Lord makes the Nicolaitanes *identical* with the imitators of Balaam (verses 14, 15).

This identity is proved by the Greek particle *houtoos* (verse 15), which means, in this *exact* way, and not, in *like* way. *In this exact way* "pray ye" (Matt. vi. 9). "When ye pray, *say*" (Luke xi. 2); say *exactly* the words of the Lord's Prayer.

This being the meaning of *houtoos* in ii. 15, this particle here identifies the Nicolaitanes with the imitators of Balaam (verse 14). By this identification, we discover what are "the works of the Nicolaitanes. They eat things sacrificed unto idols, and commit fornication" (verse 14).

Two questions now meet us:—
1. In their *literal* meaning, are Balaam and Nicolaites *identical?*
2. Does our Lord use these names *figuratively?*

Literal Identity.

1. Balaam, in its *Hebrew* derivation, means *destroyer of the people.* Nicolaites, in its *Greek* derivation, means *conqueror of the people.*

But conquest and destruction differ so little, that we may say, in their *literal* meanings, Balaam and Nicolaites *are identical.*

Figurative Use.

2. Our Lord may use these names *figuratively*. He may intend by Balaam to signify *destroyer of the people*, and by Nicolaites *conqueror of the people*, and thus unite Balaam and Nicolaites in a common *figurative signification.* He may thus use these names *figuratively*, because he uses the name "Jezebel" in this *figurative* way (verse 20).

In perfect consistency, then, with his own usage, can our Lord give to Balaam and Nicolaites a figurative sense.

As conqueror and destroyer of people, Balaam represents licentiousness and idolatry. These sins, as subjugators and murderers, have, in all ages of the world, captured and ruined more "people" than all the military devastators and scourges whose detested names blacken the pages of history.

While the church in Ephesus retains any measure of Christianity, it must "hate" the hurtful deeds of the Nicolaitanes. So long as the Son of man loves the souls of men, for whom he shed his redeeming and cleansing blood, will he abhor and oppose "the doctrine of Balaam," the destroyer of people. So long as any Christian hates the sins Christ hates, he will hate, oppose, and "reprove" (Eph. v. 11) licentiousness, and "covetousness which is idolatry" (Col. iii. 5), both in high places and in low places.

7. He that hath an ear, let him hear what the Spirit saith unto the churches. To him that overcometh, I will give to him to eat of the tree of life, which is in the midst of the paradise of God.

The Spirit: the Son of man, the speaker, transmits his words throughout to St. John by the Holy Spirit inspiring this apostle.

Unto the churches: Christ's message to each of the seven churches, he designs for all churches. "What I say unto you, I say unto *all*" (Mark xiii. 37).[1]

Overcometh: the symbolic Balaam conquers the people. Christ would have every human soul conquer Balaam.

I will give: Christ is the supreme arbiter of life and death (xxi. 6).

Tree of life: the tree of life in the Garden of Eden conferred immortality (Gen. iii. 22). Paradise, into which Christ entered at his death (Luke xxiii. 43), and to which St. Paul was once in vision caught up (2 Cor. xii. 4), has its symbolic tree of life (Rev. ii. 7, xxii. 2, 14). I will give to him *to live forever*.

The paradise: *literal*, "the king's forest" (Neh. ii. 8); *spiritual*, "Eden, the garden of God" (Ezek. xxviii. 13); the place of blessed souls between their death and resurrection.

Of God: prepared by him (John xiv. 2).

SUMMARY OF THE FIRST EPISTLE.

The first epistle has these general subjects: —

I. Christ's approvals.

1. Mission-labor. 2. Patience. 3. Rejection of evil men. 4. Trial of false apostles. 5. Regard for his name. 6. Perseverance. 7. Hatred of Nicolaitanes (verse 2).

II. Faults of the Ephesian church.

1. Loss of brotherly love. 2. Loss of high position. 3. Discontinuance of labors.

---

[1] See Rev. i. 2, p. 4.

III. Adversaries.

1. Evil men. 2. False apostles, who are advocates of *self-will*. 3. Nicolaitanes, advocates of *self-indulgence*.

IV. Duties.

1. Review of past life. 2. Repentance. 3. Renewed love and service to others.

V. Principal subjects: brotherly love, self-will, self-indulgence.

VI. Christ's threat: removal of lamp.

VII. Christ's promise: tree of life.

VIII. Adaptation of Christ's titles to the contents of the epistle.

(1) His love, "holdeth the seven stars;" (2) His omniscience, "walketh in the midst of the golden candlesticks," — make him a perfect judge.

IX. Adaptation of Christ's promised reward, "the tree of life," to the principal subject, brotherly love. Brotherly love is itself Christ's life in our souls. The possession of his life, he rewards by the preservation and increase of the same life.

PRACTICAL TRUTHS OF THE FIRST EPISTLE.

1. Christ "knows" our hearts and ways. His lightning sight reads all our thoughts, and follows us in all the paths we tread.

2. He regards all souls as priceless "gems," — priceless, because redeemed by his precious blood. When, therefore, we commit our souls to his strong and safe keeping, no power, outside of ourselves, can pluck them from his almighty hands.

3. He constantly "walks" in the midst of the personal life in which we habitually live, sees the needs of our souls, and supplies them with the necessary grace and strength to serve him.

4. Evil men and hurtful influences abound now, as always in the ages before, and must at all times be by us abhorred and resisted (2 Cor. vi. 14, 15).

5. The holiness Christ imparts to the souls he renews causes them habitually to hate sin, to oppose it, to reprove it, to avoid it.

6. The Nicolaitan spirit, *self-will*, is the source of all heresies. It is naturally connected with self-indulgence.

7. Love for Christ, and with it love for his people, is the first impulse of every heart renewed in the image of Jesus. This twofold love is the life of all inward piety, of all spiritual growth, of all work for Christ. The decay of this love is the cause and the presage of spiritual death.

8. When our first love for Christ and his people is left and lessened, it can be renewed and recovered by repentance and a new life.

9. Loss of love for Christ and for our fellow-men is its own punishment; because this loss occasions the displacement of the lamp of light and life Christ kindles and cherishes within us, and because the removal of the lamp is the extinguishment of the light of life in the soul.

10. Were there not *true* apostles, false apostles would be impossible. This is as true now as formerly. The present existence of false apostles is the proof of the present existence of true apostles. Thus Christ historically and unceasingly preserves in the world the threefold ministry — apostles, presbyters, and deacons — he originally appointed; and thus fulfils his promise, "Lo, I am with you alway, even unto the end of the world" (Matt. xxviii. 20).

11. Victory on our part is the unalterable condition of Christ's favor, and of our admission to life eternal.

12. Our possession of immortality renders necessary our admission into a world which is itself immortal, even into heaven, of which paradise is the foretaste and pledge.

THE SECOND EPISTLE: THE EPISTLE TO THE CHURCH IN SMYRNA (Verses 8-11).

This epistle is the shortest of the seven. The epistle to Thyatira is the longest. Christ does not reprove this church, nor that of Philadelphia. The subject of the second epistle is MARTYRDOM. This subject is closely connected with the subject of the first epistle, *Brotherly Love*. We are required to love all men, because Christ loves them. But Christ's love for all men caused him to die for them: hence brotherly love in following the example of Christ results in martyrdom. "Hereby perceive we the love of Christ, because he laid down his life for us: and we ought to lay down our lives for the brethren" (1 John iii. 16). "Be thou faithful unto death, and I will give thee a crown of life" (Rev. ii. 10).

8. Also to the angel of the church in Smyrna write: These things saith the First and the Last, who was for a time dead, and yet is living.

Also: except the first, each epistle begins with "and," in the sense of addition, also.

The First and the Last: the reference is to i. 17.

Second Recapitulation. — The eternity of Christ is the support and defence of his Church.

Is living: the tense is the Greek aorist. But as the aorist here is defined by the present participle "is living" (i. 18), "is living" ("is alive," English Version, A.D. 1611), is the sense of the aorist in ii. 8. Only twice more does the aorist of this verb occur in the Apocalypse (xiii. 14 and xx. 4). The present participle (i. 18) is St. John's own definition of the aorist in Rev. ii. 8, xiii. 14, xx. 4. Having thus from him the true definition, namely, "*is living*," we should in each place obediently receive and most firmly hold this authoritative definition: *is living* (xiii. 14), *are living* (xx. 4).

9. I know thine own works, even the persecution and the poverty (but thou art rich), and the blasphemy coming from those who are saying they themselves are Jews, and yet they are not, but are a synagogue of Satan.

The persecution: the existing persecution (verse 10).

The poverty: the real poverty, bordering on beggary. So the Greek.

Rich: in my love, help, and promises. Rich is emphatic, very rich.

The blasphemy: the hurtful speech spoken against thee.

Jews: since defined by "synagogue of Satan," they are bad Jews, they are not "Israelites indeed" (John i. 47).

A synagogue: this is the sense, because (a) in the Greek, the noun is without the article, (b) is the predicate.

Satan: in the Hebrew means an adversary. The Smyrnean members of his synagogue "are enemies of the cross of Christ" (Phil. iii. 18).

10. Do not fear the sufferings which thou art certainly to suffer. Behold, the Devil is certainly to cast some of you into prison, that ye may be tried. And yet ye shall have persecution during [only] ten days. Show thyself faithful even unto death, and I will give thee the crown of life.

Behold: each one of you has a deep and personal interest in my next words.

The Devil: the accuser, the slanderer. This is the Greek meaning of the word "devil."

The two names Christ here gives "the prince of devils" (Matt. xii. 24), "adversary" and "accuser," exhibit him as exerting all his power against the church of Smyrna, and as hurting it, both by artifices and open violence, and by slanderous accusations.

To all faithful Christians, the Devil is always the same malignant and deadly enemy.

Some of you: the church is addressed as *individuals*. This occasional appearance of the *individual* members of the churches proves that the angel of each church is addressed as the *representative* of the church. "Thou [the angel] shalt suffer," is in this verse 10 an instance of the relation of the angel to the church. The fact of *representation* is one of the effectual keys to open the locked meanings of the Apocalypse.

Into prison: the persecution, in the next clause, since external, forbids the spiritual sense of prison.

That ye may be tried: by temptations and sufferings, to fall away from Christ, but to be proved invincible.

During ten days: a short period of time. This sense of "ten days" is established by Bible usage. "Not ten days, nor twenty days, but a whole month" (Num. xi. 19, 20).

Show thyself: the Greek verb often has this meaning (Matt. x. 16, xxiv. 44; John xx. 27).

Unto death: this phrase occurs in Revelation, only here, and xii. 11, where the death is violent. Death by violence, by martyrdom is therefore denoted in Rev. ii. 10.

The crown: the emblem of kingship (Matt. xxvii. 29).
Of life: conferring the life eternal.

11. He that hath an ear, let him hear what the Spirit saith unto the churches: He that overcometh shall in no wise be hurt by the second death.

The second death: in xx. 14, defined to be "the lake of fire."

St. John, in the Revelation, is the only New-Testament writer who expresses contrast between first and second by using one of the words and *implying* the other.

Thus, in Rev. ii. 11, when he uses "second death," he *implies* first with "death" (verse 10).

When in Rev. xx. 5, 6, he uses "first resurrection," he *implies* the phrase "second resurrection," when he thus narrates: "Death and hades *delivered up* the dead which were in them" (Rev. xx. 13).

Thus St. John's use of *implication* is uniform. We note this fact in St. John's usage, and infer the same uniformity when he writes "first resurrection" (Rev. xx. 13).

In his contrast between the first death and the second, the first death is bodily, and *the second is spiritual.* In his contrast between the first and second resurrection, *the second is bodily.* Since, in this contrast, St. John follows the same law of uniformity which he observes in the other contrast between the two kinds of death, *the first resurrection must be spiritual.*

It is certainly *most probable* that he here uses the same law. If it is *barely possible* that St. John here uses the same law, no person is authorized, by the laws of exegesis, *to assert positively* that the first resurrection (Rev. xx. 5, 6) is a *bodily* resurrection to *precede* the universal resurrection in the last day.

The martyr-victor shall in no wise be hurt by the second death. His death will be only *bodily.* His soul will live "the life everlasting" (Luke xviii. 30).

SUMMARY OF THE SECOND EPISTLE.

The second epistle has these general subjects:—

I. Christ's approvals.

1. The acquisition of the true riches. 2. Faithfulness. 3. The endurance of sufferings.

II. Trials of the church in Smyrna.

1. Tribulation. 2. Poverty. 3. Blasphemy of Jews.

4. Imprisonment. 5. Enmity of the Devil. 6. Martyrdom, in the expression "unto death."

III. Adversaries.

1. Satanic Jews. 2. The Devil.

IV. Principal subject: martyrdom.

V. Duties.

1. Courage. 2. Fidelity.

VI. Promises of Christ.

1. The possession of courage. 2. Endurance under trials, "faithful unto death." 3. Tribulation temporary, "ten days." 4. A "crown of life."

VII. Adaptation of Christ's titles to the principal subject of the epistle.

1. "The First and the Last." Christ's eternity secures an eternal reward.

2. "Was dead, and is alive." Christ outlived his martyrdom. All who die for him will have the same deathless life, "a crown of life;" a crown conferring life eternal.

VIII. Adaptation of the promised reward, freedom from "the second death," to the principal subject, martyrdom. Christ's martyrs die but once. Their destiny and reward is life eternal.

PRACTICAL TRUTHS OF THE SECOND EPISTLE: THE REWARDS OF FAITHFULNESS TO CHRIST.

1. Life follows death. It was so with Christ: it will be so with every faithful disciple of his.

2. Temporal trials and losses often accompany fidelity to Christ.

3. The true riches: Christ's love, Christ's presence, Christ's help, Christ's image.

4. Loss of worldly expectation the consequence of fidelity to Christ.

5. Pretence proves alliance with Satan, and hostility to Christ.

6. Courage is inspired by the assurance of victory over sufferings.

7. Trials are beneficial.

8. The power of the Devil is limited, both in time and in degree.

9. Enduring fidelity to Christ secures endless honor.

10. The church in Smyrna is the martyr church.

11. Christ expects all churches to possess the martyr spirit.

12. Christ's epistle to the church in Smyrna must have armed the martyrs of the early church with undying faith and unflinching courage.

13. This epistle is *the manual* appointed by Christ for all his martyrs.

THE THIRD EPISTLE: THE EPISTLE TO THE CHURCH IN PERGAMOS (Verses 12-17).

SUBJECT: DOCTRINE OF BALAAM, SELF-WILL AND SELF-INDULGENCE.

12. Also to the angel of the church in Pergamos write: These things saith he that hath the sharp two-edged sword.

The sharp two-edged sword: the reference is to i. 16.

The Third Recapitulation. — The sword is the symbol of punishment. Christ threatens to punish the church in Pergamos.

13. I know where thou dwellest, even where is the throne of Satan; and yet thou holdest fast my name, and dost not deny the faith in me, even in the days when Antipas is my faithful martyr, who is killed in your presence; where Satan dwells.

Throne: *metonomy* for dominion.

Holdest fast my name: holdest fast the confession that Jesus is Lord (Rom. x. 9), and holdest fast prayer to my name (verse 13).

Dost not deny: the Greek aorist tense has here the force of the present. Dost not deny; that is, thou dost openly confess: emphatic negation for strong affirmation.

In the days: this is a possible sense of the expression, the days, predicted by our Lord (Matt. x. 21), and fulfilled in Pergamos.

Antipas: is not an individual, but the *representative* of a class of martyrs. Reasons for this explanation of Antipas:—

1. The angel of each of the seven churches is representative: he represents the whole church.

2. In the Book of Revelation, proper names represent classes.

(*a*) "That woman Jezebel" (ii. 20) is representative. She represents the class of fornicators, and eaters of idol-sacrifices.

(*b*) The Nicolaitanes are representative (ii. 6).

3. In the names Balaam and Nicolaites, St. John refers to the *derivative* meanings of the words, and then employs them as designations of *classes* and not of *individuals*. He may treat the word "Antipas" in the same way; (*a*) by taking it in its *derivative* sense (*against all*), and (*b*) by designating a *class* of fearless martyrs, and not an *individual*.

4. The Apocalypse is *self*-interpreting. By its own usages, Antipas is not personal, but only representative.

Antipas means, in the Greek, *against all*. The name may represent a class of brave and self-sacrificing martyrs, who could not be restrained from martyrdom by all the remonstrances and tears of all their timid and compromising relatives and friends. Hilary, Bishop of Poictiers, has an affecting description of this resolute and unyielding class of martyrs (vol. i. p. 371, 3).

This class of martyrs is constrained to submit to a violent death, rather than deny Christ, by these declarations of his: "He that loveth father or mother more than me is not worthy of me. He that findeth his life shall lose it; and he that loseth his life for my sake shall find it" (Matt. x. 37, 39); and by the hope of receiving from him the fruition of this promise: "Every one that forsaketh houses, or brethren or sisters, or father or mother, or wife or children, or lands, for my name's sake, shall receive a hundredfold, and shall inherit everlasting life" (xix. 29).

In your presence: the Greek preposition has this sense (Col. iv. 16). The presence of Christians does not prevent these unfeeling martyrdoms.

Is killed: The Greek verb is a most deadly word; it describes butchery with the sword (Rev. vi. 8, xiii. 10).

The preceding present tense, "holdest," changes all the Greek aorists in this verse 13 into present tenses.

As we now see Jewish and Pagan fathers causing their own children to be killed by the sword, we can see why our Lord, when beginning his epistle to the church in Pergamos, refers to his own sword, "These things saith he which hath the sharp sword with two edges." He will avenge the blood of his youthful saints, now being shed in Pergamos.

14. But I have against thee a few things: that thou hast

there certain men holding the teaching of Balaam, who was teaching Balak to cast a stumbling-block before the children of Israel, to eat sacrifices to idols, and to commit fornication.

Few: few faults compared with thy many virtues.

There: this particle contemplates Pergamos as distant from Patmos. Pergamos was the most northerly of the seven churches. Even there, where my name is held fast (verse 13).

Holding: in contrast with "thou holdest" (verse 13).

The teaching Balaam was teaching: an intensified expression, the teaching Balaam was earnestly teaching.

Stumbling-block: an occasion of sin.

Sacrifices to idols: the Israelites not only actually ate these forbidden sacrifices, but also "bowed down to their gods" (Num. xxv. 2).

Fornication: (Num. xxv. 1; 1 Cor. x. 8).

Like sins, like punishments: the divine inflictions in the time of Balaam, Christ is about to repeat in Pergamos, if not in kind yet in severity.

St. Paul's writings show the proneness of some of the early Christians to relapse into their former heathenish practices (1 Cor. viii. 1, v. 1).

15. In this way, thou hast, even thyself, certain men holding the teaching of Nicolaitanes in like manner.

Hast: emphatic. Thus repeating hast (verse 14), and the repetition referring the phrase, in this exact way, to verse 14.

Teaching of the Nicolaitanes: on the identity of their teaching with that of Balaam, see verse 6.

In like manner: this expression establishes the close connection between the teachings of Balaam and the Nicolaitanes.

16. Accordingly, repent. But if thou dost not, I come unto thee most certainly, and will war with them by the sword of my mouth.

Them: the Nicolaitanes.

Sword: the punishments my mouth threatens, I shall inevitably inflict.

17. He that hath an ear, let him hear what the Spirit saith unto the churches. To him that overcometh will I give to eat of the hidden manna, and will give him a brilliant gem,

and on the gem a new name engraven, which no one knoweth except the receiver.

Manna: food from heaven (Exod. xvi. 15).

Hidden: the blessing represented by the manna, even Christ himself (1 Cor. x. 4). The showbread, because made of manna, also represents Christ (Exod. xxv. 30; John vi. 49–51).

Brilliant gem: brilliant white. Gem: the gem in a signet-ring, a token of affection (Jer. xxii. 24). — *Church Review*, June, 1883 (article "Cephas").

Name engraven: names were engraved on signet-gems (Exod. xxviii. 11).

New: as a different word, and in a different sense, the new name indicates Christ's love (Jer. xi. 15, 16).

No one knoweth except the receiver: the gift of the "new name," indicating Christ's love, he accompanies by the manifestation of his love *in the soul* of every one to whom he gives the new name.

The nature and extent and preciousness of this manifested love can be known only by the person who experiences the love. This *experienced* love, unknown to others, the Scriptures call "the secret of the Lord." "The secret of the Lord is with them that fear him" Ps. xxv. 14. "His secret is with the righteous" Prov. iii. 32.

The Son of man expressly calls this secret a *manifestation:* "Him that loveth me, *I will love*, and will *manifest* myself to him" (John xiv. 21).

SUMMARY OF THE THIRD EPISTLE.

The third epistle has these general subjects : —

I. Approvals.

1. Adhesion to faith in Christ. 2. Open confession of Christ. 3. Courage (verse 13).

II. Sins.

1. Approval ("hast," verse 14) of the doctrine of Balaam. But approval of the doctrine is participation in the doctrine; hence, 2. Holding the doctrine of Balaam is the second sin.

As a *doctrine*, Balaamism is

(*a*) *Self-will.* Balaam, throughout his downward course to destruction, followed his own will.

(*b*) *Self-indulgence.* Balaam advised feasting and sensuality as traps for the Israelites.

As *a practice* ("deeds," verse 6), Balaamism is

(*a*) Idolatry. (*b*) Fornication.

Since meat offered to idols, and fornication, were prohibited by the council of Jerusalem (Acts xv. 29), these sins must have been committed by some of the early Christians, and, therefore, by some members of the church of Pergamos. Hence

III. The principal subject of Christ's epistle to the church of Pergamos is, *Self-will* and *Self-indulgence*.

These sins are "the Anakims, great and many and tall," to whom Christ gives not "so much as a foot-breadth"[1] of possession in his church; and yet they are, always and everywhere, subtle intruders, bold invaders, audacious heresiarchs, and loud-mouthed Balaams. A special epistle from Christ is imperiously needed for their reproof, resistance, expulsion, and destruction.

IV. Adversaries.

1. Satan (verse 13). 2. Balaamites.

V. Duties.

1. Repentance; which, in this epistle, includes (*a*) condemnation of Balaamism, which is, in its essence, self-will and self-indulgence; (*b*) Rejection of Balaamism in its practices, — gluttony and licentiousness. 2. The practice of (*a*) submission to God's will and institutions, the opposite of self-will; and (*b*) of self-denial (Matt. xvi. 24), the opposite of self-indulgence.

VI. Threat. Speedy punishment (verse 16). The Israelites who, by Balaam's arrangement, "committed fornication, fell *in one day* three and twenty thousand" (1 Cor. x. 8).

VII. The adaptation of Christ's title, "He which hath the sharp sword with two edges" (verse 12), to the principal subject — self-love and self-indulgence — is very obvious. These sins demand immediate extermination. Self-will annihilates revealed truth. This was most conspicuously the effect of Balaam's self-will. Self-indulgence destroys both

---

[1] Deut. ii. 5, 10.

body and soul. Balaam, the instigator of the fornication of the Israelites, who died of a plague, was himself "slain with the sword" (Num. xxxi. 8). The souls of the sinning Balaam and the sinning Israelites perished, as "fornicators do not inherit the kingdom of God" (1 Cor. vi. 9).

Sins which are as destructive as are self-will and self-indulgence ever demand a sharp and heavy sword, quickly struck, for their excision and destruction.

VIII. Adaptation of Christ's promises (verse 17) to every victor over Balaamism.

1. "The hidden manna," which is Christ's life,—the food of the soul,—is the contrasted substitute for idolatrous feasts, eaten to gratify the body. 2. Christ's secret love, symbolized by the "new name" known only to the receiver (verse 17), is the contrasted substitute for unlawful sexual love. The rewards promised by Christ in the third epistle are exactly adapted to the circumstances of the persons here addressed.

PRACTICAL TRUTHS OF THE THIRD EPISTLE.

1. A sharp sword is always needed to cut out deep-rooted sins.

2. Christ does not hold us responsible for outward conditions beyond our control.

3. Christ ever appreciates and rewards devotion shown him in the midst of dangers.

4. Every church is responsible for the heresies and sins of its members (Matt. xviii. 15-18).

5. Idolatry dethrones God. Fornication is murder in anticipation, and the prevention of family life. These sins are, therefore, most offensive to God.

6. Sins are to be measured by Christ's standard.

7. Destructive sins receive quick judgments.

8. The food Christ provides for the soul is infinitely preferable to bodily food.

9. The possession of Christ's love is not to be exchanged for illicit indulgence.

10. The more we feed on Christ, and enjoy his love, the less will be the power of our sinful inclinations over us.

THE FOURTH EPISTLE: THE EPISTLE TO THE CHURCH IN THYATIRA (Verses 18-29).

The longest epistle of the seven. The two great subjects —the *Christian Ministry*, *clerical and lay*, and *Spiritual Apostasy* — occupy this larger space.

Also unto the angel of the church in Thyatira write: These things saith the Son of God, who has his eyes as lightning, and his feet are like the flashing lightning.

The Son of God: this title of Christ is only here in the Apocalypse. Like all his titles in the Apocalyptic epistles, it is closely connected with the subjects of the epistle, and will aid us in determining what they are.

The title, "Son of God," first appears, Ps. ii. 7, where, as we learn from Heb. i. 5, it declares his *eternal generation* from the Father, and consequently his essential and absolute Deity.

When the angel Gabriel announces the birth of the predicted Immanuel (Isa. vii. 14), he names him "the Son of God" (Luke i. 35). Our Lord habitually applies this divine title to himself (Matt. xxvii. 43).

The title is thus defined by John Baptist: (*a*) as "the Lamb of God which taketh away the sin of the world" (John i. 29), and as therefore incarnate; and (*b*) as "He which baptizeth with the Holy Ghost" (verse 33), and consequently as our Almighty Sanctifier (verse 34).

Christ himself connects the new creation of the soul in his holy image with this sanctifying title: "The dead shall hear the voice of the Son of God; and they that hear shall live" (John v. 25).

Our Lord makes *belief* in himself as the Son of God the condition of discipleship (ix. 35, 38).

St. John makes *belief* in the Son of God the condition of "life through his name" (xx. 31). By Philip (*the deacon*, and therefore *a minister of Christ*) the Ethiopian eunuch was admitted to *Christian baptism*, on his profession of *faith* in the Son of God (Acts viii. 37, 38).

We may now see why, in his epistle to the church in Thyatira, our Lord calls himself "the Son of God." The title introduces him, (*a*) as divine in his nature; (*b*) as our Sanctifier; and (*c*) as the supreme Author of these *instruments of salvation*, through him as Sanctifier, (a) *faith*, (b) the sacrament of *baptism*, and (c) the gospel *ministry*.

The truths we have thus reached are all embodied in these sovereign words of his, "*All power* is given unto me in heaven and in earth" (Matt. xxviii. 18). "He that *believeth and is baptized* shall be saved" (Mark xvi. 16). "As my Father sent me, even so *I send you* [my "*disciples*," verse 20]" (John xx. 21). "*Go ye* [my "disciples," verse 16], therefore, and *disciple* all nations, *baptizing* them in the name of the Father, *and of the Son*, and of the Holy Ghost" (Matt. xxviii. 19).

By the title "the Son of God," in this epistle to the church in Thyatira, Christ exhibits himself as Sanctifier of all churches and all hearts, by these instruments of his own appointment, — *faith*, *baptism*, and the *apostolic ministry*.

His eyes: the reference is to i. 14, 15.

Fourth Recapitulation. — The lightning-vision of the Son of God denotes his *omniscience*.

His feet: His lightning-feet indicate the rapidity and promptness with which he executes his sovereign will.

19. I know thy works, even thy love, and fidelity, and service, and patience ; and so thy last works are more than the first.

Thy works: Christ expects all churches to work for him.

Thy love: Brotherly love. As the "service" in this quadruplet is *mutual* ("ministering to the saints," 2 Cor. ix. 19), the other works in this verse — love, fidelity, and patience — must be mutual.

Faith: towards each other; fidelity.

Service: the Greek word, the English Version often translates "ministry;" we may therefore regard it as the Christian ministry, both clerical and lay.

(*a*) CLERICAL. — The false ministry of the *woman* Jezebel implies a true ministry performed by *men*. The true ministry is also contained in the Greek word translated "service" (verse 19), which designates (Acts i. 17, 25, vi. 4, xii. 25, xx. 24, xxi. 19; Rom. xi. 13; 2 Cor. iv. 1, v. 18, vi. 3; Eph. iv. 12; Col. iv. 17; 1 Tim. i. 12; 2 Tim. iv. 5, 11) either the personal ministry of the apostles of our Lord, or the apostolic ministry they committed to other men.

(*b*) LAY. — But, associated as is "service" (Rev. ii. 19) with "charity," mutual love, with "faith," mutual fidelity, and with mutual "patience" of "*the church* in Thyatira" (verse 18), consisting of *lay* people as well as clergymen, the word "service" (Rev. ii. 19) must include the ministry of *laymen and laywomen.*

The inclusion, in the church of Thyatira, of laymen and laywomen among Christian workers, is no exception to the organization of the church universal in the days of St. John. The following statements of St. Paul on this point also, most conclusively, establish the Christian ministry in two forms, — *clerical*, performed by *men ;* and *lay*, performed *by men and women.*

"There is neither Jew nor Greek, there is neither bond nor free, there is *neither male nor female:* for ye are all *one* in Christ Jesus" (Gal. iii. 28).

The "oneness" of Jew and Greek, of bond and free, of male and female, is not merely the possession of a common salvation in Christ Jesus. The "oneness" is also their *common duty*, imposed upon all by the possession of a common salvation, *of working for Christ.*

This common duty resting upon all souls, because they are all redeemed by the blood of Christ, is illustrated and enforced by St. Paul, in his graphic manner.

"I beseech you, brethren, by the mercies of God, that ye present your bodies a living sacrifice, holy, acceptable to God; namely, your *word*-service [1] [that is, *the service of speech* for Christ]. For, as we have many members in one [material] body, and all [bodily] members have not the same office [Greek, "acting"]; so we, being many [individuals], are *one body* in Christ, and *every one members one of another.* Having, then, gifts [duties] differing according to the grace that is given to us, whether (*a*) *prophecy* [one form of *speech*], let us prophesy according to the proportion [the analogy] of the faith; or (*b*) ministry [of the *word*, Acts vi. 4, a second form of *speech*]; or he that (*c*) *teacheth* [a third form of *speech*], on teaching; or he that (*d*) *exhorteth* [a fourth form of *speech*], on exhortation; he that giveth, with simplicity ["liberality," 2 Cor. viii. 2]; he that showeth mercy, with cheerfulness" (Rom. xii. 1, 4-8).

According to these words of St. Paul, it is the Christian duty of every human being, who possesses the requisite knowledge and ability,

---

[1] The Greek word translated "reasonable" by the English Version (Rom. xii. 1) occurs in the New Testament elsewhere, only, 1 Pet. ii. 2, where the English Version translates the same Greek by "word." The *immediate context* (Rom. xii. 4-8) decidedly prefers *word* as the translation in Rom. xii. 1, as we shall soon show.

The Greek word translated "service" (Rom. xii. 1) means service *rendered to God.* Besides Rom. xii. 1, the following are all the places where this Greek word *latria* ("service") occurs in the New Testament: John xvi. 2; Rom. ix. 4; Heb. ix. 1, 6. That, in all of them, God is the object of the "service," there can be no doubt.

to perform *word-service for Christ.* This primary Christian duty St. Paul recognizes in another form.

"Ye are enriched by Him *in all utterance*" (1 Cor. i. 5).

"Ye abound *in utterance*" (2 Cor. viii. 7).

In Christians, God prepares a people whose special business it is *to speak for him.*

This general obligation is, however, in the New Testament, modified by special enactments. *Christian men* are, in the Church of Christ, either clergymen or laymen; "the apostles, and elders, and *brethren*" (Acts xv. 23); "the apostles and elders *with the whole church*" (verse 22).

Christian women, while excluded from teaching in churches (1 Cor. xiv. 34) and from authority over men (1 Tim. ii. 12), are *required* by St. Paul to teach *in private* (Tit. ii. 3, 4).

In Tit. ii. 3, 4, Christian women give *private instruction* to other women.

But in Acts xviii. 26, Priscilla, the wife of Aquila, does, with her husband, give Christian instruction *in private* to Apollos, "an eloquent *man.*" That the instruction is *private*, is certain from this language, "they took him unto them;" that is, took Apollos to "*their house*" (1 Cor. xvi. 19).

More: in number; "*more* than ten days" (Acts xxv. 6).

20. But I have this against thee, that thou lettest alone the woman Jezebel, who says she herself is a prophetess; and so teaches and seduces my own servants to commit fornication, and to eat sacrifices offered to idols.

Lettest alone: dost not hinder. "*Let* him *alone*" (John xi. 48).

The woman Jezebel: the name Jezebel was first borne by the Zidonian wife of King Ahab (1 Kings xvi. 31).

The historical Jezebel was a pestilence (Greek, Acts xxiv. 5) to the subjects of her Israelitish husband.

(*a*) She introduced idol-worship (1 Kings xxi. 25, 26).

(*b*) She killed the Lord's prophets (1 Kings xviii. 4), also Naboth (xxi. 15).

The historical Jezebel was the *representative* of the idolatrous and lawless portion of the kingdom of Ahab (1 Kings xviii. 13, xix. 2, xxi. 7-15).

St. John[1] calls the class of apostatizing women in the church in Thyatira *Jezebel,* on account of their resemblance to Jezebel of Tyre.

---

[1] Antipas (Rev. ii. 13) is a representative. The "man of sin" (2 Thess. ii. 3), and "antichrist" (1 John ii. 18), is each "antichrist."

In her conduct, the representative Jezebel of Thyatira resembles Miriam, the sister of Moses and Aaron.

(a) Miriam was a prophetess (Exod. xv. 20). Miriam, like Deborah (Judg. iv. 4) and Anna (Luke ii. 36), was inspired by the Holy Ghost to teach God's will. The representative Jezebel of Thyatira claims for herself the same inspiration and office (Rev. ii. 20).

(b) Miriam resisted the authority of Moses (Num. xii. 1). The representative Jezebel of Thyatira resists the authority of its apostolic ministry (ii. 2).

Since Miriam, the sister of Moses and Aaron, and a prophetess, proved rebellious, it is not incredible that in the church of Thyatira there should be a body of women (which, for their resemblance to Ahab's heathen wife, Christ calls Jezebel) raising a rebellion against the ministerial authority he constituted in the churches.

Who says she herself is a prophetess: in ii. 2 and 9, where like claims are urged, Christ denies the claims: "They are not." The same denial of the representative Jezebel's claim is here implied: she is not a true prophetess.

Teaches: Jezebel of Thyatira is a *teaching* prophetess.

Seduces: withdraws from the truth.

Fornication: here *spiritual*, for three reasons:—

(a) Contextual. The sin is called in the text both fornication and adultery, and is committed by the same individuals. The literal commission is thus impossible.

(b) Fornication is here emphatic in position. In verse 14, the phrase is "idol-sacrifices and *fornication*," where the sin is *literal:* here the phrase is "*fornication* and idol-sacrifices." The only conceivable reason why fornication has this emphatic position is its designation of *spiritual* sin.

This is a law established by Bible-Greek usage. When, in couplets *repeated*, the normal order of the words is inverted, the words become *in sense figurative*.

Example: "Pillar and ground [foundation]" (1 Tim. iii. 15). The architectural order of the words is "foundation and pillar." The inversion of the order, "pillar and foundation," renders these words *figurative*.

(c) In this book itself, fornication is often spiritual, meaning apostasy from God (xiv. 8, xvii. 2, 4, 5, xviii. 3, xix. 2).

What is the nature of the sin committed by the representative Jezebel of Thyatira?

The *woman* Jezebel claims to be an inspired prophetess. Observe: the word "woman" *precedes* the proper name Jezebel. This position of "woman" is contrary to usage elsewhere. In the only other places in the New Testament (Matt. i. 20, xiv. 3; Mark vi. 17; Luke i. 24,

ii. 5, iii. 19, viii. 3; Acts v. 1, xviii. 2, xxiv. 24), *ten* in all, where "woman" occurs in the original with a proper name, the proper name *precedes* woman.

Thus *the woman* (Rev. ii. 20) *is proved* to be *emphatic*. *The woman* is the *prominent* object in the clause.

The fact is instructive in determining the meaning of the passage.

Women in the church of Thyatira assert their *divine* inspiration, commission, office, and authority. Perhaps they adopt the argument of Korah and his rebellious company, "all the congregation are holy, every one of them, and the Lord is among them" (Num. xvi. 3).

In Rev. ii. 2, certain *men* claim to be the apostles of the Lord Jesus Christ. But in Rev. ii. 20, a different case presents itself: *women* proclaim themselves his prophetesses.

This proclamation initiates in the church of Thyatira, and in the Church at large, *a new kind of Christian ministry*. The success of this new ministry can be achieved only by the exclusion of the old. Prophetesses necessarily supersede the prophets. Victory and domination create subjugation and ruin.

We can now perceive why our Lord calls the women who occasion these radical changes, Jezebel. The heathen mistress of Ahab introduced into the nation the priests of Baal. We see not less than *eight hundred and fifty* of these usurpers at Mount Carmel. At the same time, Queen Jezebel puts to death the prophets of the Lord. The false displaces the true.

The false prophetesses of Thyatira are a Jezebel for this obvious reason: in bringing in their usurping female ministry, they drive out the male ministry of Christ's appointment. The elevation of women to the ministerial office is the downfall of men.

It is certain, from the language our Lord employs in the context, that he himself regards the male and female ministries in this very light. He approves and upholds the ministry of men: he condemns and rejects the ministry of women.

The words by which he describes the ministry of the representative Jezebel of Thyatira are condemnatory in the highest degree. In his description, her ministry is spiritual fornication and spiritual idolatry. Ministerial Jezebelism is both the rejection of the will of God, shown in his own ministerial appointments, and the adoption of the human will, shown in self-appointments, as the master and guide in religion.

St. Paul also excludes women from the public Christian ministry (1 Cor. xiv. 34).

21. And yet I am giving her a certain time, in order that

she may repent; and yet she doth not desire to repent, and turn from her own fornication.

May repent: by demanding repentance of Jezebel, our Lord pronounces her ministry *sinful*.

Does not desire: as her sin began in self-will, she does not even desire to abandon her self-worship.

22. Behold, I am casting her into a sick-bed, and those who are committing adultery with her into great affliction, unless they repent of her works.

I am casting: the punishment is already being inflicted.

Her into a sick-bed: in the Old Testament, bed was the instrument of sin (Isa. lvii. 7-9; Ezek. xxiii. 41-44). Here bed denotes bodily weakness: in Mark vii. 30, the prostrated position denotes weakness of body.

With the woman Jezebel, the symbolic bed of the Old Testament is the symbolic instrument of her punishment. Her punishment is *spiritual weakness and decline*. As in the preceding verses, so in this (verse 22), the prevailing sense is spiritual. " Into a bed," being parallel with " into great affliction," describes spiritual suffering. Jezebel's self-will is in opposition to Christ's will. She is "fighting against God" (Acts v. 39). Her self-will resists the Holy Spirit within her. As her self-will increases in obstinacy, the influences of the Holy Spirit diminish. The divine life in her is expiring. Her soul is experiencing moral death. The literal adulteress was punished with bodily death (Lev. xx. 10). Jezebel, a spiritual adulteress, is punished with the death of her moral affections. This is Jezebel's sick-bed. This is the "great tribulation" of her followers. This is her punishment. This is their punishment. Sinners perish and die spiritually in this world (2 Cor. ii. 15); "sweet savor" in the perishing.

Those who are committing adultery with her: some men in the church of Thyatira joined the secession of the apostatizing women.

Affliction: may be internal as well as external. It is sometimes distinguished from outward persecution. "Affliction *or* persecution" (Mark iv. 17).

From her works: Jezebel's works, because requiring repentance, were evil. In verse 24, they are called "the depths of Satan." A sinful mind produces a sinful life.

23. And so her children will I kill by death, and so all the churches shall fully know that I myself am the searcher of

all reins and hearts: even I will give to you, to each one, according to your works.

Her children: Jezebel of Thyatira is a spiritual harlot. Her children are therefore her spiritual children. They are her followers. St. John calls his disciples "my children" (3 John 4).

Will kill: in a spiritual sense (Rev. ix. 15, xi. 5, 7, 13, xix. 21).

By death: the repetition of the same word *intensifies* the prediction; I will utterly kill.

St. John wrote the Apocalypse about A.D. 95. During the reign of Antoninus Marcus, A.D. 138-161, perhaps only a generation after the writing of this book, Montanus, of whom Tertullian was a follower, appeared in Phrygia, a province closely adjoining the territory in which Thyatira is situated. Montanus was assisted in promulgating his wish to be regarded as the Paraclete of Christ, by two influential women, Priscilla and Maximilla, who claimed to be prophetesses inspired by the Holy Ghost.

It is thus possible that these fanatical matrons of Phrygia derived their system from the fanatical women of Thyatira, and that Montanism itself is the off-shoot and continuation of the Jezebelism of this Apocalyptic city. — EUSEBIUS, *Eccl. Hist.*, b. v., c. 16; MOSHEIM, *Eccl. Hist.*, i. 151.

This then, is the meaning of the passage: "Her converts I will by a moral death utterly kill."

Know fully: from their own experience.

The searcher: this title of God the Father (Rom. viii. 27), Christ here appropriates to himself.

Reins and hearts: this twofold specification includes every portion of the human soul (Heb. iv. 12, 13).

The Searcher of the reins and hearts sees the secret spring, both of Jezebel's sin and of the sin of her followers. This secret spring-head is pride and self-conceit (Rom. xii. 16).

"I will give to you [all the churches], to each one [to each individual member of the churches], according to your works:" the character of the sin determines the character of the punishment.

24. But to you I say, the rest who are in Thyatira, all who are not holding this doctrine, who are not personally knowing the depths of Satan (as they call them), I am not casting on you any other burden.

This doctrine: of Jezebel's.
Who: as a class.

Depths: secret purposes (2 Cor. ii. 11), ["devices"]. Not certain that there is in the word "depths" any reference to gnosticism.

Satan: the prime instigator of Jezebel and of her party (verse 9).

As they: the rest. The uncorrupted portion of the church call the new teaching Satan's purposes.

Other burden: other requirement (Matt. xi. 30); that is, the retention of your present Christian graces and the performance of your present Christian duties (verse 25).

25. Except the burden which ye have, hold fast, until I shall come.

Hold fast: hold fast my teaching; hold fast my ministry, consisting exclusively of men. The command applies to Christians in all ages of the world.

Shall come: to the final judgment in the last day.

26. Also he that overcometh, even he that keepeth my works unto the end, to him will I give authority over the nations.

He that overcometh: nominative of designation. As to each victor in Thyatira.

He that keepeth: the keeper; victory comes by keeping.

My works: the works I require; "my patience," the patience I require (iii. 10).

Authority over the nations: over the Gentiles (see ii. 9). I will make him a fellow-victor with myself over the Gentiles (see xi. 15, xii. 5, xv. 4, xix. 15). He shall be in my hands an instrument of extending my church in the Gentile world, by turning souls from sin unto holiness.

27. (And he shall rule them with a rod of iron, as the vessels which are of clay are utterly shivered) as I myself also receive of my Father.

Rule: as a shepherd (John x. 11).

Rod: sceptre (Heb. i. 8).

Of iron: irresistible (ix. 9), not oppressive.

As the vessels: as vessels of clay can be utterly shivered by a rod of iron, so utterly shall Christ's victors overcome their spiritual enemies in the hearts of men.

Receive of my Father: "all authority is given unto me in heaven and in earth" (Matt. xxviii. 18). This clause belongs to verse 26.

28. And so I will give him the morning star.

The morning star is the emblem of a king (Isa. xiv. 12). I will make my victor a king. By this star, symbol of kingship, I constitute him irresistible king over all nations. Every true disciple and faithful minister, Christ makes the instrument of his divine power and success in the world. The martyrs in all ages were such kings. What kings in the world are St. John and St. Paul to-day! This explanation of the morning star accords with the kingly language of verse 27.

29. He that hath an ear, let him hear what the Spirit saith unto the churches.

See ii. 7, 11, 17, iii. 6, 13, 22.

SUMMARY OF THE FOURTH EPISTLE.

The fourth epistle has these general subjects:—
I. Titles of Christ.
1. The Son of God (verse 18). 2. Searcher of hearts. 3. Possessor of lightning-eyes. 4. Possessor of lightning-feet. 5. Impartial judge, "I will give according to works" (verse 23). 6. Merciful judge (verse 21).
II. Approvals.
1. Mutual love, "charity" (verse 19). 2. Mutual "service" ("ministering to the saints," 2 Cor. ix. 1). 3. Mutual fidelity, "faith" (verse 19). 4. Mutual patience. 5. Increase ("more," verse 19) of all these Christian graces. 6. Ignorance of Satan's depths (verse 24).
III. Sins.
1. Of the church itself. (*a*) Toleration of the women called Jezebel, "sufferest" (verse 20). (*b*) Neglect to suppress her "doctrine" (verse 24). 2. Of Jezebel. (*a*) Spiritual apostasy, "reins and hearts" (verse 23). (*b*) Love of power (verse 26). (*c*) Assumption of the ministerial office, "calleth herself a prophetess" (verse 20). (*d*) Creation of a female ministry, "*woman* Jezebel" (verse 20). (*e*) Teaching spiritual apostasy to the church of Thyatira, "teach" (verse 20). (*f*) Practical seduction of a portion of the church, "seduce" (verse 20); "leave this doctrine" (verse 24). (*g*) Refusal to repent (verse 21).

IV. Principal subjects.

1. *The great duty:* the exercise of the Christian ministry, both clerical and lay. 2. *The great sin:* SPIRITUAL APOSTASY.

V. Adversaries.

1. Jezebel. 2. Her followers. 3. Satan.

VI. Duties.

1. Non-toleration of Jezebel. 2. Holding fast present mutual love, service, fidelity, and patience.

VII. Threats.

1. Sickness (casting into a bed). 2. Great tribulation. 3. Spiritual death.

VIII. Mercies.

1. Space for repentance (verse 22). 2. No other burden than present duties.

IX. Promises.

1. Power over the Gentiles, to convert them to Christ. 2. Equality of dominion with Christ (verse 27). 3. Morning star.

X. Adaptation of Christ's titles — (a) Son of God, (b) searcher of "reins and hearts" (verse 23), (c) eyes, (d) feet — to the general subjects, the Christian ministry, and spiritual apostasy.

1. The Son of God is the author of the Christian ministry. 2. The special design of the gospel proclaimed by the Christian ministry is to reveal the thoughts of hearts (Luke ii. 35). Christ's infinite knowledge finds the thoughts, appoints his ministers (Acts i. 24), distributes his gifts of the Holy Ghost (Acts xv. 8). Since spiritual apostasy is in the heart, the secret sin requires the Searcher of "reins and hearts" to detect it.

3. Christ's lightning eyes scan the thoughts of both ministers and people, and discern the nature and extent of the departure of each soul from his will and appointments.

4. Christ's lightning feet always go with his ministers wherever they carry his gospel, and bring its messages of

salvation to all souls, whether willing or unwilling to receive his mercies. Since his lightning feet dispense his mercies, his lightning feet also reach all sinning and apostate souls to inflict on them his just punishments.

XI. Adaptation of Christ's rewards to the working members of the church in Thyatira. The rewards of the Christian ministry are both in the present life and in the world to come. In the present life, the rewards of the Christian ministry are these three: (a) opportunity, (b) success, (c) increase of grace in the soul of each minister.

1. Opportunity. This is the field into which Christ sends every minister, both clerical and lay, to work. In Thyatira, this field was the Jews and Gentiles, who filled the city, and the members of the church itself. To men and women alike, there was the open opportunity of practising their graces, of love of souls, of services of fidelity, of enduring patience.

2. Success. "To him that overcometh, and keepeth my works unto the end, will I give power over the Gentiles" (verse 26), to convert them unto myself. This promised success Christ "received of his Father" (verse 27), and the hope it inspires in him moves him in his own ministry for our salvation.

3. Increase of grace in the soul of every worker for Christ. "He that watereth shall himself be watered" (Prov. xi. 25); "It is more blessed to give than to receive" (Acts xx. 35), — more blessed on account of the inner and personal reward.

The future rewards of the Christian ministry are so great and inconceivable that they must be described by figures: "They that turn many to righteousness are shining stars for ever and ever" (Dan. xii. 3). The church Christ is addressing in his fourth epistle knew this promise (Rev. ii. 28); and the working Christians in the Church must, for its sake, work on "unto the end."

PRACTICAL TRUTHS OF THE FOURTH EPISTLE.

1. Because divine, the Son of God is both omniscient and omnipresent (verse 18).

2. Brotherly love is a prolific root, producing service, fidelity, and patience (verse 19).

3. Christ endows Christian graces with the power of growth and increase (verse 19).

4. Although Christ does not allow women to be *public* prophetesses in his church, he appoints them teachers in *private life* (Phil. iv. 3; Tit. ii. 3, 4; Acts xviii. 26).

5. Toleration of sin is itself sinful (verse 20).

6. The love of power is a sin hard to overcome and forsake (verse 21).

7. Sins cherished always displace Christian graces (verse 22).

8. Spiritual sickness, unless cared for, occasions spiritual death (verse 23).

9. Sin in its origination in the human heart is so secret, even to our consciousness, that only the omniscience of Christ can detect it (verse 23; Ps. xix. 12, 13).

10. Christ makes our works the test of our spiritual state (verse 23).

11. The purposes of Satan are his "devices" (2 Cor. ii. 11), by which he plots our ruin (verse 24).

12. Christ imposes duties according to our strength.

13. Before we can subdue the hearts of others to Christ, we must be habitual victors over our own dispositions and affections (verses 26, 27). A Christian wilfully sinning cannot be a successful soldier of Jesus Christ.

14. The starry brilliancy with which Christ rewards his gospel servants (Dan. xii. 3) is in proportion to the Christian light they impart to others (verse 28).

CHAPTER III.

THE FIFTH EPISTLE: THE EPISTLE TO THE CHURCH IN SARDIS (iii. 1–6).

SUBJECT, SPIRITUAL DEATH.

1. Also to the angel of the church in Sardis write : These things saith he that hath the seven Spirits of God, and the seven stars : I know thy works, that thou hast a name to live, and yet thou art dead.

The seven Spirits and the seven stars: in these expressions, there is reference to i. 4 and 16, where the expressions are explained.
Fifth Recapitulation of previous titles borne by Christ.
Name: emphatic, *mere* name. Your life is not a reality.
To live: in the Apocalypse, only here in a spiritual sense. The same sense, Rom. vi. 8. In Rev. xx. 4, "live" denotes, not resurrection-life, but *manner of life ;* describes a *kingly* life.
And yet thou art dead: in a spiritual sense, because contrasted with "to live" in preceding clause. In the Apocalypse, only here in this sense. Also, Luke ix. 60; Eph. ii. 5; 1 Tim. v. 6.

Christ, as always, "uses great plainness of speech" (2 Cor. iii. 12). The first stroke of his resistless hand tears off the mask of hypocrisy. By this startling address he intends to break the fond dream of self-delusion, in which the church of Sardis is sleeping. The sudden address to this dead church is, like his loud call to the entombed Lazarus, "Come forth!" The sharp summons is a resurrection trumpet to rouse the sleeping and dreaming church to newness of life.

In the dull ears of many a church, at the present hour, is the same stirring trumpet voice now sounding, *Thou art dead !*

2. Become ever watchful, and strengthen the rest of the

works, which were about to die; for I do not find thy works perfected in the sight of my God.

"The rest" (in the Greek) refers to the preceding "works" (verse 1), just as "the rest" (ii. 24), refers to the preceding "you." Christ determines the character of *persons* by their works (Matt. vii. 16). By "the rest of the works" [workers] we may understand the rest of the persons; namely, the careless or backsliding Christians in Sardis.

Were about: in his love and hopefulness, Christ regards the death as already past (Rom. vi. 17).

To die: in a spiritual sense, as in Rom. viii. 13.

Perfected: brought to perfection, not in the full "measure" (Matt. xxiii. 32) I require.

In the sight of: in the judgment of; "before" (Luke i. 6) has this sense. God is our present Judge. He is incessantly measuring our works by his own perfect standard.

My God: in the Apocalypse, only in the epistle to Sardis, where *five* times (iii. 2, 12) in the Greek.

Our Lord utters the expression (Matt. xxvii. 46; Mark xv. 34; John xx. 17). It is taken from Ps. xxii. 1, 2, 10. The word "my" denotes the closeness of the relation subsisting between God the Father and God the Son. So close is this relation, that each knows the mind of the other. When, then, our Lord says in Rev. iii. 2, "in the judgment of my God," he, in effect, says, "in the judgment of the Father, whose judgment I myself fully know."

3. Accordingly, remember how thou art receiving and hearing and keeping; and so repent. Accordingly, if thou dost not watch, I will come against thee as a thief; and so thou art in no wise knowing in what hour I shall come against thee.

Accordingly: the particle we translate "accordingly" is both retrospective and summarizing. It is not inferential, and cannot be justly translated "therefore" (English Version). This Greek particle here reviews the declarations and exhortation in verses 1 and 2, and presents them as constraining reasons for personal and minute recollection and immediate repentance.

Remember: see ii. 5.

How: "after what manner" (Acts xx. 18). Since the manner required repentance ("repent," next clause), the manner was bad. "How" (1 Cor. iii. 10) describes manner; and the manner, "wood, hay, stubble," must also be bad.

In Rev. iii. 3, "how" is in contrast with "livest," "watchful," and "strengthen" (verses 1 and 2), and therefore has this meaning: "How lifelessly, carelessly, and feebly art thou receiving and hearing and keeping!" In Eph. v. 15, "how" (so in the Greek) means, how not foolishly, "not as fools." Supreme folly likewise marks the manner of the dying church of Sardis.

Receiving: the new name (ii. 17). This is the only kind of receiving predicated in the Apocalypse of Christian individuals.

Hearing: the voice of the Holy Spirit (ii. 7, 11, 17, 29).

Keeping: my works (ii. 26), observing, doing the works I command. The Greek verb we translate "keeping" is in the present tense, and thus makes the two preceding Greek verbs we translate "receiving" and "hearing," *in sense* present tenses, describing constant habit.

The church of Sardis is a sick man, scarcely able to walk. The grasp of his receptive hand is feeble. The hearing of his ear is dull. His active obedience, so far as he attempts it, is partial and irresolute.

As a thief: unexpectedly (Matt. xxiv. 43). The Sardian church neither looks for nor hastes unto the coming of her Lord (2 Pet. iii. 12). She neither expects his coming nor desires it.

How many Sardian Christians are there at the present time! Their expectations and desires are fixed upon all worldly objects. For Christ, and the treasures he presents to their hearts, their affections are feeble and dying.

4. Yet thou hast a few names in Sardis, that are not defiling their garments; and so they shall walk with me in white, for they are worthy.

Yet: there is a brighter fact than the deadness of the church of Sardis as a community.

Thou hast: even in the midst of the universal spiritual deadness.

A few names: persons (Rev. xi. 13; Acts i. 15).

Few, compared with the whole number; a few live Christians, "the election" (Rom. xi. 7).

Are not defiling: the Greek tense describes their usual practice.

Not defiling; that is, are most carefully preserving the unsullied whiteness of their garments. They are retaining the holiness and purity of their souls, with which Christ incessantly blesses them.

In the presence and light of Christ in our souls, may we all now continually see light!

Garments: this language is symbolic. Garments are symbols of states of soul.

(*a*) Of a *sinful* state. "Joshua the high priest was clothed with *filthy* garments" (Zech. iii. 3). "The Lord spake unto those that stood before him, Take away the *filthy* garments from Joshua. Unto Joshua the Lord said, I have caused *thine iniquity* to pass from thee" (verse 4). Thus it is proved from the Bible itself, that a soiled garment is the symbol of the *sinful* state of the soul (Jude 23).

(*b*) Of a *holy* state. "I will clothe with change of raiment" (Zech. iii. 4). "He hath covered me with the robe of *righteousness*" (Isa. lxi. 10). "To the Lamb's wife was granted that she should be arrayed in fine linen, clean and white: for the *fine linen* is [represents] the *righteousness* of the saints" (Rev. xix. 8).

Walk: that is, live (xxi. 24).
With me: John xvii. 24.
In white: in white garments (verse 5); that is, in holiness.
Worthy: of every honor (1 Tim. vi. 1).

5. He that overcometh shall be thus clothed in white garments, and in no wise will I blot out his name from the book of life; and I will confess his name before my Father and before his angels.

Overcometh: he all the time, every day and every hour, conquers his unwatchfulness and deadness. Every sin is a dangerous enemy, and therefore must be conquered.

Thus clothed: clothed as "the few" are in verse 4, in white.
Clothed: clothed about, fully clothed.
Blot out: the blotting assigns to the lake of fire (xx. 15).
Book of life: God commanded Moses to *number* the children of Israel on two occasions: (*a*) in the second year of their departure from Egypt (Num. i. 1–4); (*b*) in the plains of Moab (xxvi. 1–3).

A great sin, for example idolatry, caused the name of the sinner to be blotted out of this book of numbering (Exod. xxxii. 33). In other words, the idolater was put to death (Judg. vi. 31).

This, then, is the meaning of these words, "I will not blot out his name from the book of life;" I will not put him to death, I will not subject him to the second death (xxi. 8).

Confess his name: declare his name to be rightly written in the book of life (Ezra ii. 62; Neh. vii. 64).

Before my Father and before his angels: angels will attend our Lord when he comes to the universal judgment (Matt. xxv. 31). His confession of each conqueror will be approved by God the Father and by his angels. The decisions of God always commend themselves to the intelligence and moral judgment of all good angels.

6. He that hath an ear, let him hear what the Spirit saith unto the churches.

See ii. 29.

SUMMARY OF THE FIFTH EPISTLE.

This epistle has these general subjects:—

I. Christ's titles.

1. He that hath the seven Spirits and the seven stars (verse 1).
2. The Author of the book of life (verse 5).
3. The Judge (verse 5).

II. Evils.

1. Decline of the life of God in the soul (verse 1).
2. Decline of spiritual graces: (*a*) of self-examination ("remember"); (*b*) of watchfulness; (*c*) of the desire for restoration ("strengthen").

III. Causes: Loss of the life of Christ in the soul; (*a*) by indifference, (*b*) by sin.

IV. Remedies.

1. Renewal of the soul by the Holy Spirit.
2. Practice (*a*) of self-examination, (*b*) of watchfulness, (*c*) of former graces.
3. Restoration to former spiritual state.
4. Repentance and abandonment of sin.

V. Grounds of hope.

1. Life and graces, though dying, are not absolutely dead (verse 2).
2. A few souls are still faithful and worthy (verse 4).

VI. Threats.

1. Of Christ's advent to judge.
2. Of unexampled judgments (verse 3).
3. Of omission of warnings (verse 3).

VII. Rewards.

1. Christ's life.
2. White garments.
3. Enrolment in the book of life.
4. Acceptance.

VIII. Principal subject, spiritual death.

IX. Application of Christ's titles to the principal subject.

1. The seven Spirits can restore spiritual life.

2. Christ's love, symbolized by the seven stars, leads him to attempt the restoration.

X. Adaptation of the promised rewards to the persons addressed.

The rewards promised (VII.) will excite to the use of the remedies (IV.).

PRACTICAL TRUTHS OF THE FIFTH EPISTLE.

1. Christ now employs the Holy Spirit for restoration from spiritual deadness, as well as for growth in grace (verse 1).

2. The mention of "the stars," signet-gems, emblems of Christ's love, proves that he ever loves his people, even when they are backsliding (verse 1).

3. Great as is the blessing of registration by Christ in his book of life, the blessing may be forfeited and lost by spiritual deadness (verse 2).

4. The remedy for spiritual deadness is twofold: (*a*) habitual watchfulness; (*b*) re-establishment of Christ's life and of the dying graces in their former activity and strength (verse 2).

5. Examination precedes finding. Christ is constantly examining our works (verse 2).

6. St. Paul's exhortation embraces the only safe rule: "Let us go on to perfection" (Heb. vi. 1). His example enforces his own exhortation in Phil. iii. 13, 14 (verse 2).

7. Memory, the observer and recorder of our nominal profession, urges us to practise repentance and a new life (verse 3).

8. Neglect to watch and repent insures swift and sudden punishment (verse 3).

9. There are always, in every church, a few worthy souls who are ever faithful to Christ (verse 4).

10. The rewards of victory over sin are life with Christ, and his recognition and reception "in the hour of death, and in the day of judgment" (verse 5).

11. The voice of the Holy Spirit always enters and instructs the willing ear.

THE SIXTH EPISTLE: EPISTLE TO THE CHURCH IN PHILADELPHIA (Verses 7-13).

SUBJECT OF THE EPISTLE, THE CONVERSION OF THE JEWS.

The church in Philadelphia is a *missionary church to the Jews*. This church is Christ's own pattern for all his churches, at the present time and at all times.

---

7. Also to the angel of the church in Philadelphia write: These things saith he that is holy, he that is true, he that hath the key of David, he that openeth and no one shutteth; and shutteth, and no one openeth.

These things: which follow.

Holy: "The Holy One" is one of the names of Christ (Acts iii. 14). Holiness is more than sinlessness: it is moral perfection.

True: real, perfect. Christ is "the true [perfect] light" (John i. 9). He is "the true [perfect] God" (1 John v. 20); "*very* God of *very* God" (Nicene Creed).

The key of David: the reference is to i. 18, where the keys are "the keys of hell and of death." In iii. 7, "the key" is the key of church authority.

Sixth Recapitulation.

"The key of the house of David will I lay upon him" (Isa. xxii. 22). Key is the symbol of kingly dominion (Luke i. 32). David, as founder of the kingdom of Israel, was its head. He is thus a type of Christ (Jer. xxx. 9). David's kingdom typifies the Church of Christ. Christ *alone* has the key of the Church, the supreme authority in it (Matt. xvi. 19, xxviii. 18). No Roman pope has this key.

Openeth, etc.: from Isa. xxii. 22, which is prophetic of Christ. The quotation describes the resistless, almighty power of Christ.

8. I know thy works: behold, I am now setting before thee an opened door, which no one can shut; for thou hast

very little ability, and thou art keeping my own word, and art not denying my name.

I know thy works: that they are good. Because they are good, I now give thee additional work to do.

Behold: for thyself. Give personal and earnest attention to all I am about to say. My words are of the deepest interest to thee, to the Jews, to the Church of Christ, and all mankind. My important utterances immediately follow.

I am now setting before thee an opened door: I am now placing an opened door before thine eyes. I myself open the door. The door thus opened immediately before thee is my command for thee to enter the door at once.

The door symbolizes a large opportunity to work for Christ.

St. Luke and St. Paul not only use this symbol, but explain it: "God opened the door of faith to the Gentiles" (Acts xiv. 27). God gave the Gentiles the opportunity of believing in Christ.

"A great and effectual door is opened unto me" (1 Cor. xvi. 9): I am allowed by God to do a great and effectual work for him.

The opening and shutting, in verse 7, suggest the image of a door; and the opened door itself images an open and wide opportunity to work for Christ by extending his gospel.

The work to which Christ, by the door he opens, appoints the church in Philadelphia, is the *conversion of the Jews*, of which he assures this church when he thus promises, "I will make them to come and worship before thy feet" (verse 9).

The door which Christ, in his epistle to the church in Philadelphia, opened for the conversion of the Jews, has never been shut. This door has always been opened ever since. It is wide open at the present moment. It will not be shut until all the Jews have had the opportunity of entering it, and through it of passing into Christ's kingdom, both on earth and in heaven.

A very little: small in quantity. In the Greek, emphatic: thus 1 Cor. v. 6, "*a very little* leaven."

Ability: *pecuniary* ability. "Beyond their power," *pecuniary* ability (2 Cor. viii. 3). The pecuniary ability of the Corinthians is defined by St. Paul as "deep poverty" (verse 2).

The church in Philadelphia is therefore *very poor* in this world's goods; but the "deep poverty" of this church, Christ makes the *first* of the three reasons he gives for setting before the Philadelphians the opened door, the duty he imposes upon them of working for the conversion of the Jews. "I am setting before thee an opened door, for thou hast very little pecuniary ability: thou art very poor [first reason], and thou art keeping my own word [second reason], and art not denying my name [third reason]."

He pronounces poverty *the primary qualification* for the service.

Poverty is a comprehensive term, and may mean, (*a*) simple scantiness of temporal living, or (*b*) temporal support by others, or (*c*) may include both these states.

MINISTERIAL POVERTY is thus a subject which Christ himself places permanently in his church, and presents to our constant attention.

I. Ministerial poverty is a *Christian fact*.

1. Christ himself was a poor man. "The Son of man hath not where to lay his head" (Matt. viii. 20).

2. His twelve apostles were poor men. "They forsook all, and followed him" (Luke v. 11).

3. St. Paul was a poor man. "Ye sent once and again to my necessity" (Phil. iv. 16). "These hands have ministered to my necessities" (Acts xx. 34). "In hunger and thirst, in cold and nakedness" (2 Cor. xi. 27).

4. The ministers of Christ in the early Church were all poor men. "The ministers of Christ in necessities" (2 Cor. vi. 4).

5. As a class, Christ's ministers have in all ages been poor men.

This Christian fact, so fully established by the example of Christ and of his ministers for so many centuries, plainly indicates that the fact is his *own appointment*.

Since it is Christ's own ordinance, ministerial poverty will be a Christian fact to the end of time. It will exist always.

II. Ministerial poverty is a *Christian power*. The poverty of ministers does not hinder their success. Instead of a hinderance to ministers, poverty is a power. This was pre-eminently the fact with the ministry of Christ and his apostles.

Ministerial poverty is a mighty power, because it detaches ministers both (*a*) from the attractions and (*b*) from the instrumentalities of the world.

(*a*) Since poverty is Christ's appointment for his ministers, men will not enter the ministry through hope of personal advantage, but through the constraint of their convictions that the gospel is from heaven, and through the impulse of the call of Christ's Spirit in their hearts, which they can neither silence nor resist.

(*b*) The field of ministerial usefulness which Christ creates and appoints is devoid of worldly instrumentalities. Christ does not place in the hands of his soldiers carnal weapons. Ministers carrying with them the abiding belief in this ordinance will use only the instruments he allows; namely, (*a*) the power of his written and preached Word, (*b*) the power of believing prayer, and (*c*) the accompanying power of the Holy Ghost.

In view of Christ's own ministry and appointment, and in view of the experience of his Church in all past ages and at the present time, we do not exaggerate when we say, poverty is the instrumentality by which the gospel was at first planted; poverty is the instrumentality by which the gospel has been preserved and extended in the world; poverty is the instrumentality by which the gospel will yet overcome all obstacles, and become the belief and the law of all nations.

III. The Christian fact of ministerial poverty can never justify ministerial idleness. What is true of Christ's ministers is true of Christ's people. When other things are not hinderances to any person's Christian usefulness, his poverty is not an excuse for the neglect of the duty of speaking and laboring for Christ. Every person who has a mind can think for Christ. Every person who has a voice can speak for Christ. Every person who has hands can work for Christ. Every person who has feet can, like Christ himself, "go about doing good." When voice and hands and feet fail, every person who has a praying heart (and every person can have, and can wield, this effectual power) can, in silence and in secret, pray Christ to "make his ways known to all sorts and conditions of men, his saving health unto all nations."

The ministerial poverty Christ establishes does not at all release the laity from the obligation, under which he places them all, to provide his ministers with an adequate temporal support. "The Lord hath ordained that they which preach the gospel should live of the gospel" (1 Cor. ix. 14). "Have we not power [right] to eat and to drink?" (verse 4.)

"Have we not power [right] to lead about a sister, a wife, as well as other apostles, and as the brethren of the Lord, and Cephas?" (verse 5.)

These questions of St. Paul establish these truths: —

1. Every minister of the gospel has the right granted him by Christ to marry.

2. Himself, and wife, and children have the right from Christ of lay support.

3. The laity are required by Christ to provide ministers and their families with adequate sustenance.

The adequacy of ministerial support is to be determined by —

(*a*) The common lay expense of living, and (*b*) the unavoidable necessities of ministers and their families.

In case the laity do not give ministers adequate livings, the clergy are then bound to support themselves, so far as possible. St. Paul, when not in prison, supported himself (Acts xx. 34). Lay neglect cannot authorize ministerial neglect. When not sustained by the laity, ministers are bound by Christ to still work on for him, so far as they are able. Each minister receives his commission from Christ, and not from the people. The ministerial commission is created, not by money, but primarily by the Holy Ghost; and this commission must be obeyed until bodily ability is withdrawn by Christ.

When both lay and self support cease, even then these duties remain obligatory upon every minister of Christ: (*a*) speaking for Christ in private, (*b*) incessant prayer, giving Christ no rest till he make his Church a praise in all the earth (Isa. lxii. 7).

My own word: My own teaching.

Not denying: that is, boldly confessing. The emphatic negative is here used for the strong affirmative.

Poor churches and *poor* ministers are, by Christ's appointment, "to spend and be spent in preaching the unsearchable riches of Christ" (2 Cor. xii. 15; Eph. iii. 8).

What classes are churches and ministers to enrich by Christ's unsearchable riches?

Are "the poor of the earth" (Job xxiv. 4) to be thus blessed? or are the blessings of the gospel to be restricted to the "rich in this world" (1 Tim. vi. 17), and to "honorable men" (Nah. iii. 10) and "honorable women"? (Acts xvii. 12.)

Our Lord's answer to these questions is most direct and conclusive. The answer is but a single sentence, easily understood and easily remembered: "The Lord hath anointed me *to preach the gospel to the poor*" (Luke iv. 18).

Christ's duty is our duty: "As my Father hath sent me, even so I send you" (John xx. 21). "Go ye into all the world, and preach the gospel *to every creature*" (Mark xvi. 15). According to Christ's decision and command, we are to preach his gospel "*to every creature.*" Christ allows no exception. Neither race, complexion, nor condition can deprive any human being of the gospel.

Christ's assumption of our nature makes "every human creature" Christ's brother. Our duty to Christ thus becomes our duty to his brethren, who are all mankind. Our duty to Christ's brethren is, to feed, to clothe, to house, to visit, when sick or in prison (Matt. xxv. 35–45), in case they need our help.

By these decisions, Christ gives to the poor, the sick, the helpless, the right to a portion of the greater abundance with which he favors the rich and prosperous.

No! since Christ partakes of our humanity, and has tasted death for every man, and is thus related to every human being, the gift of his gospel is by no means the only Christian debt rich and well-to-do people owe the abject poor, even the most miserable pauper. The relief of their bodily wants forms an essential portion of the imperative obligation Christ creates and enforces.

No region can have permanent health till the swamps are drained and cultivated. The world cannot have a stable and safe civilization till the whole populace is Christianized and incorporated permanently into the State and Church. Majorities govern, if not by votes, by example and influence. A godless population will destroy any nation.

9. Behold, I will make some of the synagogue of Satan, who say they are Jews, and yet they are not, but are lying, behold, I will make them come and worship God before thy feet, and make them know that I myself am loving thee.

Some of the synagogue: Christ here promises to make a portion of these bad Jews his true worshippers. He thus pledges himself to give success to the labors of the church of Philadelphia in behalf of the Jews. This promise of Christ is the door he opens and keeps open, first for the Philadelphian church, and also for all churches in all succeeding years.

The wide door was open; and the duty commanded by Christ, to enter it and work for the conversion of the Jews, was unalterably binding upon all the churches, both Eastern and Western, during all the unchristian and disgraceful periods of the past, when, instead of trying to convert the Jews to the gospel of Christ, Christians tried to shut his open, and fastened-open, door, and persecuted the Jews with fines, disenfranchisement, expatriation, imprisonment, and death.

Even in Christian countries, at the present hour, the Jews as a class are regarded with dislike, and are excluded from all social intercourse. Christian disposition and Christian conduct towards the Jews must precede all Christian effort in behalf of their souls.

Say they are Jews, but yet they are not, but are lying: these Jews, because not "Israelites indeed" (John i. 47), are not true, but false, Jews. Their claim to this true Judaism is a falsehood. The miracle of the conversion of such enemies to the cross of Christ is the more striking.

Come and worship God before thy feet: after the word "worship," God is implied in the Greek, and for this reason: the word "God" is expressed, vii. 11, xi. 16, xix. 4.

The Greek verb translated "worship" describes the adoration of a *Divine* Person (iv. 10, v. 14, vii. 11, xi. 1, 16, xiv. 7, xv. 4, xix. 10, xxii. 9).

"Worship," and "before thy feet," are *different* actions. *Proof:* (*a*) "I fell at his feet (*b*) to worship" (xix. 10, xxii. 8).

Prostration may be the accompaniment of the worship of a *Divine* Person, but is not the worship itself.

We see this distinction broadly drawn in the request of Naaman (2 Kings v. 18). The promised conversion of the Jews fulfils Isa. ix. 14, in substance quoted in Rev. iii. 9.

Shall know that I am loving thee: My blessing upon the labors of the Philadelphian church for the conversion of the Jews will be proof to the converted Jews that I am loving this church, and that I shall give additional proofs of my love by converting still other members of the Jewish body.

10. Because thou art keeping the word respecting the patient endurance I require, I myself also will keep thee from the hour of trial, which will certainly come upon all the world to try them that dwell on the earth.

Patient endurance: this is the meaning of the Greek noun the English Version here translates "patience."

This essential requisite in all labors for the conversion of souls to Christ, the church in Philadelphia conspicuously exhibits. Its enduring patience eminently fits it for the arduous work of converting the obstinate Jews.

Patient endurance is now the indispensable qualification for the complicated missionary work Christ is demanding so urgently at the hands of all his churches. Success is impossible without the constant application of the patience which is resolved not to fail. The present conversion of the Jews is difficult by reason of their neglect of their own scriptures, and their adherence to the human system of rabbinism.

Keep: preservation from evil is one of the rewards with which Christ compensates labors in his behalf. This preservation Christ both promises and prays for. "I have given them thy word [to speak]; I pray that thou shouldest keep them from the evil" (John xvii. 14, 15). Christ neither promises nor prays in vain.

The hour of trial: the season of severe afflictions which characterized the early history of the Christian Church. "In the world ye shall have tribulation" (John xvi. 33). "We told you before that we should suffer tribulation; even as it came to pass, and ye know" (1 Thess. iii. 4). "The fiery trial which is to try you" (1 Pet. iv. 12).

To try: trials, like winds, separate the chaff from the wheat (Matt. iii. 12). Like fire, trials purify the gold from the dross (1 Cor. iii. 13).

Trials discover character. "The Lord your God proveth you, to know whether ye love the Lord your God with all your heart and with all your soul" (Deut. xiii. 3). As winds, fires, and searchers and judges of the heart and soul, trials are God's present judgment-seats, from which he is incessantly issuing his own decisions respecting our spiritual state. When trials make us better, they prove us the pure gold God treasures for his own use. When trials make us worse, they prove us the useless dross God rejects and casts away.

Christ's reward of preservation from all that is *really evil* is, as formerly and always, so at the present time, one of the strong motives he is ever presenting to all his churches everywhere to engage them actively and persistently in the evangelization of the Jews, and in the conversion of all heathen people, both at home and abroad.

The world: strictly, the inhabited world. So the Greek, metonomy for the inhabitants of the world.

In St. Paul's Epistle to the Hebrews (i. 6, ii. 5), this Greek term means *not* "habitable earth" (as explained by William Kay, D.D., in the Bible Commentary, vol. iv. p. 31), but means *the Church of Christ*. This meaning of the Greek term is derived from the Septuagint of Isa. lxii. 4, where this Greek term is for the Hebrew appellation "Beulah," the meaning of which is "married." "As a young man *marrieth* a virgin, so shall thy sons *marry* thee ["daughter of Zion," verse 11; the same city as "the holy people, the redeemed of the Lord," verse 12; that is, "Mount Zion, the city of the living God, the heavenly Jerusalem," Heb. xii. 22, which is no other city than *the Church of Christ*]; and as the bridegroom rejoiceth over *the bride* ["the *Lamb's wife*," Rev. xxi. 9], so shall thy God rejoice over thee" (verse 5). The Church, as the beloved bride of Christ, "married," *dwelt-with* (the meaning of the Greek term both in Isaiah and the Epistle to the Hebrews), "loved," is intended in Isa. lxii., and consequently in Heb. i. 6 and ii. 5, because the Greek term in these two places is the same as the Greek term in Isa. lxii. 4.

That dwell on the earth: another name for the enemies of Christ. This is proved by Rev. vi. 10, viii. 13, xi. 10, xiii. 8, 14.

While the church in Philadelphia, laboring faithfully and earnestly for the conversion of Jews, shall be preserved from every real evil, the enemies of Christ will be tried and punished with his heaviest judgments.

11. I come quickly. Hold fast the treasure thou hast, that no one take thy crown.

Come quickly: to fulfil my three great promises: 1. Conversion of the Jews (verse 9); 2. Preservation of the converting church in Philadelphia; 3. Punishment of my enemies.

Treasure: implied after "hast," because expressed after "have" (2 Cor. iv. 7). We *have* this treasure (of preaching the gospel).

In Rev. ii. 1, the verb "hold" has a treasure for its object; namely, "the seven stars," the signet-gems.

These examples from 2 Cor. iv. 7, and Rev. ii. 1, prove that both verbs "hold" and "hast" can lawfully admit "treasure" as their object.

Preaching the gospel is a precious treasure, for these most inviting reasons: (*a*) It gathers priceless souls for Christ, who are imperishable jewels in his crown (Mal. iii. 17). (*b*) It procures for the preacher the crown of life, his inestimable gift and reward from Christ.

In Rev. iii. 8, the opportunity to convert the Jews is the treasure. This precious treasure hold fast most firmly. This golden opportunity most faithfully and enduringly improve.

This urgent exhortation Christ still addresses to all his churches, of every name and in every country.

No one take: let no one prevent your taking the crown Christ promises you, the crown of life (ii. 10).

The same glorious prize Christ now places within the reach and grasp of each one of us. What an unspeakable blessing and honor to be crowned by Christ! Reader, let neither man nor woman nor evil angel take thy crown.

12. He that overcometh, I will make him a pillar in the temple of my God, and he shall go no more out; and I will write upon him the name of my God, and the name of the city of my God, the new Jerusalem, which is coming down out of heaven from God, and my new name.

Pillar: a door suggests a side-post and pillar. A pillar implies a temple. Pillars of ancient temples were sometimes carved into figures of men.[1] On the conqueror (verse 12) thus sculptured, names might be engraved.

In the Apocalypse, the Greek noun here (verse 12) translated "temple" always designates the holy of holies, the second apartment of the temple at Jerusalem; and by the figure, *a part for the whole*, this second apartment denotes the entire temple. This fact requires us to derive the imagery of the "pillar" from this temple on Mount Moriah, and thus forbids the primary reference to a heathen temple.

In the New Testament, "pillar" occurs elsewhere only Gal. ii. 9,

---

[1] The Atlantes at Pompeii is an example.

and 1 Tim. iii. 15. But as in each place "pillar" is *a figure*, the New Testament does not explain the origin of the imagery in Rev. iii. 12.

The Old Testament, however, furnishes the *literal* pillar, and this in connection with the temple in Jerusalem, and thus gives us the source of the figurative language when Christ promises to make the angel of the church in Philadelphia a pillar:—

Hiram of Tyre came to King Solomon, and cast two pillars of brass, and set up the pillars in the porch of the temple. He called the name of the right pillar Jachin (that is, *he shall be established*); he called the name of the left pillar Boaz (that is, *in it is strength*)" (1 Kings vii. 13–15, 21).

The meaning of the names of these pillars King Solomon caused to be erected, *established* and *strength*, is fully expressed in this description of the pillar (Rev. iii. 21). "He shall go no more out" (of the temple); which is the negative form of the affirmation, *he shall be strongly established* in the temple. *Go no more out* (that is, *established in strength*), obviously embodies the meanings of Jachin (*established*) and Boaz (*strength*); and signifies, by this *double* embodiment, that the angel of the church in Philadelphia is, as a pillar, as strong, firmly set, immovable, and enduring, as were *both* the pillars of molten brass in the high porch of Solomon's temple. As a representation of the vast strength and lasting stability of the church in Philadelphia, nothing in the compass of Scripture architecture can exceed this *doubled* imagery taken from the masterpiece of the skilful Hiram [1] of ancient Tyre, the city which the prophet Ezekiel pronounces "perfect in beauty" (xxviii. 12), made so by its cunning craftsmen, of whom Hiram was the most noted.

He shall go no more out: he shall always be a pillar in the temple of God, which is his church. In the historical Church on earth, the missionary example of the church in Philadelphia will ever live, and will ever prove a controlling power in the world. In the New Jerusalem, the evangelizing members of the church in Philadelphia will be pillars of beauty, as permanent and glorious as is the golden city itself.

The permanence of the truths here imaged so graphically and impressively creates the permanency of the duties Christ by this imagery so richly rewards. So long as verse 12 of chapter iii. is a part of his Apocalypse, it will be the changeless duty of his Church at all times, and in all places, to design systematically, to attempt habitually, and to seek most earnestly and permanently, the conversion of every Jewish soul and of every heathen heart.

---

[1] 1 Kings vii. 14.

The name of my God: the name of God is "the seal of God" (ix. 4). God's seal is the mark of his favor (vii. 3, 4; Ezek. ix. 4).

The name of the New Jerusalem: the inscription on a person, of the name of a city, denotes that he is a citizen of this city, and is identified with its own existence, history, riches, and honors (Acts xxi. 39).

Which is descending: is descending *incessantly:* so the Greek *present* participle decides.

The New Jerusalem is another name for Christ's kingdom. The capital city here stands for the kingdom itself.

Christ himself is *from above* (John viii. 23). His kingdom has the same origin (Gal. iv. 26; Heb. xii. 22), not only in the world, but in our hearts (Luke xvii. 21). Thus heavenly in its origin, Christ's kingdom is spiritual in its nature and influences.

The kingdom of God thus *within us* is *in power* (1 Cor. iv. 20). This power is to every believing soul "living water" (John iv. 10) and "living bread" (vi. 51).

In these ways the New Jerusalem has an *unceasing* descent. *Incessantly* is the New Jerusalem descending into believing hearts.

Out of heaven: heaven is here for the first time in the Apocalypse. It means, in this text, the residence of God.

Sometimes heaven in the Apocalypse means *the sky* (vi. 13, 14, viii. 1, x. 5, xi. 6, xii. 4, xvi. 21, xx. 11). This, therefore, may be the meaning of heaven in some other places in the Book of Revelation; for example, iv. 1, 2.

Many of the symbols and scenes in the book may be pictured and exhibited *on the face of the sky.*

My new name: Christ's new name he has already minutely described (ii. 17).

On the forehead of the conqueror described in the epistle to the church in Philadelphia, *three* names are inscribed. Three is *a full* number (Isa. xix. 24): name is identical with seal. Seal is a mark of favor. Three seals, therefore, on the forehead of the Philadelphia conqueror, are indications that Christ confers upon him *boundless* favor. No favor whatever does Christ withhold from his missionary conqueror.

But the Philadelphia conqueror is, in modern language, *a successful missionary to the Jews.*

By thus magnifying his regard for every one who labors for the conversion of the Jews, Christ not only magnifies the importance of the work, but he also magnifies his love for "his brethren, his kinsmen according to the flesh" (Rom. ix. 3). Christ has not cast away his people which he foreknew" (Rom. xi. 2). He still loves the children of Abraham: he still desires their salvation. He still commands and expects all his churches, without exception, to work incessantly for their conversion to himself.

13. (Identical with ii. 29, etc.)

SUMMARY OF THE SIXTH EPISTLE.

The sixth epistle has these general subjects : —

I. Christ's titles.

1. The holy. 2. The perfect. 3. He that hath the key of David. 4. He that openeth, and no one shutteth; and shutteth, and no one openeth.

II. Approvals.

1. Faithfulness; "kept my word" (verse 8). 2. Open confession of Christ's name (verse 8). 3. Enduring patience (verse 10).

III. Principal subject: the door Christ opens, namely, the opportunity he gives for the conversion of the Jews.

IV. Duties.

1. To enter the door Christ opens; that is, to attempt the conversion of the Jews. 2. Retention of present possessions, "hold that fast which thou hast" (verse 11); (*a*) faithfulness, (*b*) courage (open confession), (*c*) enduring patience, (*d*) occupation of the opened door, continuance of your work for the conversion of the Jews. 3. To conquer (verse 12).

V. Promises.

1. The door now opened will remain opened: "no man can shut it" (verse 8). The opportunity I give for the conversion of the Jews will always remain, even to the end of the world. 2. The work for converting the Jews will succeed; Jews will be converted: "I will make them to come and worship before thy feet" (verse 9); "My word shall not pass away" (Matt. xxiv. 35); "The natural branches shall be graffed into their own olive tree" (Rom. xi. 24); "All Israel shall be saved" (verse 26). 3. Preservation "from the hour of temptation" (verse 10). 4. Rewards, (*a*) crown (verse 11), (*b*) pillar (verse 12), (*c*) names (verse 12).

VI. Fitness of the church of Philadelphia for the work to which Christ appoints it.

1. Poverty; "little strength" (verse 8). Christ here pronounces poverty a ministerial advantage. The experience of his Church confirms the truth of his declaration. The most successful promulgators of his gospel have always been poor men. 2. Faithfulness (verse 8). 3. Courage (verse 8). 4. Endurance (verse 10).

VII. Application of Christ's titles to the principal subject.

1. His holiness prompts him to attempt the removal of the unholiness of the Jews. 2. His perfection includes love. Christ's affection for his brethren according to the flesh is the moving cause of all his efforts for their conversion. 3. His omnipotence ("openeth, and no man shutteth") secures the fulfilment of this promise, "I will make them to come and worship before thy feet" (verse 9).

VIII. Adaptation of Christ's rewards to the Philadelphian church. Christ appoints this church to be a missionary church. Mission-work among the Jews is both most important and most difficult. The rewards Christ promises his workers in this field are proportionably great and numerous (verse 4).

PRACTICAL TRUTHS OF THE SIXTH EPISTLE.

1. The promises of Christ cannot fail; because they rest upon his holiness, his perfectness, his kingship, his omnipotence.

2. The duties Christ specially rewards are firm adherence to his revealed word, open confession of his name, enduring labors in his service.

3. Both ministers and people should accept with cheerfulness and thankfulness the respective positions Christ assigns them in his Church. The service of each class he most amply rewards. This is the minister's reward (Matt. xix. 29); this, the layman's (Heb. vi. 10, xiii. 16).

4. Christ never shuts his opened doors of opportunity and duty.

5. Christ makes special provision for the salvation of the Jews, by assigning the work of their conversion *to all his churches.*

6. The conversion of the Jews is with Christ *a promised fact.* The Jews, as a body, will yet become Christians. Christ's promise cannot fail.

7. Christ's epistle to the church in Philadelphia is a MISSIONARY MANUAL, prescribing the duty of all his people, not only to the children of Abraham, but to all unconverted and heathen souls.

8. This MANUAL should be thoroughly studied and diligently practised by every Christian.

THE SEVENTH EPISTLE: EPISTLE TO THE CHURCH IN LAODICEA (Verses 14–22).

SUBJECT: LUKEWARMNESS, WANT OF SUPREME LOVE FOR GOD.

14. Also to the angel of the church in Laodicea write: These things saith the Amen, the faithful and true witness, the author of the new creation of God.

The Amen: only here in the New Testament as an appellation of Jesus Christ. From the Hebrew, with this meaning: the truth, "the God of truth" (Isa. lxv. 16).

The faithful and true witness: this expression refers to i. 5, the faithful witness."

The Seventh Recapitulation.

Faithful: trustworthy.

True: perfect.

The author: the Greek *arche* is in meaning identical with "cause" (Ecclus. xxv. 24, xxxvii. 16; Wis. of Sol. xii. 16, xiv. 27; Col. i. 18). But "cause" is nothing less than "author."

The new creation: the new creation of the soul in the image of Christ. "I make all things new" (Rev. xxi. 5). "If any man be in Christ, he is a new creature" (2 Cor. v. 17).

Christ here appeals to these appellations to show that his subsequent language respecting the church in Laodicea will most certainly be realized.

15. I know thy works, that thou art neither cold nor hot. I would thou wert cold or hot.

The reference in verses 15 and 16 may be to water in three states, — cold, boiling hot, and lukewarm. Cold water cools thirst (Luke xvi. 24). Hot water boils meat (1 Kings xix. 21). Both are thus useful. But lukewarm water nauseates ("spew," Rev. iii. 16), and is thus useless and hurtful.

In the New Testament, cold and heat describe different states of human love for God.

Examples. — "The love of many shall wax cold" (Matt. xxiv. 12). "Fervent in spirit, serving the Lord" (Rom. xii. 11).

Fervent love for God is, therefore, the supreme love for God. Christ demands of every human being, "Thou shalt love the Lord thy God with all thy heart, and with all thy soul, and with all thy mind" (Matt. xxii. 37).

We can now see the nature of lukewarm love. It loves something more than God. Men who are "lovers of their own selves, and are lovers of pleasure more than lovers of God" (2 Tim. iii. 2, 4), Judas in loving money (John xii. 6), and Demas in loving "this present world" (2 Tim. iv. 10), more than they loved Christ, are all examples of lukewarm love.

The church in Laodicea is "neither cold nor hot." It has not lost all love for Christ, but it does not love him fervently and supremely. Its love is hesitating, irresolute, reserved, partial, indifferent. When Christ says, "I would thou wert cold or hot" (verse 16), he does not desire this church to be colder than it is in its love, but he desires it to be *more fervent* in its love. Christ demands of the Laodicean church such love for himself as is supreme and exclusive.

The wish, "I would thou wert cold or hot," is *hyperbole*. This wish is by the hyperbole intensified into this expression: *Most earnestly do I desire* thee to love me supremely. God in the same manner intensifies his desire that idols would prove themselves possessed of life, when he exclaims, "Do good, or do evil, that we may know that ye are gods" (Isa. xli. 23).

16. In this way, since thou art lukewarm, and so neither hot nor cold, am I certainly about to do, namely, to spew thee out of my mouth.

In this way: in this unusual way. Christ's usual way is long forbearance (Rom. ii. 4).

To spew thee out of my mouth: this language presupposes that Christ expects satisfaction from the conduct of the church of Laodicea. He expects she will reciprocate his love, and that her love for him will be to him like food pleasant to his taste. But in place of satisfaction his experience brings disappointment. "The morsel he has eaten, he vomits up" (Prov. xxiii. 8). Christ through loathing and disgust rejects the lukewarm church; and unless she opens her heart to admit his newly proffered love (verse 20), her rejection will be final and unalterable.

17. Because thou art saying, I am very rich, and continually growing richer, and I have need of nothing; and yet thou knowest not that thou thyself art the most wretched, and the most pitiable, even poor and blind and naked.

The want of love for Christ in the church of Laodicea is occasioned by her self-love, her self-trust, and her self-satisfaction. Like her prototype, the selfish "spouse" in the Song of Solomon (chapter v.), who lost her "beloved" because, while he was knocking at her door for admission, she was through her self-love arraying her person, even to the profuse anointing of her hands and fingers (verse 5), the church of Laodicea is most amply providing for her own temporal convenience and luxury.

Rich: *already* rich.

Growing rich: becoming *richer*.

Need of nothing: this negative expression intensifies both "rich" and "richer," and in sense is the superlative, "richest," with this boastful meaning: In my own estimation I am the richest of mortals.

All this self-trust and self-boasting has both a spiritual sense and application.

It is the language of *self-righteousness*, such as the self-righteous Ephraim utters, "I am become rich, I have found out substance: in all my labors they shall find *none iniquity in me that were sin*" (Hos. xii. 8).

The church in Corinth, as described by St. Paul, is influenced by the same self-righteous spirit. "Ye are full, ye are rich, ye have reigned as kings *without us*" (1 Cor. iv. 8).

The self-righteousness of the church in Laodicea prevents her realizing her need of the righteousness of Jesus Christ. She does not love him supremely, because she does not feel her imperative need of his atoning blood to remove her guilt, and of his renewing grace to make her a new creature in him. She loves him little, because in her judgment he forgives her little (Luke vii. 47).

Totally different is the judgment of Christ, the author of the new creation, respecting the spiritual state of the self-righteous and coldly loving church of Laodicea.

Most wretched art thou: in thyself. Thy spiritual condition is most miserable.

Most pitiable: Its wretchedness excites the pity of all people truly Christian, and also of the holy angels (Luke xv. 7).

Thou art even poor, blind, naked: these words are not additional appellations, differing from "wretched" and "pitiable," but are explanations of "most pitiable."

Poor: to beggary, utterly poor. In a spiritual sense. "In me dwelleth no good thing" (Rom. vii. 18).

Blind: darkened, in a spiritual sense:—

(a) Blind to her own sins and to her spiritual poverty.

(b) Blind to the necessity of being justified by the blood of Christ, and saved by his gracious and new-creative power.

Naked: Without clothing, without the white garments Christ gives (verses 4 and 5), without the inward holiness these garments represent.

18. I counsel thee to buy of me gold-coin purified by fire, that thou mayest grow rich; and white garments, that thou mayest be clothed, and that the disgrace of thy nakedness does not show itself; and eye-salve to anoint thine eyes, that thou mayest see.

Counsel: The Greek word implies that the counsellor is intimately acquainted with the mind and state of the counselled (Matt. xii. 25; John ii. 25). Because I fully know thy wants, I counsel thee.

Buy: the meaning is not literal. The blessings Christ confers cannot be obtained by either money or service (Acts viii. 20). The true meaning of buy is *strongly to desire*. "Ho, every one that *thirsteth, come buy without money* and without price" (Isa. lv. 1).

Of me: Christ alone possesses and dispenses the spiritual blessings he counsels the spiritually poor earnestly to desire.

Purified: melted by the fire till all the dross is separated from the ore, and the gold is made pure and bright.

Rich: have "the true riches" (Luke xvi. 11), in increasing quantities. Poverty (verse 17) is want of holiness. In this world, then, holiness constitutes "the true riches."

Show itself: (John xxi. 1, 14) "showed himself."

Disgrace: Isa. xlvii. 3.

Nakedness: in spiritual sense, sinfulness.

Eye-salve: inner illumination by Christ (Luke xxiv. 45).

Eyes: hearts (Eph. i. 18, iv. 18; 1 John ii. 27; Matt. vi. 22, 23).

In verse 17, blindness is *second* in the triplet: poor, *blind*, naked. In verse 18, the removal of the blindness is *the last* in the triplet, to show that the spiritual illumination of the soul by Christ is essential to the perception of spiritual poverty, and to the desire of spiritual riches, and also to the sight of our spiritual deformities, and to our aspiration after the possession of Christ's image in our hearts.

See: have spiritual sight (Mark viii. 18; Luke viii. 10).

19. Whomsoever I love, I myself reprove and chasten. Accordingly, be fervent and repent.

Love: with personal affection.
Reprove: so as to convince him of his sin (2 Sam. xii. 13).
Chasten: to make him better (Heb. xii. 5, 6).
Be fervent: the Greek verb, and "hot" (verse 15), have the same root. Fervent, not "zealous" (English Version), is therefore the correct translation.

20. Behold, I stand at the door, and knock: if any man hear my voice, and open the door, I will come in to him, and will sup with him, and he with me.

Behold: with only one exception, "behold," in the Apocalypse, introduces either a new subject or a new illustration. In verse 19, "repent" is the concluding exhortation, which we may regard as equal to this declaration and promise to the Laodicean church, "Return unto me, and *I will return* unto you" (Mal. iii. 7). Love me with all thy heart, and thou shalt have my unreserved love. In verse 20, "behold" introduces a most graphic and most attractive picture of *the manner* of our Lord's return to the repenting soul. There is no such picture of Christ's love elsewhere in the Bible. His manner is most condescending and most winning.

I stand: I am standing on the outside of thy house (Luke xiii. 25).

In Rev. iii. 7, Christ calls himself "He that openeth, and no man shutteth;" but here he is standing on the outside of the door, as a brother (Acts xii. 13), as a servant (Luke xiii. 25), as a bridegroom (Song of Sol. v. 2), and knocks, and thus *asks for admission*. In drawing us to himself, Christ respects the freedom of the human will.

At the door: of the house (Mark ii. 1). At, close to; so near as to touch and knock the door; nearer than "about" (Mark ii. 2); nearer than "before" (Jas. v. 9); at the door of the *heart*.

And knock: am knocking continually.

Forms of Christ's knocking: —

External: by his word and providence; (*a*) rebuke (verse 19), (*b*) discipline (verse 19).

Internal: by his Holy Spirit; (*a*) illumination (Luke xxiv. 45; Rev. iii. 18), (*b*) conviction (John xvi. 8), (*c*) sense of Christ's love (Rom. v. 5).

Any one: "Him that cometh to me, I will in no wise cast out" (John vi. 37).

Hear: and obey, i. 3.

My voice: merely *the sound* of my voice. In the Greek, "voice," *genitive* with "hear," as in this place, is simply the *sound* of the voice. In Acts ix. 7, "voice," *accusative* with "hear," is *the meaning of* the voice (Acts xxii. 9).

The Lord's voice (Rev. iii. 20) is the *whispered* word, "open" (Matt. xxv. 11; Luke xiii. 25). When he simply *whispers* this entreating word, he desires and expects us to listen and obey. Returning love for Christ waits to hear this whisper, however faint, and rejoices because it heralds the near presence of Christ himself.

Open the door: in two ways.

Literal. — At the time St. John wrote the Apocalypse, the door of a dwelling-house had two valves, each called a door. This double door was fastened on the inside by two perpendicular bolts and a horizontal cross-bar. Each valve was fastened to the sill by one of the perpendicular bolts. The cross-bar resting on mortices in the side-posts also fastened both the valves. The whole door was opened by removing the bar, and raising the bolts.

Spiritual. — (*a*) Reviving love; (*b*) attention (Prov. iv. 20); (*c*) faith (Mark xi. 22); (*d*) obedience (John xv. 14).

The excluding inside bar and bolts are, therefore, (*a*) indifference, (*b*) inattention, (*c*) unbelief, (*d*) disobedience.

I will come in to him: I will enter his house and his heart.

Will sup with him: supper was, in the time of St. John, the principal meal, and was taken in the evening (Mark vi. 21; Luke xiv. 16; John xii. 2). I will *feast* with him. To eat *with a person* is *to receive* him to one's confidence and affection (Luke xv. 2; Gal. ii. 12; John xxi. 20, xiii. 25). "I will love him freely, I will receive him graciously, I will heal his backsliding" (Hos. xiv. 2, 4). This, then, is the meaning of Christ's promise: I will sup with him, namely, I will *love him*, leaning on my heart (John xiii. 23).

He with me: thus leaning and being loved, he shall *fervently love me in return for my immeasurable love* (1 John iv. 19). I will feed him with my own holy humanity (John vi. 51, 54–56), and thus make him a partaker of my own holy nature. With what a divine exhibition of his humble condescension, undying love, and exhaustless desire for the salvation of every human soul, does Christ end his seventh and last epistle to the churches! Neither lightning nor thunder accompanies his gentle approach. The only voices audible are these voices which are ever turning the world to the incarnate Son of God. "Christ's love passeth knowledge" (Eph. iii. 19). "The love of Christ constraineth us" (2 Cor. v. 14). "We love him because he first loved us" (1 John iv. 19).

The language of this verse and that of the Song of Solomon (v. 2) are so much alike, that the similarity cannot be accidental, but must be designed by the Holy Spirit who inspired both passages.

1. The persons addressed are similar. Each is an espoused bride; each is called bride, — "spouse [Greek *numphe*, bride]" (Song of Sol. v. 1). "The *bride* [Greek, *numphe*], the Lamb's wife" (Rev. xxi. 9).

2. The mind of each is in *a hesitating, irresolute state*. When the spouse rises to open the door, she hesitates, and lingers to anoint her hands and fingers (Song of Sol. v. 5). "Thou art neither cold nor hot" (Rev. iii. 15), also describes a state of hesitation.

3. Each is addressed by the bridegroom. "The *voice* of my beloved" (Song of Sol. v. 2). The voice of the bride's beloved is her bridegroom. Because the Lamb's wife is his bride (Rev. xxi. 9), he himself is the Bridegroom. Christ's wife is his Church (Eph. v. 23). The church in Laodicea, because connected with the Church universal, is his Church, and is therefore his bride.

4. Each is beloved by the bridegroom. "My love, my dove" (Song of Sol. v. 2). "Christ loves the church" (Eph. v. 25).

5. To each the bridegroom seeks admission. "My beloved *knocketh*, saying, *Open* to me, my love" (Song of Sol. v. 2). "I stand at the door, and *knock*: if any man *open* the door, *I will come in to him*" (Rev. iii. 20).

6. To each a feast is promised. "He brought me to the banqueting house" (Song of Sol. ii. 4). "I will sup with him, and *he with me*" (Rev. iii. 20).

These multiplied coincidences between the Song of Solomon and Rev. iii. 20 not only disclose the origin of St. John's language in this verse, but also establish the character of the Song of Solomon. The book is an Oriental and poetical description of the reciprocal love subsisting between Christ and his Church.

21. To him that overcometh will I grant to sit with me in my throne, as I also myself overcame, and sat down with my Father in his throne.

This verse describes the final reward Christ gives every victor over the sins mentioned in the seventh epistle. The reward is participation in the exaltation, dignity, and glory of Christ (John xvii. 24).

He that overcometh. See ii. 7.

To sit: enthroned, as Christ sits enthroned. The enthronement of the victor will *resemble* the enthronement of Christ. It will not be *the same* enthronement. "When he shall appear, we shall be *like* him" (1 John iii. 2). In the New Testament, the preposition "with" sometimes denotes, *not sameness*, but *likeness, resemblance*.

Examples. — (*a*) "Abraham dwelt in tents *with* Jacob." Abraham and Jacob were not contemporaries: Abraham, therefore, must have dwelt in tents *as* Jacob dwelt in tents.

(*b*) "Herod the king was troubled, and all Jerusalem *with him*" (Matt. ii. 3). Jerusalem was troubled *as* Herod was troubled.

(*c*) "Eat and drink *with the drunken*" (Matt. xxiv. 49). Eat and drink, *as* the drunken eat and drink, to excess.

(*d*) "Watch *with* me" (Matt. xxvi. 38). Watch *as* I watch.

(*e*) "May die *with him*" (John xi. 16). May die *as* Jesus dies.

With me: enthroned *as* I am enthroned (iv. 4).

In my throne: "the throne of God and *of the Lamb*" (xxii. 3).

Sat down: and am now sitting; "*am* set down," English Version A.D. 1611, which (2 Thess. ii. 4) translates the same aorist verb of Rev. iii. 21, as a present tense, — "sitteth."

With my Father in his throne: In this clause, "with" does not denote *likeness*, but *association and sameness*. "With" here receives this sense, from this command of God the Father to God the Son, "The Lord said unto my Lord, *Sit thou* at my right hand" (Ps. cx. 1).

After his ascension into heaven, our Lord Jesus Christ "sat on the right hand of God" (Mark xvi. 19). The right hand of God is "the right hand *of his throne*" (Heb. viii. 1, xii. 2).

The right hand of the throne of God is the right-hand seat in this throne. The two seats are *in one and the same throne*. But *one throne* is mentioned. The assumption that there is a second throne cannot, however, create a second throne. The enthroned Father and Son occupy but *one* throne.

With Christ's enthronement at God's right hand in the same throne, he was by his Father invested with universal sovereignty and dominion (Eph. i. 20, 21; 1 Pet. iii. 22).

This investment proves his occupation of the same throne with his Father.

The refusal to receive and love Christ is —
1. Ingratitude (2 Cor. v. 14).
2. Contempt (Heb. x. 29).
3. Sin (John xv. 22).
4. Loss (Acts iv. 12).
5. Danger (Heb. x. 28-31).

22. He that hath an ear, let him hear what the Spirit saith unto the churches.

1. *Seventh repetition* of this exhortation, — ii. 7, 11, 17, 29; iii. 6, 13, 22.

2. These seven repetitions invest the exhortation with the strongest emphasis, and with the greatest value and authority.

3. Christ himself pronounces the exhortation.

4. The Holy Spirit conveys the exhortation to the seven churches.

5. Because these churches are *representative*, this exhortation Christ addresses to all churches, at all times and in all places.

6. The blessing of Christ always accompanies the reception of the exhortation (i. 3), through the perpetual presence and almighty power of the Holy Ghost (1 Pet. i. 12).

SUMMARY OF THE SEVENTH EPISTLE.

The seventh epistle has these general subjects: —

I. The titles of Christ. 1. The Amen. 2. The faithful and true Witness. 3. The Author of the new creation. 4. Counsellor (verse 18. See Isa. ix. 6). 5. Reprover (verse 19). 6. Bridegroom, " stand at the door, and knock " (verse 20; Song of Sol. v. 2). 7. Friend, " sup with him " (verse 20). (8). Judge (verse 21).

II. Subject, lukewarmness, — want of supreme love for God

III. Sins. 1. Lukewarmness. 2. Self-righteousness (verse 17). 3. Self-ignorance (verse 17).

IV. Duties. 1. To buy gold, and white raiment. 2. To anoint eyes (verse 18). 3. To be zealous (fervent). 4. To repent (verse 19). 5. To hear Christ's voice. 6. To open the door. 7. To sup with Christ (verse 20). 8. To overcome all sins (verse 21).

V. Threats. 1. Rebuke (verse 19). 2. Chastening. 3. Rejection (verse 16).

VI. Dispositions of Christ. 1. Desire for the fervent love of Laodicean church (verse 15). 2. Regard for the welfare of the church (verse 18). 2. Love for the church (verse 19). 4. Love manifested (verse 20).

VII. Christ's promises. 1. To give (*a*) the true riches, (*b*) holiness, (*c*) illumination (verse 18). 2. Fellowship with himself (verse 20). 3. Kingly authority and honor.

VIII. Adaptation of Christ's titles to the general subject.

Each of the eight titles is closely connected with the great purpose of this seventh epistle, — *the creation, in the soul of every human being, of supreme love for Christ.*

IX. Application of the truths of the epistle to the case of the persons addressed. These truths are the *motives* Christ presents to induce all men, without exception, to love him supremely. These motives exhaust even the divine treasury of instrumentalities. If the threats and the promises and the surpassing love of Christ do not draw sinners to him, nothing will. Their sinfulness and their ruin are beyond remedy. Christ is free from the blood of all men. Lost souls are the authors of their own destruction.

PRACTICAL TRUTHS OF THE SEVENTH EPISTLE.

1. Love felt and acting, desires love in return.
2. The infinite love of Christ demands, from its own nature, the supreme love of every human soul.
3. The infinite love of Christ deserves the supreme love of every human soul. Love shown merits love reciprocated.
4. Christ, the Author of the human nature, creates in every human soul instinctive gratitude. We naturally love them that love us.
5. Christ, the Author of our moral nature, and of its new creation in him, not only creates the capability, but also inspires the inclination, to love him as Creator, Redeemer, Benefactor, and Sanctifier. Christ "tasted death for every man" (Heb. ii. 9). Every human soul does, in consequence, possess the gift from Christ of the efficacy of his blood. Redemption is thus universal and unlimited. With this gift, every human soul also receives from Christ the gift of moral capability, and with it the grace and power to exercise it. Were not this second gift the possession of every human soul, the first gift would be useless, and " Christ is dead in vain " (Gal. ii. 21) ; a possibility forever inconceivable.

The Christian facts that Christ tasted death for every man, and that he is " the true Light which lighteth every man "

(John i. 9), establish these Christian truths, — universal redemption, and universal participation in Christ's gift of spiritual light.

These fundamental truths of the gospel destroy a prominent position in "Natural Law in the Spiritual World," by Henry Drummond, "Spiritual life is conferred only upon a small portion of mankind;" and also this kindred dogma of John Calvin, "By the eternal decree of God, eternal life is fore-ordained for some, and eternal damnation for others" (*Institutes*, book iii. chap. 21).

6. Refusal to love Christ is opposition both to the native instinct of gratitude, and to the grace of his Holy Spirit, with which he inspires every human soul.

7. Destitution of love for Christ is destitution of his image, which is love (1 John iv. 8).

8. If we are not like Christ, we shall not see him when he shall appear (1 John iii. 2).

CHARACTERISTIC PECULIARITIES OF CHAPTERS I., II., AND III.

1. RECAPITULATIONS.

We have just listened to the sevenfold repetition of Christ's impressive exhortation to the seven churches.

In our previous attention to his words, we have heard seven other recapitulations. These deserve to be more minutely examined.

Chapters ii. and iii. repeat substantially the first chapter.

The first chapter of the Apocalypse contains a most graphic, and at the same time unique, description of the person and offices of the Son of man.

This description fills two portions of the chapter (verses 4–8 and 11–18). The second description is an expanded recapitulation of the first. Thus early in the Apocalypse does the principle of recapitulation appear. The same principle pervades the entire volume. The obvious design of recapitulation is the exhibition of the unfailing and absolute certainty of the events symbolized and predicted. Recapitulation is the emphatic repetition of this declaration. "The dream [vision] was doubled unto Pharaoh *twice;* because the thing *is established by God*, and God will *shortly bring it to pass*" (Gen. xli. 32).

Recapitulation is often-reiterated instruction and admonition, "precept upon precept, line upon line" (Isa. xxviii. 13), that the lessons may be deeply engraven upon the imagination and memory, and be forever remembered and obeyed.

St. Paul employs recapitulation with forcible impressiveness and persuasive tenderness: "Of many I have told you often, and now tell you even weeping" (Phil. iii. 18).

These illustrations from Isaiah and St. Paul will help us understand and appreciate the incessant use of recapitulation in the Apocalypse. In Rev. ii. and iii., each of the seven epistles begins by *repeating* a portion of the description of our Lord in the first chapter. That *the exactness* of the recapitulations may be easily seen, the description of our Lord and the recapitulations are here placed in opposite columns.

OUR LORD'S DESCRIPTION.	RECAPITULATIONS.
1. "In the midst of the seven golden candlesticks, one like unto the Son of man" (i. 13). "He had in his right hand seven stars" (verse 16).	*Epistle I.* — "Who walketh in the midst of the seven golden candlesticks." "He that holdeth in his right hand seven stars" (ii. 1).
2. "I am the first and the last: I am he that liveth and was dead; and behold, I am alive forevermore" (i. 17, 18).	*Epistle II.* — "The first and the last, which was dead, and is alive" (ii. 8).
3. "Out of his mouth went a sharp two-edged sword" (i. 16).	*Epistle III.* — "He which hath the sharp sword with two edges" (ii. 12).
4. "His eyes were as a flame of fire; and his feet like unto fine brass, as if they burned in a furnace" (i. 14, 15).	*Epistle IV.* — "Who hath his eyes like unto a flame of fire, and his feet are like fine brass" (ii. 18).

5. "The seven Spirits which are before his throne" (i. 4). "In his right hand seven stars" (verse 16).

6. "I have the keys of hell and of death" (i. 18).

7. "Jesus Christ, the faithful witness" (i. 5).

Epistle V. — "He hath the seven Spirits of God, and the seven stars" (iii. 1).

Epistle VI. — "He that hath the key of David; he that openeth, and no man shutteth; and shutteth, and no man openeth" (iii. 7).

Epistle VII. — "The faithful and true witness" (iii. 14).

OFFICE OF THE RECAPITULATIONS.

Each recapitulation introduces either a *threat* or a *promise*. Epistles one, three, five, seven, contain threats; epistles two, four, six, contain promises. Thus the threats and promises alternate.

EPISTLE I. — *Threat.* "I will remove *thy candlestick*" (ii. 5); repeated from "He that walketh in the midst of the *seven golden candlesticks*" (ii. 1).

EPISTLE II. — *Promise.* "I will give thee a crown *of life*" (ii. 10); repeated from "which *is alive*" (verse 8).

EPISTLE III. — *Threat.* "I will fight against them *with the sword of my mouth*" (ii. 16); repeated from "He which hath *the sharp sword with two edges*" (verse 12).

EPISTLE IV. — *Promise.* "I will give him the morning star" (ii. 28); repeated from "the Son of God hath his eyes like unto a flame of fire, and his feet are like fine brass" (verse 18).

The morning star is the emblem of a king. (Isa. xiv. 12) "I will give him the morning star;" that is, I will make him a king. "To him will I give power over the nations" (Rev. ii. 26). "He shall rule them with a rod of iron" (verse 27). In other words, his ruling power shall be irresistible. His power will be resistless, because his eyes, like mine, shall be quick to discern, like "a flame of fire," that is, like the lightning; and his feet swift to execute, like my own lightning feet, "burning" and flaming in their almighty and conquering rapidity.

EPISTLE V. — *Threat.* "I will come on thee as a thief; and thou shalt not know what hour I will come upon thee" (iii. 3); repeated in its ideal from "He that hath the seven Spirits of God and the seven stars" (verse 1). Holding the seven stars, Christ is *affectionate*. Holding the Spirits of God, Christ is both *omniscient* and *omnipotent*. These attributes enable Him to come *as a thief, suddenly, at any un-*

known instant. His *affection* will determine *the manner* of his coming. While *punitive*, it may yet be *in love.*

EPISTLE VI. — *Promise.* "I have set before thee an *open* [opened] *door*, and no man can *shut* it" (iii. 8); repeated from "He that hath *the key* of David; he that *openeth*, and no man *shutteth*; and *shutteth*, and no man *openeth*" (verse 7).

EPISTLE VII. — *Threat.* "I will *spew* thee out of my mouth" (iii. 16); repeated as the necessity of the rejection, from "the faithful and true witness" (verse 14), who has already said "I hate" false disciples (ii. 6), and who therefore will show this declaration to be "faithful and true."

These seven groups of Apocalyptic scriptures disclose the relations existing between the descriptions of our Lord in the first chapter, and their recapitulations in chapters ii. and iii.

The descriptions of our Lord are designations of *the character* of the several threats and promises pronounced in the second and third chapters.

But symbolic descriptions, which are thus definite designations, are themselves SYMBOLIC PREDICTIONS.

These, then, are the very significant and instructive relations subsisting between the descriptions of our Lord's person and offices, in the first chapter of the Apocalypse, and their subsequent recapitulations: THE DESCRIPTIONS ARE PREDICTIONS, THE RECAPITULATIONS ARE FULFILMENTS.

The recapitulations are fulfilments, because with God a threat is an execution, unless the threat is averted by repentance. With God also. a promise is a realization, unless the promise is nullified by human unbelief and disobedience.

These inherent relations between chapter i. and chapters ii. and iii. are MOST IMPORTANT. They cast invaluable light upon the structure and significance of *the remaining portions of the book.* In the sublime visions which follow the seven epistles, are both *symbolic predictions*, and *symbolic fulfilments* of these predictions. In arrangement, chapters iv.-xxii. are reflections and counterparts of the first three chapters. Recapitulation is the initiating clew into the intricate and complicated labyrinth, which it will be our next attempt to enter, and trace to the end. The fact of PREDICTION and FULFILMENT in chapters i., ii., and iii., is a strong and divine key, prepared to open, on all doors, all locks, and lift all bolts which may hereafter in their received traditions and antiquated rustiness resist our tentative hands, and bar our inquiring way.

II. INTENSIFICATIONS BY AMPLIFICATION.

These intensifications abound in the second and third chapters.

The intensifications are of two kinds.

1. *The descriptions of our Lord* in chapter i.

EXAMPLES.

Simple.	Intense.
(a) "I have the keys of hell and of death" (i. 18).	"He that hath the key of David; he that openeth, and no man shutteth; and shutteth, and no man openeth" (iii. 7).
(b) "Jesus Christ, the faithful witness" (i. 5).	"The faithful and true witness" (iii. 14).

2. *A climactic series:* —

(1) Of *threats*.

(a) "I will remove thy candlestick" (ii. 5).
(b) "I will war with the sword" (verse 16).
(c) "I will come as a thief" (iii. 3).
(d) "I will spew thee out of my mouth" (verse 16).

(2) Of *promises*.

(a) "Tree of life" (ii. 7).
(b) "Crown of life." Preservation from "second death" (ii. 10, 11).

The promise is here *doubled*.

(c) Hidden manna. White stone. New name (ii. 17).

The promise is here *tripled*.

(d) Power over nations. Rod-of-iron rule. Breakage to shivers. Morning star.

The promise is here *quadrupled*.

(*e*) Sentence of worthiness. White raiment. Name in book of life. Confession before Christ's Father. Confession before his angels (iii. 4, 5).

Here the promise is *quintupled*.

(*f*) Crown. Pillar. Immovability. Name of God. Name of New Jerusalem. Christ's new name (iii. 11, 12).

Here the promise is *sextupled*.

(*g*) Enthronement with Christ (iii. 21).

This promise is *sevenfold*, since enthronement with Christ is *the consummation* of all the *twenty-one* other promises; *twenty-one* being the multiple of *three* and *seven*, each of which is a *perfect* number. Thus their multiple is *perfect*.

These elaborate illustrations of intensified amplification disclose an unexpected literary excellence in the Apocalypse, — its *minutely artistic character*. Other instances may hereafter reveal themselves.

III. REPRESENTATION.

Recapitulation and amplification are inherent in the very nature of the Apocalypse, as a literary creation. The book is a series of visions. The visions are not realities, but the *representations* of realities. Because the visions are *representative*, they can be recapitulated and amplified.

Representation pervades and characterizes the whole volume. Nothing on its pages is literal fact, in case the object presented can be symbolized.

Instances of representation in the first division of the Apocalypse may enable us to perceive more clearly the structural character of the book.

1. The vision of the Son of man in the first chapter represents his actual character, so far as he exhibits it in the various symbols.

In the seven epistles, Christ exhibits himself in *various* symbols and in *various* characters. He is thus a *multiplied* symbol. The fact is a model. Other persons may, then, assume different symbols, provided St. John shall so determine. The scarlet woman (chapter xvi.) may be the symbol both of civil and ecclesiastical power.

2. In the seven epistles, the angels are representatives of the seven churches.

3. In their turn, the seven churches are representatives of all future churches which may possess their excellences, or may renew their faults and vices.

The recapitulations, amplifications, and representations of the first division of the Apocalypse foreshadow, predict, and insure the re-appearance of the same peculiarities in the diversified visions which succeed the epistolary portion of the book.

We await with impatient interest the presentation and development of the larger and more eventful drama. The new scenes will, in outward features, closely resemble their instructive predecessors.

RELATIONS OF THE SEVEN EPISTLES OF THE APOCALYPSE TO THE AFTER PORTIONS OF THE BOOK.

The seven epistles are not a separate and completed part of the Apocalypse. They are necessary and essential *preparations* for the subsequent portions.

I. At the beginning of the second part of the book, a throne of judgment is erected (iv. 2).

The seven epistles are the DIVINE CODE by which the decisions of this judgment-throne are ruled.

The seven epistles of the Apocalypse, although bearing different titles, constitute a COMPREHENSIVE SUMMARY, first of *all Christian duties*, and then of ALL THE SINS which oppose the creation of Christ's life in our nature, deaden this life when it exists, cause the ruin of lost souls, and perpetually weaken his Church, and hinder its growth and extension.

The contents of the seven epistles disclose their inherent

possession of these indispensable constituents of a *judgment-code*.

CHRISTIAN DUTIES PRESCRIBED BY THE SEVEN EPISTLES.

1. The first epistle enjoins brotherly love as *a habitual affection of the soul.*
2. The second epistle enjoins Christian love, which shows itself *in labors* for the spiritual good of others, even unto martyrdom.
3. The third epistle enjoins *open and persistent confession of Christ*, and *self-denial and self-restraint.*
4. The fourth epistle enjoins *submission to God's will* in all its revelations and institutions.
5. The fifth epistle enjoins *the activity, energy, increase, and controlling sway* of the life Christ imparts to the soul.
6. The sixth epistle enjoins *absolute obedience* to the command of Christ *respecting the conversion of the Jews.*
7. The seventh epistle enjoins *supreme love for Christ.*

Thus disclosing their inherent *legal* contents, the seven epistles demonstrate their nature. They are in their association and exhaustiveness *a comprehensive summary of all Christian duty, both to God and man.*

SINS FORBIDDEN BY THE SEVEN EPISTLES.

1. By the first epistle, *hatred of our fellow-men.*
2. By the second epistle, *neglect of the souls of others.*
3. By the third epistle, *self-indulgence* in the twofold forms of *gluttony and sensuality.*
4. By the fourth epistle, *self-will and apostasy from Christ.*
5. By the fifth epistle, *self-murder* in causing the death of the soul.
6. By the sixth epistle, *the neglect of Christ* by the neglect of his brethren *the Jews* (Matt. xxv. 45).
7. By the seventh epistle, *self-love*, the dethronement of supreme love for God.

So inclusive is this list of sins forbidden by the seven

epistles, that all our spiritual enemies, of whatever name, are contained in the comprehensive summation.

We thus discover *the close connection* St. John himself creates between the seven epistles and the throne of judgment (iv. 2). The judgment-throne imperiously needs a *legal code* by which to frame its decisions. A throne implies the previous existence of law. The legal code, the authoritative standard of its mandates, the throne of judgment now possesses in *the seven epistles* already prepared as *legal authority* for its use.

II. The seven epistles contribute, from their varied resources, very largely towards the construction of the second and third parts of the Apocalypse. The exhibition of the extent of this contribution is here necessary, in order to appreciate the intimate relations the seven epistles bear to the compositions which follow.

1. The *material imagery* of the seven epistles is afterwards repeated.

(*a*) The candlestick (ii. 5) appears again in xi. 4; not only in form, but also in signification, that of the Church.

(*b*) " The tree of life " (ii. 7) still bears fruit (xxii. 14).

(*c*) Christ's sword (ii. 12) re-appears (xix. 15).

(*d*) The " white stone " (ii. 17) shines anew (xxi. 11).

(*e*) The " rod of iron " (ii. 27) smites again (xii. 5), and still again (xix. 15).

(*f*) " The morning star " (ii. 28) has a second rising (xxii. 16).

(*g*) " White garments " (iii. 4) retain their signification (xvi. 15).

(*h*) " The book of life " (iii. 5) is re-opened (xx. 12).

(*i*) " The key of David " (iii. 7) " opens " treasures no other key can open (v. 5).

(*j*) The " open door " (iii. 8) is seen a second time (iv. 1).

(*k*) " Throne " (iii. 21) is almost constantly visible in the remaining divisions of the Apocalypse.

2. The *immaterial figures* of the seven epistles occur in the subsequent chapters.

(*a*) The second death (ii. 11) is also mentioned (xx. 14).

(*b*) "The New Jerusalem," the Church (iii. 12) descends from heaven once more (xxi. 2).

(*c*) The promised enthronement (iii. 21) is fully realized (xx. 4).

3. The *same persons* appear both in the seven epistles and portions following.

(*a*) Jezebel (ii. 20) is newly created in the "woman sitting on the scarlet-colored beast" (xvii. 3).

The resemblances between Jezebel and this woman are so striking and numerous, that they must be drawn by the finger of God.

(1) Each woman is moved by pride.

(2) Both women are controlled by self-will (Jer. 1. 29, 31).

(3) Each woman claims to be the head of a church.

(4) Both women collect followers.

(5) Each woman teaches false doctrines.

(6) Each woman is a spiritual adulteress, and is thus unfaithful to God.

(7) Each woman is guilty of apostasy from God.

(8) Both women are associated with Satan.

(9) Both women refuse to repent (Rev. ii. 21; Jer. li. 9).

(10) Both women are punished with spiritual death.

(*b*) The faithful portion of the church in Thyatira is the model of "the woman clothed with the sun" (xii. 1), "the Lamb's wife" (xxi. 9).

(*c*) The faithful martyrs represented by Antipas (ii. 13) re-appear in vi. 9–11, xviii. 20, xix. 2, xx. 4.

(*d*) The seven conquerors (ii. 7, 11, 17, 26; iii. 5, 12, 21) re-appear by implication, with the first symbolic appearance of Christ as conqueror (vi. 2); and re-appear actually, when clothed in fine linen, white and clean, they upon white horses follow the victorious and triumphing "Word of God" (xix. 13, 14).

(e) The searching declaration, prefacing each epistle, "I know thy works," recognizes Christ as *supreme Judge* of all churches and of all mankind. *He fills the rest of the volume with his judicial acts.* He is supreme Judge, in breaking the seven seals; in imaging on the seven scrolls the coming history of his Church and of the world; in blowing the seven trumpets; in pouring out the seven censers; in defeating and punishing his enemies; in vindicating and rewarding his followers; in annihilating Babylon; in harvesting the earth; in calling the dead, small and great, before his great white throne; in preparing the New Jerusalem for the eternal residence of the blessed, and "the lake of fire" (Rev. xx. 14) for the Devil and his angels and adherents.

These multiplied repetitions of the seven epistles, in the subsequent writings of the Apocalypse, demonstrate that the connection of these epistles with the sections which follow is not only *real, intimate,* and *pervading,* but is *intended and created by the inspiration and guidance of the Holy Spirit.*

SECOND DIVISION (CHAPTERS iv.–xx. 1–10).

THE second division of the Apocalypse has both a chronology and a purpose.

I. The chronology begins with the commencement of the Church of Jesus Christ, and ends with the destruction of this present earth. This is the extensive period included in the chronology. But, while thus comprehensive, the chronology is not an enumeration of exact dates. These are known only to the omniscience of God, and can be determined only by the fulfilment of his predictions.

II. The purpose of the Apocalypse is twofold : —

1. First, to exhibit the *sovereignty* of Jesus Christ, both in his Church and in all worlds.

Just before his ascension, he assumed the possession of all power in earth and heaven (Matt. xxviii. 18). The second division of the Apocalypse is, in part, the symbolized exhibition of this supreme sovereignty.

2. Second, to exhibit Christ's *administration* of his sovereignty, in rewarding his true disciples, and in punishing his enemies. This discriminating administration is portrayed by series of symbols most appropriate and most instructive.

Both the chronology and the purpose are symbolized by the erection of the "throne," at the opening of the fourth chapter, and by the succession of symbols which closely follows.

The sovereignty of Christ is denied: his administration is resisted. This denial and this resistance cause opposition and conflict. The maintenance of Christ's sovereignty, and the preservation of his administration, are, in the Apocalypse, represented by the conditions of warfare and its military instrumentalities, horses and horsemen, the bow and the sword.

The second division has two parts. The first part (iv.–ix.) is characterized by the seals (iv.–vii.) and the trumpets (viii., ix.).

The second part (x.–xxii.) contains the symbolic Bridegroom (chap. x.); the two witnesses (xi.); the bride of Christ, and her enemies (xii. and xiii.); the victor Lamb and his victor Church; the fall of the apostate Church, symbolized by two harvests (xiv.) and by the seven censers (xv., xvi.); the scarlet woman and her ruin (xvii., xviii.); alleluias; the marriage of the Lamb; the enthronement of the martyrs (xix., xx. 1–10).

The seals are symbolical predictions. The trumpets, the harvests, the censers, are the symbolical fulfilments of the predictions.

SECOND DIVISION, PART I. (CHAPTERS iv.–ix.).

CHAPTER IV.

This chapter is a preparation for the introduction and opening of the " seven seals " (v. 1).

A throne of judgment is set in heaven. God the Father is seated on this throne. Encircling his throne are twenty-four other thrones. On these thrones twenty-four human elders are sitting as associate judges.

Before the supreme throne, seven torches of fire are blazing, representing the seven Spirits of God.

The pavement before the throne is, in its whiteness and purity, like a sea of glass.

The executioners of the decisions of the thrones are cherubim.

VISION OF GOD'S THRONE OF JUDGMENT (Verses 1–11).

1. After these things I saw. And behold, an opened door in heaven, and the first voice, which I heard as a trumpet speaking with me [spake again] saying, Ascend thither, and I will show thee the events which must certainly come to pass hereafter.

After these things: after the delivery and reception of the seven epistles.

Opened door: "the heavens were opened" (Ezek. i. 1; Matt. iii. 16; Acts x. 11, vii. 56).

The first voice: that is, the same voice which addressed St. John (i. 10), the voice of the Son of man (verse 13).

Ascend: St. John ascended "in the vision" (ix. 17; see xi. 12).
I will show: the Son of man is the Revelator (John i. 18).

2. And immediately I was in the spirit: and behold, a throne was set in heaven, and upon the throne, a Judge sitting.

A throne was set: of the *judicial* character of this throne, the following proofs in the context are sufficient: (*a*) "the lightnings and thunderings" proceeding from the throne (Ps. xviii. 14); (*b*) the presence of the living creatures (verses 6, 7), who are the executioners of God's judgments (Ezek. x. 2, 6, 7).

A Judge sitting: "Thou *satest in the throne judging* right" (Ps. ix. 4). The Judge enthroned is God the *Father*, because (vii. 10) distinguished from "the Lamb" and (iv. 5) from the Holy Spirit.

3. And he who is sitting is in appearance like a jasper, and a cornelian, and a rainbow around the throne is in appearance like an emerald.

Jasper: the precious stone intended is probably the *diamond* (*Dict. of the Bible*). The white diamond is an emblem of the purity and impartiality of God.

Cornelian: emblem of his justice.

Rainbow: God's own "token" of his mercy and faithfulness (Gen. ix. 12; see Ezek. i. 28).

Emerald: emblem of peace (Ps. xxiii. 2). As the green of the emerald tempers the red of the cornelian, so the bow of promise tempers God's judgments.

4. And encircling the throne are twenty-four thrones, and upon the thrones I see twenty-four elders sitting, clothed in white garments, and upon their heads golden crowns.

Twenty-four thrones: the imagery of the throne encircled by twenty-four other thrones is derived from the Jewish Sanhedrin. In this court, the high priest presided (Matt. xxvi. 62), and was therefore the *supreme* judge. His associate judges were twenty-four in number, corresponding to the twenty-four classes into which the Jewish priests were divided (1 Chron. xxiv. 7-18).

The Sanhedrin sat in the form of *a half-circle* (SMITH, *Dict. Bible*, iv. 2839, a.). The twenty-four judges were thus under the eye of the principal judge.

Our Lord himself (Rev. i. 1) furnishes St. John with the imagery of iv. 2-7. Of this imagery our Lord may, therefore, have made the court of the high priest Caiaphas (Matt. xxvi. 57), and the judgment-seat of Pilate with its paved court, the suggestive model.

If so, then our Lord makes the very tribunals which condemned him, the pattern of the higher tribunal he has created in this world, and is now sustaining and administering.

Golden crowns: a golden crown is the badge of a king (Ps. xxi. 3). The executive Judge, representing the Son of man, wears a golden crown (Rev. xiv. 14). The twenty-four elders wear golden crowns on account of their judicial office.

By Christ's appointment, his gospel ministers are incessantly acting as judges in his Church (Matt. xviii. 18; John xx. 23). The enthronement of twenty-four *human* judges (Rev. iv. 4) symbolizes the abiding and perpetual exercise of judgment by the ministers of Christ's Church. In Rev. xxi. 12, 14, "the twelve tribes of the children of Israel" and "the twelve apostles of the Lamb" are conjointly the foundations of the holy Jerusalem, the Church of Christ. This representation repeats the symbolism of the Christian ministry, also symbolized in iv. 4.

5. And out of the throne are going forth lightnings and thunderings, and voices: and seven torches of fire are burning before the throne, which are the seven Spirits of God.

Lightnings and thunderings: "thunderings and lightnings" is the normal order of the Bible expression for the audible and visible manifestation of electricity (Exod. xix. 16; Ps. xviii. 13, 14).

But in the Apocalypse the order is changed, and the expression is exaggerated. Lightnings, and voices, and thunderings (iv. 5, xi. 19, xvi. 18). Thunderings, and voices, and lightnings (viii. 5). The order is thus changed, and the expression intensified, to show the scenes are *not literal,* but unearthly and symbolic.

Voices: words uttered by the thunders (vi. 1, x. 3, 4).

The lightnings, voices, and thunderings are symbols of God's judgments. "He shot out lightnings, and *discomfited* them" (Ps. xviii. 14). "*A fire* goeth before him, and *burneth up his enemies*" (xcvii. 3).

Seven torches: (John xviii. 3; Rev. viii. 10).
Are: that is, represent (i. 20; Matt. xxvi. 26, 28).
Spirits of God: (Zech. iv. 10; Rev. i. 4, v. 6).

6. And before the throne, a sea of glass, like crystal; and in the midst of the throne, and round about the throne, four living beings full of eyes before and behind.

A sea of glass: the pavement of polished marble before the sovereign's throne is the origin of this language.

"Thick sheets of glass of various colors were laid down for paving floors" (SMITH, *Dict. Gr. and Rom. Antiq.*, p. 1212, a).

Roman judges placed their judgment-seat, their official chair, on a tessellated pavement of different colors. Pilate had such a seat (John xix. 13).

Julius Cæsar, on his campaigns, carried with him this kind of pavement.

Moses once saw a vision resembling this shown St. John. "Under the feet of the God of Israel, as it were a paved work of a sapphire stone, and as it were the body of heaven in clearness" (Exod. xxiv. 10).

Crystal: (Ezek. i. 22; Rev. xxi. 11, xxii. 1) the rock-crystal.

Four living beings: identical with the "four living creatures" (Ezek. i. 5) and the cherubim. "The living creatures are the cherubim" (Ezek. x. 20).

The cherubim are the ministers of God's judgments (Ezek. x. 2, 7; Rev. vi. 1-8, xv. 7).

The cherubim in the Book of Revelation are also ministers of the judgments of God. "One of the four living beings gave unto the seven angels seven golden censers *full of the wrath of God*" (Rev. xv. 7).

As the executioners of God's judgments, each of the four living beings (Rev. iv. 6) corresponds to "the officer" (Matt. v. 25): "The *judge* deliver thee to the *officer*." The Jewish Sanhedrin had a band of these officers, attending, like cherubim, our Lord when before Caiphas (Matt. xxvi. 57).

Full of eyes: thus symbolically full of knowledge, the cherubim can execute with certain wisdom.

In Rev. vii. 11, the cherubim are distinguished from "*all* the angels." The cherubim are, therefore, *not angels.*

A cherub is the symbol of the life God imparts to his material creation (Ezek. i. 20, 21, x. 17).

The four cherubim are not symbols of the Four Evangelists. This explanation is purely imaginary.

7. And the first living being like a lion, and the second living being like a bull, and the third living being having the face of a man, and the fourth living being like a flying eagle.

In the Book of Genesis, the land-animal creation appears in *four* forms, — wild beasts, tame cattle, man, and birds (Gen. i. 20, 25, 26). These four classes re-appear in Ezek. i. 10 and Rev. iv. 7.

1. The "lion" represents the wild beasts. 2. The "ox" of Ezekiel, the "calf" of Revelation, the "bullock" (bull) of Judg. vi. 25, represent tame cattle. 3. "Man" represents the human race, in its different "kindreds, tongues, peoples, and nations" (Rev. v. 9). 4. The "eagle" represents the birds.

The cherubim, thus representing the life of God in the whole animated creation, are the ministers of God's *judicial providences.*

In this very character of God's judicial messengers, the several classes of animated beings, represented by the cherubim, present themselves, either directly or by necessary inference, in the Book of Revelation.

1. *War* is one of the agencies the punitive cherub wields.

The descriptions of the war-horse by the patriarch Job (xxxix. 19–25), and by St. John himself (Rev. ix. 17–19), rank this animal, certainly not among tame cattle, but with wild beasts. Whenever the horse appears in the Apocalypse, he is a war-horse. A horse with the head of a lion and the tail of a serpent (ix. 17, 19) is, in representation, a wild beast.

2. *Tame cattle* administer to the prosecution of war, (*a*) by producing the grain that feeds the soldiers, (*b*) by moving army-stores on marches (1 Chron. xii. 40). The service of tame cattle is, therefore, implied in the Apocalypse whenever battles occur.

3. Men, as the chief combatants, are present in the Apocalypse as often as horsemen and armies move before us.

4. Among birds as instruments of God's judgments in the Apocalypse, locusts, classified with birds by Moses (Lev. xi. 22), are first prominent because generating pestilence, one of God's judgments in the Book of Revelation; and then eagles, who devour the carcasses of the slain in battle (xix. 21).

We thus see why the judicial cherub is compounded of lion, bull, man, and eagle. Each component part of his symbolic structure indicates the peculiar agency he employs as the executioner of God's penal judgments.

8. And the four living beings, each one of them having apiece six wings encircling all round, and within are full of eyes; and no intermission have they day and night, saying, Holy, holy, holy, Lord God Almighty, who was, and is, and is to come.

Six wings: six, definite, for many, indefinite; "six troubles" (Job v. 19): *full*-winged. The many wings denote rapidity of flight. Their rapidity equals the lightning (Ezek. i. 14).

Connection of the Cherubim with God's Throne.

In the prophet Ezekiel's description of the cherubim, they are connected with four wheels (i. 15), the "rings," or rims, of which are "so high" and vast, "that they are dreadful" (verse 18). These wheels, so terrific in their height, sustain and move the throne of the Lord Almighty. His throne is moved by these immense circles, which themselves are moved by the cherubim; "for the spirit of the living creature is in the wheels. When the cherubim go, the wheels go by them" (verses 19, 20).

As the movements of the cherubim are as "flashes of lightning" (Ezek. i. 14), the movements of the wheels and of the judgment-throne they bear and propel, have the same immeasurable speed.

Thus giving motion to wheels of such magnitude, the cherubim must be equally great in size. Moved by wheels so vast, and by living creatures so immense, the throne of judgment itself partakes of the like vastness and immensity.

Of what are these superhuman objects, filling the material heavens with their encompassing outlines, the symbols?

(*a*) They are most instructive symbols of God's *omnipotence*, acting through his animated creation.

(*b*) Neither throne, nor wheels, nor cherubim have *locality*. In their electric swiftness they are *everywhere*. They are thus also symbols of God's *omniscience* and *omnipresence*.

The cherubim in Revelation are the representatives of the same truths respecting God as are the cherubim in Ezekiel.

Holy, holy, holy: in Isa. vi. 3, the *seraphim*, ministers of God's *mercies*, praise him for his *love and mercy*. In Rev. iv. 8, the *cherubim*, ministers of God's *judgments*, praise him for his *justice*.

"Justice and judgment are the foundation of thy throne" (Ps. lxxxix. 14).

9. And when the living beings give glory and honor and thanksgiving to him who sits upon the throne, to him who liveth for ever and ever;

Glory: glorious condition.
Honor: exalted state.
Glory, honor, thanksgiving, explain "Holy, holy, holy."
Three forms of doxology in the Apocalypse,—threefold (iv. 9, 11), fourfold (v. 13, xix. 1), sevenfold (vii. 12). Each form is perfect in itself. The different forms indicate that God deserves all possible forms of perfection.

10. The twenty-four elders fall down before him who sits

on the throne, and worship him who liveth for ever and ever, and cast their crowns before the throne, saying:

The prostrations of the elders reflect their dispositions, — humility, reverence, gratitude.

11. Worthy art thou, O Lord, to receive the glory and the honor and the power: because thou thyself didst call into being all things; and so on account of thy will they existed, and were called into being.

The glory: just given by the cherubim.
On account of thy will: because thou didst so determine. Thus the original and sole Creator of all things, God is able to execute all the decisions which proceed from his righteous throne (iv. 2).

THE APOCALYPTIC SYMBOLS SUCCEEDING THE FOURTH CHAPTER.

Of symbols repeated *seven* times, *three* kinds present themselves to our attention in the second division of the Apocalypse, — scrolls, trumpets, and censers.

1. The scrolls (chapter vi.) symbolize the triumph and exaltation of the martyr church.
2. The trumpets (chapters viii., ix.) symbolize the punishment and ruin of the *heathen* enemies of the church.
3. The censers (chapter xvi.) symbolize the punishment and overthrow of the *apostate* church.

The *seventh* of the scrolls (viii. 1), of the trumpets (xi. 15), and of the censers (xvi. 17), is used for *transition to a new subject*. The seventh scroll introduces the trumpets. The seventh trumpet introduces the censers. The seventh censer announces the fall of the great city Babylon.

CHAPTER V.

THE LAMB, THE REVELATOR, THE PRINCIPAL SUBJECT (John i. 18).

1. Also I saw upon the right hand of him who is sitting on the throne a scroll, pictured inside and backside, fast-sealed with seven seals.

Upon the right hand: the occupant of the throne is in appearance like a man, — *anthropomorphism*. The right hand indicates absolute control. The scroll lay upon the *open* hand, thus ready to give it to the "worthy" claimant.

A scroll: resembling that described by the prophet Zechariah (v. 2): "A flying roll, the length is twenty cubits [thirty feet], and the breadth thereof ten cubits [fifteen feet]."

In Acts x. 11, the vessel descending from heaven to the Apostle Peter is as a *great* sheet, so great as to contain *all* [so the Greek] *the* four-footed beasts of the earth, and *the* wild beasts, and *the* creeping things, and *the* fowls of the air" (verse 12).

The scroll St. John sees (Rev. v. 1) may in size, then, equal the *microcosm* St. Peter saw.

Pictured: portrayed. The scroll (Rev. v. 1) is covered with the figures of the horses and their riders exhibited (vi. 2, 4, 5, 8).

Both the scroll itself, and the pictures portrayed on it, indicate *permanency* and *unchangeableness*. The visions shown St. John are not of a transient and temporary character, but the events they prefigure are all enduring and unalterable. The Scriptures ascribe this character to the productions of the pen and the brush.

"Write this for a memorial" (Exod. xvii. 14).

"Note it in a book, that it may be for the time to come" (Isa. xxx. 8).

Inside and backside: when the inside of the parchment or papyrus was filled, then the backside was also used. The expression "inside and backside," is equivalent to saying, "The contents of the scroll are very large" (Ezek. ii. 10; Zech. v. 3). "The two tables of the testimony were written on both sides" (Exod. xxxii. 15).

Fast-sealed with seven seals: the scroll, because thus sealed, consists of seven convolute scrolls. Each seal is attached to a separate scroll. The seven scrolls are rolled successively around the seventh or inner scroll. A seal is appended to the outer edge of each scroll. The seals denote that the contents of the scrolls are utterly secret and absolutely unknown (Deut. xxxii. 34).

The imagery here is taken from Isa. xxix. 11, 12. See Dan. xii. 4, 9; Rev. x. 4, xxii. 10.

Breaking the seals *includes* unrolling the scrolls, and disclosing their contents. This is certain from these texts in Revelation: "Seal up those things which the seven thunders uttered, and write them not" (x. 4). "Seal not the sayings of the prophecy of this book; for the time is at hand" (xxii. 10).

(*a*) "This book" consists of several written scrolls. (*b*) Because "not sealed," they are *unrolled*. (*c*) Because unrolled, their *contents are disclosed.*

2. And I saw a strong angel proclaiming with a loud voice, Who is worthy to unroll the scroll and to break its seals?

This question magnifies the unfitness of all angelic and human agents, and the exclusive worthiness of the Lamb.

Worthy: morally worthy (John i. 27; Matt. viii. 8). The incarnate Son of God is worthy in his perfect humanity as the sacrifice for our sinfulness and guilt.

3. And no one in heaven, nor on the earth, nor under the earth, was able to unroll the scroll, or even to imagine its contents.

Heaven, earth, under the earth: the expression includes the universe.

Under the earth: denotes "the place of departed spirits."

Imagine its contents: the Greek verb has this sense (Col. ii. 5).

"Who can *think* what the will of the Lord is?" (Wis. of Sol. ix. 13).

4. And I myself was bewailing greatly, because no one was found worthy to unroll the scroll; even to imagine its contents.

Was bewailing: with the voice (xviii. 19), not by tears. The scene which excited St. John's distressing lamentation is a representative picture. It exhibits the hopeless wretchedness of our fallen and sinful human nature, apart from the incarnation of the Son of God, and his sacrificial death, to redeem us from our guilt and to save us from unholiness.

Imagine: see verse 3.

5. And one of the elders saith to me, Lament not: behold, the Lion who is out of the tribe of Juda, the Root of David, conquered, so as to unroll the scroll, even its whole seven scrolls.

Lion: "Judah is a *lion's* whelp" (Gen. xlix. 9).
Juda: "Our Lord sprang out of Juda" (Heb. vii. 14).
The Root of David: the offspring of David (Isa. xi. 10).
Conquered: by his blood (Rev. v. 9), the right to open the entire future history of his Church.

John the Baptist first calls Christ the sacrificial Lamb: "Behold the Lamb of God, that taketh away the sin of the world" (John i. 29). We can never fully perceive the extent and value of the divine truths contained in this declaration. Except for the revealed truth, that, by the appointment of God, Christ is "the Lamb slain from the foundation of the world" (Rev. xiii. 8), the redemption of the fallen and sinful race of mankind would not have been accomplished, the church of the redeemed would not have existed, and the Church of Christ could not have had a history. For the redemption of sinning and guilty man, not only is the incarnation of the Son of God necessary, but also his assumption, from the moment Adam and Eve transgressed the law of God, of the sacrificial character of the "Lamb slain" in place of the disobedient human pair. In their guilt and sinfulness, our first parents could not be pardoned, and restored to the holy image of God they had lost, except by the "worthiness" (Rev. v. 2, 4, 9), the incarnation, the sacrificial death, the renewing power, of the "Lamb slain from the foundation of the world."

For a season St. John contemplates these necessities as not provided for. The bare thought torments his soul with the bitterest anguish.

The assurance of the elder, "the Lion of the tribe of Juda, the Root of David," the Incarnate Son of God, "the Lamb slain" and yet standing alive, *conquered* by his blood, to open the sealed scrolls, and to unfold the history of his Church, stops forever all lamentation from the exulting and grateful heart of the apostle. If he does not sing with his own mouth, the swelling song of the heavenly hosts stirs him with emotions too deep for words.

Neither in his Gospel nor in his Apocalypse does St. John reveal his own feelings excited by the wonders he saw and heard. That his soul was strongly stirred, we discover from this declaration in one of his epistles: "We *love* him, because he first loved us" (1 John iv. 19).

When the four living beings, and the twenty-four elders, perceive that these necessities are all most fully met by the "Lamb slain," they break forth into ecstatic joy, and thank and praise God for the redemption and salvation (v. 6, 9) he has forever perfected. The living beings and the elders rejoice and exult for the same reason, that Christ is the revelator of the history of his Church.

Scrolls: Greek, seals; seals by *metonomy* for scrolls; the sign for the thing signified.

Opening the seal of a letter is opening the letter. Christ breaks the seven seals; Christ unrolls the seven scrolls. *By anticipation*, the cherubim, the elders, the angels, and every creature in the universe (v. 8-13), thank and praise the Lamb for *opening the entire scroll* (v. 9).

In chapter vi. 1, the Lamb begins the opening of the seven seals; that is, the unrolling of the seven scrolls, and *the full exhibition of their pictured contents.*

The remainder of the sixth chapter describes the opening, the unrolling, and the exhibition of *all* the scrolls except the seventh.

The character of the revelations thus made by Christ, we shall see when we examine the contents of the sixth chapter.

6. And I saw in the midst of the throne, and of the four living beings, and in the midst of the elders, the beloved Lamb standing, as having been slain, having seven horns and seven eyes, which are the seven Spirits of God sent into all the earth.

The beloved Lamb: our Lord uses the Greek form of the word as a term of affection (John xxi. 15: "Feed my beloved lambs"). St. John adopts the term, with the love our Lord imparted to it (1 John iv. 19). St. Paul calls Christ "the beloved" (Eph. i. 6).

Standing: alive, upright, and strong. A slain lamb is prostrate. Although once slain, the Lamb of God now ever lives (Rom. vi. 9).

As having been slain: indicated by marks of blood on him (verse 9, vii. 14, xii. 11, xix. 13).

Seven horns: emblems of omnipotence (Deut. xxxiii. 17). The Lamb is able to create the history of his Church.

Seven eyes: emblems of omniscience (2 Chron. xvi. 9). The Lamb is able to foresee and predict the history of his Church.

7. And he comes and receives the scroll out of the right hand of him who is sitting on the throne.

Comes: in a couplet, as here, "comes" gives graphic effect to the language.

8. And when he receives the scroll, the four living beings, and the twenty-four elders, fall down before the Lamb; each elder holding a harp, and each living being holding a golden altar-basin full of incense-offerings, which are the prayers of the saints.

Fall down: to worship the Lamb. Prostration is one act, worship is another.

Harp: commemorates victory (xiv. 2, xv. 2). The Lamb is the victor (verse 5). He is here praised for his anticipated triumphs, as well as his past victories. The elders only have the harps. They nowhere in the Apocalypse burn incense.

Altar-basin: in the Mosaic ritual, the Greek *phiale*, English Version "vial," was a large basin, used in the service of the great altar for the reception of the blood of the animals there sacrificed (Exod. xxvii. 3. BUSH, *note;* GESENIUS, *Heb. Lex.*, p. 462, *sub mizrak*).

This altar-basin was much larger than the "censer" (Rev. viii. 3), and may be used (verse 8) elsewhere to indicate the large quantity of incense burned.

The altar-basin may be used for still another reason, which accords with the context.

As the receptacle of the blood of the sacrificed animals, the altar-basin was an "instrument of death" (Ps. vii. 13). Incense burned in such an instrument must partake of its nature, and be itself deadly. Deadly nature is the exact possession of the incense offered and consumed in Rev. v. 8.

Only the four living beings have the altar-basins (xv. 7).

Themselves chief executioners, the four cherubim very significantly burn incense in the large basins in which the slayers of oxen before the out-door altar caught their blood.

Incense-offerings: this is the meaning of the Greek (Exod. xxx. 34–36).

Are the prayers: that is, represent the prayers. The prayers. This phrase in Revelation, only here and viii. 3, 4. Whatever, then, is the character of the prayers in viii. 3, 4, is the character of the prayers in verse 8. But the prayers in viii. 3, 4, are prayers for *vengeance:* they are the prayers we hear in vi. 10, "How long, O Lord, holy and true, dost thou not *judge and avenge* our blood on them that dwell on the earth?"

Of the saints: identical with "them that were slain for the word of God" (vi. 9): they are Christ's *martyred* saints.

The incense-offerings represent these prayers of the martyred saints for vengeance.

Incense, in the Apocalypse, is beyond doubt an emblem of *wrath and judgment*.

The censers of the two hundred and fifty rebels (Num. xvi.) caused their death. "The censers [the incense in the censers] of these sinners against their own souls" (verse 38).

"Take you censers, Korah and all his company, and put fire therein, and *put incense* in the censers before the Lord to-morrow" (verses 6, 7).

"Bring ye before the Lord every man his censer, *two hundred and fifty censers.* They took away every man his censer, and put fire in the censers, and laid incense thereon" (verses 17, 18).

"There came out a fire from the Lord, and *consumed the two hundred and fifty men*" (verse 35).

Thus, in the case of Korah and his associate rebels, *incense was the instrument of their destruction.*

Hence (Rev. v. 8, viii. 3, 4) censers (the incense in them) are symbols of *judgments and punishments.*

This is most certain with Rev. viii. 3, 5, as verse 5 proves: "The angel took the censer, and filled it with fire of the altar, and cast it into the earth; and there were *voices, and thunderings, and lightnings, and an earthquake,*" which are all unmistakable tokens of God's judgments.

Here also sharply notice: the two hundred and fifty rebels of Num. xvi. are *members of the Israelitish church.* The destroying incense, in their case, acted *within God's church.*

Thus incense is a *church* instrument of destruction. The objects incense affects in the Book of Revelation are, therefore, *ecclesiastical.* The persons on whom the censers are poured are *within the church of God* in its two forms, *Jewish and Christian.*

9. And they sing a new song, saying, Worthy art thou to receive the scroll, and to unfold its scrolls; for thou wast slain, and didst redeem to God by thy blood, out of every tribe and tongue and people and nation.

They sing: *with the voice,* but not accompanied by the harp. The imagery here is taken from the choirs arranged by King David (1 Chron. xv. 19-22).

New: renovated (2 Cor. v. 17); that is, better, superior.
Redeem: it is Greek usage to omit the accusative after the verb, when the phrase *out of* follows (Rev. ii. 10). The phrase, with *out of*, takes the place of the accusative. This usage renders " us " (Rev. v. 9, Eng. Ver.) superfluous, and the insertion of the Greek for " us " a clerical blunder arising from ignorance of usage.
Tribe, etc.: fourfold enumeration denotes completeness (Gen. x. 5, 31).

10. And thou didst make them a kingdom, even priests: and so they shall reign on the earth.

Kingdom: see i. 6.
They shall reign: Christ's martyrs, as a continual succession, from generation to generation, are intended. So also xx. 4, 6.
On the earth: by this phrase, the present material earth is in the Apocalypse always intended. No *changed and renovated* earth is ever indicated.

11. Also I saw, and I heard the voice of many angels encircling the throne, and the living beings and the elders, even thousands of thousands;

I saw: in vision. The angels are visible, as well as audible. They respond to the anthem of the cherubim and the elders.
Even thousands of thousands: the expression denotes numbers innumerable.

12. Saying with a loud voice, Worthy is the Lamb who was slain to receive this praise, this Alleluia [namely], power, and riches, and wisdom, and might, and honor, and glory, and blessing.

Riches: fulness of every grace (Eph. i. 23). This sevenfold doxology denotes the completeness of Christ's worthiness, and of the praise as his due.

13. Also every creature which is in heaven, and in the earth, and under the earth, and the creatures which are on the sea, even all in them, I heard saying, To him who is sitting on the throne, and to the Lamb, be given blessing, and honor, and glory, and might, for ever and ever.

In Rev. xix. 3, the Alleluia is repeated by the "people" a second time. In the same way, verse 13 repeats verse 12. This *fourfold* ascription is also complete in its structure and purpose.

14. And all the four living beings were saying, Amen. Also the elders fall down and worship.

Were saying, Amen: to each of the ascriptions (verses 12. 13).
The elders: unite with the worship in heaven and in earth.

CHAPTER VI.

THE SIX SCROLLS: IMAGERY, CONTENTS.

THE six scrolls, in chapter vi., must be examined in connection, in order to be understood.

The *first* scroll (verses 1, 2) discloses the imagery and purpose of the whole.

The predicted Conqueror (verse 2) *implies previous* warfare, and devastations from the enemy. The proposed expedition is occasioned by the injuries already inflicted upon the cause of the future Conqueror. He arranges to defeat his enemies in *three* ways, — war (verse 4), famine (verse 5), and pestilence (verse 8).

The imagery, in each case, may be taken from the Bible history of the Jews.

1. *War.* — Babylon was the successful invader of Judæa, and the resistless captor of Jerusalem with great slaughter (Jer. xxxix. 1-8). Yet Babylon itself was afterwards destroyed by the Medes (Jer. li. 11). In the avenging war of the Medes against Babylon, there is the pattern of the war-imagery of Rev. vi. 4. Cyrus (Isa. xliv. 28, xlv. 1-6) may be the model after which the representative of the Conqueror (Rev. vi. 2) is constructed. The resemblance between Cyrus and the rider of the white horse is remarkable. (1) Both are kings. (2) Both are conquerors. (3) The conquests of each are extensive. (4) The enemy of each is Babylon. (5) Each is to subdue Babylon.

Proofs. — (*a*) Cyrus: "Besiege, O Media" (Isa. xxi. 2); "Babylon is fallen, is fallen" (verse 9). (*b*) The *represented* Conqueror is the Lamb (Rev. xiv. 1). No sooner does he appear with his followers on Mount Zion, than an angel repeats the same annunciation of Babylon's overthrow Isaiah uttered, "Babylon is fallen, is fallen" (Rev. xiv. 8).

The prophet Jeremiah utters predictions against Babylon of the same character: "Babylon is taken" (l. 2); "Out of the *north* there cometh up a nation against her" (verse 3); "I will raise up against Babylon an assembly of great nations from the north country" (verse 9).

2. *Famine.* — This infliction is the accompaniment of war. Jerusalem, when besieged by the Babylonians, was distressed and weakened by famine. Babylon, when in turn besieged by the Medes, must have experienced the same wasting process, and furnished the imagery of Rev. vi. 5, 6.

3. *Pestilence.* — This frightful evil is the rapid sequence of famine. The Jews had witnessed a memorable instance of its power. When the king of Assyria besieged Jerusalem, the angel of the Lord relieved and ended the siege: a pestilence he inflicted destroyed in one night one hundred and eighty-five thousand Assyrian soldiers. The memory of St. John would recall this example of divine rescue, when, in Rev. vi. 8, he predicts the ravages of pestilence.

We thus find, in the history of the Jews and of the adjoining nations, the sources from which the striking imagery of scrolls one, two, three, and four, may, in chapter vi., have been derived.

These four warlike and destructive scrolls prepare the road for the sudden appearance of *the fifth scroll* (Rev. vi. 9–11).

The affecting imagery of this scroll may be repetitions of these bloody histories: "The king of Babylon slew *the sons* of Zedekiah before his eyes: also the king of Babylon slew *all the nobles* of Judah" (Jer. xxxix. 6); "Their blood have they shed like water round about Jerusalem" (Ps. lxxix. 3).

Pilate mingled the blood of certain Galilæans with their

sacrifices (Luke xiii. 1). In the confusion of the sacking of Jerusalem by the Babylonians, worshipping Jews may have been butchered at the foot of the altar of burnt-sacrifice, and have thus furnished the imagery of prostration and supplication in the fifth scroll.

The first, second, third, and fourth scrolls prepare the instrumentalities for relieving the miseries depicted in the fifth scroll. The fact of this previous preparation is most instructive and encouraging. The fact reveals one of God's methods of dealing with his persecuted children. *He provides beforehand for the removal of their sufferings.* Their distresses never take God by surprise.

The sixth scroll (vi. 12-17) is the symbolic confirmation of the symbolical prophecies in the first four scrolls. Thus *the martyr-church is the great and absorbing subject* of the six scrolls in chapter vi., and in consequence, of the entire second division of the Apocalypse.

The sixth scroll is prophetic of the seven trumpets (chapter viii.). The sealing (chapter vii.) is preparatory to their sounding. The seventh trumpet (xi. 15) is prophetic of the seven censers (xvi.).

Since, under the scrolls, Judæa and Jerusalem, the modal imagery, are supposed to be nationally in ruins, all legal forms of redress are impossible. The only available relief is the *supplication of the martyred saints* to Almighty God (vi. 10), who loves justice and mercy, and promises to hear and answer the prayers of his people. Legal processes, because possible, are used under the censers (xvi.).

THE UNROLLING OF THE FIRST SCROLL (Verses 1, 2).

1. Also I saw, when the Lamb unrolled the first of the seven scrolls. And so I heard the first of the living beings, as the voice of thunder, saying [to the first horse and horseman], Come.

Also I saw: I had another vision.
The first of the living beings: like a lion (iv. 7) he re-appears (xv. 7).

The lion-like cherub is now the herald of the representative of Christ, "the Lion of the tribe of Judah" (v. 5). The lion-faced cherub is the symbol of resistless power. The prophetic symbols he now summons to present themselves cannot be defeated.

As the voice of thunder: as though the thunder spake, the lion-cherub utters this command, "Come." "A sound of battle is in the land, and of great destruction" (Jer. l. 22).

Come: addressed, not to Christ, as xxii. 20, but to each of the four riders in succession (verses 1, 3, 5, 7). The cherub, the minister of God's justice, calls each of the horsemen to come and do his appointed work.

This explanation of "come" agrees with "went forth" (verse 2), and "went out" (verse 4); and with "Come, and he cometh" (Matt. viii. 9, where "come" is the address of the centurion to the soldier, to present himself and do the work commanded him). This, and no other, is the meaning of "come" in Rev. vi. 1, 3, 5, 7. The scene now before our eyes is a military muster. The thunder-voice we hear is a startling war-cry.

2. Also I saw, and behold a white horse, and the rider on him having a bow, and there is given him a crown, and he is going forth conquering, and that he may conquer.

Horse: is an emblem of war (Prov. xxi. 31; Jer. li. 27; Ezek. xxvi. 10, 11). "A people shall come from *the north;* they shall ride upon *horses*" (Jer. l. 41, 42).

The imagery of the four horses (Rev. vi. 2, 4, 5, 8) resembles that of Zech. i. 8–10.

White: brilliant white, "as snow" (i. 14). White is emblematic of victory (xix. 11–18), indicated by "conquering and conquer" (last clause of verse 2).

The rider: is not Christ himself, but is a prophetic symbol of Christ, "the Word of God" (xix. 11–13).

Nowhere in Bible Greek is victory personified. The crowned rider in this verse cannot be the symbol of victory, for this insuperable reason: he cannot be the symbol of a personification which in Bible usage does not exist.

Having a bow: the bow was specially the *Oriental* weapon. The bow implies arrows. In an engagement, the archers on horses *began* the battle (2 Kings xix. 32; Ps. lxxvi. 3; Jer. vi. 23, l. 42). Our Lord is, in Old-Testament prophecy, an archer (Ps. xlv. 4, 5). In Isa. xiii. 18, the Medes, the destroyers of Babylon, use "bows to dash the young men to pieces." The coincidence is one of many that indicate "Cyrus, king of Persia" (2 Chron. xxxvi. 23), as the original of the representative conqueror in Rev. vi. 2.

"All ye that bend the *bow*, shoot at Babylon, spare no *arrows*" (Jer. l. 14).

"Call together the archers against Babylon" (verse 29). This, then, is the inspiriting truth symbolized by the conquering archer in Rev. vi. 2: Our Lord now *begins* every fight in which his Church is lawfully engaged; he *leads* in every spiritual battle. This truth applies to Christians as *individuals*, as well as to his corporate Church.

A crown is given him: the symbol of victory (xiv. 14), in anticipation of his certain triumph. In xix. 19-21, Christ is *actual* victor: as such, he has "many crowns."

He is going forth: to battle (1 Sam. xxviii. 1).

Conquering: is now conquering.

That he may conquer: his purpose in going forth to battle is to conquer. His purpose will be fully realized (1 Cor. xv. 27).

THE UNROLLING OF THE SECOND SCROLL (Verses 3, 4).

3. Also when he unrolled the second scroll, I heard the second living being saying [to the second horse and horseman], Come.

The second living being: like a bull (iv. 7). The symbol of work, execution. "Ox strong to labor" (Ps. cxliv. 14).

4. Also goes forth another horse, fire-red, and to his rider is given to take away all peace from the earth, even that the combatants shall kill each other: and there is given him a great sword.

Fire-red: symbol of destructive war (Zech. vi. 2). This meaning of the symbolism is established by the remainder of the verse.

The rider: personifies war. Instances of personification in the Bible: "Sword, go through the land" (Ezek. xiv. 17); "I send my judgments, *the sword, and the famine, and the pestilence*" (verse 21). The same judgments are the riders in Rev. vi. 4, 5, 8, by personification (Matt. x. 34).

Kill each other: mutual destruction of the combatants is the effect of all wars.

Sword: implies close and deadly combat.

THE UNROLLING OF THE THIRD SCROLL (Verses 5, 6).

5. Also when he unrolled the third scroll, I heard the third living being saying [to the third horse and horseman], Come.

And so I saw. And behold, a black horse, and his rider holding a balance in his hand.

The third living being: "has a face as a man" (iv. 7). Man is the emblem both of intelligence and kindness (Dan. vii. 4).

A black horse: blackness is the image of terror (Job iii. 5).

The rider: personifies famine.

Balance: beam of the balance (Lev. xix. 35, 36). Symbolizes food weighed on account of its scarceness. "Meat *by weight*" (Ezek. iv. 10).

6. And I heard a voice in the midst of the four living beings, saying, A quart of wheat for a penny, and three quarts of barley for a penny; also hurt not thou the oil and the wine.

In the midst of the four living beings: they surround the throne (iv. 6). The voice, then, comes *from the throne.* The voice comes from God, who sits on the throne. In accordance with the symbolism furnished by the man-faced cherub symbolizing intelligence and kindness, God's voice mitigates the severity and horrors of famine by fixing the price of food to a *living* standard.

A quart of wheat for a penny: the price of wheat must not be greater. A penny was the price of a day's labor (Matt. xx. 20). Among the Greeks, a quart of wheat was the daily allowance to a common laborer. God forbids the diminution, in time of famine, of the daily allowance of wheat, and also forbids the increase of its price.

Three quarts of barley for a penny: three denotes fulness (Isa. xix. 23, 24; Zech. xiii. 8). Barley is a less valuable grain than wheat. A penny shall buy the usual full measures of barley.

The oil and the wine: by *metonomy*, for the olive-tree and the vine.

Thou shalt not hurt: the address is to personified famine. The rider of the black horse is thus forbidden to lessen the production of oil and wine, since both, like wheat and barley, are articles of bodily nourishment (Ps. civ. 14, 15; Joel i. 10–12).

Hurt: ii. 11, vii. 2, 3.

These divine limitations of the evils of famine prove that God is a merciful Judge. In wrath he remembers mercy (Hab. iii. 2). Whenever famine prevails, he forbids the rich to oppress the poor by raising the prices of provisions, and by curtailing wages.

Were this benevolent law of God universally obeyed, there would be few conflicts between capital and labor.

THE UNROLLING OF THE FOURTH SCROLL (Verses 7, 8).

7. Also when he unrolled the fourth scroll, I heard the voice of the fourth living being, saying [to the fourth horse and horseman], Come.

The fourth living being: "like a flying eagle," symbolizing the rapidity with which the pestilence depopulates.

8. And I saw, and behold a pale horse, and his rider over him. His name is Death, and Hades follows with him, and authority is given him over the fourth part of the earth, to kill by sword, and by famine, and by death, and by the wild beasts of the earth.

Pale horse: the color is the first light-green shoot of plants in the spring of the year (Mark vi. 39). With the prophet Isaiah, the color is the paleness occasioned by fright (Isa. xxix. 22).

His rider: pestilence personified.

Over him: (Matt. xxiii. 22) "over" describes the sitting of the *invisible* God. In Rev. vi. 8, there is no *visible* form, as a skeleton, representing death, as sometimes in pictures. So invisible is pestilence in its coming and ravages, that it can have no visible symbol.

His name is Death: nothing here but a mere name of an *invisible* power guiding the "pale horse," the symbol of pestilence; and therefore *over* the horse, and not *on* him as his visible rider.

Hades: the unseen world of departed human souls personified.

The fourth part of the earth: the earth, by *synecdoche*, for mankind. In Rev. xx. 8, "the four quarters of the earth" include the *whole earth.* "The fourth part of the earth" lacks three parts of being the whole. Through the unfailing mercy of God, the ravages of pestilence are never total.

To kill: the infinitive expresses the unlimited action of the verb.

Again in wrath God remembers mercy (Hab. iii. 2).

By sword: by *metonomy*, for war symbolized by the "red horse" (verse 4).

By famine: symbolized by the "black horse" (verse 5).

By death: that is, pestilence, symbolized by the "pale horse" (verse 8).

By the wild beasts of the earth: "I send my four sore judgments, — the sword, the famine, and the noisome beast, and the pestilence" (Ezek. xiv. 21). This reference by St. John to God's four judgments is, in sense, this declaration: The ravages of pestilence shall equal the ravages of all the four judgments combined. In other words, the ravages of pestilence shall exceed the united ravages of war, famine, and wild beasts. St. John here employs the imagery of the prophet Ezekiel (Ezek. xiv.). The experience of the world confirms the truthfulness of this desolating prediction. War, famine, wild beasts, in turn slay their thousands: pestilence slays its ten thousands.

Since *three* is a complete number (Isa. xix. 24, 25), the three horses following the white horse and his rider, and achieving all the exterminating victories, form a *complete* army, both in its constitution and outfit, and in its ability and successes. No other forces are necessary. Were other troops gathered and marshalled, there would be no object in massing them for a battle. *There would be no enemy to be attacked and conquered.*

Thus finished and absolute is the victory of our Lord over all his enemies, which is symbolically predicted by the red, black, and pale horses following his triumphant march through this world.

THE UNROLLING OF THE FIFTH SCROLL (Verses 9–11).

THE SUFFERING CHURCH OF CHRIST.

Our Lord, having predicted the occurrence of "famines, and pestilences, and earthquakes," after the destruction of Jerusalem by the Romans, describes the treatment his Church shall receive from "all nations:" "They shall deliver you up to be afflicted, and *shall kill you*" (Matt. xxiv. 7, 9).

The fifth scroll, which he now unrolls and displays, repeats, in most impressive symbols, the startling prediction he pronounced upon the Mount of Olives (Matt. xxiv. 3, etc.).

The four living beings do not herald the opening of the fifth scroll. The act would not accord with their office as the executioners of Christ's judgments. His Church is now to be vindicated, not punished. The vindication belongs to Christ, not to the cherubim. Accordingly, Christ, without cherubic heralding, unfolds the fifth scroll.

---

9. Also, when he unrolled the fifth scroll, I saw under the altar the souls of the slain on account of the word of God, even on account of the testimony which they were holding.

I saw: in the vision (ix. 17).

Under: down under.

The altar: of burnt sacrifice (Exod. xxx. 28). The blood of the sacrifice was poured out "at the *bottom* of the altar" (Lev. iv. 7).

To be down "under the altar," is, then, to lie slain at the foot of the altar of burnt sacrifice. These slain saints are lying in their blood. Lying slain in their blood, *at the foot of the altar of burnt sacrifice*, these saints are *themselves sacrifices to God*. They sacrificed their lives in his service, and for his sake. St. Paul uses the same imagery (Phil. ii. 17), and illustrates it in his own life (Acts xv. 26).

Their shed blood is crying for vengeance (Gen. iv. 10). Their unavenged blood is itself a pleading supplication.

I saw the souls of the slain: this sight was, according to the psychology of the Jews, not impossible. In their psychic theory, the soul was not so changed by the death of the body as to become invisible.

The dead in Hades *see* the soul of the king of Babylon when it comes into their place (Isa. xiv. 4, 9, 16).

Even St. Paul ascribes to the soul "joints and marrow" (Heb. iv. 12).

In accordance, then, with Jewish representations, does St. John say, "I *saw the souls* of the slain."

But his language here is *highly figurative*. The souls, although visible, are not *real* souls. They are merely souls *in vision*. They are *representative* souls. They represent the suffering Church of God in all ages of the world. Because *representative*, and not *real* souls, they have no *locality*. They are *not* souls *in paradise*. They are not *personal individuals*, but only a *representative class*.

The cause of the martyrdom of these prostrate and slaughtered saints deserves to be closely and habitually studied.

They are slain on account of the word of God, even the testimony they are holding.

These martyrs constitute a class of God's servants, who in succession from age to age proclaim to their fellow-men his revealed will. They are firm believers in *divine revelation*, and fearless heralds of its entire contents.

The essence of their constant proclamation is the faithful testimony they incessantly bear to the nature, character, and redeeming and saving work of the incarnate Son of God, our Lord Jesus Christ.

This Christian testimony is both a historical fact, and a constraining, undying, and binding example.

The historical fact records itself in the deaths of the illustrious line of martyrs from St. Stephen through the centuries of shed blood down to the martyrs of the English Reformation, Cranmer, Latimer, and Ridley, and their fellow-sufferers.

The sublime example of these martyrs for Christ's truth is our rich inheritance, and our daily and authoritative lesson.

Like this "noble army," we are to hold Christ's entire gospel most firmly; proclaim it in its full integrity most faithfully and fearlessly; and to recommend it to others, and force it upon their attention and love, not only by word of mouth, but by our own self-denying, prayerful, and holy lives.

Testimony: see i. 2.

Were holding: most firmly and faithfully. The testimony Christ gives them, they ever retain and hold.

THE PRAYER OF THE SACRIFICED SAINTS.

10. And they were praying with a loud voice, saying, How long, O Lord, holy and true, dost thou not judge and avenge our blood on them that dwell on the earth?

The personification of Gen. iv. 10 here becomes a drama.

Were praying: the Greek verb has this meaning (Rom. viii. 15; Gal. iv. 6; Jas. v. 4).

How long: delay deplored (Ps. lxxix. 5; Zech. i. 12).

O Lord: as Head of the Church (1 Tim. vi. 15).

Holy: cannot allow sin to be unresisted.

True: will fulfil his promises.

Judge: this prayer for judgment proves that "the throne" (iv. 4) is a throne of *judgment*.

Avenge: same prayer, Ps. lxxix. 10, and Luke xviii. 7. Thus the words are the incessant prayer of God's suffering Church, by his appointment. Vengeance is invoked (Rev. vi. 10); vengeance has been inflicted (xvi. 5-7, xix. 2).

Dwell on the earth: the persecutors of God's Church (xi. 10, xiii. 8, 12, 14, xvii. 8).

Rev. vi. 10, the martyrs pray for *themselves;* xi. 18, the twenty-four elders pray for *the martyrs;* xvi. 5-7, "the angel of the waters" announces the infliction of the vengeance.

11. And there is given them each a white robe. Also it is commanded them to rest utterly yet for a season, until are completed in number both their fellow-servants and their brethren, who are about to be killed as they themselves also were killed.

White robe: worn by a victor-king (1 Chron. xv. 27).

The "great multitude which no man can number" (Rev. vii. 9,

13), identical with martyr-saints, "are clothed with white robes." But this innumerable host are *victors*. Their character of victors is proved by this song of *victory* they sing, " *Salvation* [Vulgate, *victoria*] to our God which sitteth upon the throne, and unto the Lamb" (vii. 10).

The "white robe" given to each of the slain under the altar is, then, *the symbol of victory*. They are regarded as suppliants *whose prayers are answered*. The gift of the white robe of victory follows the answer to their prayers. Had God not answered their prayers, he would not mark them with a symbol of victory.

Since they are victors, they are kings. Priests are not victors, because they do not fight battles.

Because the martyrs are here regarded as victor-kings, the white robes they wear are *kingly* robes.

The gift of the white robes entitles the victor-saints to the future dignity of *enthroned* kings. *White-robed*, they are *candidates* for kingly enthronement, when God shall determine the time (xx. 4, 6).

Rest utterly: in their present condition of approval by God, and of expectation of the kingly dignity promised (xiv. 13).

For a season: which ends (xx. 4).

Fellow-servants: as present witnesses for Christ (xix. 2).

Brethren: future witnesses for Christ. They are brethren because members of the one body of which Christ is the Head (Rom. xii. 5; Eph. iv. 15). Fellow-servants and brethren form two classes.

To be killed: there will be martyrs while the Church is militant.

They themselves: the martyrs of vi. 10.

THE UNROLLING OF THE SIXTH SCROLL (Verses 12-17).

SYMBOLIC CONFIRMATION OF THE PRECEDING SCROLLS.

Confirmation by *recapitulation*.

In the first three chapters, recapitulation is structural usage. The several aspects of our Lord's first manifestation in the first chapter are minutely *repeated* in the second and third chapters.

Recapitulation, as a *structural principle*, appears in the sixth scroll, itself being in substance the repetition of the preceding scrolls.

Specifications by *sevens*: a complete list; earthquake, sun, moon, stars, heaven, mountain, and island, — all classes of men.

12. Also I saw when he unrolled the sixth scroll, and there is a great earthquake, and the sun becomes black as sackcloth of hair, and the whole moon becomes as blood.

The prophecy of Isa. xiii. 1-22, that Babylon shall be destroyed by the Medes, contains the same images of desolation and terror that are depicted by the sixth scroll. This scroll is, in substance, the copy and repetition of Isa. xiii.

The Medes may be the prototypes of the Northern hordes which destroyed the Roman Empire. Babylon is the prototype of the Roman Empire itself.

Earthquake: whenever occurring in the Apocalypse, is the symbol of *punitive judgment*.

Sun: another symbol of punitive judgment (Matt. xxiv. 29).

Sackcloth: Isa. l. 3.

The whole moon: this third punitive judgment intensifies Joel ii. 31; Matt. xxiv. 29. The imagery of the darkened sun and moon is derived from solar and lunar eclipses.

13. And the stars of heaven fall to the earth, as the fig-tree casts its unripe figs because shaken by a mighty wind.

Stars: are symbols of rulers (Num. xxiv. 17; Isa. xiv. 12). The imagery is taken from falling meteors.

Unripe figs: Nah. iii. 12.

14. And the heaven passes away as a rolled scroll; and every mountain and island is moved from its place.

By these strong and frightful representations, great political and social destructions are predicted. So Isa. xxxiv. 4.

15. And the kings of the earth, and the princes, and the military chiefs, and the property-holders, and the conquerors, and every bondman, and every freeman, hide themselves by fleeing into the caves, and into the rocks of the mountains.

Enumeration by *sevens*, a complete list. Portions of this enumeration are from Jer. l. 35, 36. "Princes" (verse 35) is identical with "great men" (Rev. vi. 15). Kings, great, rich, chief, mighty, bond, free. Startling description of universal fright. Terror makes all classes absconding and hiding cowards. "They shall become as women" (Jer. l. 37). "Men's hearts failing them for fear" (Luke xxi. 26).

Same imagery, Isa. ii. 21. Its origin is found in Zech. xiv. 5, "Ye fled from before the earthquake." "Two years before the earthquake" (Amos i. 1).

This earthquake occurred in the reign of Uzziah, King of Judah (Zech. xiv. 5), B.C. 500. This earthquake was so violent as to divide in halves a mountain near Jerusalem, and to move a part of the mountain from its place (JOSEPHUS, *Antiq.* li. § 4).

16. And they are saying to the mountains and the rocks, Fall on us, and hide us from the face of him that sitteth on the throne, and from the wrath of the Lamb.

So overwhelming is their fright, that they prefer death to life (Jon. iv. 3).

Mountains, etc.: repetition of Hos. x. 8.

17. For the great day of his wrath is come; and who is able to stand?

Day: time, season. The only instances where the expression "great day" occurs in Revelation are vi. 17 and xvi. 14. In xvi. 14, it is a day *of battle on this earth*. On *this earth*, therefore, is the day (vi. 17), and is not the day of the last and universal judgment.

Who is able: rhetorical, for "none can."

Stand: opposed to flight (Eph. vi. 13). Who can stand against fright and flight? God's judgments are irresistible. Man is powerless when they fall upon him. This is the final teaching of the sixth scroll.

The sixth scroll is in its terrific specifications a repetition of the scrolls which precede it. Its repetitions *confirm* the previous prophecies, to show that their fulfilment is *infallibly certain*.

The imagery throughout the sixth scroll is the imagery of wrath. The great earthquake, the black sun, the blood-moon, the falling stars, the departing heaven, the trembling mountains, the swaying islands, the horrified and fleeing *men* (women and children are, from unendurable fright, all previously dead); their shrieks of terror as they enter the dens and rocks, and call upon the mountains to crush them, — are the most appalling images, manifestations, and predictions of the divine wrath, here symbolically predicted to be inflicted on this sinful world, so long as it shall continue to disobey the laws of God. Of the utter defeat and irreparable ruin of all the enemies of Christ, the sixth scroll is the most conclusive as well as the most appalling prophetical demonstration.

The period of time occupied by the scrolls will equal the continuance of the martyr church on earth. The scroll-period will therefore be coeval with the periods assigned by God to both the trumpets and the censers. We thus ascertain that the second division of the Apocalypse, in its succession of changing symbols, is not an unbroken and continuous chronological series. The book is rather a succession of prophetically shifting scenes, repeating for amplification, impressiveness, and the establishment of certainty under different symbolic forms, the same history of the Church and the world in both its records already written, and its records to be hereafter written.

CHARACTER OF THE SCROLLS.

Each of the scrolls is a symbolic prophecy. The fulfilments of the prophecies are in two forms, — trumpets and censers.

The trumpets are judgments upon *secular* Babylon, and thence upon the *heathen* enemies of the Church of God. The censers are judgments upon his *apostate* Church, the *spiritual* Babylon. The martyr-church is confronted and assailed by each class of enemies, — heathen, and apostate Christian.

The assault will end only with the termination of this present probationary system, in which God places us for our moral trial and spiritual perfection.

So far as this assault can be illustrated by history, the evils have thus far been both material and spiritual. The future history of the world will, we may conclude, resemble its past history, at least for a while, but not always.

While, under the trumpets, *secular* Babylon and the heathendom she represents are being subdued, a portion of the true Church becomes secularized, and changed, while outwardly Christian, into the old hostile Babylon in spirit and character.

Thus Babylon, either secular or spiritual, is throughout the Apocalypse the enemy and assailant of the martyr-church.

CHAPTER VII.

THE SEALING OF THE ONE HUNDRED AND FORTY-FOUR THOUSAND (Verses 1–8).

BEFORE the great and prolonged battle (doubly prefigured in the six scrolls by the horses and the earthquake) begins, the preservation of the faithful Church is symbolized by the sealing of the same number (twelve thousand) of persons in each of the twelve tribes of the Israelites.

Israelites are sealed, not in contrast with Gentiles, but in conformity to the previous symbolism, chapter vi., in which, on behalf of the Israelites, the representative Medes are preparing to wage war upon the Babylonians, the representative foes of God's Church.

---

1. *Also, after this, I saw four angels standing on the four corners of the earth, holding the four winds of the earth, that the wind should not blow on the earth, nor on the sea, nor on any tree.*

Four angels: are *avenging* angels, because they "hurt the earth and the sea" (verse 2). Four angels (ix. 14, 15) "prepared to slay the third part of men."

The four angels in vii. 1, 2, and ix. 14, 15, are, we may conclude, the *same angels*; since their business is the same, "to hurt and to slay."

Four corners: the winds come from the four corners of the earth (Jer. xlix. 36).

Standing on the four corners of the earth: that is, encompassing the whole earth. The four corners indicate the entire circuit

(Isa. xi. 12; Rev. xx. 8). Standing is the attitude of execution (Heb. x. 11). They stand ready to let all winds loose.

Holding: holding in, restraining the winds, that they "should not blow."

The four winds: *all* the winds. This restraint is for the work of sealing. The infliction of the threatened judgments is suspended during the time of the sealing.

2. And I saw another angel ascending from the rising sun, having the seal of the living God; and he cries with a loud voice to the four angels, to whom it is given to hurt the land and the sea;

Another angel: the minister of God's favor to the sealed.

Ascending: like the rising sun with blessings.

Seal: of approval. The affixing of a seal is approval (Jer. xxxii. 44).

Of the living God: the seal he seals. Since ever living, God can during all time affix the approving seal.

3. Saying, Hurt not the land, nor the sea, nor the trees, until we seal the servants of our God on their foreheads.

Hurt not: by letting the winds loose. The perfect stillness of the winds indicates the perfect security of the sealed. Not a zephyr breathes, not a leaf stirs, not a wave whispers. The absolute security from evil of all sealed souls, symbolized by the absolute hush of air and land and ocean, Christ confirms by this promise: "No man shall pluck them out of my hand" (John x. 28).

We: myself and the four angels.

Seal: for preservation. The persons not sealed are to be destroyed (Ezek. viii., ix.).

Servants of our God: his true worshippers (Gen. l. 17; Isa. lxi. 6).

Their foreheads: "a plate of pure gold, with the engraving, *Holiness to the Lord*, shall be upon Aaron's *forehead*, that the children of Israel may be *accepted* before the Lord" (Exod. xxviii. 36, 38). The *inner* seal is the indwelling of the Holy Spirit (John xiv. 23; 1 John i. 3).

The sealing, though not described by St. John, now takes place (Ezek. ix. 4, 11). He then hears the number of the sealed.

The sealing is *moral and spiritual* approval, the reward of the previous battles and triumphs forshadowed and foretold in chapter vi.

The nature of the approval decides the nature of the battles themselves. The battles and their victories, although prefigured and predicted by outward war, famine, and pestilence, are moral and spiritual. The real contest prophetically described (chapter vi.) is between Christ's own truth and appointments, and human errors and devices. In the daily strife, the holiness of heart which Christ requires and creates is ever contending for the mastery over the sinfulness the Devil inspires, and the depraved affections of mankind prefer and cherish.

This is the present contest of every human soul.

THE NUMBER OF THE SEALED.

4. And I heard the number of the sealed; a hundred and forty-four thousand sealed out of every tribe of the sons of Israel.

One hundred and forty-four thousand: a definite number for an indefinite. A thousand is often in the Bible used in this indefinite sense (Ps. l. 10, lxxxiv. 10, xc. 4; 2 Pet. iii. 8). The indefinite one hundred and forty-four thousand equals the "great multitude which no man can number" (verse 9).

Every tribe: the twelve tribes in the following list represent the *entire* Church of God, both *Jewish and Christian*, according to our Lord's own words, "Ye yourselves who are following me shall, in the regeneration when the Son of man shall sit on his throne of glory, *sit*, even ye yourselves, *upon twelve thrones*, because *judging the twelve tribes of Israel*" (Matt. xix. 28).

With St. Paul, "the seed of Abraham" (Heb. ii. 16) is identical with the twelve tribes of Israel.

Thus all-embracing, the twelve tribes of Israel are both typical and inclusive. They are types of Christ's Church universal; and like it they include his servants gathered from all nations, during all periods of time.

5. Out of the tribe of Judah, twelve thousand sealed.

The same language in the Greek is used of the remaining eleven tribes, and therefore needs not to be here repeated.

List of Tribes (Rev. vii.).

Juda, Reuben, Gad, Aser, Nepthalim, Manasses, Simeon, Levi, Issachar, Zabulon, Joseph, Benjamin.

This list does not agree with any other Bible-list of the twelve tribes.

Of these lists there are five, all in the Old Testament: one by Jacob, two by Moses, two by Ezekiel.

First, by Jacob: —

Reuben, Simeon, Levi, Judah, Zebulun, Issachar, Dan, Gad, Asher, Naphtali, Joseph, Benjamin (Gen. xlix. 3-27). Of Jacob's twelve sons, Leah was the mother of six, — Reuben, Simeon, Levi, Judah, Issachar, Zabulon; Rachel, of two, — Joseph, Benjamin; Zilpah, Leah's maid, of two, — Gad, Asher; Bilhah, Rachel's maid, of two, — Dan, Naphtali.

In this list, the order is in part the succession of birth: Reuben, Simeon, Levi, Judah (Gen. xxix. 32-35).

Second, by Moses: —

Judah, Simeon, Benjamin, Dan, Manasseh, Ephraim, Zebulun, Issachar, Asher, Naphtali, Reuben, Gad (Num. xxxiv. 19-28).

In this list, Judah has displaced Reuben, according to the prediction of Jacob (Gen. xlix. 4, 10).

Third, by Moses: —

Reuben, Judah, Levi, Benjamin, Ephraim, Manasseh, Zebulun, Issachar, Gad, Dan, Naphtali, Asher (Deut. xxxiii. 6-24).

This list exhibits in its first three names the natal, civic, and ecclesiastical superiority among the tribes.

Fourth, by Ezekiel: —

Dan, Asher, Naphtali, Manasseh, Ephraim, Reuben, Judah, Levi, Benjamin, Simeon, Issachar, Zebulun, Gad (thirteen; Ezek. xlviii. 2-27).

Fifth, by Ezekiel: —

Reuben, Judah, Levi, Joseph, Benjamin, Dan, Simeon, Issachar, Zebulun, Gad, Asher, Naphtali (verses 31-34).

Ezekiel's lists differ, not only from each other, but from all other lists; perhaps, to indicate that the predicted measurements enumerated by the lists will not be *literally* fulfilled (verses 8-30).

Peculiarities of St. John's List.

1. Both Dan and Ephraim are omitted from this list, although contained in each of the lists given by Moses, and in Ezekiel's first list. (*a*) Dan is omitted because "Dan shall *judge* his people" (Gen. xlix. 16.) The enrolment (Rev. vii. 5-8) is not for *judgment*, but for the contrary purpose, *preservation*. (*b*) Ephraim's place is taken by Joseph his father (verse 8). Perhaps Ps. lxxviii. 9-11 gives the reason for this omission of Ephraim, *his unfaithfulness to God*.

"The children of Ephraim, armed, carrying bows, turned back in the day of battle. They kept not the covenant of God, and refused to walk in his law; and forgot his works, and his wonders that he showed them."

Thus unfaithful, Ephraim is not fit to *represent* any portion of the one hundred and forty-four thousand, all of whom are sealed and approved on account of their fidelity to God.

2. *Judah* heads the list of the sealed (Rev. vii. 5). "Our Lord sprang out of Judah" (Heb. vii. 14). The list in Rev. vii. 5-8 is therefore a *Christian* list. The one hundred and forty-four thousand sealed are *Christians*, the representatives of faithful Christians until the end of this present world.

These sealed Christians receive, in chapter vii., a twofold recognition from our Lord, the presiding Judge. The second recognition (verse 9) explains the first (verse 4). Their numbers are not limited, but are boundless. The twofold recognition shows how precious the sealed are in the estimation of Christ. They are treasures so priceless, that his love constrains him to count them more than once. The miser's affection for his gold and silver, his notes and securities, leads him to give them repeated countings. A saved soul is dearer to Christ than all material creations.

SYMBOLIC REPRESENTATION OF THE CHURCH OF CHRIST VICTORIOUS AND TRIUMPHANT (Verses 9-17).

The Church represented in these verses is the same body as that composing the one hundred and forty-four thousand sealed. "The multitude no man can number" is the *recapitulation* of the sealed twelve tribes. The structural usage which pervades all portions of the Apocalypse creates the recapitulation in the present instance.

---

9. After this I saw, and behold a great multitude which no one could number, out of every nation, even out of all tribes and peoples and tongues, standing before the throne and before the Lamb clothed with white robes, and palms are in their hands.

Multitude: innumerable. The sight St. John saw of an innumerable multitude of sealed, approved, and accepted Christians answers the great question, once asked our Lord, "Are there few that be saved?" (Luke xiii. 23.) The saved are so many that they cannot be numbered. No numbers can count the vast and increasing throng. The goodness of God in the present day leads to repentance (Rom. ii. 4). Christ ever travels in the greatness of his strength, *mighty to* *save* (Isa. lxiii. 1). The preaching of the cross is everywhere "the power of God" (1 Cor. i. 18). Now, as always, multitudes of believers are being added to the Lord (Acts v. 14). The churches throughout the habitable earth are continually "edified, and walking in the fear of the Lord, and in the comfort and renewal of the Holy Ghost," are incessantly "multiplied." Sanctified souls, dying in the faith of Christ, and sleeping in Jesus, are every moment being added to the "great multitude no man can number." In the countless and swelling assembly, Christ sees the triumphs of the travail of his soul, and is satisfied (Isa. liii. 11).

Standing: is the attitude of praise. "Stand up and bless the Lord" (Neh. ix. 5).

The throne: the throne erected (iv.), and remaining (v. 1, 6, 13, vi. 16).

Clothed with white robes: re-appearance of the martyr-saints (vi. 11, vii. 13, 14).

Palms: emblems of joy, not of victory.

The imagery of palms is derived, not from Greece and Rome, but from the usages of the Israelites.

On the annual festival of tabernacles, commemorative of the passage of the Israelites through the wilderness, and of the goodness of God in the return of seedtime and harvest (Deut. xvi. 13-15), "they took branches of palm-trees, and *rejoiced* before the Lord seven days" (Lev. xxiii. 40). "There was *very great gladness*" (Neh. viii. 17). "They kept *with gladness* the feast of tabernacles. They bare *branches of palms*, and sang psalms unto Him that had given them good success" (2 Macc. x. 6, 7).

The "great multitude innumerable" rejoice in the possession of the security, rest, and peace resulting from Christ's *tabernacling* with them (verse 15); and they express their joy by waving palm-branches, and shouting, "Salvation to our God" (verse 10).

10. And are crying with a loud voice, saying, The victory to our God who is sitting upon the throne, and to the Lamb.

The victory: the deliverance (1 Sam. xiv. 45; 2 Sam. xix. 2; 2 Kings v. 1; Hab. iii. 8). "They sang psalms unto Him that had given them good success" (2 Macc. x. 7). The worshippers ascribe their victory both to the Father and to the Lamb; thus "honoring the Son even as they honor the Father" (John v. 23).

11. And all the angels had placed themselves in a circle around the throne and the elders and the four living beings, and fall before the throne, on their faces, and worship God.

Antiphonal response of angels.

Had placed themselves: while the "great multitude" is shouting. Angels sympathize with the Redeemer and the redeemed (Luke ii. 9-14; Matt. iv. 11, xxviii. 2; John xx. 12; Acts i. 10). The elders and the four cherubim are not here worshippers. They are in v. 8. Both classes are distinguished from "all the angels." Neither elders nor cherubim are angels.

12. Saying, Amen. The blessing, and the glory, and the wisdom, and the thanksgiving, and the honor, and the power, and the might [due, be given] to our God for ever and ever. Amen.

The words of the response are in two parts.
(a) Amen, which is assent to the human multitude (verse 10).
(b) The sevenfold doxology.

13. And one of the elders speaks, saying to me, These who are clothed with white robes, who are they? and whence came they?

Speaks: "answered," English Version. This elder is not previously addressed. "Answer" has here this sense, *begins* to speak. (See John v. 17.)

Who? and whence? the questions fix attention upon the objects, and obtain more minute descriptions.

This elder, as a representative of the Church of Christ, makes, by his questions, this consoling truth most prominent, that Christ *most richly rewards all sufferers for his sake.*

14. And I said to him, My master, thou thyself knowest. And he said to me, These are they who are coming out of the great tribulation, and they washed their robes and made them white by the blood of the Lamb.

My master: honorary title of address to a superior (John xii. 21).
Thou knowest: that is, I know not (Ezek. xxxvii. 3).
Who are coming: the present for the certain future (John xvi. 13, Greek).
The great tribulation: "In the world ye shall have tribulation" (John xvi. 33); "There shall be great tribulation" (Matt. xxiv. 21).

The white-robed victors represent Christ's militant, suffering, and victorious people, in all ages of his Church.

Washed: the Greek verb implies the *personal action* of the agent.
Robes: that is, themselves.

Made them white: made themselves, through faith in Christ crucified, pure and holy. "The blood of Christ cleanseth from all sin" (1 John i. 7).

15. On this account they are before the throne of God, and are serving him day and night in his temple, and he who sitteth upon the throne shall cause his tabernacle to rest upon them.

On this account: because they are sanctified.

Are before the throne: the white-robed throng (verse 9) are before the throne *in this present vision*. This is a symbolical representation of the position Christ's faithful servants occupy at all times, and in every period of the world. They "come boldly unto the throne of grace" (Heb. iv. 16).

Serving him day and night in his temple: their service symbolizes the service we are all now exhorted by St. Paul to render. "Let us serve God acceptably with reverence and godly fear" (Heb. xii. 28).

In his temple: which is, in this verse, the holy of holies, where is the mercy-seat, the throne of grace, to which we can all now come boldly and acceptably, since by his own blood (Heb. ix. 12) Christ has made manifest to us all the way into this holiest of all seats of his mercy (verse 8).

The possession of Christ's mercy and image in this world foreshadows and secures the possession of his presence and glory in the world beyond this (John xvii. 24; 1 John iii. 2).

Cause his tabernacle to rest upon them: shall spread his own habitation over them; shall defend them by his everlasting presence (Exod. xxix. 45; Isa. iv. 5, 6).

In symbol, this assurance is Christ's promise renewed to each believing and obedient soul. "If a man love me, my Father will love him, and we will come unto him, and *make our abode with him*" (John xiv. 23).

16. They shall not hunger more, and they shall not thirst more, and in no wise shall the burning sun hurt them, nor any kind of heat.

These four assurances are amplified repetitions of God's promises, by the prophet Isaiah, of blessings *in this life*. "They shall not (1) hunger, nor (2) thirst; neither shall (3) the heat nor (4) the sun smite them" (Isa. xlix. 10).

"The blood of the Lamb" (Rev. vii. 14) imparts to these assurances *Christian* senses, which the Bible explains as indicating *spiritual blessings* he is *at present continually bestowing.*

(1) "Blessed are they which do *hunger* and (2) *thirst* after righteousness: for they shall *be filled*" (Matt. v. 6).

Both the sun and heat are emblems of spiritual evils.

(3) "The sun shall not smite thee by day. The Lord shall preserve thee *from all evil:* he shall *preserve thy soul*" (Ps. cxxi. 6, 7).

(4) "Thou, O Lord, hast been a *shadow from the heat*" (Isa. xxv. 4).

17. Because the Lamb who is in the midst of the throne shall tend them, and shall lead them unto life-fountains of waters. Also God shall wipe away every tear from their eyes.

This verse embodies a triplet of Christian blessings, since conferred by the Lamb: two positive, shepherd-tending and leading; and one negative, wiping away tears.

1. **Shepherd-tending**: includes defending and feeding. Christ is "the good Shepherd" (John x. 11). (*a*) He defends us from all evil (John xviii. 9); (*b*) he feeds us with himself (John vi. 51).

2. **Shepherd-leading**: unto life-fountains of waters (Ps. xxiii. 2; John iv. 14).

3. The wiping-away of tears (Isa. xxv. 8) is the negative form for the positive bestowal of peace and joy. "Peace I leave with you, my peace I give unto you" (John xiv. 27).

"I have spoken unto you, that my joy might remain in you, and that your joy might be full" (John xv. 11). "Your joy no man taketh from you" (xvi. 22).

"They that sow in tears shall reap in joy" (Ps. cxxvi. 5).

Christian poets and divines very properly employ Rev. vii. 14–17, to portray the bliss of paradise. The words may, indeed, have this *secondary* application, although the *primary* reference seems to be to the spiritual joys Christ provides for Christian pilgrims in their journey through this imperfect world to the perfection of his heavenly presence.

St. John himself employs portions of this imagery to picture the increased happiness of the citizens of the New Jerusalem after the universal resurrection, and the annihilation of this present earth (Rev. xxi. 3, 4, xxii. 3). Our Lord's prophecies in Matt. xxiv. have a nearer and a more remote perspective. Rev. vii. 15-17 must have the same twofold reference. Our Lord himself *doubles* the rewards he promises to faithful devotion to his service (Mark x. 29, 30).

CHAPTER VIII.

THUS far in chapters iv.-vii., all is *preparation*,—the throne of judgment, the Judge, the associate judges, the executioners, the judgments to be inflicted, the preservation of the Church of Christ, its thanksgiving and praise.

With chapter viii., *executions* begin, in the forms of trumpets and censers. The executions are wholly confined *to this present world*.

The executions end with chapter xx., verse 10; thus extending through *thirteen* chapters.

Thus with chapter viii. begin the symbolical *fulfilments* of the preceding symbolical *predictions* in chapters iv.-vii.

The Apocalypse has, like the Book of Ezekiel, these forms of prophecy and fulfilment, in order to indicate and proclaim *the absolute certainty* of the events which Christ by these graphic representations foreshadows and predicts (Gen. xli. 32; Ps. lxii. 11).

THE UNROLLING OF THE SEVENTH SCROLL.

We must now notice and remember that the seventh scroll is *itself a scroll*. It does not differ in nature from the preceding scrolls. It does not change their subjects. Its special office is *perpetuation*. Retaining the essential nature of the former scrolls, and holding most firmly their own purpose, the seventh scroll expands their subjects, and presents them in new aspects and with more definite applications. This scroll bears the same relation to its predecessors as our Lord bears to the Old-Testament prophets. The business and duty of the seventh scroll is TO FULFIL.

1. *The trumpets* are previous prophecies fulfilled upon *heathen nations.*

This fact, so important to the right interpretation of the trumpets, is clearly demonstrated by subsequent records.

The blasts of the fifth and sixth trumpets "hurt" and "kill" *heathen* men (chapter ix.). They are heathen, because they "have not the seal of God in their foreheads" (verse 4), and because they "worship" both "*devils and idols*" (verse 20).

2. The censers are antecedent predictions fulfilled upon *ecclesiastical persecutors*, both Jewish and Christian. This fact will appear in chapter xvi.

---

1. And when he unrolled the seventh scroll, there is silence in heaven about the space of half an hour.

Silence: implies (*a*) preparation, "the seven angels *prepared* themselves to sound" (verse 6); (*b*) waiting, "praise *waiteth* [Heb., "is silent"]" (Ps. lxv. 1); (*c*) dread, "the earth *feared*, and was still" (Ps. lxxvi. 8).

The silence is connected with the offering of the incense (verse 3). So Luke i. 10: the people are in silent prayer "at the time of incense."

2. And I saw the seven angels who are standing before God, and there are given them seven trumpets.

The seven angels: the seven designated for the seven trumpets. All angels are ministering spirits (Heb. i. 14).

Standing: prepared for their work.

Seven trumpets: are war-trumpets (Num. x. 9, xxxi. 6; Job xxxix. 25; Hos. viii. 1; Joel ii. 1; 1 Cor. xiv. 8). Thus the seven trumpets herald war in its executive horrors.

With Rev. viii. 2 compare Josh. vi. 4, "*Seven priests* bear *seven trumpets.*" These priests blow their trumpets against the *heathen* city of Jericho.

Judas Maccabæus follows the example of Joshua: "O God, be our help! *The heathen* are assembled together against us to destroy us. Then *sounded they* with trumpets" (1 Mac. iii. 52, 54). So in Rev. viii. 7, 8, 10, 12, ix. 1, 12, the six trumpets announce Christ's judgments on *heathen* nations.

3. And another angel comes and stands upon the altar, having a golden censer; and there is given him much incense that he may give it to the prayers of all the saints, on the golden altar which is before the throne.

This verse contains the *symbolic answer* to the prayers of the saints in the fifth scroll (vi. 9).

In this verse 3, there are two altars, — the altar of burnt sacrifice in the first clause, and the golden altar of incense in the last clause.

A golden censer: for burning incense on the golden altar within the temple.

May give it [much incense] **to the prayers**: the usage in the Apocalypse, of the Greek verb meaning "give," requires the preposition *to*, and not *with* (English Version).

There is not an instance in this book where the verb is followed by the dative of *coincidence*, which requires the preposition *with*. On the contrary, when "give" is succeeded by the dative, the dative is that of *the recipient*, and must be translated *to*, and not *with*.

Much incense is necessarily the accusative *implied* after "may give" in this sentence: there is given him much incense, that he may give it [much incense] to the prayers.

All the saints: the prayers of all saints, and the prayers of saints (v. 8), are identical. The prayers themselves are there offered by the slain under the altar (vi. 10),—these prayers for vengeance, "How long, O Lord, holy and true, dost thou not judge and avenge our blood?"

The incense (viii. 3) *is itself the answer* to these prayers of the martyr saints. Incense is the symbol of *prayer answered*. This is Hebrew usage. "*Give ear* unto my prayer," *answer* my prayer. (Ps. cxli. 2) "Let my prayer be set forth *incense*," let my prayer *be incense;* let my prayer be *answered*. "*As* incense" is not permitted by the Hebrew, which *omits* the *as* of the English Version.

This answer of vengeance (verse 3) is *twofold*, — trumpets (viii. 7, 8, 10, 12, ix. 1, 13), censers (xvi. 2–4, 8, 10, 12).

4. And so the smoke of the incense ascends by the prayers of the saints, out of the hand of the angel, before God.

Smoke: *avenging* smoke. This may be the sense of smoke everywhere in this book (ix. 2, 3, 17, 18, xiv. 11, xv. 8, xviii. 9, 18).

By the prayers: no instance in Bible Greek where the verb translated "ascend" is used with the prepositions representing "with." We must therefore reject "with" of the English Version, and use "by."

In Ezek. xxvi. 3 (Septuagint), the Greek verb to ascend is followed by an *instrumental* dative. The sea rises *by* its waves.

Thus Greek usage provides no other meaning for "prayers" than the *instrumental*. The smoke of the incense ascends *by* the prayers.

Incense, as we have just seen (verse 3), is *prayer answered*. The ascent of the incense is *the answer obtained*. This, then, is the meaning of Rev. viii. 4, first clause. Answer is obtained *by* the prayers of the saints.

5. And the angel takes the censer, and fills it from the fire of the altar, and casts it to the earth, and there were voices and thunders and lightnings and an earthquake.

Lev. xvi. 12, 13, provides the imagery of Rev. viii. 4. This verse 5, because symbolizing spiritual judgments, describes actions which are not mentioned in the Mosaic ritual; namely, *the return* of the priest to the great altar, and his use of the golden censer. The loud responses which followed are most impressive *confirmations of the answer* the prayers of the saints have already received (verse 4).

The imagery of these loud responses, "voices, thunders, earthquake," may be derived from the shouts of the priests, the sounds of the trumpets, and the voices of the singers which formed the "finishing the service at the altar," as narrated by the "Son of Sirach:" "Then shouted the sons of Aaron, and sounded the silver trumpets, and made a great noise; the singers also sang praises with their voices" (Ecclus. l. 14, 16, 18).

Cast it to the earth: this pouring-out of the contents of the golden censer, namely, the glowing coals and the smoking incense, is an impressive symbol of God's wrath, and is also prophetic of the severe judgments inflicted by the trumpets and by the censers.

See Ezek. x. 2; Luke xii. 49.

6. And so the seven angels who are holding the seven trumpets are preparing themselves to sound.

The seven angels: mentioned in verse 2.

Are preparing themselves: by the actions of the angel with the incense (verse 3).

THE FIRST THREE TRUMPETS (Verses 7-11).

The bowman on the white horse (vi. 2) is the symbol of victory. Like him, the first three trumpets symbolize conquests.

THE FIRST TRUMPET.

7. And the first angel sounded. And there follows hail and fire, both mingled with blood, and they are cast unto the earth. And the third part of the earth is burned up, and the third part of the trees is burned up, and every green herb is burned up.

The imagery of this verse is taken from the plague of hail in the Book of Exodus. "The Lord sent hail, the fire ran along upon the ground; the hail smote both *man* and beast; the hail smote every herb of the field, and brake every tree of the field" (ix. 23, 25).

In the two passages, the agents and the objects affected are essentially the same. The passage in Exodus will help us interpret the passage in Revelation. In this important respect, however, the passages differ. That in Exodus is a *literal* narrative: this in Revelation is a symbolic representation.

In this verse 7, the only effective agent is fire. Its action is threefold, to show that its destruction is utterly remediless.

Of the three objects irremediably burned, —

1. "The earth" denotes the inhabitants of the earth (xi. 6, 18, xix. 2); the common people.
2. "The trees" symbolize *civil rulers* (Ezek. xxxi. 2-18).
3. The "green herb" is an emblem of the weakness and helplessness, both of people and rulers, before the fire of God's indignation. "Evil doers shall wither as *the green herb*" (Ps. xxxvii. 2).

THE SECOND TRUMPET (Verses 8, 9).

8. Also the second angel sounded. And as it were, a great mountain, burning with fire, is cast into the sea; and the third part of the sea becomes blood.

This language is made symbolic by the expression, "as it were." The symbols are, —

1. "A great mountain," symbolizing a great kingdom (Dan. ii. 35-45).

A **burning mountain**: a mountain rent from its high range, and thrown into the sea by a volcanic earthquake; symbolizing the destruction of the great kingdom.

With the prophet Jeremiah, this mountain symbolizes the kingdom of Babylon on the Euphrates: "I am against thee, O destroying mountain; and I will roll thee down from the rocks, and will make thee a burnt mountain" (li. 25).

In the Apocalypse, Babylon is (*a*) Rome ecclesiastical (xiv. 8), derived from (*b*) Rome civil (xiii. 3). The mountain, therefore, in this verse 8, represents the *civil* Roman empire, destined to dislodgement, overthrow, and ruin. Our Lord (Matt. xxiv. 15; Luke xxi. 20) identifies the fourth beast of Dan. vii. 7, with the Roman empire. But this fourth beast ("kingdom," verse 23) "wears out the saints of the Most High" (verse 25). The Pagan Roman empire caused the ten persecutions of the early Christian Church. The denunciations of the trumpets are directed, first of all, against this persecuting Pagan empire, symbolically destroyed (Rev. xviii. 21; repeated from Jer. li. 63, 64).

2. The sea is often, in the Bible, the image of political confusion and revolution.

In the Book of Daniel, the four beasts, which are symbols of four kingdoms (vii. 23), "come from *the sea*" (verse 3); from political turmoil and change.

Our Lord, when foretelling the destruction of Jerusalem, intensifies his prediction by adding this image of unrest and removal: "The sea and the waves roaring" (Luke xxi. 25). In this sense, then, political confusion and revolution, may we understand "sea" (Rev. viii. 8).

3. **Blood**: imagery taken from Exod. vii. 20. We cannot misunderstand the signification of this word as a symbol. Blood is the image of death. "The third part of the creatures *in the sea died*" (verse 9).

9. And so the third part of the creatures which are in the sea, and which have lives, die; also the third part of the ships perish utterly.

This verse, like its predecessor, has three subjects.

1. **Creatures in the sea**: participants in military rebellions and governmental revolutions.

2. **Have lives**: the most active agents in the civil wars and political changes. "We are willing to impart unto you our own *lives*" (1 Thess. ii. 8).

3. **Ships**: for sailors, by *metonomy*. "*Howl*, ye *ships* of Tarshish" (Isa. xxiii. 1). "*The ships* of Tarshish *did sing* of thee" (Ezek. xxvii. 25).

Perish utterly: when kingdoms and empires decay, navies are inactive and useless, and sailors cease to be a class of laborers. The declining Roman empire illustrated this beginning of its extinction.

THE THIRD TRUMPET (Verses 10, 11).

10. Also the third angel sounded. And there falls from heaven a great star, burning as a torch, and it falls on the third part of the rivers, and upon the fountains of waters.

Star: an angel (Judg. v. 20; Job xxv. 5, xxxviii. 7).

Falls: an act of injury (vii. 16, viii. 10). The great burning and shining star is a *destroying angel*.

Burning: each of the first three trumpets causes burning (verses 7, 8, 10).

Torch: blazing as a torch, to intensify the purpose of his fall.

Rivers and waters: other names for *the common people* (xvii. 15). The common people are "the fountains" of national life.

11. The name of the star is called Wormwood. And so a third part of the waters become wormwood, and many of the men die by means of the waters, because they are made bitter.

Wormwood: the star has this name on account of the effects he produces.

In the Old-Testament prophets, wormwood is a punishment threatened *the people*.

"I will feed *this people* with *wormwood*" (Jer. ix. 15).

The effect of wormwood when eaten is to produce *drunkenness*. "Make *drunken with wormwood*" (Lam. iii. 15). *The nature* of the drunkenness is thus described by the prophet Jeremiah: "I will fill all the inhabitants of this land, the kings, the priests, the prophets, and all the inhabitants of Jerusalem, with *drunkenness*. And I will *dash them one against another, even the fathers and the sons together*, saith the Lord: I will not pity, nor have mercy, but *destroy* them" (xiii. 13, 14).

Wormwood is thus, in the Old Testament, the most frightful symbol (*a*) of popular infatuation, and (*b*) of mutual destruction by the infatuated and besotted *people as a nation*.

In chapter vi. of the Apocalypse, the three *prophetic* symbols, war, famine, pestilence, — these destroyers are *from without*.

In the three symbols of *actual* destruction, introduced by the three trumpets, the destroyers are *from within*. The people as a nation all combine to kindle spontaneous combustion, and work internecine annihilation.

The men: implied in the preceding trumpets, and thus revealing the reference of the symbols to *human beings*. The waters represent the common people, here injuring the men, and therefore of a different class. The men are consequently the upper classes corrupted and ruined by the demoralized lower classes.

The first three trumpets prophetically and most instructively symbolize the Roman empire in its decay and overthrow. It is a burning forest (verse 7); it is a consuming mountain (verse 8); it is a deadly sea (verses 8, 9). It is a poisoned spring-head of human life. Without conscience, the people commit suicide by self-indulgence. Without mutual confidence, the higher orders disappear with the disappearance of the only sustaining basis in the social edifice, — *an honest constituency*.

The history of Rome, after the time of St. John, gives remarkable confirmation of his symbolic predictions respecting this doomed empire.

Previous to the year A.D. 222, less than one hundred and thirty years after St. John had his visions in the isle of Patmos, *thirteen* Roman emperors had died a violent death. An imperial death every ten years! Within *fifty* years after this date, not less than *fifty* emperors had ended their perilous days in the same manner. The reign of an emperor averaged only a single year (MILLOT, *Elements Hist.*, ii. 269, 275).

"Wars, famine, pestilence, contempt of the laws, and insurrections of the army, set the empire *in combustion* [p. 281]. The laws sunk into chaos [p. 275]. Unbridled licentiousness put an end to all subordination" [p. 271].

The prophetic symbols of St. John apply to every civil power that adopts the vices and sins of the Pagan empire of Rome.

The frightful symbolism of these three trumpets has ever its evident application and its unmistakable notes of warning. No human organization can long endure which is animated and controlled by a self-indulgent, unprincipled, and contentious population.

The symbolic star, *popular infatuation*, as in ancient Rome, so in all countries, is inevitably self-destructive.

"The madness of the people" in the French Revolution is an obvious and an admonitory illustration.

When time shall so clear the public eye of sectional prejudice as to let it look heavenward, the people of the United States of America will see, in the fratricidal war of A.D. 1861–1865, the re-appearance of the burning and flaming star "Wormwood."

The incipient strike in these Northern States, A.D. 1877, which threatened to become a general insurrection, is alarming proof that the bad angel "Wormwood" still hovers in our own ominous sky.

THE FOURTH, FIFTH, AND SIXTH TRUMPETS.

The fourth, fifth, and sixth trumpets announce *the instruments* by which the first, second, and third trumpets will be accomplished.

THE FOURTH TRUMPET.

12. Also the fourth angel sounds. And the third part of the sun is smitten, and the third part of the moon, and the third part of the stars, that the third part of their light may be darkened; even the daylight in its third part may not shine, and the night-light in the like manner.

To the locked meaning of this figurative verse, these words of Moses provide the opening key: "The precious fruits *brought forth* by the sun; the precious things *put forth* by the moon" (Deut. xxxiii. 14).

According to this declaration of Moses, the sun and moon are the causes of vegetable growth.

In Rev. viii. 12, one-third part of the sun, moon, and stars is darkened, so that the daylight (Luke vi. 13; 1 Thess. v. 5, first clause) and the night-light (John xi. 10: 1 Thess. v. 5, last clause), is diminished one-third.

This diminution of daylight and of night-light would occasion proportional diminution of vegetable growth.

The darkened sun, moon, and stars are, therefore, most undoubtedly symbols of *famine*.

The causes of famine are, —

1. Drought, which is God's infliction. Two present causes of famine are human and largely self-inflicted.

2. The production of tobacco and opium instead of grain. By this substitution, the quantity of grain is diminished, and its price increased, and the people are rendered poor in purse and health.

3. The distillation of grain into intoxicating liquors. This consumption of food creates the twofold evil of poverty and of possible and inevitable drunkenness, — the cause of increased poverty and of multiplied wretchedness.

Drought is only an occasional infliction from God.

The substitution of narcotics and alcohol for bread, the staff of life, is a deep and open volcano, dug by human hands, ever burning, ever belching, ever covering unmeasured districts of all continents with its barren lava, and ever consuming with its incessantly ejected flames millions of blighted sufferers of all nations of mankind.

Of the cause of famine in these its threefold manifestations, the eclipsed sun, the black moon, and the quenched stars, are most appropriate and most significant symbols. The ever-falling showers of human tears are in most instances the ascended clouds which hide the luminaries of heaven.

The Herald Eagle.

13. Also I saw and heard an eagle flying in the place of the noonday sun, saying with a loud voice, Woe, woe, woe to the inhabitants of the earth, by the other voices of each trumpet of the three angels who must soon sound!

An eagle: the emblem of a swift messenger (Jer. xlviii. 40).

Place of the noonday sun: this is the meaning of the Greek word erroneously translated "the midst of heaven" by the English Version. The eagle, in this verse, flies in the zenith at noonday, that he may be seen by all eyes, and heard by all ears.

Saying: the loud and high scream of the flying eagle heralds the infliction of *three* separate woes (ix. 12).

(*a*) ix. 1-11. Pestilence.
(*b*) ix. 13-21. War.
(*c*) ix. 14. The contents of censers (xv. 7, xvi. 2-16).

As three is a *full* number, God will inflict no more woes than these.

CHAPTER IX.

The imagery in this chapter is amplified and intensified to an extent unknown in any preceding portion.

THE FIFTH TRUMPET.

The woe now trumpeted is *pestilence*. This character of the first woe is required both by the context, and by the symbols employed.

(*a*) *By the context.* The fourth trumpet (viii. 12) announces *famine*. The sixth trumpet (ix. 14-17) announces *war*. The prophetic and natural triplet, war, famine, pestilence (vi. 4, 5, 8), demands its own fulfilment to be (since famine is the voice of the fourth trumpet, and war is the voice of the sixth trumpet) famine, *pestilence*, and war. The context thus assigns unalterably *pestilence* to the *fifth* trumpet. *The natural order* of the judgments is changed, because they are here *symbolic*.

(*b*) *By the component symbols.* The "star" (ix. 1) and the "locusts" (ix. 3), the meaning of which we shall soon see.

1. Also the fifth angel sounds. And I see a star from heaven fallen to the earth, and there is given him the key of the bottomless pit.

A star from heaven fallen to the earth: the star is an angel. (See viii. 10.) In some sense, the star is actually on the earth. The *fall* of the star is a *judgment* (viii. 10). The sun *falls*, and hurts by its *influence* (vii. 16). The "star" (ix. 1) may also have fallen, and hurt *by its influence*.

This star personified has the key of the bottomless pit. He uses the key. He opens the door of the bottomless pit. From the opened door, ascend columns of smoke (verse 2). Smoke implies fire. Fire implies heat.

Thus, by opening the door of the bottomless pit, the star fills the whole atmosphere with *burning heat*. The fifth trumpet heralds pestilence. The fallen star produces the burning heat. The burning heat produces the pestilence. The fallen star therefore produces the pestilence.

The fallen star in its deadly influence resembles the deadly influence of one of the planets.

In the time of St. John, it was the prevalent opinion, that the excessive heat and the increased mortality of summer were caused by the dog-star, Sirius (in Greek *Seirios*, which means *scorching*).

This is the opinion of the principal Greek and Latin writers during the period of *a thousand years* from the poet Homer, B. C. 900, to the naturalist Pliny, the contemporary of St. John.

These are the possibilities that St. John derived the imagery, by which he portrayed the power of the pestilence, from the common opinion of his day.

St. John may have been familiar with the popular belief respecting Sirius. For

1. He resided many years in Asia Minor, where Greek ideas prevailed, and Greek literature was accessible.

2. He may have read the Greek poets. St. Paul had read some of them: St. John had the same opportunity.

3. St. John must have read the Septuagint, the Greek translation of the Old Testament. It was the Bible of the apostles. In the Septuagint, *Orion*, the name of the constellation of which Sirius forms a part, occurs (Job xxxviii. 31).

4. St. John may have seen this very place in the Book of Job. In Rev. iii. 7, St. John refers to Job xii. 14. In Rev. xii. 10, St. John refers to Job i. 9 and ii. 5. He was therefore not a stranger to the book.

5. St. John repeatedly quotes the prophet Isaiah. This writer ranks Orion with the stars (xiii. 10, "the constellations thereof;" Hebrew, their Orions). Thus, in St. John's time, and in a volume he often quotes, Orion, the constellation containing Sirius the dog-star, was itself known *as a star*.

St. John may, then, have been familiar with the current belief respecting Sirius. If familiar, he may by "the star" (Rev. ix. 1) refer to Sirius.

Is given: by Christ.

Bottomless pit: this expression in the Apocalypse (ix. 1, 2, 11, xi. 7, xvii. 8, xx. 1, 3) not identical with "lake of fire and brimstone' (xix. 20, xx. 10, 14, 15, xxi. 8).

2. And he opens the bottomless pit, and there ascends

smoke out of the pit, as the smoke of a great furnace, and the sun is darkened, and the air, by the smoke of the pit.

Smoke: accompanied by *heat* (xviii. 9, 18).
Furnace: like the "burning fiery furnace" (Dan. iii. 6).
The air: the atmosphere. (Exod. x. 15) the air is darkened by locusts. The atmosphere is *heated* by the hot smoke, as well as darkened. It is thus proved that "the star" (verse 1) is the cause of *burning heat*.

3. Also out of the smoke come locusts upon the earth; and there is given them power, as the scorpions of the earth have power.

The fifth trumpet introduces pestilence. It is thus defined: "the offspring of inclement skies, and of legions of putrifying locusts" (*World's Progress*, article "Plague").

Jerome (fifth century) thus describes the deadly influence of these decaying insects:—

"Putredo mortuorum locustarum et factor in tantum noxius fuit, ut æram quoque corrumperet, et pestilentia tam jumentorum, quam hominum gigneretur" (on Joel ii. 20).

"Locusts, when dead, so corrupt and infect the air, that it often occasions dreadful pestilences." — JOHN THEVENOT (French traveller), A.D. 1667.

Power is given them: permission to poison; dead locusts poison the air.
Scorpions: the sting of the scorpion is not always fatal. While it is a torment, it is not a deadly infliction. Thus the scorpion's sting is a just representation of the pestilence. When it prevails, while many of its victims die, death is not universal.

4. And it is said to them: Not to hurt the grass of the earth, nor any green thing, nor any tree, but only the men who have not the seal of God on their foreheads.

Is said: by Christ.
Hurt not: thus, unlike all other locusts. These locusts are therefore *dead*. They can eat neither "grass," nor "green thing," nor "tree," the special depredation of live locusts. Their present abstinence the direct opposite of their clean work in Egypt (Exod. x. 15).

Objection.

Pestilence cannot be the woe introduced by the fifth trumpet, because pestilence assails the sealed as well as the unsealed.

Answer.

1. Pestilence may be taken in a large sense. Pestilence may include every waste of the health of the human being, except its original mortality.

2. The violation of the laws of health shortens human life. "The wicked shall not prolong his days" (Eccles. viii. 13).

3. The observance of the laws of health prolongs human life. "Godliness hath the promise of the life that now is" (1 Tim. iv. 8).

4. God employs bodily diseases as medicines of the soul.

5. The wicked, the unsealed, are "hurt" instead of blessed by these medicines.

6. The righteous, the sealed, are blessed by their bodily inflictions, and in this way are "not hurt" by the pestilence.

7. The Book of Revelation predicts *spiritual* evils and *spiritual* blessings, and not merely *bodily* injuries and *bodily* advantages.

8. In connection with human freedom, and human imperfection and wickedness, the laws God appoints often appear as *destined tendencies* rather than as *absolute certainties*.

9. Bodily diseases, the outgrowth of human sinfulness, may be included in the subjects of symbolic prediction under the fifth trumpet.

10. The waste of human life by (*a*) drunkenness, by (*b*) use of tobacco, opium, morphine, hasheesh, and other narcotics, by (*c*) sexual sin, is a *perpetual pestilence* by which God is punishing the transgressors.

The general destruction of female virtue among the Romans of the first centuries of the Christian era was one of the principal causes of the utter fall and hopeless ruin of the Roman empire.

The Scriptures themselves ascribe loss of bodily health to drunkenness and licentiousness. "Whoredom and wine take away the heart" (Hos. iv. 11).

Wine "biteth like a serpent, and stingeth like an adder" (Prov. xxiii. 32).

"Remove thy way from the strange woman, lest thou mourn at the last, when thy flesh and thy body are consumed" (Prov. v. 8, 11).

Thus pronounced by the Scriptures to be destructive of bodily health, these sins may, by St. John, be most properly symbolized as a pestilence.

5. And permission is given the locusts, not to kill the men, but that they shall be tormented five months. And so their torment is as the torment of the scorpion when he strikes a man.

The men shall be tormented: the locusts do not torment. The men are tormented by the pestilence. The Greek verb elsewhere describes the "palsy" (Matt. viii. 6). Since thus used, this verb may legitimately describe pestilence.

Five months: the life-time of the locust. He is hatched in the spring, and dies in the fall, when his decaying body produces pestilence. The five months symbolize the limited duration of pestilence as a divine judgment. Health is the daily sun of human life: disease is the passing cloud.

Their torment: the torment the locusts inflict, not the torment of the sufferers (ALFORD).

6. Also in those days the men shall seek death, and shall not find it; and shall long to die, and yet death shall flee from them.

This verse forms an intensive parallelism.

The men: described in verse 4.

Shall seek death, etc. : a graphic picture of despair and hopeless misery (Jer. viii. 3; Job iii. 21). The pestilence, in its various kinds, may assume the chronic forms predicted by Moses. "The Lord will make thy plagues great plagues, and of *long continuance*, and sore sicknesses, and of *long continuance*" (Deut. xxviii. 59).

Description of the Locusts (Verses 7-10).

The description consists of a series of unexampled intensifications, for the purpose of showing the greatness and hurtfulness of the pestilence in its numerous ramifications and manifestations. The exaggerated imagery cannot denote *material objects*. Such exaggerations are natural impossibilities. *Moral evils must be intended.*

---

7. And the images of the locusts are like horses prepared for battle; and upon their heads, as it were, crowns like gold; and their faces, as it were, the faces of men.

The images: suggested by the locusts.

These images are: —

1. **Horses** (Joel ii. 4) **prepared for battle**: caparisoned (Zech. x. 3; Jer. vi. 23). This equipment implies strength. Feeble horses would not be arrayed for battle.

2. **Crowns like gold**: a crown is the symbol of *kingship*. "The soldiers put a crown of thorns upon the head of Jesus, saying, Hail,

King of the Jews!" (Matt. xxvii. 29.) The locusts have power like kings.

Like gold: the crowns of the locusts are not *mock* crowns, like the thorns our Saviour wore, but crowns of *real gold*. Their power is not in appearance, but is actual and most efficient.

3. **The faces of men**: the face is the index and expression of intelligence. The pestilence, under the figure of the locusts, St. John represents as intelligent. Intelligence is the ability to execute. The pestilence can execute according to the measure of its power.

8. And they were having hair like the hair of women, and their teeth were like the teeth of lions.

4. **Hair of women**: have long hair (1 Cor. xi. 15). There is a species of locust with hair (Jer. li. 27); "*rough* caterpillars," English Version. Because covered with hair, the locusts are here represented as large and strong as quadrupeds, perhaps as lions, next clause.

5. **Teeth of lions**: the fifth similitude, like the preceding four, describes *the power* of the symbolized pestilence. The prophet Joel applies the same illustration to the locusts (i. 6).

9. And they were having breastplates like breastplates of iron; and the noise of their wings was like the noise of chariots drawn by many horses rushing into battle.

The imagery in this verse describes the irresistible character of the power wielded by the pestilence.

Breastplates: making the locusts invulnerable. "When they fall upon the sword, *they shall not be wounded*" (Joel ii. 8).

Iron: symbol of hardness (Deut. xxviii. 23). The breastplate was usually made of brass. Iron is harder than brass, and more impenetrable.

Wings: denote swiftness of execution. The hairy locust has wings (Nah. iii. 16).

Chariots: "Like the noise of chariots on the tops of mountains shall they leap" (Joel ii. 5).

The chariots and horses here represent *irresistible* power (Isa. lxvi. 15; Jer. iv. 13; Dan. xi. 40).

10. Also they are having tails like scorpions, and stings; and in their tails their power is to hurt the men five months.

Tails: "head and tail" (Isa. ix. 14), is a phrase for completeness. The heads, verse 7, begin the description of the locusts; tails, verse 10, end the description.

Stings: poisonous stings; this meaning of "sting" (1 Cor. xv.

55, 56). This is the meaning of "sharpness" (a sharp point) in the *Te Deum*, as this word is taken from the passage in First Corinthians.

Power: *delegated* power. God himself ever commissions the pestilence.

11. **They have over them as king the angel of the bottomless pit. His name in Hebrew is Abaddon, and in the Greek tongue he has the name Apolluon.**

King: political chief of the tribe. Here, predicate, *as* king. Locusts *natural* have no king (Prov. xxx. 27). The king, therefore, in this verse, must be *immaterial*. The king cannot be the commander, even in symbol, of armies of *human soldiers*. The immaterial cannot symbolize the material. The locusts (Rev. ix. 3-11) cannot represent *flesh-and-blood* military hosts.

The angel of the bottomless pit: the pestilence personified, which comes from the bottomless pit (verses 2, 3). The patriarch Job has a similar personification (xxviii. 22). "Destruction and death, say."

Abaddon: the destroyer.

Apolluon: the destroyer.

The name is repeated for emphasis. The repetition equals a superlative, — most destructive destroyer. The repetition explains the intensifications in the imagery investing the locusts. The intensifications magnify the deadly nature of the pestilence.

When we consider the frightful extent to which human life has been continually wasted, and is now continually wasted, by pestilence, *in its Bible sense*, we perceive that the intensified imagery St. John employs to depict the desolating evils is by no means exaggeration. The great and accumulated obstacles which at the present time hinder personal and social happiness, and oppose civilization and the influence and extension of Christianity, are the very pestilential vices and destructive sins so graphically and minutely portrayed under the fifth trumpet.

12. **The first woe is past. Behold, there are coming yet two woes after this.**

This is the announcement of St. John.

First woe: of the three predicted (viii. 13). The first woe is the plague of the locusts, symbolizing pestilence (ix. 1-11).

Is passed: in symbol and prediction.

Two woes: one given immediately (ix. 13-21) by the sixth trumpet, the woe of war; the other by the seventh trumpet (xi. 14), that is, by the contents of the censers it introduces (xv. 7, xvi. 2-16).

These three woes finish the symbolic representations of God's judgments in the Apocalypse.

In Bible arithmetic, the number *three* equals an integer, or whole number. "Israel shall be *the third with* Egypt and *with* Assyria, *even a blessing* [*full* blessing] in the midst of the land: whom the Lord of hosts shall bless, saying, Blessed be (1) *Egypt* my people, and (2) *Assyria* the work of my hands, and (3) *Israel* mine inheritance" (Isa. xix. 24, 25).

In this passage, Israel is a third, Egypt is another third, Assyria is still another third; and yet the united three are *one* full blessing.

In this way, the "three woes" (Rev. ix. 12) are in their destination *one full and exhaustive* curse. They completely empty the cup of God's indignation.

THE SIXTH TRUMPET (Verses 13-21).

The Judgment of War.

13. Also the sixth trumpet sounds. And I hear a voice out of the horns of the golden altar, which is before God;

Voice: *an answer* to the prayers of the saints for vengeance (viii. 3).

Horns the space enclosed by the horns of the golden altar (Exod. xxx. 2) was the surface where the incense was burned, which is a symbol of vengeance; a voice, then, of *vengeance*, from the incense-altar.

14. Saying to the angel who is holding the trumpet, Loosen the four angels, who are bound on the great river Euphrates.

Trumpet: the avenging trumpet.

Loosen: the opposite of "bound," next clause. The angels restrained from inflicting God's judgments are now loosened from this restraint.

Four angels: (see vii. 1, note). They are the avenging *cherubim* (iv. 6-9). In Ps. lxxx. 1, 4, cherubim and hosts are identical. In Ps. ciii. 20, 21, hosts and angels are identical. The "four angels" (Rev. ix. 14) are, therefore, cherubim. The river Chebar (Ezek. i. 1, 3, x. 22) is a branch of the Euphrates. The location of the four angels on the Euphrates thus identifies them with the cherubim on the Chebar.

Bound: held back from their work of destruction.

Euphrates: was the north-eastern boundary of the promised land (Gen. xv. 18; Deut. i. 7, xi. 24; Josh. i. 4; 1 Kings iv. 21). The

Euphrates was the battle-border between contending armies (2 Sam. viii. 3; 2 Kings xxiii. 29).

The Euphrates is the symbol of *invading* armies (Isa. viii. 7, 8).

Thus associated in the Old Testament, the Euphrates is (Rev. ix. 14, xvi. 12) most appropriately the symbolic barrier against military invasion.

15. And the four angels are loosed, who had been prepared for the period of an hour, and a day, and a month, and a year, to kill the third part of the men.

An hour: the definite words in this specification of time prove the period is definite. The usual order of designating a period of time, namely, year, month, day, hour ("year and four months," 1 Sam. xxvii. 7), is reversed for emphasis, to show that the period here designated would be definite *to an hour, at the beginning of the period*. Since thus *measured by hours*, and *begun* at a definite hour, it would also *end* at a definite hour. The phrase is an emphatic form of expressing this truth, "God hath *determined* the times before appointed" (Acts xvii. 26). The time included in the phrase is a little more than a year, and therefore a brief period. God limits the destructive work of the four angels to this space. Through his mercy, wars are usually short.

Kill: the locusts (v. 5) only *torment*. The horsemen sent by the four cherubim *kill* their victims.

The third part: God thus limits the ravages of war, as he limits the ravages of famine (viii. 12) and of pestilence (ix. 5). The effects of the first three trumpets are also limited to the same extent (viii. 7-10).

16. And the number of the embattled hosts of the horse-army is two hundred millions. Even I hear their number.

The appalling imagery (ix. 16, 17) is taken from the following places in the Old Testament:—

"A people cometh from the *north* country [beyond the Euphrates, Jer. xlvi. 6, 10], and a *great* nation. They shall lay hold on bow and spear. They are cruel, and have no mercy. Their voice roareth like the sea. They *ride upon horses, set in array as men* for war" (Jer. vi. 22, 23).

"King of *Babylon from the north*, with *horsemen;* the *abundance* of his *horses; the hoofs* of his *horses*" (Ezek. xxvi. 7, 10, 11).

The number: this word marks the sublime beauty of the passage. The numbering of the horsemen is the very first indication of their presence. They are already gathered and marshalled, waving their spears, and aiming their arrows.

Two hundred millions: to such immeasurable numbers, effectual resistance is impossible. They are victors before striking a blow.

17. And in this outlook I saw the horses in the vision, and their riders: they have breastplates fire-red, purple and yellow; and the heads of the horses are like the heads of lions, and out of their mouths issue fire and smoke and brimstone.

St. John must take his imagery from the ascension of the prophet Elijah. "Horses of fire; he went up by a whirlwind into heaven" (2 Kings ii. 11).

The invulnerable breastplates flash with rays fire-red, purple, and brilliant yellow. The utter uselessness of striking such polished armor is the admonition thus symbolized.

Like the heads of lions: the prophet Jeremiah compares warhorses to swift eagles (iv. 13). The prophet Habakkuk compares warhorses to swift leopards and fierce wolves (i. 8). Thus compared to eagles, to leopards, to wolves, horses in St. John's imagery may, without excessive exaggeration, have heads like lions, to symbolize their overwhelming power of charge and assault in battle.

18. By these three plagues are killed the third part of the men, by the fire, and by the smoke, and by the brimstone, which is issuing out of their mouths.

This verse describes the effect of the triform stream the monster horses breathe from their open mouths.

19. For the power of the horses is in their mouth, and in their tails; for their tails are like serpents, by having heads, and so by them they inflict hurt.

The locusts have tails like scorpions (verse 10). The horses have tails with heads, the tails being thus like serpents.

The origin of the intensified imagery in verses 17, 18, 19, is obvious.

1. The horse fights *with his mouth*. When fighting he breathes strongly, and his breath is visible. This hot breath St. John aggravates into "fire, smoke, and brimstone."

2. The horse also fights *with hind hoofs*. The horse thus fighting "head and tail" (Isa. ix. 14) may by *hyperbole* be said to fight with his tail; and his tail becomes by exaggeration "a serpent."

Thus ends the frightful portrait of the *second woe*, — the punitive judgment of war.

The *fulfilment* of this symbolic prediction may have begun with the invasion and overthrow of the Roman empire by the Northern hordes, hosts of whom came from regions beyond the river Euphrates.

The past history of the world demonstrates the indescribable severity of this universal and long-continued judgment. War can never be robbed of its horrors.

Wars are created by human passions. God, while disapproving wars, ever uses them as manifestations of his displeasure against the sins of nations. As punitive inflictions, wars will continue in the world so long as states, kingdoms, and empires are selfish, ambitious, unjust, and aggressive.

The Impotence of Mere Punishment to produce Reformation is the subject of verses 20, 21.

20. And yet the rest of the men, who are not killed by these plagues, do not repent and forsake the works of their hands, not to worship devils and idols, which are of gold, and of silver, and of brass, and of stone, and of wood, which can neither see, nor hear, nor walk.

The rest of the men: the rest, in contrast with the third part of the men (verse 18), who are killed.

Of the men: the men who have not the seal of God on their foreheads (verse 4). Only one-third are killed (verse 18). The rest God spares, that they may repent, and become his true worshippers. God's mercy shines conspicuously throughout the Apocalypse.

By these plagues: inflicted by the horsemen.

Devils: fallen angels.

Works of their hands: the idols they make of gold, silver, brass, stone, wood.

Gold, etc: this enumeration repeated from Dan. iii. 5, and v. 4. The idolatry of the Babylon on the Euphrates is continued by the Babylon on the Tiber.

See: Ps. cxv. 5.
Hear: verse 6.
Walk: verse 7.

21. And yet they do not repent, and forsake their murders, nor their sorceries, nor their fornication, nor their thefts.

Murders: of the early Christians during the ten persecutions; in war against Jerusalem (Matt. xxiv. 6); by acts of violence against individuals (Acts xii. 2).

Sorceries: the practice of divination, augury, oracles (SMITH, *Dict. Antiq.*). See notes on xviii. 23.

Fornication: Rom. i. 26. In Rome, as well as in Greece, the State not only tolerated fornication, but protected it, and obtained profit from it (*Dict. Greek and Roman Antiq.*, 605 a).

Thefts: perhaps of men (1 Tim. i. 10). The plural denotes a large number. The Greek word means the thing stolen. This, then, is the sense of the assertion in the text: They will not forsake their thefts; they will not surrender their stolen possessions; they will not return to its lawful owners the property they acquire by stealing or by unlawful means.

The refusal of these spared unbelievers to forsake their sins illustrates our Lord's assertion in Luke xvi. 31. They despise the forbearance of God (2 Pet. iii. 9).

1. When pestilence is by symbol predicted (ix. 1-11), other methods of depredation upon health and life are likewise predicted. In this extensive catalogue must be placed all bodily inflictions arising from *the abuse* of our animal appetites, — gluttony, alcoholism, narcotic poisoning, and the wasting death of unbridled lust.

2. War is the outward manifestation of inward passions, — ill-will, hatred, malice, deadly purpose.

These inward passions often become to us instruments of self-punishment. God may employ the unrestrained lusts of our hearts as scorpions by which he chastens us within for our sins. In our souls, these secret tormentors may be sorer judgments than even the calamities of war itself.

Most necessary every moment is this prayer in our Litany, "Good Lord, deliver us from *hatred* and malice; from all *inordinate and sinful* affections; from all *the deceits of the flesh*," as well as "of *the world and the Devil*."

Ever since God had a separate people, they have been opposed by the ungodly world, which, if not actually, is practically, a heathen world.

The opposition presents itself in two principal forms. One form is *war;* the other form is *ungodly manners.* Ungodly manners always prove a more formidable enemy than even the desolations of war.

Illustrations of this fact abound in the history of the past, and in the condition of human life at the present time.

The personal sins of King David, and of his voluptuous son Solomon, were more injurious to Israelites than their wars with the surrounding nations.

In our own body politic of to-day, depravation of morals, and our prevalent vices, are more destructive evils than even the ravages of our great fratricidal war. An internal cancer is more pestilent than a gun-shot.

SECOND DIVISION, PART II. (CHAPTERS x.–xx. 10).

In the first part of the second division of the Apocalypse (chapters iv.–ix.), there are these visions: God's throne of judgment; the cherubim, his executioners; the unrolling of the seven scrolls; the six trumpets, predicting judgments upon the *heathen world*.

The second part of the second division of the book presents a *different subject*. THE CHURCH OF CHRIST APPEARS. The whole scene is new. The symbols change from trumpets to censers. The seventh and last trumpet (xi. 15) predicts victory (Num. x. 10).

This third form of symbolism by censers is historical.

It reflects *past* history; it foreshadows *future* history.

Both the *reflection* of history, and the *prediction* of history, are *without specific dates*.

The symbols in this second part are, as in the antecedent portions, not realities. They are *representations* of realities. The Apocalyptic symbols are nothing more than strong shadows.

The censers symbolize Christ's judgments upon his *apostate Church*.

The great subjects occupying chapters x.–xx. are the following:—

(x.) The Bridegroom, Jesus Christ.

(xi.) The two witnesses, representing the perfect Church, as Christ's herald in the world to the end of time.

(xii.) The Church, in its faithfulness to Christ, as his pure bride.

(xiii.) The hostility of the dragon to the Church. His agents, the two wild beasts; their efforts to injure and corrupt the Church.

(xiv.) The true Church victorious. The victors and their enemies.

(xv.) Preparation for the final conflict.

(xvi.) The effusion of the seven censers.

(xvii.) The apostate Church.

(xviii.) Her destruction.

(xix.) The alleluias; the marriage of the Lamb; *Armageddon* heralded.

(xx. 1–10) Imprisonment of Satan; the enthronement of the martyrs; defeat of Gog and Magog; and punishment of the Devil, the beast, and the false prophet.

From this brief summary, it is evident that chapters x.–xx. form a closely connected symbolic exhibition of the earthly history of the Church of Christ from his incarnation to the end of the probationary state of the world of mankind. As we survey the multiplied and unrivalled symbols of these wonderful and divine chapters, this changeless truth should take full and tenacious possession of our deepest convictions, namely, *All that these symbols were to St. John and his contemporaries, they are to every soul of man at the present moment.* Every truth symbolized lives continually, and has an incessant application to each one of us. To us all, Christ is the same Judge and Saviour he was in the isle of Patmos. On each of our foreheads is now either the seal of Christ, or the mark of the lamb-dragon. In reserve for each one of us is either a crown or a curse.

CHAPTER X.

ANGELIC SYMBOL OF CHRIST THE BRIDEGROOM (Verses 1-12.)

1. AND I saw another mighty angel coming down from heaven, clothed with a cloud, his face as the sun, and yet a rainbow is on his head; and his feet as pillars of fire.

The term "another" is, in the second division of the Apocalypse, applied to the word "angel" *nine* times. But in no instance is the angel *one of a group of angels.* Consequently, "another" (x. 1) refers back to "another" (viii. 3), where the angel *imprecates judgments.* The office of "another angel" (x. 1) is, therefore, of the same kind, that of *imprecation.*

Mighty: applied to an angel, v. 2, x. 1, xviii. 21, only. The appellation does not in any instance determine the rank and character of the angel.

Angel: *Who* is symbolized by this mighty angel? This is the answer *required by the context.*

In chapter xii. 1, *a woman* is the symbol of Christ's Church. The Church is "the Bride, the Lamb's wife" (xxi. 9). Christ is, then, *the Bridegroom.*

The mighty angel (x. 1) *symbolizes Christ as the Bridegroom,* for these conclusive reasons : —

1. A bride (xii. 1) *implies* and *requires* a bridegroom.

2. A bridegroom *precedes* a bride : "Adam was *first* formed, then Eve" (1 Tim. ii. 13).

In Bible practice, the man chooses and takes the woman to be his wife: the woman does not choose and take the man to be her husband.

These facts involve this conclusion: The bridegroom, Christ, is symbolized, in point of time, *before* his bride, the Church, is symbolized.

3. As *an angel*, Christ was with the children of Israel in the wilderness (Exod. xxiii. 20, 21; 1 Cor. x. 4).

4. Our Lord was, at that time and in that place, "a *husband* unto them" (Jer. xxxi. 32). He is also the husband of the *Christian* Church: "I have espoused you *to one husband, to Christ*" (2 Cor. xi. 2).

5. He, as their husband, *reproves* the children of Israel (Jer. iii. 20).

These five Bible facts authorize this assertion. The mighty Angel (Rev. x. 1) symbolizes Christ as Bridegroom. The assertion accords with the facts.

1. Since an angel, the mighty angel most appropriately symbolizes the angel with the Israelites, who was Christ.

2. Christ was the husband of his Church from its foundation. Thus a husband, he is most properly symbolized as a bridegroom.

3. Christ, as the reprover of his ancient Church, is most justly represented, when he re-appears symbolically in the mighty angel, whose "little book" (x. 2) is a record of *reproofs* against Christ's present Church.

The identity of the symbols designating the mighty angel, with the symbols designating Christ, make the mighty angel a symbol of Christ.

1. The mighty angel is "clothed with a cloud." He is thus clothed to indicate that he is the herald of *terrific judgments*. "A great *cloud* and a *fire*" (Ezek. i. 4). "Out of the fire went forth *lightning*" (verse 13).

The Son of man is thus announced: "Behold, he cometh with *clouds*" (Rev. i. 7). "He cometh with *clouds*" to *punish*. "The Lord rideth upon a swift *cloud* into Egypt" (Isa. xix. 1). "The Lord shall *smite* Egypt" (verse 22).

The symbolism investing the mighty angel, and the symbolism investing the Son of man, are thus identical.

2. "The face" of the mighty angel is "as it were the *sun*" (x. 1). This face of fire is identical with this description of the Son of man. "His eyes are as *a flame of fire*" (i. 14).

3. The feet of the mighty angel are "as *pillars of fire*" (x. 1). The feet of the Son of man are "like *lightning*" (ii. 18).

These symbolic identities between the mighty angel and the Son of man are resemblances which enforce this conviction: The mighty angel symbolizes Christ, who is the Bridegroom of his Church, and who now appears to punish his adulterous wife, — his *apostate Church*.

The adulteress is, by the law of Moses, punished with death (Lev. xx. 10). The husband of the adulterous wife institutes the legal proceedings against her, as authorized by Moses (Jer. iii. 8, v. 7; Ezek. xvi. 38, 48), where the husband inflicts death as the punishment.

It is certain, therefore, that the appearance of the mighty angel (Rev. x. 1.) symbolizing Christ as the avenging Bridegroom of his faithless Church, and the death-penalty he inflicts upon the apostate Babylon (Rev. xviii. 8), accord perfectly with the provisions of the law of Moses for the treatment of the adulteress. She is to be put to death; and the injured husband is to *institute the proceedings*, and see that the required punishment is inflicted.

5. There is another resemblance between the mighty angel and the Lamb, which certainly prepares the angel to symbolize Christ. The mighty angel holds in his hand a scroll unrolled. In the entire Book of Revelation, the Lamb is the only other person who unrolls scrolls, and holds them in his hand. The Lamb alone unrolls the seven scrolls. Indeed, by unrolling the seventh scroll, and causing six trumpets to be blown, he creates the very visions which *immediately precede* the descent of the mighty angel, holding in his hand an unrolled scroll.

Since the Lamb is the only being in the universe worthy and able to unroll scrolls, the sole relation the descending angel, who is not Christ, can bear to the Lamb, is that of *representative*. On account of this relation, therefore, the mighty angel represents and symbolizes the Lamb, who is the Bridegroom (Rev. xxi. 9).

6. In another aspect does the symbolizing mighty angel resemble the Son of man. The mighty angel is *in the act* of "coming down out of heaven." So the Greek of this verse 1. This act of continual descent the Son of man is also performing: "The bread of God is *he which cometh down from heaven, and giveth* life to the world" (John vi. 33).

In Rev. iii. 12, the New Jerusalem, which is the Church of Christ, is characterized as the "city which *is coming down* out of heaven."

Thus closely and remarkably does the mighty angel resemble, in his continual descent from heaven, the continually descending Son of man, and his continually descending Church, of which he is the Head and the Bridegroom.

Since resemblances authorize symbolism, the symbolical connection of the mighty angel with Christ, the Bridegroom of his Church, is most amply established.

Rainbow: In Revelation, only here and iv. 3, where, as here, it is the symbol of *mercy* (Gen. ix. 13-15; Ezek. i. 28). Although the symbolizing mighty angel is descending from heaven to inflict judgments upon the apostate Church of Christ, judgment is modified by mercy.

Pillars of fire: the straight and brilliant white lines of lightning (i. 15, ii. 18), so often seen on the dark face of a thunder-cloud. His feet have lightning swiftness to run and to execute.

The explanation which regards the mighty angel (x. 1) as *the rep-*

resentative of Christ, the Bridegroom of his Church, *fully harmonizes* (chapter x.) with the imagery of the bride (chapter xii.); also with the virginity (spiritual) of the followers of the Lamb (xiv. 4); and likewise with the fornication (spiritual) of the woman (the unfaithful bride) sitting upon the scarlet-colored beast (xvii. 3); and lastly, with the "marriage-supper of the Lamb" (xix. 7), accompanying his union wth his faithful bride.

2. And while holding in his hand a small scroll, unrolled, he also places his right foot on the sea, and his left on the earth.

In his hand: in v. 1, the scroll is *on* the *right* hand of the Judge on the throne. The *right* hand of the angel may, therefore, be holding "the little book open." He may also lift his *right* hand when he utters his oath. In swearing, the Orientals raised the right hand (Ps. cxliv. 8, 11; Isa. xliv. 20, lxii. 8). The swearing hand of the angel grasps the scroll containing God's judgments.

Small scroll: containing accusations (Isa. xxx. 8, 9). The imagery of the "small scroll" may be derived from the "bill of divorcement" (Deut. xxiv. 1).

The symbolic Bridegroom holds the accusing scroll. It may contain an indictment for adultery against his wife, "arrayed in scarlet" (xvii. 4). She is "burned with fire" (xviii. 8). Burning was the punishment of the adulteress (Gen. xxxviii. 24; Lev. xx. 14).

Before the infliction of the burning, there must be a previous (*a*) indictment, (*b*) trial, (*c*) conviction, (*d*) sentence, (*e*) execution. This fivefold process of justice fully discloses itself (chapters x.–xviii.).

(*a*) In the Jewish courts, charges are brought *in writing* (Job xiv. 17; Dan. vii. 10; Rev. xx. 12). The "little book" is the indictment.

(*b*) The two witnesses (xi. 3) establish the charges.

(*c*) Conviction (xiv. 7).

(*d*) Sentence (xiv. 8).

(*e*) Execution (xiv. 9–11, xv. 6, xvi., xvii. 1, 14, xviii. 2, 5, 8, 20).

Then, in the midst of the symbolic drapery of these nine chapters, the usual proceedings of a court can be plainly detected and regularly traced.

Unrolled: indicating that the charges are ready to be made *at once*.

Sea and land: in the creation of this earth, the sea was *first* seen; hence, here first mentioned.

The angel stands on both sea and land, to show that Christ is universal Judge, and that his judgments affect all parts of this world where his Church exists.

3. And he cries with a loud voice, even as a lion roars. And when he cries, seven thunders speak their peculiar words.

Roars: the voice of the angel is frightful; carries terror with it.

Thunders: responsive. The voice of the angel utters threats. The voices of the seven thunders utter their peculiar threats. The repetition of the utterances intensifies the denunciations.

4. And when the seven thunders had spoken their peculiar words, I was about to write; and I heard a voice from heaven, saying unto me, Seal up the words which the seven thunders have spoken, and write them not.

From heaven: from God.

Seal: roll up and seal the scroll; that is, reserve for the present the publication of the threats (xxii. 10; Isa. viii. 16). "The words of God" (xvii. 17) may refer to the subjects contained in the "little book."

The predictions of God's judgments are symbolically announced in these *three* forms: (a) the "little book," (b) the voice of the mighty angel, and (c) the voices of the seven thunders, to emphatically affirm *the certain fulfilment* of *all* the predictions.

The fulfilments of these threefold predictions are symbolized by the censers, chapters xv. and xvi.

First, predictions; then fulfilments.

This method is but the repetition of preceding methods in the Apocalypse.

Examples. — (a) The three horses, red, black, pale (vi. 4-8), *predict* war, famine, pestilence.

(b) The darkened sun, moon, and stars (viii. 12), and the locusts, and the horsemen (ix. 1-19), symbolically *fulfil* the predictions symbolized by the tri-colored horses (vi. 4-8).

Recapitulation is the movable bolt which opens many a door, otherwise shut, in this figurative and elaborate book.

5. And the angel whom I saw standing on the sea and on the earth raised his hand to heaven;

The raising of the hand was the accompaniment of an oath (Gen. xiv. 22; Dan. xii. 7). The upraised hand calls God to witness the truth of the oath.

6. And he sware by Him that liveth for ever and ever, who

created the heaven and the things in it, and the earth and the things in it, and the sea and the things in it, that delay shall be no longer;

Sware: the angel's oath, calling God to witness the truth of his declaration, is his most solemn confirmation of his assertion respecting time, in the last clause of this verse.

The insuperable difference between resemblance and identity renders these comments of Dean Alford irrelevant: —

"The angel in Rev. x. 1 is not Christ, for Christ could not swear by himself. This he would do (verse 6), if he were this angel" (ALFORD, *in loco*).

But, although the angel is not Christ, yet as the angel *represents* Christ, and therefore is *not identical with Christ*, he may *in symbol* swear by Christ.

Created: the sole Creator of the universe ("heaven, earth, sea"), is able to control and limit time in its progress.

Delay: the Greek word is translated "space," respite (ii. 21). When the noun is embodied in a verb, it is translated "delayeth" (Matt. xxiv. 48; Luke xii. 45). There has been delay, "a little season" (vi. 11). But now delay shall cease. The predictions by the "little book," by the voice of the mighty angel, and by the voices of the seven thunders, shall be fulfilled *shortly*.

The cessation of delay is followed by fulfilment. This fulfilment is embodied in "finished" [fulfilled], (verse 7), the finish being "in the days of the voice of the seventh angel, when he shall begin to sound" the seventh trumpet, heralding the censers, chapter xvii.

7. But in the days of the trumpet of the seventh angel, when he must sound, and so is made effectual the mystery of God as he declares the good news to his servants the prophets.

Days: the period following the seventh trumpet (xi. 15), announcing the complete establishment of the kingdom of Christ.

Must: the Greek verb often denotes necessity; that is, accordance with the divine appointment, and therefore certain, destined by God to take place.

Is made effectual: This translation is justified, —

1. By derivation: —

The Greek noun, which is the root of the Greek verb we translate "is made effectual," has the sense of *effect*, in these places: —

"The *effect* of those things is death" (Rom. vi. 21).

"The *effect* everlasting life" (v. 22).

"Christ is the *effect* of the law" (x. 4).
"The *effect* of that which is abolished" (2 Cor. iii. 13).
"The *effect* of the commandment" (1 Tim. i. 5).
"The *effect* of your faith" (1 Pet. i. 9).
2. By usage:—
"When they *shall make effectual* their testimony" (Rev. xi. 7).
"In them *is made effectual* the wrath of God" (xv. 1).
"Till the seven plagues of the seven angels *are made effectual*" (v. 8).
"Until the words of God *are made effectual*" (xvii. 17).

The mystery of God: by comparing Col. i. 23, "mystery of God," with Col. ii. 2, "the gospel," we discover that "the mystery of God" (Rev. x. 7) is "the gospel," in the strict sense given it by its derivation, namely, *good news*.

The gospel in this sense, "the gospel" identical with "the mystery of God," is the root of the Greek verb which the English Version inadequately translates "declared," but which should be translated as follows: "makes known the glad tidings," that is, joyful prophecies, which abound in the Apocalypse (xi. 15, xii. 10, xiv. 1-4, 6-8, 13, xv. 2-4, xviii. 20, xix. 1-9, xx. 4-6), and are included in the word "glad tidings."

Prophets: New-Testament prophets are intended (xxii. 6, 9); and St. John is among the number.

8. And the voice which I heard from heaven is again speaking to me, and saying, Go, take the small scroll which is unrolled in the hand of the angel, who is standing upon the sea and upon the earth.

Take: to publish (verses 8, 9); take to read, as eating (verse 9) is reading.

9. And I went to the angel, and said to him, Give me the small scroll. And he saith to me, Take, and eat it up, and it shall make thy stomach bitter, but in thy mouth it shall be sweet like honey.

Eat it up: eat it entirely; read it carefully; fully comprehend the meaning of the scroll. This direction is Ezek. iii. 3 repeated.

Bitter: the contents of the scroll are, in themselves, woeful and destroying.

Sweet: the knowledge of the contents of the scroll is at first pleasant to St. John. He was pleased to be assured that God will avenge his martyred saints; but the manner and the severity of the vengeance sadden his spirit.

10. And I took the small scroll out of the angel's hand, and ate it up; and it was in my mouth sweet like honey; and yet when I had eaten it, my stomach became bitter.

In this verse, the emphatic position of the words gives this sense: The sweetness was greater than predicted.

11. And yet they say to me, It is necessary for thee again to prophesy against many peoples, and nations, and tongues, and kings.

And yet: notwithstanding the good news (verses 7-10).
They: the voices heard (verses 4, 8).
Necessary: because God commands.
Prophesy: reproofs and warnings (Ezek. xi. 4, 5, 9).
Again: the previous prophecies (viii. 12, ix. 1-19) were of the woes of famine, pestilence, and war. The word "again" gives, therefore, to the word "prophesy," this sense: predict *reproofs and warnings.*
Against: "Set thy face *against* Mount Seir, and *prophesy against* it" (Ezek. xxxv. 2).
Peoples: nations, tongues: "peoples, nations, tongues" (xvii. 15).
Kings: "With the great whore the kings of the earth have committed fornication" (xvii. 2) "Eat the flesh of kings" (xix. 18).

St. John, in subsequent portions of the Apocalypse, utters prophecies against all classes of the unbelieving and disobedient.

CHAPTER XI.

THE eleventh chapter of the Apocalypse contains these subjects: the measurement of the temple; the rejection of the outer court; the two witnesses; the sounding of the seventh trumpet.

THE MEASUREMENT OF THE TEMPLE.

1. There is given me a reed, like a staff; and he said, Arise, and measure the holy of holies of God, and the altar, and the worshippers in the court.

The angel here, as in chapter x., represents Christ. The angel gives St. John a reed, and commands him to measure the temple.

Measurement is the symbol of preservation.

"Measuring reed" (Ezek. xl. 3). Temple measured (xli. 1). Result of measurement: The glory of the Lord fills the temple (xliii. 4). "I will dwell in the midst of the children of Israel forever" (verse 7).

"A man with a measuring line in his hand; to measure Jerusalem; Jerusalem shall be inhabited; towns without walls for the multitude of men. For I, saith the Lord, will be unto her a wall of fire round about" (Zech. ii. 1-5).

In Rev. xi. the first act of the representative angel, and the first words he speaks, are symbols of *mercy*. By him, Christ still continues and preserves his true Church. Its faithful members still "look for the mercy of our Lord Jesus Christ unto eternal life" (Jude, verse 21).

The precious objects St. John is commanded by the angel to measure, and thus preserve, are these two, — the temple and its court. The temple includes its worship, and the court includes its worshippers.

This is the symbolical process of the twofold inclusion. (*a*) The holy of holies is used for the entire temple, by *synecdoche*, — a part for the whole. (*b*) The altar of incense is used for the worship offered on the altar; a *metaphor*, — the container for the contained. (*c*) The worshippers are used for the court they occupy; namely, the court of the Israelites, closely adjoining the temple; *metaphor*, again, — the contained for the container, the reverse of the preceding figure.

The temple of God is his Church (1 Tim. iii. 15), in which are his worship and his worshippers.

The true worship of God includes, (*a*) his ministry, (*b*) his sacraments, (*c*) his creeds, (*d*) his ritual (Acts ii. 42). His true worshippers are Christians, whose souls are renewed in the image of Christ, and who thus "worship him in spirit and in truth" (John iv. 24).

The symbols in the first clause of verse 1 resemble, both in design and in persons, the sealing of the one hundred and forty-four thousand (Rev. vii. 4). There, Christ's judgments upon the *heathen world* are about to be predicted. Here, his judgments upon his *apostate* Church are at once to be prophetically symbolized (xi. 2). The faithful portion of the Church will be saved. Its measurement is the symbol of its salvation, just as the numbering is the symbol of the salvation of the one hundred and forty-four thousand.

Both the thousands numbered (vii. 4), and the worshippers in his preserved temple, are *the same Church of Christ numbered twice.* They are numbered the first time to assure them that they shall be preserved from *heathen* enemies. They are numbered the second time (for measurement of living men is numbering) to assure them of their preservation from the assaults of *apostate* Christians.

The *double* numbering is a *repeated* assurance of the fidelity and omnipotence of Christ (Gen. xli. 32). "Heaven and earth shall pass away, but my word shall not pass away" (Matt. xxiv. 35). "The gates of hell [whether heathen, or nominally Christian] shall not prevail against my Church" (xvi. 18). "There is a remnant according to the election of grace" (Rom. xi. 5).

THE REJECTION OF THE OUTER COURT.

2. And yet the court, which is without the temple, cast it without, and do not measure it, because it is given to the Gentiles; and so the holy city they shall tread forty-two months.

The court: is here used for the occupants of the court which was outside of the court of the Israelites, and, thus situated, is, in this verse, the court of the Gentiles. This use is *metaphor*, — the container for the contained.

Cast it without: that is, cast the *Gentiles* without the court of the Israelites, who, in verse 1, are "the worshippers in the temple."

Do not measure it: do not measure, do not number, the Gentiles; that is, reject the Gentiles from the number of "the worshippers." Although the Gentiles occupy the court bearing their name, and thus occupy a portion of "the holy city," they are not *true* worshippers.

Is given to the Gentiles: the language of this part of the verse is derived from these prophetic words of our Lord: "Jerusalem shall be trodden down of the Gentiles" (Luke xxi. 24).

But the word "Gentiles" in Rev. xi. 2 cannot be taken in a *literal* sense. Its sense is here figurative, because the preceding portion of the verse is figurative. Literalness and figure cannot be commingled in the same passage.

The exact figurative sense of the word "Gentiles" in this verse 2 is given it by its contrast with "the worshippers" (verse 1). "The worshippers" are *true* Christians. The "Gentiles" are, consequently, *false* Christians.

The holy city: is defined by Rev. xxi. 2 as the "new Jerusalem," which, according to St. Paul, is *the Church of Christ* (Gal. iv. 26).

Tread: not in a *literal* manner, as the present Jerusalem is trodden by the feet of the Gentile Turks. *To tread the holy city, is to occupy it with worship.* "When *ye appear before me, to tread my courts*" (Isa. i. 12). The apostate Church will, with its own worship, occupy the true Church. The modernized liturgy of the Church of Rome has displaced the ancient liturgies of the Western Church, the Gallican, the Mozarabic, the Sarum.

Forty-two months: three years and a half. Three and a-half years is *the half of seven years*, a *full* period. Thus forty-two months denotes a *limited* period. The wild beast, the compound of leopard, bear, and lion, continues the same *limited* period (Rev. xiii.). This monster represents the Roman Empire *Christianized.* The *apostate* Church and the Church of Rome are *identical in the length of time* they are to continue in this world. The time will come when they will not be. The true Church will yet rejoice at their departure. The Lord in mercy hasten the time he promises!

In the scenery of the judicial court, which the Apocalypse establishes, the *apostate* Church is the culprit to be tried, condemned, punished and forever removed.

THE TWO WITNESSES.

3. And I will give to these two witnesses of mine, to prophesy. And so they shall prophesy, one thousand two hundred and sixty days, clothed in sackcloth.

I will give to prophesy: the insertion of "to prophesy" with "give" is required by usage in the Apocalypse itself.

Examples.

"I will give" is followed by the infinitive *expressed*, ii. 7, "to eat;" and iii. 21, "to sit." The infinitive "to drink" is *implied* after give (in the Greek), xxi. 6. This infinitive is therefore *implied* after "give" in this verse 3, "I will give *to prophesy.*"

These two witnesses of mine: the pronouns (Greek) "these" and "mine" necessarily identify the two witnesses with two objects in *the immediately preceding context*.

The pronoun "these" (the Greek article before "witnesses") proves that two objects which can be called "two witnesses" have, in the near past, been *already mentioned*.

The pronoun "mine" proves that the "two witnesses" were, *previous* to their being mentioned here, *in the possession of the angel and in his service*.

It is thus a *constructural demonstration*, that the "two witnesses" exist *in the previous* context, and are to be sought *there and nowhere else*. The "two witnesses" cannot possibly be any objects whatever *out of the previous context*.

In the previous context, there are *only two associated objects*, (a) *The worship of God*, and (b) *His worshippers*. THESE TWO OBJECTS are, therefore, exclusively the "two witnesses." To state the fact in a more definite form:—

The "two witnesses" are, THE WORSHIP OF GOD, and THE WORSHIPPERS OF GOD IN THE CHURCH OF CHRIST.

Worship and worshippers in being called "witnesses" are personified. As worship is for the *incense-altar*, and worshippers for the *court of the Israelites*, altar and court are *material* objects, and capable of personification. The material nature of the incense-altar and of the court of the Israelites deprives the "two witnesses," represented by the altar and the court, of all *personality*. The "*two witnesses*" *cannot be persons*, either scriptural or historical, either ancient, primitive, mediæval, modern, or future.

The positions we give "these" and "mine" are fully justified by the English Version in its translation of the Greek article and of the Greek personal pronoun.

(*a*) This version thus translates the Greek article with the number two, "these two" (Rev. xix. 20).

(*b*) "Friend *of mine*" is the expression of the English Version, (Luke xi. 6).

St. John thus exhibits the Church of Christ in two forms, — its worship and its worshippers. By this exhibition the Church becomes "two witnesses," and by being two witnesses can give legal testimony according to the requirement of the law of Moses. "At the mouth of *two* witnesses, shall the matter be established" (Deut. xix. 15).

In these two forms of worship and worshippers, the testimony of the Christian Church to its divine original and authority is most ample and conclusive.

1. The *worship of the Church* embraces ministry, sacraments, creeds, ritual (Acts ii. 42).

Each of these institutions of Christ is, in its historical life, a reliable witness that the Church of Christ is from heaven.

(*a*) The Christian ministry includes both a body of officiating men, and the divine message they deliver.

(*aa*) As a *body of officiating men*, the present ministers of the historical Church can trace their origination along an unbroken historical line, back to this first commission from the sole Author of the ministry: "As my Father sent me, even so I send you" (John xx. 21).

(*bb*) The *message* the ministers of Christ deliver is his gospel, contained in the twenty-seven books of the New Testament. The historical evidence that these books are authentic and genuine is vastly stronger than the evidence any other book in existence can bring to prove its own authenticity and genuineness.

(*b*) The *Christian sacraments* of baptism and the Lord's Supper have existed in all ages, from the present to the time of Christ. Their historical existence makes him their only Author, and as such a divine Person.

(*c*) The *Christian creeds*, the Apostles' and the Nicene, also have an historical life which identifies them with the historical beginning of the gospel itself.

(*d*) The *Christian ritual* of the historical Church consists largely of the Lord's Prayer and the Book of Psalms.

Christ enjoins the habitual use of his Prayer (Matt. vi. 9). St. Paul commands the responsive use of the Psalms (Eph. v. 19).

Both the Lord's Prayer and the Book of Psalms are historical witnesses for Christ. Like the ministry, the sacraments, and the creeds, the Lord's Prayer and the Psalms are component parts of all Church history; and as such they recognize Christ as their Author and Institutor, and therefore as divine.

2. *Christian worshippers* are witnesses for Christ, first as a Church, and then as individuals.

(a) *As a Church.* — The Church of Christ has existed historically for nineteen centuries. It appears as an organized institution from the present day back to the primal day when Christ said "*My* Church" (Matt. xvi. 18). During all these centuries, the Church has verified these words of his, "I *build* my Church:" for, had he not *continually* built his Church from century to century, his Church could not have existed continually; and because he thus ever builds it, he is divine.

(b) *As individuals.* — Every individual Christian who possesses and exhibits Christian graces in his heart and life is himself a witness that Christ is divine.

Christian graces are not human in their origin and growth. Christ alone creates and preserves his holy image in our souls. His new creation within us proves and establishes his own deity.

"Ye shall be witnesses unto me, both in Jerusalem and in all Judæa, and in Samaria, and unto the uttermost parts of the earth," (Acts i. 8), are our Lord's last words to his apostles, just before his ascension into heaven.

As Christ's appointed witnesses, the apostles include not only the Christian ministry, since next to Christ himself they are its founders; but also the Christian sacraments, creeds, and ritual, because, when the apostles organized the Christian Church, they administered its sacraments, embodied in writing the facts forming the creeds, and also performed the ritual Christ prescribed for the perpetual use of his Church (Acts ii. 41, 42).

The testimony the apostles, as Christ's chosen witnesses, give for him, thus including the books of the New Testament, and its creeds and ritual; these books and their embodiments of the Christian faith, and their forms of Christian worship,— become the standards by which the "two witnesses" in the Apocalypse try and test the ministry, the sacraments, the creeds, and the ritual, of all the churches existing from the beginning of the gospel, and thus determine whether or not these churches are actually apostolic, really primitive, and purely Christian.

As constituted by St. John, the "two witnesses" are not rhetorical figures, not dramatic illustrations, not inexplicable puzzles, not concealed personages, to be forever wrapped in impenetrable mystery; but the "two witnesses" of the Apocalypse are the *infallible criteria* fixed by Christ himself for the incessantly needed process of detecting all that is false, and of establishing and vindicating all that is true, in the multiform Christianity of the historical periods and of the present day.

One thousand two hundred and sixty days: this number identifies the "two witnesses" with "the woman in the wilderness," the bride of Christ, His true Church, where she is fed for exactly the same period of days (Rev. xii. 6), "a thousand two hundred and threescore days." Because limited by the identical duration of time, "forty-two months," the *apostate* Church (xi. 2) and the beast from the sea (xiii. 5) are identical. Since the same duration of time thus identifies the *apostate* Church and the marine beast, the same duration of time identifies the true Church and the two witnesses.

One thousand two hundred and sixty days equals forty-two months; *with this important difference*, the period of these *months* is *shorter* than this period of *days* by *twenty-eight* days. With the Jews, a term of time *partly* completed is counted as though *fully* completed. Our Lord thus predicts of himself, "The Son of man shall be in the heart of the earth *three days and three nights*" (Matt. xii. 40). He was actually in the tomb of Joseph only *parts* of three days. Forty-two months may be merely forty-one months and *one* day. One thousand two hundred and sixty days cannot be less than forty-one months, *twenty-nine days*, and *one hour*. The difference between the two periods is *twenty-eight days*, or *four weeks;* a period in prophetical time extending through several years.

The true Church of Christ will, therefore, in this world outlive the *apostate* Church.

Shall prophesy: only twice does this verb occur in the Apocalypse. In x. 11, the verb means *to testify against:* this, consequently, is its meaning in xi. 3.

Clothed in sackcloth: the dress of "the two witnesses" discloses their office. Their message is *warning*. Thus clothed, Elijah, Isaiah, John the Baptist, were *warning* messengers (2 Kings i. 8; Isa. xx. 2; Matt. iii. 1-4).

4 These are the two olive-trees, and the two candlesticks, standing before the Lord of the earth.

This description of the two witnesses is obviously derived from the vision of the prophet Zechariah: "Behold a candlestick all of gold, with a bowl upon the top of it, and his seven lamps thereon, and seven pipes to the seven lamps, which are upon the top thereof" (Zech. iv. 2).

"And two olive-trees by it, one upon the right side of the bowl, and the other upon the left side thereof" (Zech. iv. 3).

According to the explanation an angel gives Zechariah of the use of these two olive-trees, they yield an incessant supply of oil for the golden candlestick.

In this minute representation, the two olive-trees and the candlestick are in official structure *one* object, contributing to *one* effect, *the production of light*.

In St. John's representation (Rev. xi. 4), evidently borrowed from that of Zechariah, each olive-tree is also a candlestick, *producing light.*

Both Zechariah and St. John symbolize this great truth, each olive-tree produces light *by the appointment of God.* By *his appointment,* the olive-tree is *a light-bearer.*

This truth St. John applies to "the two witnesses." *Each witness is, by Christ's appointment, a light-bearer.* Since the two produce but *one* effect, the two witnesses are virtually *one light-bearer.*

Light-bearing is the especial office of the true Church of Christ, both in its Head and in all its members.

1. Christ the Head of the Church is "the *light* of the world" (John viii. 12).

2. The ministers of his Church "are the *light* of the world" (Matt. v. 14).

3. All the members of his Church are light-bearers. "Ye shine as *lights* in the world, *holding forth the word of life*" (Phil. ii. 15, 16).

As a light-bearer, the Church enlightens and dispels all moral and spiritual darkness. "The *light* shineth in *darkness*" (John i. 5). "Have no fellowship with the unfruitful works of *darkness*, but rather *reprove* [*testify against*] them" (Eph. v. 11).

Standing: ready to serve the Lord (Heb. x. 11).

Before the Lord of the earth: since the two witnesses are his servants, sin against *them* is sin against *him* (Luke x. 16).

The next verse (Rev. xi. 5) illustrates this startling truth.

5. **And so, if any one desires to hurt them, fire comes forth from each of their mouths, and devours their enemies. And so, if any one desires to hurt them, in this way is it necessary for them to die.**

Desires: the Greek verb has this sense (John v. 6, ix. 27).

Even the desire to hurt the two witnesses offends God (Exod. xx. 17).

Fire: is the *consuming message* the two witnesses utter (2 Kings i. 10, 12; Jer. v. 14, 23, 29).

Devours: God punishes the inflicters of hurts upon his two witnesses (Luke x. 16).

"They shall be devoured as stubble fully dry" (Nah. i. 10).

Enemies: of God (Jas. iv. 4), of the cross (Phil. iii. 18). Children of the Devil (John viii. 44; 1 John iii. 8, 10).

In this way: by fire.

Necessary: by the will of God. "With the froward, thou wilt show thyself froward" (Ps. xviii. 26).

6. These have authority to shut the heaven, that the rain wet not the earth, in the days of their prophecy, and they have authority over the waters to turn them into blood, even to smite the earth with every kind of plague, as often as they will.

Authority: the power God gives the two witnesses.

1. **Shut heaven**: God grants his two witnesses the same power he gave the prophet Elijah (1 Kings xvii. 1; Jas. v. 17). This prophet punished, by God's appointment, the Israelites with famine. With some form of curse, God still punishes the despisers of his Church and gospel.

Days of their prophecy: in the same sense as "prophesy" (verse 3); in the time of their utterance of reproofs and warnings.

2. **Turn waters into blood**: turn blessings into curses (Exod. iv. 9, vii. 17-20; 2 Cor. ii. 16).

3. **Smite the earth**: mankind (Gen. vii. 11).

Every kind of plague: Deut. xxviii. 15, etc.

As they will: the two witnesses are God's representatives and agents. Under his guidance, their will is his will. He adapts his punishments to the nature of the sin.

7. And when they shall make effectual their testimony, the wild beast ascending from the bottomless pit shall make war with them, and shall overcome them and kill them.

Shall make effectual: for justification of this translation, see x. 7.

The deadly wound this wild beast receives (xiii. 3, 14) is *the effect of* the testimony of the two witnesses.

The wild beast: his appearance is here *prophetically* announced. He does not *actually* appear till xiii. 1. Strictly, the *wild* beast, because (Acts xi. 6) distinguished from a "four-footed beast," a tame, domesticated beast.

The word is here in the Apocalypse for the *first* time. Not to be confounded with "another beast," the lamb-dragon (xiii. 11).

The article, *the* wild beast (Rev. xi. 7), does not refer this beast to "fourth beast" (Dan. vii. 19).

In Rev. xi. 7, the article "the" is required by the participial adjunct "ascending from the abyss." This participial adjunct is in effect an *attributive* adjective, to which the article belongs, and forms this phrase: The ascending (from the abyss) wild beast. Instances of this usage are "The coming king" (Luke xix. 38); "The walking men" (Mark viii. 24).

The article (Rev. xi. 7) is *restrictive*. The particular wild beast is distinguished from other wild beasts, by the words connected with it, "ascending, from the abyss." Here the *limiting* expression, "ascending — from the abyss" (attributive) unites with the one limited subject (wild beast), and forms *one complex idea;* namely, the ascending (from the abyss) beast.

In this view, the article (Rev. xi. 7) has its *generic* use, which includes the instances where a single object (the wild beast) *forms a class by itself.* There is no other such wild beast as this (Rev. xi. 7).

Who is the ascending (from the abyss) wild beast?
Wild beast is the Bible-symbol of a *kingdom.* "These great beasts, which are four, are four kings" (Dan. vii. 17). "The fourth beast shall be the fourth *kingdom*" (v. 23). A *kingdom,* then, is intended by the wild beast (Rev. xi. 7), the *Pagan* kingdom (empire) of Rome. See xiii. i.

To make war: this phrase in the New Testament only, Rev. xi. 7, xiii. 7, xix. 19); often in the Septuagint. The phrase is stronger than the simple word *to war,* which merely indicates the fact of war; while to make war implies deliberation, purpose, preparation, conflict.

With: is always the sense of the Greek proposition with "to war" and "to make war," when *opposition* as here is *expressed.* The opposition is from the preaching of the two witnesses. The wild beast from the bottomless pit appears *prophetically* in Rev. xi. 7. He appears *actually* in xiii. 1, but is there the creation and agent of the dragon. Because he and the dragon are agent and principal, the warfare of both and the enemies of each are precisely the same. In consequence of this identity, "the two witnesses" (xi. 7) and "the remnant of the woman's seed" (xii. 17) are *the very same objects.*

These identities of warfare and enemies determine that the periods of the time when "the two witnesses" are overcome and killed, and "the remnant of the woman's seed" is warred with by the dragon, are also identical.

The two witnesses, as the representatives of the worship of the Church of Christ and of its worshippers, begin their symbolical life with the very beginning of the gospel itself. The remnant of the woman's seed also has a beginning equally early.

These identities of warfare and enemies likewise determine the period of time when the wild beast from the sea and from the bottomless pit receives his deadly wound and his partial healing. The time is identical with the time of the two witnesses and of the remnant of the woman's seed.

The exegetical facts now before us respecting the wounding and healing of the first wild beast the dragon creates and employs, do not authorize the explanation that the sword-stroke of the first wild beast, and the cicatrization of the gash, have their realization in the decline of the Pagan Roman empire, and in its revival in papal Rome. The numerical difficulties inhering in this venerable explanation, it is neither the ability nor the duty of the Greek exegesis of the Apocalypse to explain: the attempt is entirely outside of her legitimate province.

War: the verbs "make war," "conquer," "kill," are in the New Testament used both in a material and in a spiritual sense.

"Make war" has a material sense, Luke xiv. 31; the sense is spiritual, Rev. xix. 19.

"Conquer" is material, Luke xi. 22; is spiritual, Rev. xii. 11, xv. 2.

"Kill" inflicts bodily death, Rev. ii. 13; spiritual, Rev. ii. 23, 16.

The twofold meanings of these verbs create this fact. The warfare, the defeats, and the deaths, which "the two witnesses," the representatives of the true Church, suffer from the wild beast, — the representative of the false Church, — are also both material and spiritual. The injuries inflicted by the wild beast (Rev. xi. 7) are *prophetic*. There are historical fulfilments of these prophecies which irrefutably ascribe these twofold injuries exclusively to the Church of Rome. (See xiii. 15).

THE LIFE AND DEATH OF THE TWO WITNESSES.

Success is figurative life; failure is figurative death. Figurative life and figurative death may be contemporaneous.

The Figurative Life of the Two Witnesses.

1. As heralds of Christ's revealed truth, and as his reprovers of all human sin, the "two witnesses" are ever living in *a ministerial succession*, where, while individuals die, the succession itself continues with a deathless life.

2. The "two witnesses" are also ever living, as the conservators and expositors of the books of the Old and New Testaments. The duties and prohibitions contained in these divine records, the "two witnesses," as ministers of the gospel, are ever applying to the lives and consciences of their hearers.

3. The "two witnesses," as gospel ministers, also live incessantly in the Christian creeds, sacraments, ritual, and canons. Living this diversified life, they are not only teachers and advisers, but oftentimes judges and administrators. The rubrics of the Prayer-book, and the canons of the Church, embody injunctions and denials, of which ministers are, by their sacred office, the sole exponents and administrators.

When their instructions, acts of discipline, and their own Christian example are effectual and edifying, they have their figurative and official life.

The Figurative Death of the Two Witnesses.

The death of the two witnesses is as varied as are the ingenuity and perverseness of human nature.

A few specifications may be instructive and admonitory.

When their apostolic ministry is rejected; the books of the Old and New Testaments are denied a divine original, pronounced forgeries, superseded by Church traditions, displaced by human dogmas, exchanged for false philosophies; the Christian creeds are neglected; the Christian sacraments are discarded; the Christian ritual is abandoned; the Christian catechism enjoining temperance and chastity "for every male child" as well as "for every female," and the Christian canons defining consanguinity and restraining divorce, are disobeyed, — then the two witnesses themselves die, because their crushed hopes and their disappointed desires die, because ruined souls die to all hope of holiness and bliss, and because Christ himself dies by a new crucifixion in the failure of his own "means of grace" and salvation.

8. **And so each of their dead bodies lies on the broad way of the great city, which is called, spiritually, Sodom and Egypt, where also their Lord is crucified.**

The imagery of this verse assumes, —

(*a*) The *actual* death of the two witnesses, and of the persons they represent. "I will bring *a sword* upon you. I will cast down your *slain* before your idols. I will lay *the dead carcasses* of the children of Israel before their idols" (Ezek. vi. 3–5).

(*b*) *The contempt* with which the two dead witnesses are treated. "They shall not be lamented, *neither shall they be buried*; they shall be *as dung* upon the face of the earth" (Jer. xvi. 4).

These prophetic symbols, describing the actual death and profound contempt of the two witnesses, were strictly fulfilled in the murders and burnings inflicted in the middle and more recent ages by the Church of Rome.

The broad way: in ancient Rome, on the east bank of the Tiber, was a street of this name, *Via Lata*, extending from the Capitol to the north-west angle of the city.

The carcasses of the two witnesses are laid on the principal street, that they may be seen and mocked by the passing crowds. "All that pass by clap their hands at thee, they hiss and wag their head. They open their mouth at thee; they hiss and, gnash their teeth" (Lam. ii. 15, 16).

The great city: Jerusalem material is *never* so called in the Bible. The term is only, elsewhere, Rev. xvi. 19, xvii. 5, 18, xviii. 2, 10, 16, 18, 19, 21, where Babylon, the "harlot woman," the *apostate* Church, is meant; and xxi. 10, where "the *holy* Jerusalem, descending out of heaven from God," the Church in post-resurrection glory, is intended.

Spiritually: only here, and 1 Cor. ii. 14, where the word is defined by the phrase, "by the Spirit." "Is called spiritually," means, therefore, is called, is named, by the Holy Spirit, who shows St. John the visions in the Apocalypse, and explains to him their meaning.

Sodom and Egypt: Sodom. Were Jerusalem intended, the phrase would be "Sodom and *Gomorrah*" (Isa. i. 10). As this is not here the phrase, by Sodom the harlot Babylon is meant (xvii. 1. 5). Sodom literal was characterized by fornication. Here (xi. 8) the fornication is *spiritual;* that is, unfaithfulness to Christ, the husband of his Church (Eph. v. 23). "Babylon, *the great city*, made all nations drink of the wine of the wrath of her *fornication*" (Rev. xiv. 8).

Egypt: is characterized by plenty (Acts vii. 12), by wealth (Heb. xi. 26). The possession of riches creates spiritual pride (Rev. iii. 17). This is one of the sins of the harlot Babylon: "She glorified herself. She saith in her heart, I sit a queen" (Rev. xviii. 7).

The name Sodom, *a burning*, prefigures the nature of her destruction: "She shall be *utterly burned with fire*. The kings of the earth shall see the smoke of her *burning*" (xviii. 8, 9).

Where also our Lord is crucified: the word "crucified" also shows that the crucifixion is a sin in addition to the sins of *spiritual* fornication and *spiritual* pride.

The fact that the crucifixion is an addition to *spiritual* sins introduces and establishes three other facts: —

(*a*) The crucifixion is *spiritual*, as in Heb. vi. 6.

(*b*) The crucifixion is committed *at the present time*, since the crucifixion (Heb. vi. 6) is described by a *present* participle.

(*c*) Is crucified, is the Greek aorist of habitude, the equivalent of our *present* tense: is crucified *continually*.

The nature of this crucifixion is described Heb. x. 29, where, as here, the Greek aorists have the force of *present* tenses.

For the fact that our Lord is crucified by Babylon, see Rev. xvii. 6; Matt. xxv. 40. He is crucified in the death of his martyrs.

Their Lord: this appellation only here in the Apocalypse. The Lord of the two witnesses; the "Lord Jesus" (xxii. 20), who made them witnesses, and commissioned them to testify in his name.

The crucifixion of their Lord is a greater outrage than the murder of his witnesses.

The Church of Rome now crucifies the Lord Jesus by every dogma of hers which detracts from his offices of Redeemer, Mediator, and Intercessor.

9. And certain men of the peoples and tribes and tongues and nations joyfully behold their dead bodies three days and a half, and will not suffer their dead bodies to be laid in a sepulchre.

Certain men of the peoples: a mob, composed of all nations and classes of people.

Joyfully behold: contemplate with exulting delight the spectacle of the exposed carcasses.

Three days and a half: the time the two witnesses remained dead (verse 11). The half of a week, a short period. The exultation and mockery of the motley crowd will be very brief. The dead witnesses will soon live again. The blood of the martyrs is the seed of the Church.

Will not suffer: the mob would leave the lifeless and derided witnesses to be devoured by prowling birds and the wild dogs of the city.

Dead bodies: the words are repeated, to mark the inhumanity of forbidding interment.

Laid: a burial-word (Matt. xxvii. 60).

Sepulchre: of stone (Luke xxiii. 53). The Jews did not bury "in graves" (English Version). St. Paul does not teach immersion in Rom. vi. 4: "We are buried with Christ by baptism." Christ was not buried in a grave, but "laid in a tomb hewn out in the rock." (Matt. xxvii. 60).

10. Also, all the inhabitants of the earth rejoice over them, and make themselves merry. They will also send gifts to each other, because these two prophets torment all the inhabitants of the earth.

Also: the joy of the city-mob spreads widely, and seizes all the inhabitants of the earth.

Torment: cause the wicked world to be tormented by the inflictions of God's punitive judgments, mentioned in verses 5 and 6 of this chapter.

"Whereas, men have lived dissolutely and unrighteously, thou hast *tormented* them with their own abominations" (Wis. Sol. xii. 23).

The torments of the inhabitants of the earth are *retributive*. They are illustrated by this prayer against Antiochus Epiphanes: "Think not that our nation is forsaken of God; abide a while, and behold his great power, how he will *torment* thee" (2 Macc. vii. 16, 17); and by this answer to the prayer, "The Lord Almighty, the God of Israel, smote the king with sore *torments;* and most justly: for he had *tormented* other men" (ix. 5, 6).

Rejoice: "the carnal mind is *enmity* against God" (Rom. viii. 7). All nations hate Christ's messengers (Matt. xxiv. 9). "Men love darkness rather than light, because their deeds are evil. Every one that doeth evil hateth the light" (John iii. 19, 20). For these reasons, when Christ's messengers — represented by the two witnesses — are killed, "all nations" rejoice.

Send gifts: marks of excessive joy. Feasting is implied. "The Jews made days of *feasting and joy*, and *sent portions* one to another" (Esth. ix. 22).

Prophets: in the same sense as prophesy (verse 3), teachers and reprovers.

Historical Illustration.

In 1572, the massacre of St. Bartholomew's Day was the subject of boasting throughout Roman Christendom. At Rome, pope, cardinals, and bishops went mad *with joy* over the intelligence. The messenger who brought the news from Paris was rewarded with *a gift* of a thousand crowns. The cannon of St. Angelo thundered a *grateful* salute; the bells rang from every steeple; bonfires turned night into day. The Pope, Gregory XIII., attended by cardinals and lesser dignitaries, went in procession to the Church of St. Louis, and joined in a *Te Deum* of *ecstatic praise*. As they entered, they read, over the portals of the church, the words, *Angelo Persussore Divinitus Immisso;* that is, the avenging angel is *divinely* sent, — a blasphemous application of Isa. xxxvii. 36, "The angel of the Lord smote, in the camp of the Assyrians, one hundred and eighty-five thousand; and in the morning they were all dead corpses," to King Charles IX. of France, by whom the great slaughter of St. Bartholomew's Day was effected ("Edinburgh Review," vol. xliv., 1826; "Massacre of St. Bartholomew," by Henry White. London: Murray, 1868).

Our Lord assures us that he shows his Church the prophetic visions of the Apocalypse, to reveal her future history (Rev. i. 1, 19, iv. 1). Civil history records the fulfilment of Apocalyptic prophecy. The voice of history, when once uttered, can never be silenced. Prophetical and historical coincidences are not accidents. They are the creations of God's superintending Providence. The world, in its progress, is not controlled by chance. The light God's providences disclose, we may safely follow. Historical light is the beacon-fire God kindles and keeps burning on the hilltops of the passing centuries. Because God creates and maintains these inextinguishable fires, they are not phantoms. The lights of history are God's illuminations for our sure guidance.

11. And after three days and a half, the Spirit of life from God comes into them, and rests upon them, and they stand upon their feet; and great terror falls upon the wondering spectators.

Nothing divine can die.
The Spirit of life: this phrase in the New Testament, only Rom. viii. 2. The Holy Spirit giving life, "quickeneth" (John vi. 63, where "the Spirit" is the Holy Spirit, as the Nicene Creed rightly judges). Whenever our Lord calls a person of the Trinity "the Spirit," he *in every instance* means the Holy Spirit, the *Third* Person.

Comes into them: this expression is evidently taken from the prophet Ezekiel's description of the resurrection of the "dry bones;" "the breath [spirit] came into them" (xxxvii. 10).

Rests upon them: this addition to the English Version is required by the Greek.

The Holy Spirit both enters the two witnesses, and rests upon them continually.

Stand upon their feet: language taken from Ezekiel's vision of the "dry bones" (xxxvii. 10). Standing on the feet is restoration to full life, and to perfect health and strength (Acts xiv. 10, xxvi. 16).

Fear: panic-fear, terror, outward show of fear. Divine manifestations awaken fear (Matt. xvii. 6, xxvii. 54).

12. And the two witnesses hear a loud voice from heaven, saying, Come up hither. And they go up to heaven in the cloud. And yet their enemies merely behold them with wonder.

Come up hither: exaltation to heaven describes symbolically the highest prosperity. "Thou, Capernaum, art exalted unto heaven" (Matt. xi. 23). "Sit together in heavenly places" (Eph. ii. 6). "The man thought he could reach the stars of heaven" (2 Macc. ix. 10). *Cæsar in cœlum fertur* (CICERO, *Phil.* iv. 3, 6).

The cloud: a cloud may be implied with the voice from heaven, in the first clause of this verse, "a voice out of the cloud" (Matt. xvii. 5).

THE RESURRECTION OF THE TWO WITNESSES.

"There is hope of a tree, if it be cut down, that it will sprout again" (Job xiv. 7). "The tree of life in the garden of Eden" never dies. "Because I live, ye shall live also" (John xiv. 19). Christ imparts his own immortality to his Church, and thus secures its endless perpetuity and universal prevalence. Because Christ lives in his Church, its battlefields, although for a season covered with bleaching skeletons, are soon thronged with revived armies, ready and strong to renew the conquering fight.

Thus animated and sustained, the Church cannot die. Its seeming death is another life. It is victor over all assaults. Spear-thrusts cannot kill its vitality. Exploding cannon cannot hit its impalpable deathlessness. Fires cannot stop its revivification. Its scattered ashes are the live germs of new forests, in themselves self-perpetuating, and the sprouting pledges of larger harvests, possessing the deathless principle of indefinite reproduction.

Historical Illustrations.

1. The Romish Inquisition did not, in the thirteenth century, exterminate the Albigenses. A remnant fled to Bosnia, near the Adriatic Sea. Their descendants are a part of its present Christian population.

2. The Waldenses were not converted to Romanism by the sword, in the sixteenth century. Large numbers remained faithful to their primitive faith. The present government of Italy grants them religious freedom.

3. The horrors of St. Bartholomew's Day did not destroy Protestantism in France. At the present time there are *one hundred and fifty* consistories of the reformers. The Central Council of the Reformed Churches holds its sittings in Paris, the very city where the butcheries of St. Bartholomew's Day began their devastations.

4. Bishops Latimer and Ridley were, by order of Queen Mary, burned at the stake in the city of Oxford, A.D. 1555. As they were burning, Latimer said to Ridley, "We are kindling to-day a flame in England which will never go out."

In the largest measure has the prediction been realized. *Only three years* after its utterance, the Protestant Queen Elizabeth succeeded the Romish Mary. With the reign of Elizabeth, the great glory of England, both in Church and State, began its unexampled career.

Then the number of the bishops of the Church of England was not twenty: now the bishops of this Protestant Church, in all its branches, are more than two hundred, and are found on every continent of the habitable earth.

Not till the year 1784, was there a bishop of the Protestant Episcopal Church in the present United States of America. The principal cause of this exclusion was State legislation against this Church, which was thus virtually dead. In 1885 this Church has *seventy* bishops.

And yet: the enemies of the two witnesses do nothing more than behold them with wonder. They are satisfied to fear, to behold, and to wonder. Although not simply "one" witness, but "two witnesses," rise from the dead, the affrighted and wondering beholders do "not repent" (Luke xvi. 30, 31).

"*Behold*, ye despisers, and *wonder*, and perish" (Acts xiii. 41).

13. Also in that hour there is a great earthquake, and the tenth part of the city falls, and in the earthquake seven thousand persons are killed; and so the rest are affrighted, and give glory to the God of heaven.

Earthquake: a symbol of God's indignation (vi. 12, viii. 5, xi. 19, xvi. 18). "The earth shook and trembled, *because he was wroth*" (Ps. xviii. 7).

The indignities offered the persons of the "two witnesses" greatly aggravate the condemning and inexpiable accusations symbolized by "the little book" in the angel's hand (Rev. x. 2, 8-10).

Like the persons of all official servants, the persons of the two witnesses are sacred in the eyes of the law. Indignities to witnesses are indignities to the judge, to the court, to the officers, to the government itself.

History illustrates this fact. When the messengers of King David to Hanun, King of Ammon, were by him "villanously entreated" (caption of Bible chapter), David avenged the insult to his kingdom by a desolating war upon the Ammonites (2 Sam. x. 1-7, 14).

When, in our Lord's parable of the husbandmen, they killed not only the servants of the owner of the vineyard, but also his son, his treatment of the murderers is justified by the law of nations: he "miserably destroyed those wicked men" (Matt. xxi. 41).

The conduct of King David and of the owner of the vineyard shows how lawless and past forgiveness are the multiplied insults heaped upon "the two witnesses."

God's punishments surely and swiftly follow.

As in the vision of the prophet Ezekiel, the symbolic exhibition of the different forms of idol-worship by the Jews (viii. 5, 10, 12, 14, 16) warrants and ushers in this awful decision of God, "Mine eye shall not spare, neither will I have pity" (viii. 18); so the symbolic treatment of "the two witnesses" by the jeering rabble demands and hastens this infliction upon the murderers and abusers of his special servants and representatives. Also in that hour there is a great earthquake (xi. 13).

The city: mentioned in verse 8, called Sodom and Egypt, "the harlot Babylon."

Names: *metonymy* for persons (iii. 4).
Seven: a *full* number. Here, definite for indefinite (Lev. xxvi. 18; Ps. xii. 6; Prov. xxvi. 10). The "slain" are in great numbers, are *innumerable*.

The harlot city killed the two witnesses: now her own citizens are killed in countless numbers. God avenges the blood of his servants (Deut. xxxii. 43.)

Historical Illustration.

In 1572 the Church of Rome massacred in France at least thirty thousand Protestants. At this very time there were, in Japan, two hundred thousand converts to Romanism. In 1587, only *fifteen* years after the massacre of St. Bartholomew's Day, the Emperor of Japan began to persecute his subjects who adhered to the Church of Rome. All historians pronounce this the direst persecution the world has ever seen. The persecution ceased only with the extermination of Christianity. The Japanese government required universal return to paganism, on pain of death. The decree was rigorously enforced. All the Japanese Christians either renounced their religion, or were put to death.

Are we mistaken when we see in this unparalleled persecution the *retributive* hand of God, fulfilling his own prediction? "There is a great earthquake, and the tenth part of the city falls, and in the earthquake are killed seven thousand" (xi. 13).

The rest are affrighted, and give glory to the God of heaven.
The rest: of the inhabitants of the city, the citizens who are not killed.
Give glory: become God's true worshippers. His judgments prove instruments of mercy and salvation.

Has the Church of Rome renounced in conviction and purpose her persecuting policy? Is she, through God's transforming grace, returning to primitive and original Christianity? The last clause of this verse 13 contains the promise, "All things are possible with God."

14. The second woe is past. Behold, the third woe cometh quickly.

In viii. 13, three woes are predicted. Three is a *full* number.
The three woes are all the woes with which God will afflict this world.

1. The *first* woe is the plague of locusts (ix. 1–11). "*One* woe is past" (verse 12), — the infliction of the *fifth* trumpet.

2. The *second* woe is the infliction of the *sixth* trumpet (ix. 13-xi. 13). "The *second* woe is past" (xi. 14).

3. The *third* woe is the infliction of the *seventh* trumpet (xi. 15-xiv. 20), and includes the seven censers (xv. 1-xvi. 20). Chapters xvii.-xx. 6 are amplifications of the *seventh* censer (xvi. 17-21).

Swiftly: denotes *certainty* (2 Pet. ii. 1; 1 Thess. v. 3).

THE SEVENTH TRUMPET (Verses 15-19).

The preceding trumpets repeat themselves. Trumpets four, five, and six are repetitions of trumpets one, two, and three. The seventh trumpet is the outgrowth of the preceding six, and the herald of the six censers.

The seventh trumpet introduces the third and last woe. The seventh trumpet is thus a *war* trumpet (Num. x. 9), and a trumpet of *judgment and warning* (Joel ii. 1).

The seventh trumpet is here also a trumpet of *victory* (Num. x. 10). The seventh trumpet is followed by "great voices in heaven," announcing prophetically the victory of the kingdom of Christ over all its enemies.

Trumpets of triumph were blown at the dedication of Solomon's temple (2 Chron. v. 12, 13); also when the foundation of the second temple was laid (Ezra iii. 10).

We have already seen, in the Apocalypse, judgments *preceded* by symbols and proclamations of victory.

1. The white horse of victory *precedes* the red, black, and pale horses of war, famine, and pestilence (vi. 2-8).

2. The sealing of the one hundred and forty-four thousand *precedes* the judgments announced by the six trumpets upon the *heathen* world (vii.-ix. 21).

3. The measurement of the temple of God, the repetition of the sealing, *precedes* the judgments denounced against the *apostate* Church for its treatment of "the two witnesses," the representatives of the *true* Church (xi. 1-13).

By these several symbols of triumph, Christ designs to strengthen the faith and animate the courage of his Church in its incessant and varied conflicts with sin, the world and the Devil. In worldly battles, victory is never certain. Before every battle truly Christian, Christ, by all the symbols of victory he shows us, proclaims our duty and heralds our success. "Fight you must; suffer you must; but triumph is the fixed result by my promise and help."

Encouragement, accordingly, is the loud note of the great voices from heaven we now hear.

---

15. Also the seventh angel sounds. And there are great voices in heaven, saying, The kingdom over the world is become our Lord's; also his Christ's, and he shall reign forever and ever.

Voices: that is, speakers, — part for the whole. Thus "ears" (Ps. xl. 6), "eyes" (Luke x. 23), "feet" (Rom. x. 15), for persons.
The kingdom: predicted (Dan. vii. 14, 27).
The world: the inhabited world.
Our Lord: God the Father (xix. 1).
His Christ: the kingdom has also become his Messiah's (Ps. ii. 2).
He shall reign: namely, our Lord, God the Father (xix. 6).

16. And the twenty-four elders, who before God are sitting upon their thrones, fall upon their faces and worship God.

The twenty-four elders who appear in iv. 4, 10, v. 8, 14, vii. 11, appear again. They are the representatives of the Church of God in both its forms, — the Jewish and the Christian.
Fall and worship: two different acts.
Worship: in the Apocalypse, the object worshipped is either really divine, or regarded as deserving honor as though divine.
The elders now thank and praise God for his unlimited victory.

17. Saying, We thank thee, Lord God Almighty, who art, and who wast, because thou hast taken thy great power, and art reigning.

This verse contains the eucharistic language of the elders.
Art reigning: the reign of God resulting from his victories.

18. And so the Gentiles are angry, and thy wrath is come, and the time promised the dead to be avenged, even to give the recompense due thy servants, the prophets and the saints, and the worshippers of thy name, small and great, and to destroy the destroyers of the earth.

Verse 17 is a thanksgiving. Verse 18 is *a series of petitions* for (*a*) judgment, (*b*) recompense, (*c*) destruction. Verse 19 contains the symbolical answers to these petitions.

In vi. 10, the martyrs pray for *themselves*. In xi. 18, *the Church of Christ*, by its representatives, the twenty-four elders, prays for vengeance upon the *heathen* foes of the same martyred saints. In xi. 18, the twenty-four elders pray that the *false Christians* who kill the martyrs may be punished.

Thus prayers for vengeance introduce two series of punishments, — the series symbolized by the trumpets, and the series symbolized by the censers.

And so: in consequence of the contents of verses 15, 16, and 17.

The Gentiles are angry, and thy wrath is come: these facts excite and create the petitions.

The Gentiles: in the same sense as in verse 2 of this chapter xi.; namely, false Christians. The phrase has the same sense in xvi. 19, xix. 15.

Angry: the word is in the Apocalypse only here and xii. 17, where the dragon is angry with the woman, who represents the Church of Christ. Thus, in each instance, the anger has for its object the true Church.

Thy wrath: the *execution* of thy wrath. The same sense in vi. 17.

THE THREE PETITIONS.

1. For *judgment*. The time *promised* the dead martyrs in vi. 9, 10, and 11; the vision of the fifth scroll. There God promises the martyred dead a time of vengeance. The twenty-four elders, in their first petition (xi. 18), plead the promise in vi. 9-11, where "judged" (English Version, xi. 18) means *avenged*. The verb has the sense of vengeance in xviii. 20. In vi. 10, "judge" is defined by "avenge."

The vengeance implored in the first petition consists of two divine manifestations, — recompense and destruction.

2. For *recompense*. Recompense implied in vi. 11; recompense expressed, xviii. 12. The recompense follows the temporary rest of these martyrs.

This twofold nature of the vengeance gives the Greek conjunction before "to give recompense," etc., the meaning of *even*, and also renders "thy servants . . . small and great," *explicative* of the dead in the first petition.

Thus the second petition entreats recompense for the dead martyrs under the name of "servants," which is their name in vi. 11; "fellow-*servants*," a name here in xi. 18, expanded into prophets, saints, and fearers of God's name.

In xix. 5 is this classification: his servants and his fearers. This classification proves that prophets and saints (xi. 18) are *specifications* of servants, requiring the *explicative* "*even.*"

Prophets: the dead martyrs were themselves *prophets*. They were slain on account of the word of God they proclaimed [prophesied], and on account of the testimony, which they would not change (vi. 9).

Saints: the dead martyrs are often elsewhere called saints (v. 8, viii. 3, 4).

Worshippers of thy name: in Acts xiii. 26, the worshippers of God are distinguished from the "children of the stock of Abraham." The "worshippers of thy name" in xi. 18 are, therefore, *Gentile* worshippers of God.

Fearers of God are his *worshippers*. "Cornelius, a *devout* man that *feared* God, and *prayed to God always*" (Acts x. 2). "*Fear* God, and *worship* him" (Rev. xiv. 7).

Small and great: this class includes *both* "thy servants and thy worshippers." This inclusion is proved by "all ye his servants, and ye that fear him, both small and great" (xix. 5).

Small and great: small here means *young;* great means *old,*— young and old, children and adults.

Among *children* who were martyrs for God, we must include the children of the Albigenses, Waldenses, and Huguenots. Among adult martyrs must be forever ranked the Christian men and women put to death by the Romish Inquisition, whatever may have been their nationality. Their innocent blood utters an incessant cry for vengeance.

3. The destroyers of the earth.

Their methods of destruction, as described by the Bible, are,—

1. Following other gods (Judg. ii. 19).

Example in the Church of Rome: Mariolatry.

2. Forsaking God (Jer. xv. 6).

Instances in the Church of Rome: Its doctrines, which are additions to the primitive creeds.

3. Sinful lives (Ezek. xx. 44). "It is a shame even to speak of those things which are done of them in secret" (Eph. v. 12).

The earth: by *synecdoche*, for the inhabitants of the earth, sinful mankind (Gen. xi. 1; Rev. vi. 8, xi. 6, xiii. 3, xix. 2).

19. And so the sanctuary of God which is in heaven is opened, and the ark of his covenant shows itself, and there are lightnings and voices, and thunders, and an earthquake, and great hail.

The Three Answers to the three petitions (verse 18) now follow.

First Answer.

1. The sanctuary of God in heaven is opened. This is the first time this sanctuary is opened in the Apocalypse. Over the mercy-seat were the cherubim, symbolizing the messengers of God's judgments. The sanctuary is now opened *for the egress of his avenging angels* (xiv. 15, 17, xv. 5, 6). The first petition was for the infliction of judgments (v. 18). The opening of the sanctuary is, then, the symbolic answer to this first petition.

Second Answer.

2. The manifestation of the ark of the covenant. This ark was in the sanctuary, the most holy place (Exod. xxvi. 34).

Covenant is the appellation of the ark, because it contained —

(*a*) The two tables of the Ten Commandments, which are called the two tables of *the covenant* (Deut. ix. 15).

(*b*) The mercy-seat, the cover of the ark (Exod. xxv. 21). Covenant and mercy being thus associated, the ark of the covenant is also the ark of mercy. On the mercy-seat, sacrifices were offered which procured mercy (Lev. xvi. 15).

(*c*) In the gospel, the covenant of which Christ is the Author (Matt. xxvi. 28) contains *promises* (Gal. iii. 17; Heb. ix. 15). Thus the New Testament gives to "the covenant" (Rev. xi. 19) this meaning, the covenant of *promise*.

The manifestation of the ark of the covenant of promise is, then, a most impressive symbol of the *fidelity* of God in fulfilling his promises; and also a symbolic answer to the second petition, the petition for *recompense*.

Third Answer.

3. A storm of great hailstones, accompanied with flashing lightnings, loud voices uttering woes, crashing thunders, and a convulsing earthquake, form the symbolic answer to the third petition (verse 18), the petition for *destruction* (viii. 7, xvi. 21; Ps. xviii. 7, 12, 13).

These symbolic answers are also symbolic *prophecies*. Their *fulfilments* are the contents of the chapters which now immediately follow chapter xi.

CHAPTER XII.

The twelfth chapter introduces by most graphic symbols the history of the Church of Christ in this world.

THE WOMAN CLOTHED WITH THE SUN (Verses 1, 2).

1. Also a wonderful sign appears in heaven; a woman clothed with the sun, and the moon is under her feet, and upon her head a crown of twelve stars.

Sign: presage foreshadowing future events (Matt. xvi. 3, xxiv. 3). A vision exhibits *a temporal period* of a peculiar character. The period is exhibited *as a whole*. Its beginning may have already transpired, when the vision is first disclosed. Historically, a vision may be *retrospective*, as well as prospective.

Thus, in the vision of "the man-child" (Rev. xii. 5), events are exhibited, *antecedent* as well as subsequent to his birth.

This *twofold perspective* characterizes other visions in the Apocalypse.

In the visions exhibiting *the powers resisting* the true Church, the narrative shows the *beginning* of the destructive process, as well as its progress and its completion (Rev. xii. 7–17).

These explanations anticipate and remove difficulties otherwise formidable.

Great: connected (xv. 1) with "marvellous," wonderful; great therefore because exciting wonder, a wonderful sign.

In heaven: the visible heaven.

Woman: symbol of the Church (Isa. liv. 6; Ps. xlv. 9). The model of the woman here pictured is Eve, the first woman, in her original holiness, innocence, and faithful allegiance to God. In Rev. x. 1, a mighty angel has already appeared as the symbol of the *husband* of this representative woman. Now the symbolic *wife* herself appears. No aspects of the symbol are necessarily derived from Mary, the wife of Joseph (Matt. i. 18). The Old and New Testaments furnish the essential outlines. The church here represented is the perfect Church (Eph. v. 27).

Clothed: as a bride (Isa. xlix. 18). The attire of a bride is "fi linen, clean and white" (Rev. xix. 8), fine linen *shining* and cle So the Greek. In verse 14, the fine linen is *white* and clean. T. *whiteness* of the fine linen is *shining*. White is *shining* white. This shining whiteness of the fine linen resembles the light of the sun, — resembles sunlight: "His face did *shine* as the *sun*, and his *raiment* was *white* as the *light*" (Matt. xvii. 2).

In the Song of Solomon, the beauty of the maiden is there portrayed in language most figurative. She is compared to the moon and to the sun. "Who is she that looketh forth [from the window] as the dawn [dawning morning], shining as the white [moon], pure [bright] as the heat [sun], formidable as furnished with banners [as a camp of soldiers]?" (Cant. vi. 10.) The maiden here described wears an outer robe, called "veil" (Cant. v. 7), similar to the outer robe of pale tint worn by the bride (Rev. xii. 1).

The descriptions of this maiden are not so much of her *person* as of the *adornments* of her person. "Thy cheeks are comely *with rows* of jewels, thy neck *with chains* of gold" (i. 10). Her complexion was not fair: "I am *black*" (verse 6). When, then (Song of Sol. vi. 10), she is said to be "fair as the moon, clear as the sun," the fairness and the clearness may be referred to her *dress*. Like the bride (Rev. xii. 1), she may in her linen tunic have been clothed with sunlight, and in her "veil" (Song of Sol. v. 7), her outer robe, with moonlight. If this reference is admissible, the resemblance between the maiden in Canticles and the bride in Revelation becomes still more close and remarkable.

In both women, their loveliness was *moral* beauty. "The fine linen is the righteousness of saints" (Rev. xix. 8).

St. John may from this figurative passage in Solomon's Song take his imagery in Rev. xii. 1.

By the sun he may here mean sunlight, — light. "Sun" has this meaning in 2 Sam. xxiii. 4; Ps. lxxiv. 16; Isa. xxx. 26, lx. 19; Jer. xxxi. 35.

Instead, then, of "a woman clothed with the sun" (English Version, Rev. xii. 1), we may translate, "a woman clothed with *light*." Her fine linen garment will be like the raiment of Christ when transfigured, "shining, white as the light" (Matt. xvii. 2), and thus bright as the sunlight (Cant. vi. 10).

The Old Testament clothes a bride in *two* garments (Ps. xlv. 13, 14; Ezek. xvi. 10). The first and principal garment was "fine linen"

(Rev. xix. 8; Ezek. xvi. 10). This garment covered the feet (Jer. xiii. 22). The second garment called (Ezek. xvi. 10) "silk," and (Cant. v. 7) "veil," was a thin translucent tissue, probably of silk, as St. John (Rev. xviii. 12) mentions "silk."

This outer robe of silken tissue covered principally the lower portions of the body, and fell in flowing compass far below the feet.

These forms of the bridal dress amply explain St. John's additional description of the woman clothed with moonlight, namely, "the moon under her feet." Since the sun is sunlight, is light, the moon is moonlight, is pale light. The open-work robe of thin silk would dim the brilliant white of the inner linen garment, and thus give to its lower portions a paler light.

The moon, that is, the moonlight, is, then, the outer robe of thin open silk; and, because it dims the brilliant whiteness of the inner garment of fine linen, this glossy tissue clothes the inner tunic with the pale hue of moonlight. Because the delicate silken robe encircles the feet with graceful folds, this garment is "under the feet."

A crown of twelve stars: this imagery St. John takes from these words of Ezekiel, describing God's bride of the Old Testament: "I put a beautiful crown upon thy head" (xvi. 12). As a queen, this Old-Testament bride wears a crown (Esth. ii. 17). Since Christ is king, as well as a bridegroom, his bride is queen, and wears a crown.

The stars on her crown may refer to the gems with which the crown is studded and adorned.

The number "twelve" refers the stars to the twelve tribes of Israel, which are themselves symbols of the Church of Christ in its membership (Matt. xix. 28).

The symbolic bride (Rev. xii. 1), thus arrayed, adorned, and dignified, is "a glorious church" (Eph. v. 27), even "all glorious" (Ps. xlv. 13).

2. And being with child, she cries out, because in travail and in pain to bring forth.

Even this definite language does not designate any *actual* woman. The woman here is merely a symbol of Christ's Church. The minute description is solely for graphic effect.

The same use of minute specifications in the Old Testament fully justifies the explanation just given of the language of this verse.

The prophet Ezekiel (chapter xvi.) exhibits a woman as the symbol of Jerusalem (verses 1 and 2). For intensification this symbolic woman is most minutely portrayed, first as an infant, and then as a wife. But the infant foundling and the faithless wife of Ezekiel is not a real woman: she is nothing but figure.

In the same way the woman of St. John (Rev. xii. 2) is not a real woman: she is wholly figure. She is not the personal Mary the Virgin, the mother of Christ.

THE GREAT RED DRAGON (Verses 3-17).

3. And still another sign in heaven shows itself; and behold a great dragon, fire-red, having seven heads and ten horns, and upon his heads seven diadems.

The cry of the suffering woman does not bring another woman to her help (Gen. xxxv. 17). Not even an Egyptian hag comes in ready to kill the expected child (Exod. i. 16). Quite a different murderer presents himself. He is the instigator of all murders (John viii. 44), a great dragon, fire-red. The dragon here is the symbol of Satan (Rev. xx. 2, where he is called a "serpent"). The imagery of the dragon is thus taken from "the serpent" that tempted Eve, the first woman (Gen. iii. 1-6; 2 Cor. xi. 3). Having in the Garden of Eden destroyed the holiness of the wife of Adam, the dragon hopes now to destroy the entire person of the bride of Christ. When he cannot annihilate this bride, then he plots for her spiritual destruction, and succeeds in producing the apostate Church, the harlot Babylon. Eve herself, in disobeying God's prohibition not to eat the tree of the knowledge of good and evil, became an apostate and a spiritual adulteress and spiritual harlot. His ruinous success with Eve prompts the dragon to attempt the alienation of a portion of the Church from its affection for Christ.

Fire-red: bent on destruction; red in blood (Ps. lxviii. 23).

Seven heads and ten horns: this *dragon* has but *one* mouth (xii. 15). The *beast* (xiii. 2) with seven heads and ten horns has but *one* mouth. The dragon's seven heads may therefore be seven protuberances of his one head. A serpent's head is often covered with plates. Head is the symbol of *wisdom* (Eccles. ii. 14). Horn is the symbol of *power* (Luke i. 69).

Both the numbers seven and ten are definite for indefinite. The seven heads and the ten horns of the dragon are symbols of his deep cunning and of his great power.

Seven diadems: diadem is simply a head-*band* of linen or of silk, sometimes adorned with pearls or precious stones. A crown is a head-*wreath*, originally of leaves or flowers, afterwards of gold. In origin and use, the diadem *precedes* the crown. A diadem is the symbol of royal dignity (Ecclus. xi. 5). Kings sometimes wore more than one diadem: (1 Macc. xi. 13) "two crowns upon his head, the crown of Asia and of Egypt."

4. And his tail draws away the third part of the stars of heaven, and casts them to the earth. And the dragon stands in front of the woman who is on the point of bringing forth, that when she brings forth he may devour her child.

Draws away: present tense, draws *continually*. The dragon's power is incessant. The verb in the New Testament always implies force: draws by force.

Third part: this amount of destruction often in Apocalypse (viii. 7-12, ix. 15, 18).

Stars: may denote civil rulers (Dan. viii. 10; Matt. xxiv. 29).

In the Septuagint, dragon is the constellation called the Serpent. "He garnished *the heavens;* his hand formed the *serpent*" (Job xxvi. 13). Possibly reference is here made to this constellation of the northern sky. The dragon's displacing the stars indicates his power over civil rulers.

Stands: half erect. Pliny thus describes the dragon: "celsus et erectus in medio incedens" (*Historia Naturalis*, viii. 3).

5. And she brings forth a mighty son, who is certainly to rule all the nations with an iron sceptre. And her child is caught up to God, even to his throne.

She brings forth: the mother bringing forth is the Church. "Jerusalem is the mother of us all. She hath many children" (Gal. iv. 26, 27). Although Jerusalem is the Church, yet St. Paul calls her a *bearing* ("gendereth," verse 24) mother.

A mighty son: "man," English Version, means manly, strong, mighty; "*manly* stomach" (2 Macc. vii. 21). Mighty, the title of the son the symbolic woman brings forth, is the very title the prophet Isaiah gives Christ, "*mighty* to save" (Isa. lxiii. 1). Clement of Alexandria, second century, calls Christ the mighty child.

To rule: as *a shepherd* (John x. 11).

Iron: that is, irresistible.

Is caught up to the throne of God: is rescued from the power of the dragon (xi. 12).

The occupant of a throne is a king. Christ was king while he was in this world (John xii. 15, xviii. 37).

6. And the woman flees into the wilderness, where she hath a place prepared by God, that there they may nourish her a thousand two hundred and sixty days.

Flees: through fright.

Wilderness: not on the earth; the vision is in the visible heaven (verse 1).

In the Bible, the "wilderness" is

(*a*) An uninhabited and uncultivated region; a *solitary* place (Isa. xxxv. 1).

(*b*) A place of refuge and safety (1 Kings xix. 4). This is the meaning of "the wilderness," Rev. xii. 6.

(*c*) The resort of evil spirits, devils, demons, and their associates (Matt. iv. 1, xii. 43; also Rev. xvii. 3).

Nourish: that is, men implied. In sense, the equivalent of "is nourished" (verse 14). By perpetual succession of members, the Church is nourished and preserved in the world.

Days: a longer time than forty-two months (xi. 3, xiii. 5. See xi. 3).

The period is a limited one. The time will come when the true Church will cease to be persecuted, either by Romanism or by infidels.

THE DESCENT OF SATAN AND HIS ANGELS TO THE EARTH
(Verses 7-12).

Digression from the previous narrative. Narrative resumed, verse 13.

7. And there is war in heaven: Michael and his angels to war against the dragon; and the dragon wars and his angels.

Verses 7-12 describe a symbolic scene shown to St. John, to explain the sudden appearance of the dragon in front of the woman (verse 4). The symbolic scene must be derived from real transactions. When and where they occurred, the Bible does not reveal. The Scriptures furnish only the following intimations respecting the actual events here referred to:—

1. Certain "angels kept not their first estate, but left their own habitation" (Jude 6).

2. "Pride" was the cause of their "fall and condemnation" (1 Tim. iii. 6).

3. "The serpent beguiled Eve through his subtlety" (2 Cor. xi. 3).

4. "The Devil was a murderer from the beginning" (John viii. 44).

There is war: not, there had been war. The context forbids the pluperfect. The verbs, "I heard" (verse 10), and "rejoice ye" (verse 12), make St. John a witness of the scene, which, consequently, is *within his hearing and sight*.

War: *a representation* of war. The entire scene (verses 7–12) is symbolic. Since the scene is symbolic, the events are consistently represented as occurring partly in heaven and partly on earth.

Michael: this name means, He who is like God. Like God in his *punitive* actions, not in his nature. The name occurs only in Dan. x. 13, 21, xii. 1; Jude 9; Rev. xii. 7.

His angels: the angels Michael commands, as "prince" (Dan. x. 13, 21, xii. 1), as "archangel" (Jude 9). Since Michael and his angels are (Rev. xii. 7) fighting angels, they are *cherubim* (Ps. lxxx. 1-3).

To war: the war in heaven was for this purpose, — for Michael and his angels to war against the dragon and his angels.

8. And yet he does not prevail. Not even their place is longer found in heaven.

Does not prevail: the Devil and his angels have not internal strength to resist the assault of Michael and his angels. Disobedience weakens even an angelic nature.

Their place is not found: there is no place they can hold. So complete is their defeat and expulsion, that not even one dragon-angel is left in heaven.

The utter defeat of the dragon, thus symbolically exhibited, is a prediction and an assurance of his utter defeat here on earth.

9. And so the great dragon is cast out, the old serpent, who is called the Devil and Satan, who is deceiving the whole world, he is cast out into the earth; also his angels are cast out with him.

Is cast out: is thrown out.

Old serpent: who deceived Eve (2 Cor. xi. 3).

Old: he was in the Garden of Eden (Gen. iii. 1-6).

Is called: in the Bible. Devil, in Matt. iv. 1, means "slanderer" (1 Tim. iii. 11); is called Satan, adversary (Matt. iv. 10).

Who is deceiving: xx. 3, 8, 10.

The whole world: all the inhabitants of the world (Rev. iii. 10) are subject to "his devices" (2 Cor. ii. 11).

Is cast out: repeated for emphasis.

Into the earth: for the probation of the human race. "In the world ye shall have tribulation" (John xvi. 33). "Temptation is common to man" (1 Cor. x. 13).

His angels are cast out: into the earth, for the same purpose the

Devil is cast into it. His angels are demons (Rev. ix. 20; Jas. ii. 19; 1 Cor. x. 20). There is but one Devil: demons are many.

THE MARTYRS WITNESS THE CONFLICT AND ITS RESULTS. THEIR EXULTATION OVER SATAN'S DEFEAT, PAST AND ULTIMATE (Verses 10-12).

10. And I heard a loud voice in heaven, saying, Now is the salvation and the power and the kingdom our God's, and so [is established] the authority of his Christ; for the accuser of our brethren is cast out, who is accusing them before our God, day and night.

This voice in the material heaven is the voice of the martyrs, whose prayer for vengeance we heard (Rev. vi. 10).

The answer God gives their prayer contains this declaration:—

"*Their* [Christian] *brethren*" would be "killed," as they themselves had been "killed for the word of God, and for the testimony which they held" (vi. 9).

Among the utterances of "the voice in heaven" (xii. 10), this is one: "The accuser of *our brethren.*" Thus "their brethren" (vi. 9), and "our brethren" (xii. 10), *are identical.* In consequence of this identity, the martyrs of vi. 9, and the speakers of xii. 10, are *themselves identical.*

The martyrs of vi. 10 re-appear in xii. 10. In their exultation (xii. 10-12), they anticipate their own full vindication, and also the full vindication of all their fellow-martyrs, as well as the absolute triumph of the Church of Christ.

By these processes of investigation, we discover *the nature of the rest* promised the martyrs (vi. 11). The rest promised them is the rest and exaltation of soul inspired by their faith and hope in the certainty of their ultimate enthronement.

The Special Purpose of Rev. xii. 10–12.

This passage, expressing victory and triumph, strongly resembles vii. 10, 12, and xi. 15, 17, 18. Each of these three exclamations of victory *precedes* the infliction of judgments upon the enemies of Christ, and the endurance of trials and sufferings by his Church. The purpose of each exclamation is the same: to assure the Church of its complete triumph at last.

Rev. xii. 10–12 *precedes* the account of the Devil's most deadly machinations and assaults: (*a*) his pursuit of the woman (xii. 13); (*b*) his war upon her seed; (*c*) his creation of the triform beast, leopard, bear, lion (xiii. 1, 2); (*d*) his intrusion of the lamb-dragon

(xiii. 11). To prepare the Church for these Satanic enemies, and to strengthen her for the terrible conflict, the martyrs in their secure and hopeful rest exclaim, —

"Now is come salvation and power, and the kingdom of our God."

Now: at this very moment, even now: we take the very first instant after the victory to express exultation and joy.

Salvation: victory, including deliverance; in this sense, also, vii. 10, xix. 1.

Power: the manifestation of the power, "from his power" (xv. 8).

The kingdom: the establishment of the kingdom, of the reign of Christ. Kingdom means reign (xvii. 17); English Version, "dominion."

Our God's: the context requires this sense, which is confirmed by vii. 3, "the servants of our God," servants *belonging to* our God.

Is accusing: of being guilty and sinful (Job i. 7–11).

11. And yet they themselves conquer him by reason of the blood of the Lamb, and by reason of the word of their testimony; and so they love not their life unto death.

They themselves: the earthly combatants; the succession of Christian martyrs. Mortal and sinful, weak, and assaulted by Satan himself, they yet conquer.

The blood of the Lamb: removes their guilt, and cleanses them from all sin (Eph. i. 7; 1 John i. 7).

The word of their testimony: the word they testify respecting Christ. They persevere in their confession of Christ. Their endurance secures their victory.

They love not: they disregard.

Unto death: their endurance results in the sacrifice of their lives.

12. On account of this, rejoice, ye heavens, and ye that dwell in them. Woe to the earth and to the sea, for the Devil is come down against you, having great wrath, because he knoweth that he hath but a short time.

This: the endurance and triumph of the martyrs, and the defeat of Satan.

Heavens: this address to inanimate objects denotes the most exultant joy in the martyrs (Isa. xlix. 13).

Dwell: permanently, to abide, to live.

In them: in the heavens. Angels are here addressed; angels dwell in heaven (Matt. xviii. 10).

Woe: introduces a state the opposite of joy, the distress of the present Church of Christ.

The land and the sea: is (*a*) an expression for this entire world, and (*b*) for the inhabitants of this world; "you," next clause.

Is come down: cause of the woe. The Devil, cast out of heaven, comes down to afflict mankind, a creation next in rank to the angels (Ps. viii. 5).

Wrath: his defeat in heaven fires his wrath.

Short: this world is not to be always subject to the assaults of the Devil. The shortness of his time stimulates his malice and activity.

THE CHASE OF THE DRAGON AFTER THE WOMAN
(Verses 13-17).

Resumption of the narrative, verses 4-6.

13. And when the dragon sees that he is cast out into the earth, he pursues the woman who brought forth the mighty son.

Pursues: "persecuted," English Version, is too indefinite. The primary sense of the verb, cause to run, hunt, chase, pursue, should be retained in the translation.

Mighty son: the mighty shepherd King (verse 5).

14. And to the woman are given the two wings of the great eagle, that she may fly into the wilderness, into her place, where she is nourished a time, and times, and half a time, through fear of the serpent.

Are given: by God.

The two wings: the wings of the great eagle, when they are expanded, measure nine feet. The imagery is taken from Exod. xix. 4.

The great eagle: is the *aquila heliaca*, the sun-eagle, who flies high even in the eye of the sun (viii. 13, notes).

The woman, furnished with the long and broad wings of the sun-eagle, is ready to fly swiftly, loftily, and far away from the mouth of the pursuing dragon. But he anticipates her flight by close pursuit.

Time, times, and half a time: three years and a half (Dan. iv. 16, 23, 25, 32 (29), vii. 25); an indefinite period, but of limited duration.

For fear: the English Version (Judg. ix. 21) translates by this expression, "for fear," the same Greek phrase that occurs here (Rev.

xii. 14), where the English Version has "from the face of." Before she can spread her wings, the dragon is close to her with his belching mouth.

15. And the serpent casts out of his mouth, behind the woman, water, as a river, that he may cause her to be carried away by the river.

Behind: so (i. 10) "behind me."
River: image of destruction (Ps. xviii. 4; Matt. vii. 25).
The behemoth may be the origin of this imagery. "He drinketh up a river: he trusteth that he can draw up Jordan into his mouth" (Job xl. 23).

16. And the earth helps the woman, and the earth opens its mouth, and swallows up the river which the dragon casts out of his mouth.

Helps: quickly, as the verb in its composition intimates.
Swallows up: Greek, drinks down. This imagery marks *the impotence* of the dragon's effort to destroy the fleeing woman. A dry desert of sand instantly absorbs his large mouthful of water.

The incessant attempts of infidels to destroy the gospel of Christ ever prove equally impotent and useless.

17. And the dragon waxes wroth with the woman, and departs to make war with the rest of her seed, who are keeping the commandments of God, and holding the testimony respecting Jesus.

Waxes wroth: the dragon is burning with wrath because he cannot kill the woman and her mighty son. The life of this son is the death of the dragon, who avenges himself for his failure and disappointment by waging war with the rest of the woman's seed.

Departs: this is a weighty word. It embodies both purpose and inception. The dragon here *resolves* to make war; the dragon here *begins* to make war.

New-Testament usage gives each of these meanings to the Greek verb we translate "depart."

"They *went* to buy" (Matt. xxv. 10): they *resolved* to buy. "The woman *went* and saith" (John iv. 28): she *began* her narrative.

The rest: implies contrast with the portion of the seed which does not "keep the commandment of God," and which does not "hold the testimony of Jesus." The word "rest" is here equal to "remnant" (Rom. ix. 27, xi. 5), and implies the existence of the harlot Babylon (Rev. xvii. 1), the apostate Church.

The word "rest" marks contrast in the parable of the Ten Virgins. "Came the *other* virgins," the *rest* of the virgins (Matt. xxv. 11).

St. John calls the true Church "the seed of the woman," on account of its vital relation to Christ, "the seed" predicted (Gen. iii. 15). Since Christ is this "seed," Eve is the original of the woman who (Rev. xii. 1, 2, 5, 13, 17) represents the Church of Christ.

"The rest of her seed," are, by another figure, "the *good* seed, the children of the kingdom" (Matt. xiii. 38).

Keeping the commandments of God: this is the first time this expression occurs in the Apocalypse. Its contents identify it with this command of our Lord, "Keep the commandments" (Matt. xix. 17); a command, the essence of which, he says, consists in habitual obedience to another injunction of his, "Give to the poor" (verse 21).

We know how very diligent the first Christians were in obeying this injunction of their divine Master.

Zaccheus gave the half of his goods to the poor (Luke xix. 8).

The original church of Jerusalem "sold their possessions and goods, and parted them to all, as every man had need" (Acts ii. 45, iv. 34, 35).

"Barnabas, having land, sold it, and brought the money, and laid it at the apostles' feet" (Acts iv. 37).

"Remember the poor" (Gal. ii. 10).

"Concerning the collection for the [poor, Rom. xv. 26] saints, upon the first day of the week let every one of you lay by him in store, as God hath prospered him" (1 Cor. xvi. 1, 2).

"Whoso hath this world's good, and seeth his brother have need, and shutteth up his bowels of compassion from him, how dwelleth the love of God in him?" (1 John iii. 17.)

From these Scriptures, it is most certain that *care for the poor* is a command of Christ of incessant and universal obligation.

The duty of caring for the poor has these special applications:—

1. To give the poor the gospel of Jesus Christ. "The poor have the gospel preached to them" (Matt. xi. 5).

This gift embraces Christian missions, both at home and abroad.

2. To provide for the sick and helpless poor. "They brought unto him all *sick* people, and he healed them" (Matt. iv. 24).

"Jesus saith unto the *impotent* man, Rise and walk. And immediately the man was made whole, and walked" (John v. 8, 9).

This is an imperative duty which every Christian congregation, and every Christian individual, is required by Christ to perform systematically and with unfailing fidelity.

Christian missions and Christian charities are the potent instrumentalities our Lord ordains for the conversion of the whole world, Jews and Gentiles, the ignorant, the unbelieving, the sinful, the lost, the diseased and the dying, unto his loving and saving self.

Holding the testimony respecting Jesus: what testimony did the first Christians hold and proclaim respecting Jesus, the incarnate Son of God? St. Peter and St. Paul answer this great question: "There is salvation in no other. There is no other name under heaven given among men, whereby we must be saved" (Acts iv. 12).

"He is able to save them to the uttermost that come unto God by him, seeing he ever liveth to make intercession for them" (Heb. vii. 25).

The maddened dragon well knows the nature of the commandments of God, the rest of the seed of the woman are keeping, and the character of the testimony they are holding and proclaiming respecting the only Saviour, Jesus, incarnate, and enthroned and interceding in heaven. The dragon is quick to perceive that the loving servants of Christ who help the poor, and the bold heralds of Christ who proclaim an almighty and successful Saviour, will themselves prove strong and swift eagles to bear innumerable human souls beyond his grip of death. The knowledge and the sight intensify his raging anger. He fears his kingdom of darkness will not longer be preferred to the kingdom of Christ.

The dragon resolves at once, and begins at once, to make war upon these dangerous dispensers of kindness and love, and upon these detested messengers of light, holiness, and salvation.

The dragon creates, appoints, and employs the wild beast from the bottomless pit (xi. 7) through the sea (xiii. 1). The dragon and the sea-beast are thus *principal and agent*. This relation between them imparts identity to their warfare and to their enemies.

In xi. 7, there is *a prophecy* that the wild beast from the bottomless pit will overcome and kill "the two witnesses."

In xii. 17, the dragon resolves and begins to "make war with the remnant of the woman's seed." Here is *the fulfilment* of the prophecy in xi. 7.

xiii. 1, 2, 4, 7, describes *the manner* in which the prophecy is fulfilled. The dragon conducts the war through his agent, the sea-beast, to whom he gives "power and authority to make war" (verses 2, 4). Thus commissioned and empowered, the sea-beast actually "makes war with the saints, and *overcomes them*" (verse 7).

In the prophecy (xi. 7), the objects of the predicted warfare are "the two witnesses." In the fulfilment of the prophecy, the objects of the warfare are "the remnant of the woman's seed" (xii. 17), and "the saints" (xiii. 7). The persons who are the objects both of the prophecy and of its fulfilment are the same persons. "The two witnesses, the remnant of the woman's seed, and the saints" are identical. The Apocalyptic history and experience of either one of the three classes are the Apocalyptic history and experience of the other two classes. When the wild beast from the bottomless pit overcomes and kills "the two witnesses," he at the same time overcomes and kills "the remnant of the woman's seed, and the saints." When the dragon makes war upon "the remnant of the woman's seed," he at the same time makes war upon the two witnesses and upon the saints. When the beast from the sea overcomes the saints, he at the same time overcomes the two witnesses and the remnant of the woman's seed. The two witnesses, the remnant of the woman's seed, and the saints, are *all one and the same class of persons.*

18. And the dragon stops on the sand-shore of the sea.

The dragon can stop nowhere else. He has not the two long and broad wings of the great sun-eagle. He cannot use the air, and fly in pursuit of the escaping woman. The earth is her friend and helper, and his enemy, and will open its mouth wider than his jaws, and swallow him up. The narrow sand-shore is his only standing-place. The deep sea, the prolific nest of savage monsters like himself, is his only resort and arsenal. His dragon-kindred affect deserts and loneliness (Matt. xii. 43; 1 Pet. v. 8). This desolate dragon, banished from sky and land, stands on a congenial and hopeful spot. There is a wild beast in the bottomless pit, figured by the fathomless sea, that will hear and answer the dragon's imperative call.

The two witnesses, the dragon confronts and opposes by two wild beasts.

The Church of Christ represented by the two witnesses is both "a congregation of faithful men," and the "keeper and witness of Holy Writ." The social organization of the Church, the dragon opposes by the wild beast from the bottomless pit, the symbol of civil power hostile to the Church. The Church as "the keeper and witness of Holy Writ," the inspired record of God's revealed truth, the dragon opposes by the wild beast from the earth, the lamb-dragon, who as "false prophet" perverts God's truth, and occupies its place by his own inventions and errors.

The kingdom of Christ, the dragon now aspires to overthrow by worldly kingdoms and states, anti-Christian in their policy and administration, and by churches nominally Christian, as Romanism and Unitarianism, and by religious bodies renouncing Christianity, as Lootseeism, Confucianism, Buddhism, Brahmanism, Mohammedanism, Rabbinism, Mormonism.

CHAPTER XIII.

The structural continuity of chapters x.–xiii. requires that the prophetic symbols of chapter xiii. be referred, for their incipient fulfilment, to the early periods of the gospel.

In chapter x., there appears an angelic symbol of Christ, the Bridegroom of His Church.

In chapter xi., two witnesses testify for Christ, and are about to be killed by the wild beast from the bottomless pit.

In chapter xii., the murderous dragon attempts in vain to destroy the symbolic woman and her mighty infant son.

Here, then, *at the very beginning* of the life of the incarnate Christ, does the dragon *begin* his deadly persecutions of the Church both in its body, and in its head Jesus Christ. Dragon-hostility begins and runs parallel with incarnate love. *There is no intermission* in the enmity of Satan.

THE TWO WILD BEASTS.

In this chapter, two wild beasts appear, one out of the sea (verse 1), the other out of the earth (verse 11). The wild beast from the sea is a composite nondescript, part leopard, part bear, part lion. Both wild beasts are God's *punitive* agents.

Punitive wild beasts are in the Bible in two forms.

Literal: Lev. xxvi. 22; Deut. xxviii. 26, xxxii. 24; 1 Kings xiii. 24; 2 Kings ii. 24; Ps. lxxix. 2; Isa. lvi. 9; Jer. v. 6, vii. 33, xii. 9, xv. 3; Lam. iii. 10; Ezek. v. 17, xxix. 5, xxxii. 4.

Figurative: Ezek. xxxiv. 8, xxxix. 17–20; Hos. v. 14, xiii. 7, 8; Dan. vii. 3, 17.

An inspection of the references will disclose the sources from which the prophets Ezekiel, Hosea, and Daniel, as well as St. John, derived their images of *punitive* wild beasts.

At the present time, in Hindostan, wild beasts every year destroy thousands of human beings.

The first wild beast, the one from the sea (xiii. 1), from the abyss, "bottomless pit" (xi. 7, xvii. 8), is mentioned without the second wild beast, the one from the earth, the lamb-dragon, the false prophet, ten times; namely, xi. 7, xiii. 1, xvii. 3, 8, 11, 12, 13, 16, 17, xix. 19.

On the contrary, the second wild beast, the one from the earth, the lamb-dragon, the false prophet, is associated with the first wild beast in these places: xiii. 11, 12, 14, 15, 17, 18, xvi. 13; and is his subordinate.

These facts prove the superiority of the first wild beast to the second. Pagan imperialism has always been the controlling power of the Church of Rome.

Subjects of the chapter. — The enraged dragon summons to his help two other spirits as wicked as himself, (*a*) the leopard-bear-lion wild beast (verses 1–10), (*b*) the lamb-dragon (11–18).

The imagery of the compound wild beast is taken from the prophet Daniel (vii. 3–7), with this difference: in Daniel, each beast represents a separate kingdom; in Revelation, the tri-bestial monster represents a single kingdom, the *Pagan* Roman empire. The imagery of the lamb-dragon is derived from these words of our Lord: "Beware of *false prophets*, which come to you in *sheep's clothing*, but inwardly they are *ravening wolves*" (Matt. vii. 15).

The lamb-dragon is called "the false prophet" in Rev. xvi. 13, xix. 20, xx. 10.

The mongrel wild beast represents the *Pagan* Roman empire. The lamb-dragon represents the same empire *nominally* Christian.

THE FIRST WILD BEAST (Verses 1-10).

1. Also I saw, out of the sea, a wild beast coming up, having ten horns and seven heads, and upon his horns ten diadems, and upon his heads names of blasphemy.

I saw: this vision, out of the sea, a wild beast coming up.

The sea: Isaiah explains this symbolism of the sea. "*The wicked are like the troubled sea* [negative for the positive, continually causing destruction], *when it cannot rest*" (lvii. 20). The sea represents the troubled wicked world. Out of its confusion, wicked governments originate. Also from the sea the four beasts, lion, bear, leopard, and the beast dreadful and terrible and strong exceedingly, described by the prophet Daniel, arise (Dan. vii. 3–7).

Only here does the first wild beast come from the sea. In xi. 7, xvii. 8, he comes from "the bottomless pit," the prison of the dragon (xx. 3), who gives him his power and throne (xiii. 2). The first wild beast comes from a *lower* depth than the sea, his *apparent* birthplace.

Ten horns: only in two other places, namely, xii. 3, and xvii. 3, are there beasts with seven heads and ten horns. But in xii. 3, and xvii. 3, the heads *precede the* horns. On the contrary, in xiii. 1, the heads *follow* (Greek) the horns. This order is against nature. There must be a head before there is a horn. There cannot be a horn without a head. This order also conflicts with St. John's own usage (xii. 3, xvii. 3).

Why does he here (verse 1) *change the order?* This is the only possible *contextual* answer. He designs to indicate that the wild beast (xiii. 1) is *in symbol* the repetition of the *fourth* beast in Daniel, as only this beast has "ten horns," its only bodily mark save its "iron teeth" (vii. 7).

Other Explanations of the Reversed Order.

Dean Alford thus explains: "Ten horns put first, because they are crowned."

Usage does not justify this explanation. Usage establishes itself by comparing xiii. 1 with xii. 3 and xvii. 3. If the "ten horns" (xiii. 1) "are put first because they are crowned," then the "seven heads" (xii. 3) stand *before* the "ten horns" because the seven heads are crowned; "seven crowns upon his heads" (xii. 3). But crowning is not the reason for the precedence of the seven heads (xii. 3); because in xvii. 3, the "seven heads," although *not* crowned, *precede* the "ten horns."

Thus the only usage there is decides that the crowning (xiii. 1) is *not* the reason for the reversed order.

"The horns of the beast are mentioned *before* the heads, because, when the beast was arising from the sea, the horns would first appear."—BISHOP WORDSWORTH.

But it is *not certain* that the horns appeared *first*. The appearance of the beast *in a vision* would be *instantaneous*, and not *gradual* as Bishop Wordsworth supposes.

Until a better reason than the *contextual* can be given, this must hold its immovable position.

Ten horns and seven heads: ten and seven, definite for indefinite; many horns, symbols of power; many heads, symbols of intelligence (Eccl. ii. 14).

Ten diadems: symbols of kingly dignity (xii. 3).

Names of blasphemy: the heads of the sea-beast bear *titles* which are blasphemous, because claiming for him the character and power of *Deity*. A Roman emperor had the title *Divus*, divine. (Matt. xxvi. 65; Mark ii. 7; 2 Thess. ii. 4.)

2. And the wild beast which I saw was like a leopard, and his feet as the feet of a bear, and his mouth as the mouth of a lion; and the dragon gives him his power and his throne, even great authority.

Leopard: remarkable for swiftness (Hab. i. 8), for voracity (Ecclus. xxviii. 23).

Bear: with his long and sharp claws tears his prey in pieces.

Mouth of the lion: mouth for teeth. "Their teeth as the teeth of lions" (ix. 8).

In verse 1 of chapter xiii., St. John connects the sea-beast with the *fourth* beast (Dan. vii. 7). In this verse 2, he connects the sea-beast with the first, second, and third beasts of Dan. vii. 4-6. He thus connects the sea-beast with *all* the beasts Daniel exhibits. Thus connecting the sea-beast with *all four*, St. John does not, in symbol, connect the sea-beast with any *single one* of the four. According to the prophet Daniel, his four beasts represent these four kingdoms:—

1. Babylon (Dan. i. 1; 2 Chron. xxxvi. 6, 22).
2. Media (Dan. xi. 1).
3. Persia (Dan. x. 1).
4. Greece (Dan. viii. 20, 21, x. 20, xi. 2).

Since the sea-beast is connected with *all* these kingdoms, he is not connected with *any single kingdom*. He is not connected *with Greece*. The kingdom the sea-beast symbolizes *is not Greece*. The *immediate* successor of Greece was *the Roman empire*. The sea-beast symbolizes *the Pagan empire of Rome*. THE SEA-BEAST CAN SYMBOLIZE NO OTHER.

A wild beast agile, fleet, and voracious as the leopard, stout and sharp-footed as the bear, lion-mouthed, and ten-horned, "dreadful and terrible," is a most formidable monster. In describing him, horrid symbolism exhausts itself in the word "exceedingly" (Dan. vii. 7). Such a complicated wild beast is the fit representative of the Pagan Roman empire, which for emperors had these human monsters Nero, Domitian, Severus, and for soldiery and people the counterparts of their imperial tyrants.

As the wild beast from the sea represents the *Pagan* kingdom or empire of Rome, other truths follow: —

I. The sea wild beast does not represent any *individual person* in the empire, whether emperor, or pope, or any other imperial officer.

II. As the representative of the Roman empire, the sea wild beast can represent the empire only in its nature, spirit, character, condition, and influence. He represents it in its idolatrous heathenism, in its immoralities, in its imperiousness, in its selfishness, in its ambitions, in its injustice, in its oppressions, and in its cruelties.

III. Since the wild beast from the sea is thus an *abstraction*, he cannot be either "wounded" or "die," or be "healed" (Rev. xiii. 3), or have a "mouth" (verse 5), except *figuratively*. The sea wild beast has not a *material body:* he is simply a *symbolical monster*, and must be so interpreted and understood.

IV. *The same symbolical character* belongs to several other *apparent personages* in the New Testament; namely, the lamb-dragon (Rev. xiii. 11), the harlot woman (xvii. 1), the man of sin (2 Thess. ii. 3), and Antichrist (1 John ii. 18, 22, iv. 3; 2 John 7).

V. As the sea wild beast is nothing but an abstraction, and cannot therefore be wounded *bodily*, the "sword" (xiii. 14) must be *a figurative* sword, and as such can be nothing else than "the sword of the Spirit, which is the word of God" (Eph. vi. 17), — his revelation by Jesus Christ.

3. And I saw one of his heads, as though slain unto death ; and yet the wound causing his death is healed, and so the whole earth greatly admires the wild beast, and follows after him.

One of his heads: the sea wild beast, like the dragon (xii. 15), has but *one* mouth (xiii. 2), and therefore but *one* head, — the seat of life. His other heads are mere emblems of multiform wisdom (Eccl. ii. 14).

As a representative abstraction, this wild beast can be wounded only *figuratively;* and, as his figurative wounding is in the seat of his intellect, this wounding must be the loss of a measure of his wisdom.

The wisdom of the sea wild beast is the wisdom of the *heathen* world, which is *religious* wisdom, because contrasted by St. Paul with Christian wisdom. "After that the world by wisdom knew not God, it pleased God, by the foolishness of preaching Christ crucified, to save them that believe" (1 Cor. i. 21).

Pagan Rome is wounded and weakened in its *idolatrous heathenism* by the preaching of the gospel of Jesus Christ.

The New-Testament history exhibits the depth of these wounds and the extent of this weakening.

The Church of England, in her Bible published A.D. 1611, predicts that the "blow will *not be healed*" (*Epistle Dedicatory*).

The prediction was inspired by faith in Christ, and is still repeated and cherished by the same inspired faith, sustaining this Church and all her children the wide world over in their opposition to the false Church of Rome.

As early as A.D. 57, a Christian church is firmly established in the city of Rome itself; for St. Paul wrote his Epistle to the Romans to this church.

Afterwards St. Paul "dwelt two whole years in his own hired house," in the city of Rome, "and received all that came in unto him, preaching the kingdom of God, and teaching those things which concern the Lord Jesus Christ, with all confidence, no man forbidding him" (Acts xxviii. 30, 31).

So great is the blessing of God upon St. Paul's preaching, that he is able to make these remarkable records in his Epistle to the Philippians, written from his prison in Rome:—

"I would ye should understand, brethren, that the things which happened unto me have fallen out rather *unto the furtherance* of the gospel; so that my bonds in Christ are manifest *in all the palace*, and in all other places; and many of the brethren in the Lord, waxing confident in my bonds, are much more bold to speak the word without fear" (Phil. i. 12-14).

"All the saints salute you, chiefly they that are of *Cæsar's household*" (iv. 22).

At still a later date, the ministry of St. Paul in the city of Rome continues to be greatly successful. "In my gospel I suffer trouble, as an evil doer, but *the word of God is not bound*" (2 Tim. ii. 9).

Previous to his imprisonment in the city of Rome, and to the wonderful success of his preaching in the palace of the emperor, he had, to use his own account of his extensive travels in the Roman empire, "fully preached the gospel from Jerusalem round about unto Illyricum" (Rom. xv. 19), a thousand miles farther west than the "holy city."

The last time St. Paul visited Jerusalem, he found there *myriads* of Christian Jews (Acts xxi. 20).

Before his death St. Paul sent epistles, not only to the church in Rome, but also to the churches in Corinth, Galatia, Ephesus, Philippi, Colosse, and Thessalonica.

St. Peter addresses his epistles to Jewish Christians "in Pontus, Galatia, Cappadocia, Asia, and Bithynia" (1 Pet. i. 1).

"So mightily grew the word of God" throughout the Roman empire, before the death of St. Paul, A.D. 65, "and prevailed" (Acts xix. 20).

The general prevalence of the gospel in the Roman empire is a spiritual wound in the heathenism of the wild beast from the bottomless pit, so deep and vital that though for a time cicatrized and seemingly healed, the sword-stroke will yet prove fatal. The heathenism still pervading the Church of Rome is sure to die and disappear.

As though slain: the Greek particle we translate "as though," makes the participle "slain" *figurative*.

Proofs of this effect of the particle upon the participle: —

"*As dying*, and, behold, we live" (2 Cor. vi. 9).

"Remember the prisoners, *as bound with* them" (Heb. xiii. 3).

As an abstraction, the wild beast from the bottomless pit can be slain only *figuratively*. We now see that New-Testament usage allows the participle "slain" to be used in a figurative sense.

The word "slain" does not conflict with the figurative explanations we give of this verse.

Unto death: this expression occurs also in Matt. x. 21; Luke xxii. 33; Rom. vi. 16, vii. 10; 2 Cor. ii. 16, iv. 11. The slightest inspection of these places will satisfy us that the expression "unto death" means unto *utter and absolute death*.

The wild beast from the bottomless pit can die only *figuratively*. His figurative death is the utter extirpation from the Roman empire of idolatrous heathenism and its inevitable accompaniments.

Is healed: the wild beast from the bottomless pit is wounded by the general prevalence of the gospel of Jesus Christ in the pagan Roman empire. He is healed by the suppression of the gospel of Christ, and by the restoration of the worship of idols by the authority of the Roman emperors.

St. Paul, and all the apostles of our Lord save St. John, are victims to the bloody persecutions which assail and afflict the early Christian Church.

The healing, however, of the wild beast representing the Pagan empire, is neither thorough nor permanent.

1. It is not thorough.

Christianity is not totally suppressed: waters cannot drown it; fires cannot consume it; magisterial enactments and executions cannot annihilate it.

2. It is not permanent.

The worship of idols gradually ceases. Heathen temples become Christian churches. Paganism no longer has in Western Asia and in Europe an external life.

The spirit of the old heathenism still survives in the imperialism, the assumed infallibility, the claims to universal dominion, which characterize the Church of Rome, and the civil governments which inherit and adopt her selfish and aggressive policy.

The past conflicts between the gospel of Christ and the wild beast from the bottomless pit are most instructive, most admonitory, and, in their lessons, most obligatory and most encouraging.

The first, the early, and the subsequent victories of the Christian Church were won by two outward instrumentalities, made successful by the accompanying power of the Holy Ghost: (*a*) *the preaching of Christ crucified, and* (*b*) *practical Christian love*.

When the clergy became philosophers and rhetoricians, when they quarrelled with each other, and when externalism took the place of love of Christ and love of souls, the lamb-dragon rises out of the earth, and the harlot woman rides queen on the scarlet wild beast.

The ambitious, contentious, worldly, and degenerate clergy are often the real "men of sin;" the actual "antichrists;" the associates of the dragon in summoning ravaging wild beasts from the sea and the earth; the adopting fathers of the spiritual harlot; the æsthetic brokers who exchange the pure and life-giving gospel of Christ for absorbing and deadening formalism. And yet the gospel itself is *not dead*. It is now, as always, the power of God unto salvation. Christ is now present with his Church, as ever of old. No more now than at the beginning, does God give to Christ and his people the Spirit *by measure* (John iii. 34).

The Church of to-day ought to be, and can be again, a Church inflicting deadly and killing wounds on all Satanic wild beasts, on all apostatizing churches, on all forms of heathenism, on all modern infidelity and prevalent sin, and make herself the victorious, conquering, and renovating "arm of the Lord" in the whole world.

The first conquests of the gospel can now be repeated by the resumption of its first instrumentalities appointed by Christ himself: "Preach the word" (2 Tim. iv. 2); "Love the brotherhood" (1 Pet. ii. 17); "Love thy neighbor as thyself" (Gal. v. 14); "Love thine enemies" (Matt. v. 44). Christ's truth will overcome human error. Love will conquer hatred. Holy example will purify viciousness of life.

The whole world greatly admires: in xi. 10, "they that dwell on the earth," the ungodly world, rejoice and make merry, because the two witnesses are dead. Here, in this verse 3, the whole ungodly world, in their joy that the gospel is suppressed, and that heathenism is restored, greatly admires the wild beast, because he is the author of the change which inspires their joy and swells their merriment.

4. And they worship the dragon, because he gives the authority to the wild beast; and so they worship the wild beast, saying, Who is like the wild beast? and who can war with him?

The revived Roman empire, though gradually becoming nominally Christian, continues essentially Pagan in its spirit and policy.

Who is like: this question is rhetorical for this denial: There is no one like the wild beast; he is incomparable.

Who can: rhetorical question equalling this negation: No one is able to war with the wild beast; he is invincible.

5. And there is given him a mouth speaking impious words, even blasphemies. Also there is given him authority to do his work, forty-two months.

Is given him: by the dragon, verse 2, last clause.
Impious words: Dan. vii. 8, 20; Ps. xii. 3.
Blasphemies: 2 Thess. ii. 4.
Authority: by God. The context demands this sense.
To do his work: this sense of "do" allowed by ii. 5. Kind of work given, Dan. viii. 24, " to destroy."
Forty-two months: three years and a half.

With the Hebrews, seven years were, in reference to the duration of slavery, a complete period (Exod. xxi. 2). The hurtful work of the sea-beast will last only the half of such a period. See xi. 2, 3.

6. And so he opens his mouth for blasphemy against God; namely, to blaspheme his name and his tabernacle, even the dwellers in heaven.

Opens his mouth: begins to speak, Dan. x. 16; Matt. v. 2; Acts viii. 35.
For blasphemy: the purpose for which he speaks.
Against God: the Supreme God, the Father of our Lord Jesus Christ.
To blaspheme: the objects following.

(*a*) **His name**: God himself in all his attributes and relations (Exod. ix. 16; Luke xi. 2); a deadly sin (Lev. xxiv. 16).

(*b*) **His tabernacle**: his Church (xv. 5, xxi. 3).

Even: the tabernacle, the Church, is defined by the phrase introduced by "even."

In heaven: because attributive, and thus emphatic, is identical with "heavenly places" (Eph. i. 3, ii. 6), which are spiritual blessings *in Christ* (Eph. i. 3); "heaven" in a figurative sense (Rev. xi. 12).

Dwell: to dwell in heavenly places, is, then, to dwell in spiritual blessings *in Christ*. To dwell in Christ, is to dwell in God, and for God to dwell in us (1 John iv. 16).

As a definition, then, of "tabernacle," the phrase "dwellers in heaven" discloses the *character* of the tabernacle, the Church. It is the *spiritual* Church. This the sea-beast "blasphemes," misrepresents, hates, opposes, and injures.

7. Also authority is given him over every tribe and nation, and tongue and people.

Is given: by the dragon.
Tribe: community of common *blood*.
Nation: community of common *name*.
Tongue: community of common *speech*.
People: community of common *customs*.

Universal sovereignty was the *aspiration* of the Pagan Roman empire.

Universal dominion is the audacious *claim* of the present Church of Rome.

8. And so all that dwell upon the earth will worship him, of whom not one name is written in the Lamb's book of life, who was slain from the foundation of the world.

Worship him: the mongrel wild beast (verse 1) which represents the *Pagan* Roman empire.

The emperors of *Pagan* Rome were addressed as gods, and were worshipped as gods.

This proof is furnished by an inscription in Greek, found at Assos, A.D. 1881, containing a decree of the town of Assos, passed on the accession of the Emperor Caligula, A.D. 37.

The following is from the vote of the people: —

"Every city and every nation is eager to behold the face of the god" (namely, Caligula).

The following is from the oath of allegiance to Caligula, taken by the people of Assos, same date, A.D. 37: —

"We swear by the Saviour and God, Cæsar Augustus, that we will be faithful to Gaius Cæsar Augustus" (that is, to Caligula).

(*Paper of the Archæological Institute of America*, pp. 133-135, Boston, 1882. SUETONIUS, *Caligula*, 22, etc.)

Name: for person (Acts i. 15); distributive singular.

Book of life: book giving eternal life (Phil. iv. 3).

Who was slain: as a sacrifice for sin. "Thou wast *slain*, and hast *redeemed us to God by thy blood*" (Rev. v. 9).

From the foundation of the world: this phrase belongs not to "written," but to "who was slain."

The connection of "from the foundation of the world" is immovably established by the following unchangeable and authoritative usages.

Usage is the law and rule of speech. — HORACE, *Art of Poetry*, 72.

1. A prepositional clause ("*from* the foundation of the world" is a prepositional clause) belongs to the *nearest* participle, and not to the remote verb.

Examples. — (*a*) "I will utter things kept secret from the foundation of the world" (Matt. xiii. 35).

In this passage, "will utter" is the verb, "kept secret" is the participle, "*from* the foundation of the world" is the prepositional clause.

Since "will utter" predicts *future* action, and "from the foundation of the world" denotes *past* time, the verb and the participial clause cannot be connected until the distinction between *future* and *past* ceases. The *only possible* connection the prepositional clause "from the foundation of the world" (Matt. xiii. 35) can have is with the participle "kept secret."

(*b*) "The blood shed from the foundation of the world may be required of this generation" (Luke xi. 50).

In this verse, "shed" is the participle; "*from* the foundation of the world" is the prepositional clause; "required" is the verb.

The prepositional clause and the verb cannot be connected, for this invincible reason: —

Their *times* are different. The time of the prepositional clause is *past;* the time of the verb is *present.* Past and present time cannot be united.

The usage, thus most firmly established by the two examples just given, connects, in Rev. xiii. 8, "from the foundation of the world," *not* with the remote verb "written," but *alone* and *inseparably* with the *adjacent* participle "slain."

Rev. xvii. 8 does not destroy this usage, but strongly confirms it.

The words of xvii. 8 differ *essentially* from the words of xiii. 8. This essential difference is shown most clearly by placing the two passages by the side of each other. "Of whom not one name is written in the book of life of the Lamb who was slain from the foundation of the world" (Rev. xiii. 8). "Whose names were not written in the book of life from the foundation of the world" (xvii. 8).

This, then, is the essential difference between the two passages: Rev. xiii. 8 has the words, "of the Lamb who was slain;" Rev. xvii. 8 has not these words. The passages are, then, not identical. Rev. xvii. 8 cannot explain Rev. xiii. 8. It is both irrelevant and useless to refer to Rev. xvii. 8 as an illustration and interpretation of Rev. xiii. 8. Rev. xiii. 8 can be truly explained only by the words and usages it actually contains.

2. The expression "who was slain" is the equivalent of a relative sentence.

The Vulgate, and the Latin Fuldensis Codex, *qui occisus est*, as well as the Greek, regard the expression as a relative sentence.

But the phrase in Rev. xiii. 8, "from the foundation of the world," is by Matt. xiii. 35, and Luke xi. 50, made, as we have already seen, *an inseparable part of this relative sentence*. No power on earth can detach the phrase from the relative sentence. This relative sentence cannot be attached to "written." The relative sentence has no *relation* to this verb "written." As a *relative* sentence, all the *relation* "who was slain" can possibly have is to "the Lamb." So long as "who was slain" is a relative sentence, — and it will be forever, — it will belong to "the Lamb," and not to "written." "Who was slain from the foundation of the world," will always remain the same sentence it is at present. The assertions of all Christendom cannot annihilate the steel welding St. Matthew, St. Luke, and St. John create between the prepositional clause "from the foundation of the world," and the relative sentence "who was slain." The conjunction is divinely constructed, and eternal.

The connection we have just exhibited is also established by St. Peter.

"Ye were not redeemed with corruptible things, but with the precious blood of Christ, who verily was fore-ordained before the foundation of the world" (1 Pet. i. 18–20).

Because "fore-ordained," Christ was in God's purpose "slain before the foundation of the world."

The animal sacrifices which God appointed from the beginning of the human race, are closely connected with this promise, "The seed of the woman shall bruise the serpent's head" (Gen. iii. 15).

The animal which Abel sacrificed took away his sin, but not by its own virtue.

"The blood of bulls and of goats cannot take away sin" (Heb. x. 4).

The animal sacrifice offered by Abel must have *represented* "the seed of the woman," and derived all its efficacy to remove sin from the *represented seed*, who is thus "the Lamb who was slain *from the foundation of the world*" (Rev. xiii. 8).

9. If any man have an ear, let him hear.

Also Rev. ii. 7, 11, 17, 29; iii. 6, 13, 22.
In substance, our Lord's words (Mark iv. 23).
This call summons attention to the words *following* as most significant.

10. He that leadeth into captivity shall go into captivity: he that killeth with the sword must be killed with the sword. Here is the patience and the faith of the saints.

The persecutors of the Church will themselves be destroyed. The language is the repetition and intensification of our Lord's words, "They that take the sword shall perish with the sword" (Matt. xxvi. 52; see Jer. xv. 2, xliii. 11).

These predictions are here uttered to encourage his people to perseverance and faith.

Leadeth captivity: leadeth captives. Abstract for concrete. Sense of the first clause of the verse: Captors shall become captives.

Sense of the second clause: The victor who shall with his deadly sword so strike through the bodies of his enemies in fight as not to leave even one alive, shall yet be himself killed outright by the sword.

Sense of the whole verse: God shall cause his Church, though captured and killed, to triumph over all opposition.

Here is the patience and the faith of the saints: by the truths and promises just uttered by God, the endurance and the faith of his people survive all assaults (xiv. 12).

THE APPEARANCE OF THE LAMB-DRAGON (Verses 11-18).

A more subtle enemy than the sea-beast. The apt symbol of *Papal* Rome; outwardly a lamb, inwardly a dragon. "There shall arise *false* Christs, and *false* prophets, and shall show great signs and wonders, and shall deceive many. Behold, I have told you before" (Matt. xxiv. 11, 24, 25).

11. Also I saw another wild beast coming up out of the earth; and he was having two horns like the horns of a lamb; and yet he was speaking like a dragon.

Another: the third monster afflicting the true Church. The dragon is the first (xii. 3). The sea-beast is the second (xiii. 1). Three is a full number. A fourth monster will not appear. The third is the last of the desolating trio.

Out of the earth: the first wild beast (verse 1) comes apparently from the sea, but really from the bottomless pit. A second wild beast (verse 11) comes from the earth. "The earth" is here a term for this wicked world of mankind. "He that is *of the earth* is earthly," is sinful (John iii. 31).

Papal Rome in its worldly spirit and outward form has its origin in Pagan Rome. The lamb-dragon represents the succession of the Roman hierarchy. The woman in purple and scarlet (xvii. 3) represents the Church of Rome in her apostasy from Christ.

The horns of a lamb: the horns of a lamb are short and harmless, unlike the strong and dangerous horns of the bull (Exod. xxi. 29) and of the first wild beast (xiii. 1).

Was speaking: the Greek tense, the imperfect, was speaking, describes his habitual speech. The two witnesses speak for Christ. The lamb-dragon speaks for Satan.

Like a dragon: the dragon is "the Devil and Satan, which *deceiveth* the whole world" (xii. 9). "The Devil is a liar" (John viii. 44). The dragon's speech, and the speech of his imitator the lamb-dragon, is therefore deceitful, lying, false. The lamb-dragon is identical with the "*false* prophet" (xvi. 13, xix. 20, xx. 10).

The lamb-dragon "*deceiveth* them that dwell on the earth" (verse 14).

False speech is false doctrine. "Beware of *false prophets* which come to you in *sheep's clothing*, but inwardly they are ravening wolves" (Matt. vii. 15).

Historical verifications of the false doctrines of the Church of Rome are, —

1. The creed of Pope Pius IV., A.D. 1564.
2. Jesuitism, sixteenth century.
3. The dogma of the immaculate conception of the Virgin Mary, A.D. 1854.
4. The dogma of the Pope's infallibility, A.D. 1870.

12. And he executes all the authority of the first wild beast before him, and makes the earth, even the dwellers in it, to worship the first wild beast, whose death-wound was healed.

Executes: the lamb-dragon performs all the acts authorized by the wild-beast from the bottomless pit. Papal Rome, represented by the lamb-dragon, is, as an organization, the creation, the repetition, the successor, of Pagan Rome.

The succession is too obvious to be gainsaid.

1. The Pope succeeds the Roman emperor.

2. The present Roman *Curia*, the councillors of the Pope, succeeds the Roman senators who formed the council of state for the Roman emperor.

3. The Roman cardinals, the representatives of the Pope in foreign countries, are the successors of the proconsuls under the Roman empire.

Authority: when Satan tempted our Lord, the tempter claimed authority over "all the kingdoms of the world." Our Lord himself calls Satan "the prince of this world" (John xii. 31), because he inspires and controls wicked men.

A portion of the authority the dragon claims, he intrusts to the wild beast from the bottomless pit (Rev. xiii. 2). In his turn, the wild beast from the bottomless pit authorizes the wild beast from the earth to act in his place.

The wild beast from the bottomless pit represents the civil and religious power of Pagan Rome. This twofold power is embodied in Papal Rome.

The present Pope (Leo XIII.) is not satisfied with the possession of ecclesiastical power. He is at the present time exciting such governments in Europe as he can influence, to demand of all the powers the restoration of his civil power. He thus re-asserts the old Papal usurpation that Popery has authority over all civil governments.

Even: explanatory.

Healed: see verse 3.

13. And he doeth great signs, even to make fire come down from heaven to the earth in the sight of men.

Great signs: Matt. xxiv. 24; 2 Thess. ii. 9. The Church of Rome claims the power of working miracles (ARCHBISHOP WHATELY, *Errors of Romanism*).

In 2 Thess. ii. 9, the signs are characterized as false, "lying wonders." The miracles wrought by the lamb-dragon, the symbol of Papal Rome, are mere pretences.

Doeth: "Nothing is more common than to speak of professed jugglers as *doing* what they *pretend* or appear to do." — REV. DR. HUGH FARMER (the pupil of Dr. Philip Doddridge).

Exod. vii. 11, 22, viii. 7, 18, are instances which confirm Dr. Farmer's assertion.

Fire: reference to Elijah, who called fire from heaven,—
(1) To vindicate revealed truth (1 Kings xviii. 36–39).
(2) To punish God's enemies.
(a) The Church of Rome professes to work miracles to justify her exclusive claims.
(b) The Church of Rome *annually* (every Maunday Thursday) invokes God's vengeance on all heretics. "Excommunicamus et anathematizamus omnes hereticos."— PERCEVAL, *Roman Schism*, p. xxxvii.

14. And so he deceiveth the dwellers upon the earth by reason of the signs which it is permitted him to do to please the wild beast, because saying to the dwellers upon the earth to make an image for the worship of the wild beast, which has the wound of the sword, and yet lives.

And so: deception follows the exhibition of pretended miracles.
Deceives: this verb proves that the miracles (signs) are deceptions, impositions, and frauds.
Permitted: by God.
Because saying: the command to make an image to the sea-beast pleased him. The adoption of Pagan worship by Papal Rome was most agreeable to the Pagan emperors, and to the ignorant masses of people.
An image for the worship of the wild beast: this is the expression, verse 15: "King Nebuchadnezzar required the image he made to be worshipped" (Dan. iii. 5).
Even Christians were compelled to worship the image of the Roman emperor.
The testimony of Pliny establishes this fact: "Cum præeunte me deos appellarent, et *imagini tuæ*, quam propter hoc jusseram cum simulacris nummum afferri, thure ac vino *supplicarent*, preterea maledicerent Christo, quorum nihil cogi posse dicuntur, qui sunt revera Christiani, dimittendos esse putavi" (PLINY's *Letter to Trajan*, Ep. x. 97).
Adoratio pontificis, prescribed by the *Cæremoniale Romanum*, is now performed after each papal election. The adoration was performed to Pope Pius IX., Wednesday, June 17, 1846.
Sword: the thrust of the sword is mortal (Heb. iv. 12).
Lives: the present tense "has" imparts the same time to "lives" (verse 3). Pagan Rome lives for the present in Papal Rome. But the sword-thrust in the head of the first wild beast will yet cause his utter and lasting death. Christian civilization will be the destruction

of Roman imperialism, both in all churches and in all civil governments. The spirit of Pagan Rome is the spirit of selfishness, is the spirit of self-indulgence, is the spirit of self-aggrandizement, is the war-spirit, which now afflict both rulers and people, and retard and hinder the extension of the gospel of Christ.

15. Also it is permitted to give breath to it, the image of the wild beast, that the image of the wild beast may even speak, and cause that whoever shall not worship the image of the wild beast may be killed.

Permitted: by God. The Greek does not warrant the English version, "he had power."

Breath: the Greek noun sometimes has this sense: "Thou takest away their *breath*" (Ps. civ. 29).

The superstition which can worship an image will easily regard it as alive and breathing. This strong denial, "There is nó *breath* in the mouths of idols" (Ps. cxxxv. 17), may oppose the actual belief of "the heathen," that their idols did breathe.

To give breath to the image of the wild beast, is a specification of the deception ("deceives," verse 14). St. John does not assert the reality of the breath in the image.

Speak: an image which is assumed to breathe can also be assumed to speak. The Psalmist, in denying speech to idols, seems to imply that their worshippers claimed for them the power of uttering words. "They *speak* not" (Ps. cxxxv. 16).

The pretended life and speech of Roman *Madonnas* are fulfilments of the predictions in this verse.[1]

Killed: the Lateran Council expressly requires the death of heretics by the hands of the civil power. "Monearetur sœculares potestates, quod de terris suæ jurisdictioni subjectis *universos hæreticos* EXTERMINARE" (Lateran IV., A.D. 1215; Canon III.[2] PERCEVAL, *Roman Schism*, pp. 134, 135.)

The injuries contemplated by the Lateran Council are both material and spiritual, and are, contrary to the law of Christ, "Love one another" (John xv. 12), *inflicted by Christians upon other Christians*.

Material Inquiries.

Of injuries *material*, inflicted by Christians upon other Christians, there are no examples in history *until the mediæval period of the Christian Church.*

---

[1] Watson, Theological Institutes, I. 163, etc.
[2] Called Lateran, because held in the Church of St. John Lateran in Rome.

The Inquisition. — Previous to the twelfth century (xiii. 15) Christians had various controversies, but their weapons were always verbal. Not till the thirteenth century was there an organized and established *Christian* system of imprisonment, torture, and death for heretics. This system was *the Inquisition*, which was created by the Church of Rome, and which continued its deadly work for at least five centuries.

1. By order of the Inquisition in the thirteenth century, the whole race of the Albigenses in Languedoc and Toulouse, France, were hunted by fire and sword: neither sex, age, nor condition was spared. The towns became heaps of burning ruins, and the country a wilderness.

In modern France, the spirit of the wild beast seeking the bodily death of the members of Christ's Church still survives.

"The Anti-Clerical League" of Paris, in its annual report, 1884, maintains an *exterminatory* intolerance for all *Christian* ideas and persons, and asserts the power of *persecution even unto death.* — *Churchman*, Sept. 6, 1884: "Prospects of Reform in the French Church."

2. The Waldenses in Dauphine and Piedmont, between France and Italy, were, in 1560, conquered by a Spanish and French army instigated by Pope Paul IV. Many prisoners were buried alive, and women and children ruthlessly slaughtered.

The poet Milton has given disgraceful immortality to this inhuman carnage perpetrated by the Church of Rome: —

> "Avenge, O Lord, thy slaughtered saints, whose bones
> Lie scattered on the Alpine mountains cold;
> Even them who kept thy truth so pure of old,
> When all our fathers worshipped stocks and stones,
> Forget not: in thy book record their groans,
> Who were thy sheep, and in their ancient fold
> Slain by bloody Piedmontese, that rolled
> Mother with infant down the rocks. Their moans
> The vales redoubled to the hills, and they
> To heaven. Their martyred blood and ashes sow
> O'er all the Italian fields, where still doth sway
> The triple tyrant; that from these may grow
> A hundred-fold, who, having learned thy way,
> Early may fly the Babylonian woe.
> (JOHN MILTON, A.D. 1674: *Sonnet xiii.*)

3. Massacre of St. Bartholomew, Sunday, Aug. 24, 1572.

Thousands of Huguenots (French Protestants) were on that day murdered in France.

The reigning Pope, Gregory XIII., commemorated and justified the horrid massacre by striking a medal, bearing on the obverse the face of the Pope, and this inscription: "GREGORY XIII.; PONTIFEX MAXIMUS. *Anno primo.*" On the reverse, the destroying angel, bearing in her left hand a cross, in her right a sword; before her are flying and prostrate Huguenots of both sexes and various ages; and this inscription: "UGONOTTORUM STRAGES, 1572." ("The slaughter of the Huguenots.")

This medal is reproduced in fac-simile under the auspices of The American Association of Numismatists, 1877, Lagrange, Ky.

4. During the short reign of Queen Mary of England, A.D. 1553-1558, Bishops Ridley, Latimer, and Cranmer were burned at the stake, and nearly *three hundred* other persons.

Spiritual Injuries by the Church of Rome.

1. Decrees of the Council of Trent, 1545–1563.
2. Creed of Pius IV., 1564.
3. Jesuitism, sixteenth century, by which large numbers of Protestants were recovered to Romanism.
4. Dogma of immaculate conception, 1854.
5. Dogma of papal infallibility, 1870.

Thus the history of the Church of Rome furnishes most infamous fulfilments of the symbolical prophecies of Rev. xiii. 15. No other Church furnishes such coincidences between prophecy and history. The fact demonstrates the wild beast from the earth as the symbol of this persecuting and erroneous Church.

The Lamb-dragon's Slave-marks (Verses 16, 17).

16. Also he causeth all, both small and great, rich and poor, free and bond, to receive a mark on their right hand, or on their forehead.

Mark: *eight* times in Revelation (xiii. 16, 17, xiv. 9, 11, xv. 2, xvi. 2, xix. 20, xx. 4); in every instance imposed by the *lamb-dragon.*

Mark: brand burned in.

"These enrolled to be *branded* even *by fire* into the body with the ivy-leaf mark of Bacchus" (3 Macc. ii. 29).

Right hand: the hand for work (Judg. v. 26; Ps. cxxxvii. 5).

"The marks of soldiers are in their hands" (ÆLIAN, third century).

Forehead: "Slaves are inscribed with the mark of their lord, and soldiers are inscribed with the mark of their leader" (ST. AMBROSE, fourth century).

"On the forehead for profession, in the hand for work" (St. Augustine, fifth century).

Ptolemy Philopater, second century, compelled the Jews in Alexandria to be enrolled in his army, and to be branded with a hot iron.

Philo Judæus, first century, mentions idolaters who confessed their idolatry by branding its mark on their bodies with a hot iron.

The infliction of marks by the lamb-dragon, upon all classes of men, is both a symbol and a prophecy of the universal dominion the Papacy claims and asserts. The Papacy would even now enforce these claims, were it not for the want of civil power.

The acknowledged records of the Church of Rome itself are undeniable proofs of these claims and assertions.

We copy from these records of history:—

1. "The Roman pontiff alone is rightly called universal."
2. "All princes should kiss his feet."
3. "He may dethrone emperors."
4. "The Pope is able to release subjects from their allegiance to evil men."

(Dictates of Pope Gregory VII., Hildebrand, eleventh century.)—Wordsworth, *Rev.*, p. 225.

"Diffinimus sanctam Apostolicam Sedem, et Romanum pontificam, in universam orbem terrere primatum" (Council of Florence, A.D. 1438).—Perceval, *Roman Schism*, p. 153.

17. And that no one may buy or sell, save he that has the mark; namely, the name of the wild beast, or the number of his name.

Buy or sell: transact business (Jas. iv. 13).

The mark: was the name of the lamb-dragon. The name of the popedom. The name of each pope in the succession of popes which the lamb-dragon represents.

Papal Rome adopted these interdicts from Pagan Rome:—

"Non illis emendi quidquam, aut vendendi copia, nec ipsam haurire aquam dabatur licentia, antequam sacrificerent detestandis idolis. (Interdict of the Roman Emperor Diocletian, fourth century.)—Alford, iv. part ii. p. 678.

The number of his name: St. John refers to an actual practice. Numerical values were given to the letters of the name. Mercury or Thoth was invoked under the name of 1218; Jupiter, under the name of 717; the sun, under the name of 608 (*Dictionary of Bible*, "Antichrist," p. 111).

Here several questions arise.

1. What was this number?

The reference given above proves that the number was the *number of the letters* in the name, to each of which a numerical value was given.

Tharion, the Greek noun for wild beast, has in Greek the numerical value of only *sixty-nine*.

2. Is the *number* of the wild beast's name to be understood *symbolically*, or *literally?*

As the Apocalypse is throughout a book of symbols, the literal number *sixty-nine* is not intended. Were the literal sense admissible, *sixty-nine* is not *six hundred and sixty-six* (verse 18). When, therefore, St. John, in verse 18, says, "the number of the beast is six hundred threescore and six," he cannot possibly mean the literal number.

3. Since the number of the wild beast is not literal, the number must be *symbolical*. But in what sense? Are the *letters* of the wild beast's name symbols? or is *the action* of burning, indicated by the use made of the letters, the symbol? The letters composing the names were, when heated red-hot, *burned* into the quivering flesh of the slave. *The burning*, and not the letters composing the name, is the symbol of the slavery.

The language itself of verse 17 demands this sense for the number of the wild beast. The symbolism of the verse consists of two parts, "the name, and the *number* of the name;" that is, the numerical values of the name as a *different* brand. *The repetition* of the symbols intensifies the symbolism. St. John, by repeating the symbols in verse 17, magnifies the arbitrariness and severity of the wild beast as a tyrannical despot.

18. Here is The Wisdom [Christ]. Let him, who has the mind of revelation, determine the number [of the years] of the wild beast, for the number is a man's number. And so his number is *six hundred and sixty-six*.

Here: our Lord by "here" (Matt. xii. 6, 41, 42, xxiv. 23) calls attention to *himself*. St. John may, therefore (Rev. xiii. 18), repeat Christ's manner of designating personality.

The Wisdom: the article "The" must here be noticed, and allowed its full force. Perhaps this article will disclose the hidden meaning of wisdom (Rev. xiii. 18). Wisdom *with* the article "the" occurs in Bible Greek *only* in these *three* places: Matt. xi. 19, Luke vii. 35, and Rev. xiii. 18. In Matt. xi. 19, Luke vii. 35, our Lord appropriates this title, The Wisdom, *to himself*. The Wisdom, for The Wise One, that is, God; abstract for concrete.

This is our Lord's own usage.

Examples. — "I am the way," the Leader; and "the truth," the True One; and "the life," the Living One (John xiv. 6).

"I came into the world, that I should bear witness to *the truth*," the true God [in opposition to idols]. "Every one that is *of the truth*" ("of *God*," John viii. 47) "heareth my voice" (xviii. 37).

"Right hand of *the power*," the Powerful One (Matt. xxvi. 64).

Since it is thus Christ's own usage to use the abstract for the concrete, and especially since he (Matt. xi. 19; Luke vii. 35) applies "*The Wisdom*" *to himself*, "The Wisdom" (Rev. xiii. 18), the only other place in Bible Greek (besides Matt. xi. 19, and Luke vii. 35, where our Lord decides "The Wisdom" means himself) where "The Wisdom" occurs, it is proved (since Matt. xi. 19 and Luke vii. 35 impart their meaning to Rev. xiii. 18) that "The Wisdom" (Rev. xiii. 18) is no other than *Christ himself*. The lamb-dragon, the deceiver (Rev. xiii. 14), is the author of false dogmas in the Church. Most fitting is it for Christ, who is The Wisdom, the wise God, to expose the deceits of the cunning deceiver, and decide the number of his years.

He who has the mind: this expression may also be a title of Christ. The Septuagint of Isa. xl. 13 has this phrase, *the mind of the Lord*. St. Paul (Rom. xi. 34 ; 1 Cor. ii. 16) repeats these words in his Christian arguments ; while in the second passage (1 Cor. ii. 16), he makes "the mind of the Lord" and "the mind *of Christ*" *identical*.

"The mind of Christ" is the mind *belonging* to Christ. But the mind *belonging* to Christ is the mind Christ "has" (Rev. xiii. 18).

Thus Christ is proved by New-Testament usage, to be He who has the mind; and the expression becomes one of his own titles.

But when Isaiah asks, "Who knows the mind of the Lord?" (Isa. xl. 13), the prophet regards the Lord as a *Revelator* (see verse 14). In this way we discover the *character* of the mind of Christ (Rev. xiii. 18). His mind is a *revealing* mind. He has the *revealing* mind.

St. John in the Book of Revelation itself describes Christ as this very possessor of the *power of revelation*.

"The Son of God hath his *eyes like unto a flame of fire*" (ii. 18). "He *hath the seven* Spirits of God" (iii. 1).

The expression, "He that hath the mind" (Rev. xiii. 18), is in meaning the intensified repetition of the expression, "If any man have an ear" (xiii. 9); that is, have a mind to understand.

The identity of verse 9 and verse 18 (Rev. xiii.) is not merely in form, but also in subject and purpose.

In verse 8, the first wild beast ("him") is sovereign conqueror, as *civil* ruler.

In verse 17, the lamb-dragon, as *religious* ruler, is in like manner universal despot.

Verses 9 and 10 predict for the wild beast coming out of the sea defeat and punishment. This prediction is for the encouragement of the faith and endurance of the saints.

Verse 18 contains, as we shall be able to prove, similar predictions of defeat and punishment of the lamb-dragon coming out of the earth.

The predictions in symbol (verse 18) have the same object as the previous predictions (verse 10); namely, to strengthen and render unconquerable the faith and patience of Christ's people, renewed in his holy image.

Let Christ decide the number [of the years] of the wild beast.

In attempting to justify this translation of a portion of the Greek of verse 18, we must first of all broadly distinguish the following expressions, which resemble each other, and, on account of their resemblance, are often confounded and taken to denote the same thing.

1. The *wild beast* (verse 17).
2. The *name* of the wild beast (verse 17).
3. The *number* of his name (verse 17).
4. The *number* of the wild beast (verse 18).

These four expressions are thus distinguished: —

(a) The wild beast is the lamb-dragon, distinguished, by coming from the earth, from the wild beast coming from the sea (verse 1).

(b) *The name* of the wild beast is lamb-dragon (verse 11).

(c) The number of his name is the *numerical value* given to the *letters* of his name.

(d) *The number* of the wild beast is the number of his years on earth.

The Number of the Wild Beast.

Of the nature and design of the symbolism of this language, Scripture usage furnishes most ample and conclusive proofs.

The same word has different meanings.

In xii. 16, the word "mouth" has two meanings.

In xiii. 10, the Greek word translated "captivity" has two meanings, — captivity and captive.

Since these Greek words (xii. 16, xiii. 10) have two meanings, *arithmos* (number, verses 17 and 18) may have two meanings, in case the context so permits.

The context certainly gives permission.

In verse 17, number is *numerical value.*

In verse 18, number is the number *of years.*

In verse 17, the wild beast uses numbering for *injustice.* In verse 18, Christ uses numbering for *justice.*

Proofs that Number is a Symbol of Destruction.

1. Proofs derived from the word itself.

(a) In Rev. vii. and xiv., numbers are symbols of *future condition.*

In these chapters, the future condition is *preservation*. The future condition may be the *opposite* of preservation. Number, as a symbol of *destruction*, is therefore, in Rev. xiii. 18, *possible*.

(*b*) Number, as a figurative word, is sometimes the equivalent of *fewness*. "Years of number," that is, few (Job xvi. 22).

(*c*) Numbering is designation to destruction; that is, *a sentence to destruction*. "I will *number* [*sentence*] you to the sword" (Isa. lxv. 12).

(*d*) Number sometimes means to *complete*, to *finish*. The prophet Daniel thus explains *Mene* in the divine inscription on the inner wall of Belshazzar's palace: "God hath *numbered* thy kingdom, and *finished* it" (Dan. v. 26). *Mene*, therefore, as a symbolical number, expresses a *finished numbering*. Thus Bible usage decides that *the number* of the wild beast may mean a *finishing* number, a number which *finishes* the career of the lamb-dragon. The number 666 will *finish* his kingdom and domination in this world.

(*e*) The word "number" is used, in the Bible, with *years*, to designate *a period of time*.

"The number *of his years*" (Job xxxvi. 26).
"The number *of the years*" (Dan. ix. 2).

The Book of Ecclesiasticus uses the word "number" in connection with a *definite* designation of years. "The *number* of a man's days at the most are *a hundred years*" (xviii. 9).

Bible usage, therefore, permits St. John to say definitely, "The number of the years of the wild beast are *six hundred and sixty-six*," and to designate by the language the destruction of the wild beast as determined and defined by Christ.

2. Proofs derived from the Greek verb *psephizo* (translated "count," English Version). In Bible Greek, this verb occurs but *twice*, here and Luke xiv. 28, "counteth." The verb is derived from *psephos*, a pebble, a vote. In classic Greek, the verb means not only "to count," "to reckon," but also "to vote," "to decide."

Meaning of the Greek expression, *Psephisto ton arithmon* (Rev. xiii. 18):—

This expression is not, either in its form or in its meaning, the same as either of these four Greek expressions:—

(*a*) "Take the number" (Num. iii. 40). That is, *count* the number.

(*b*) "Number the number" (2 Chron. ii. 17). That is, carefully number the number.

(*c*) "Know the number" (2 Sam. xxiv. 2; 1 Chron. xxi. 2). That is, know the *exact* number.

(*d*) "Understand the number" (Dan. ix. 2). That is, understand the *meaning* of the number.

Had St. John intended to give either of these four directions, (a) *take* (count) the number, (b) carefully number, (c) know the exact number, (d) understand the meaning of the number, he would have used either "take," "number," "know," or "understand." But in Rev. xiii. 18 *he uses neither:* he *rejects* each of these four verbs, and selects in their place the verb *psephizo.* By this rejection, and by this selection, St. John most plainly indicates, that by the Greek expression, *psephisato ton arithmon,* he does *not* mean either (a) count *the letters* in the name of the wild beast, or (b) carefully number them, or (c) know their exact number, or (d) understand their meaning. By his selection of *psephizo,* he not only *rejects* the four verbs, "take [count]," "number," "know," "understand," and their meanings, but also rejects from this Greek verb itself, *in Rev. xiii. 18, each and all of these meanings.* According to St. John's own decision, *psephizo* cannot, in Rev. xiii. 18, mean "count," cannot mean "number carefully," cannot mean "know exactly," cannot mean "understand the meaning."

(e) "The number of years" is, as we have seen, a Bible term for a definite period of time.

But, whenever a period of time is numbered in the Bible, the verb used to express the numbering is never *psephizo,* the verb in Rev. xiii. 18; but, on the contrary, is *without variation, in every instance,* either *arithmeo,* to *number,* or its compound with a preposition.

We subjoin all the places:—

Simple verb, Lev. xxiii. 16; Job xxxix. 2.

Compound, Lev. xv. 13, xxv. 8; Deut. xvi. 9.

It is thus a *Bible demonstration,* that *psephizo* (Rev. xiii. 18) does not mean merely "to number," but has an *additional* and *different* signification.

Nor is this the entire effect of St. John's *rejection* from *psephizo* the meanings of "take [count]," "number," "know," "understand." He by anticipation utterly and forever rejects from Rev. xiii. 18, all the explanations, prophecies, discussions, and controversies which have arisen during the subsequent centuries from the prevalent assumptions that this Greek verb may have its impossible sense in the passage, of either "take [count]," "number," "know," or "understand."

Since *psephisato* (Rev. xiii. 18) cannot mean "take [count]," cannot mean "number," cannot mean "know," cannot mean "understand," cannot mean *merely* "to number," we have yet left us the task of finding, if possible, the true and full meaning of the verb in this verse 18 of chapter xiii.

The Bible meaning of *psephizo:*—

Inasmuch as this verb occurs but twice in Bible Greek (Luke xiv.

28, and Rev. xiii. 18), the *only* Bible illumination remaining to enlighten our exegetical darkness is the noun *psephisma*, the only derivative this verb has. Since it is a Septuagint word, its authority is decisive and binding.

Psephisma is thus defined: "A decree of the people, binding upon all classes" (SMITH, *Dict. Antiq.*, p. 211 a.).

Thus defined, *psephisma* was, with the Greeks, a binding decree for a whole community.

In the Septuagint, this judicial word occurs five times, and in these *three* senses: —

1. In the Grecian sense, three times (2 Macc. x. 8, xii. 4, xv. 36), a decree binding the whole community.

2. A decree, *with the penalty of death*.

"There went out a decree [*psephisma*] to the neighboring cities of the heathen, by the suggestion of Ptolemee, against the Jews, that they should observe the same fashions, and be partakers of their sacrifices; and whoso would not conform themselves to the manners of the Gentiles *should be put to death*" (2 Macc. vi. 8, 9).

3. A decree *for the actual destruction of life*.

"Haman, the enemy of all the Jews, devised against the Jews to destroy them, and cast Pur, that is, the lot [*psephisma*, Sept.], *to consume them and to destroy them*" (Esth. ix. 24).

Thus, in 2 Macc. vi. 9, and Esth. ix. 24, *psephisma* means *a deadly decree*.

This deadly meaning *psephisma* derives from its verb, *psephizo*, which must, therefore, mean (Rev. xiii. 18) *to determine a deadly decree*.

Because *psephisato* (verse 18) must have this meaning, we are authorized by the usages of Bible Greek to translate the second portion of the verse in this form: —

"Let Christ, who has the revealing mind, determine the number of the wild beast. For it is a man's number."

The wild beast from the earth is the symbol of a *kingdom* (Dan. vii. 23). For this reason, this beast cannot be an *individual king*. The beast cannot symbolize *any one man whatever*, either king or emperor, either bishop or pope.

The consequence is most important. Man, in the phrase "man's number," cannot refer to the symbolizing wild beast, the lamb-dragon. The word "man" cannot refer to any civil officer or ecclesiastical ruler of Rome, either ancient or modern.

Meaning of the Phrase.

The meaning of "man's number" is determined by the phrase, ' man's measure" (Rev. xxi. 17), as it there means a measure *used* by man. Hence "man's number" can mean nothing else than a number *used* by man, used by mankind. The number is a human, common, *usual* number. The sense of "a man's number" cannot be a number *pointing out* a man. This is the only possible sense of "a man's number;" namely, a number, numerals every man uses and understands. And so his number is six hundred and sixty-six.

His: that is, his *appointed* number; appointed by Christ.

Six hundred and sixty-six: in Second Maccabees, there are various division of large numbers, which are indefinite, and which determine the character of the number six hundred and sixty-six.

Examples. — (*a*) A fourth. "Five and twenty thousand" (2 Macc. xii. 26).

(*b*) Half. Two hundred and forty (verse 9) [*about* half] five hundred and five thousand (verse 10).

(*c*) Three-fourths. Seven hundred and fifty (verse 17).

(*d*) Two-thirds. Six hundred (verse 29).

In the canonical books of the Bible, six hundred is the same *indefinite* two-thirds of a thousand. "*About* six hundred" (1 Sam. xxiii. 13); afterwards, the same body of men, who are thus only "*about* six hundred," are called *exactly* six hundred (xxvii. 2, xxx. 9).

These facts respecting the Bible use of numbers prove that "six hundred and sixty-six" (Rev. xiii. 18) is *two-thirds* of a thousand.

But as this number, a thousand, is *indefinite* ("*about* a thousand," Judg. ix. 49), its two-thirds, six hundred and sixty-six, is also *indefinite*.

The fact is decisive in the explanation of our present passage. Since *six hundred and sixty-six* is *indefinite*, it *cannot* designate *the numerical values of the letters* composing any man's name. The numerical value of such letters is *definite*. But six hundred and sixty-six (Rev. xiii. 18) is *indefinite*. An *indefinite* number cannot possibly define and denote a *definite* number. *Indefinite* six hundred and sixty-six cannot by any process be embodied in the *definite*. — (*Lateinos*. ALFORD, iv., part ii. p. 679. WORDSWORTH and WEBSTER and WILKINSON, on Rev. xiii. 18, *Bible Commentary on Rev.*, p. 697.)

All words, whether Latin, Greek, Hebrew, or some other tongue, are *definite* in the number of their letters. No definite word can match the *indefinite* six hundred and sixty-six. No defined casting can fit an *indefinite* mould.

The old attempts to explain Rev. xiii. 18 must be abandoned.

Why St. John regards *six hundred and sixty-six as two-thirds of a thousand:* —

In Zech. xiii. 8, an *integer* is divided into *three* parts, *two* of which are *cut off*.

St. John employs the triform enumeration of Zechariah to indicate that the number six hundred and sixty-six is itself a symbol of *excision*.

This symbolical excision of the lamb-dragon is most instructive, and also most animating to the faith and patience of Christ's true people. The existence, the domination, the oppression, of Popedom are *not perpetual*. Their period of six hundred and sixty-six, whatever of *actual* time these may be, *will surely come to an end.* Both the world of mankind and the Church of Christ *will outlive all popes.* The happy time will come when Popery will be known only as a usurpation and an affliction *of the past.* Christ alone will yet be universal Bishop, and the sole Head of his liberated and purified Church on earth. God, in his infinite mercies and unfailing love and power, hasten the advent of the long-desired and glorious day!

"The Lord of heaven and earth defend us from the tyranny and pride of the popes and prelates of Rome; that they never enter his vineyard again, but that they may be utterly confounded and put to flight in all parts of the world: and he of his great mercy so work in all men's hearts by the mighty power of the Holy Ghost, that the comfortable gospel of his Son Christ may be truly preached, truly received, and truly followed, in all places, to the beating-down of sin, death, the pope, the Devil, and all the kingdom of Antichrist, that like scattered and dispersed sheep, being at length gathered into one fold, we may in the end rest all together in the bosom of Abraham, Isaac, and Jacob, there to be partakers of eternal and everlasting life, through the merits and death of Jesus Christ our Saviour. Amen." — *Homilies.* Second part of sermon for Whitsunday. Article of Religion, xxxv.

The Spiritual Warfare of the Lamb-Dragon.

On several preceding pages, there are memorable instances of the *external* warfare of the lamb-dragon.

But we largely fail to estimate his power, if we regard the destructive warfare he incessantly wages as wholly external, or wholly in times gone by.

The lamb-dragon is a *deceiver* (Rev. xiii. 14). In order to detect his numerous deceptions, and by their detection measure his influence in the Church of Christ, and discover his character, we must first of all closely examine the words of Christ and his apostles, in which they either describe the existence in their own times of spiritual adversaries, or predict their advent in the future.

Our Lord and his first ministers invariably ascribe the prevalence of moral evil in this world to Satan and his subordinate demons.

Our Lord attributes his own temptations in the wilderness to the Devil.

"Get thee hence, Satan." "Then the Devil leaveth him" (Matt. iv. 10, 11).

"The Devil is a liar, and the father of it" (John viii. 44).

"Satan cometh immediately, and taketh away the word that was sown in their hearts" (Mark iv. 15).

"The enemy that sowed the tares is the Devil" (Matt. xiii. 39).

"Simon, Satan hath desired to have you" (Luke xxii. 31).

"Ye are of your father the Devil, and the lusts of your father ye will do" (John viii. 44).

When Christ commissions St. Paul to preach the gospel, it is for this purpose, "To turn the Gentiles from *the power of Satan* unto God" (Acts xxvi. 18).

The apostles of our Lord everywhere repeat his declarations respecting the hurtful influence of Satan upon the souls of men.

St. Paul thus addresses Elymas the sorcerer: "O full of all subtlety and all mischief, thou child of the Devil, thou enemy of all righteousness, wilt thou not cease to pervert the right ways of the Lord?" (Acts xiii. 10.)

St. Paul elsewhere utters the same alarming truths.

"Give not place to the Devil" (Eph. iv. 27).

"Be able to stand against the wiles of the Devil" (vi. 11).

"Lest he fall into the snare of the Devil" (1 Tim. iii. 7).

"Some have already turned aside unto Satan" (v. 15).

St. James is equally decided in his warning.

"Resist the Devil" (iv. 7).

The trumpet of St. Peter is even louder in its warning.

"Be sober, be vigilant; because your adversary the Devil, as a roaring lion, walketh about, seeking whom he may devour" (1 Pet. v. 8).

St. John is even more explicit.

"He that committeth sin is of the Devil" (1 John iii. 8).

The roaring lion does not walk about without seizing his prey of human souls. His ruin of Judas, one of the disciples our Lord himself chose to be his personal attendant, was the introduction to the ruin of many others who ranked themselves among the followers of Christ.

Through the dictation of Satan, heresiarchs and apostates start immediately into life, succeed each other in rapid succession, and perpetuate their perversions and errors to future periods.

The discovery and delineation of the several abettors of Satan pertain to the history of the Church of Christ. As spring-heads of poisonous streams, many of which are still running in desolating current, they are as records full of instruction and admonition.

We must not pass them by. Faithfulness to truth and to history demands their accurate recognition.

"There shall arise false Christs" (Matt. xxiv. 24).

The prediction seems from its improbability almost incredible. St. Paul, however, not only reiterates substantially the prediction, but so definitely explains it that we are obliged to recognize "the man of sin" (2 Thess. ii. 3), the false Christ, in the Roman Papacy. To no other historical body can these words of this apostle possibly apply: "There shall come a falling away first, and that man of sin be revealed, the son of perdition; who opposeth and exalteth himself above all that is called God, or that is worshipped; so that he as God sitteth in the temple of God, showing himself that he is God" (2 Thess. ii. 3, 4).

The translators of the Bible of King James I., A.D. 1611, refer 2 Thess. ii. 3, 4, to the Roman popedom:—

"The zeal of Your Majesty toward the house of God manifests itself abroad in the farthest parts of *Christendom*, by writing in defence of the truth (which hath given such a blow unto '*that man of sin*,' as will not be healed)." — *The Epistle Dedicatory.*

These English translators not only identify "that man of sin" (2 Thess. ii. 3) with the Roman popedom; but in using the word "healed," they identify the Roman popedom with the first wild beast (Rev. xiii. 3).

1. "The temple of God" is the Church of Christ (1 Tim. iii. 15). Christ is the supreme Head of the Church (Col. i. 18). He that sitteth as God in the temple of God, sitteth there as supreme head, sitteth there as *a false Christ*. But, of all organized bodies in the whole world, only the Roman papacy claims to be the supreme head of the Church. By the simple assertion of this untenable claim, the Roman papacy proclaims itself *a false Christ*, and thus fulfils the prediction of our Lord himself, "There shall arise *false Christs*."

"All the popes and prelates of Rome, for the most part, are worthily accounted among the number of false prophets and false Christs which deceived the world a long while" (*Homilies*, second part of sermon for Whitsunday).

"The Spirit speaketh expressly, that in the latter times some shall depart from the faith, giving heed to seducing sprits, and doctrines of devils, *forbidding to marry*" (1 Tim. iv. 1, 3).

The prohibition, "forbidding to marry," is itself forbidden by St. Paul by this question of his, which proves that "apostles," and even "Cephas" (who is St. Peter himself), and the "brethren of the Lord," were all married ministers of Christ; and, because they were, also proves that he himself authorizes the marriage of all his ministers without exception:—

"Have we not power to lead about a sister [Christian] wife, as well as other apostles, and the brethren of the Lord, and Cephas?" (1 Cor. ix. 5.)

That the Church of Rome forbids the marriage of all her ministers, is a fact too well known to require here any evidence.

It is to our present purpose, which is to show *the existing influence of the Devil in the Church of Christ*, to refer again to this declaration of St. Paul: "Forbidding to marry is taking heed [is obedience] to *seducing spirits and doctrines of devils*," that we may appreciate its comprehensive and appalling signification.

St. Paul continues the frightful list of existing spiritual adversaries.

"False apostles, deceitful workers, transforming themselves into the apostles of Christ" (2 Cor. xi. 13).

These men are "false apostles," because, —

1. Christ does not appoint them to be his ministers. They appoint themselves, "transforming *themselves* into the apostles of Christ."

2. They are "deceitful workers." They "handle the word of God *deceitfully*" (2 Cor. iv. 2).

These marks of falsehood adhere most closely and undeniably to the ministers of the Church of Rome: —

1. Their assertions that St. Peter is the source of apostolic authority, and that the ministry of the Church of Rome is derived from St. Peter, are totally incapable of proof.

2. The ministers of the Church of Rome pervert and change the revealed word of God, (*a*) by unwritten and worthless traditions, and (*b*) by papal decrees contrary to the Scriptures.

"They which creep into houses, and lead captive silly women laden with sins" (2 Tim. iii. 6).

This designation has a present as well as a past history. The imprisoned nuns in all Romish countries and communities, and the sinful histories of nunneries, affix this description of St. Paul upon the ministry of the Church of Rome, beyond denial and beyond removal.

"Try the spirits, whether they are of God; because many false prophets are gone out into the world. Hereby know ye the spirit of God: Every spirit that confesseth that Jesus Christ is come in the flesh is of God; and every spirit that confesseth not that Jesus Christ is come in the flesh is not of God" (1 John iv. 1–3).

When St. John created this test of truth and error, there were men claiming to be Christian teachers who denied the incarnation of the Son of God. All such teaching St. John pronounces false.

Since the time St. John thus decided, there have been, and are now, well-known imitators of this false teaching, which, inasmuch as it is not of God, proceeds from the lamb-dragon, the Church-deceiver.

Mohammed in his Koran denies the incarnation of Jesus Christ, and of course all Mohammedans everywhere now embrace and promulgate the same blasphemous dogma.

Large numbers of Unitarian Christians, because they withhold from our Saviour the possession of Deity, also refuse to admit the truth that he "came in the flesh;" that "the Word who is God" (John i. 1) became a man by taking our human nature.

The errors we now expose are indeed held and advocated by large bodies of estimable people who are our own neighbors and acquaintances.

But truth is not created either by a greatly multiplied or by a popular vote. Nor can the same kind of vote destroy the origination of the errors from the lamb-dragon. Both the errors themselves, and the truths they confront, exist solely by the permission and authority of Christ, and by the decision of the apostles whom the divine Saviour Jesus Christ himself inspires, and thus makes our infallible teachers.

CHAPTER XIV.

This chapter contains predictions (verses 1–12) and fulfilments (verses 13–20).

The exhibition of both predictions and fulfilments denotes the *certainty* of the events thus symbolized.

I. In the predictions are *three divisions*, indicated by the three angels. Three is here a *full* number, and indicates *completeness*.

II. The fulfilments are also three, required by the three predictions, (*a*) verse 13, (*b*) verses 14–16, (*c*) verses 17–20.

Among the fulfilments are *two harvests;* the grain (verses 15, 16), the fruit (verses 17–20). The reference is to the two harvests in Palestine. This *twofold* harvesting renders the reaping of the earth *complete*. The enemies of Christ's Church are forever exterminated. "The harvest" of the world is forever "past;" and "the summer" of reaping, ingathering, and burning, is absolutely "ended."

The two reapers are directed by two angels. Each angel denotes *God's time* for reaping. "The times and seasons, *the Father* puts in his own power" (Acts i. 7).

In chapter xiv., symbols of victory and triumph follow the symbols of persecution and suffering in chapter xiii.

Subjects of this chapter. — 1. The Lamb, and his victories over the apostate Church (1–5). 2. A succession of angels announcing blessings and woes (verses 6–20).

THE LAMB AND HIS VICTORIES (Verses 1-5).

1. Also I saw [in vision], and behold, the Lamb standing upon the Mount Sion, and with him a hundred and forty-four thousand, having his name and the name of his Father engraven upon their foreheads.

The Lamb: *the* Lamb of v. 6. *The Lamb*, symbolized as victor (vi. 2), here appears victor over the *old* dragon and his two wild beasts. The symbolic *prediction* (vi. 2) is here (xiv. 1) *realized*. The Lamb in prophetic symbol overcomes the apostate Church, created by the wild beast from the bottomless pit, and headed by the lamb-dragon.

Standing: firmly and triumphantly. "Stand" (Eph. vi. 13), as victors.

Sion: in the New Testament, only here and Heb. xii. 22; in Revelation, only here. The city of David (1 Kings viii. 1). Christ is David's son and successor (Luke i. 32). Sion is the emblem of the true Church (Heb. xii. 22), opposed to Babylon (Rev. xiv. 8), the city of the sea wild beast (verse 9).

Sion and Jerusalem are *identical*. Babylon cannot possibly, therefore, be Jerusalem, as is sometimes said.

The Lamb that was slain in Jerusalem, who once entered it as King, in meekness and lowliness (Matt. xxi. 5), now as symbolic victor occupies and holds Sion, his capital city, and with it his kingdom. He thus by symbol gives victory to his Church, and symbolically fulfils his own promise, "The gates of hell shall not prevail against my Church" (Matt. xvi. 18).

A hundred and forty-four thousand: the persons here enumerated are symbolic, not real. As symbols they represent the true Church victorious over the *apostate* Church. In Rev. vii. 4, the same symbolic number represents the victory of the Church over its *heathen* adversaries.

His name, and the name of his Father: in strong contrast with the "mark" by the lamb-dragon (xiii. 16).

The one hundred and forty-four thousand victors are by numbering and sealing *doubly* honored and *doubly* secure.

Christ's name is "the Word of God" (xix. 13). His Father's name is "I Am That I Am" (Exod. iii. 14). The engraven names are divine pledges of endless preservation. Each name embodies eternity. "The Word of God" is eternal (John i. 1). "I Am That I Am," asserts self-existence, and consequently affirms the Father's eternity.

2. And I heard a voice out of heaven, as the voice of mighty waters, and as the voice of great thunder; and the voice which I heard was as the voice of harpers, harping with their harps.

Voice: one combined harmonious voice. St. John repeats the word five times; thus indicating the captivating and absorbing attraction of the loud and united harmony.

Waters: the resounding waves of the ocean (Ps. lxv. 7; Isa. v. 30; Jer. vi. 23).

Thunder: its reverberating peals.

Harpers: as the ear of St. John becomes accustomed to the sounds, he perceives the music is both vocal and instrumental. While harping, the harpers are at the same time singing. The commingled voices and harps are creating an anthem of exultation and praise in anticipation of the complete victories of the Lamb over all his enemies. "They take the *harp*, and *rejoice*" (Job xxi. 12).

3. And so they are singing as it were a new song before the throne, and before the four living beings, and the elders: and yet no one was able to learn the song, but the hundred and forty-four thousand, who were redeemed from the earth.

New: in contrast with their former trials and prayers (v. 9, vi. 9, 10).

Redeemed: by the blood of Christ (v. 9). Gratitude to Christ inspires their song. Without the sense of his love, no one can sing this song (ii. 17, xix. 12).

From the earth: from the sinful people of the earth (xiii. 3).

"Look unto the rock whence ye are hewn, and to the hole of the pit whence ye are digged" (Isa. li. 1). The deepest emotions of which the soul of man is capable are the perceptions of the lost condition and ruinous companionship from which Christ saves us. These perceptions find utterance in the exclamations of men who had these perceptions, "Who maketh thee to differ?" (1 Cor. iv. 7;) "Is not this a brand plucked out of the fire?" (Zech. iii. 2;) "I am not meet to be called an apostle" (1 Cor. xv. 9).

4. These are they who are not defiled with women; for they are virgins. These are they who follow the Lamb wherever he goeth. These are redeemed from men, the first fruits to God and to the Lamb.

These ... are virgins: the one hundred and forty-four thousand, here said to be virgins, *represent* the *entire* Church of Christ, *in all time*. To predicate *literal* virginity of such a representative class, is simply to formulate an impossibility, which as a proposition refutes itself. The predication is imposed upon the passage by the common mistake of regarding the Apocalypse as a record of real events, and of overlooking its actual character, a book of symbolic predictions.

In the language of the Bible, idolatry is spiritual adultery.

"Through her whoredoms Israel defiled the land, and committed *adultery with stocks and stones*" (Jer. iii. 9).

"*With their idols* have they committed *adultery*" (Ezek. xxiii. 37).

In the Apocalypse, the great city Babylon (xiv. 8) is called "the great harlot" (xvii. 1), with whom "the kings of the earth commit fornication" (verse 2); and this fornication is the worship of the wild beast from the sea, and his image (xiv. 9).

When, therefore, St. John asserts that not at all with women the one hundred and forty-four thousand are defiled, he merely asserts that they do not either in form or in spirit practise the worship of idols, introduced by the wild beast, and cherished by the harlot Babylon.

The "ten virgins" (Matt. xxv. 1) are not virgins in a *literal* sense, but in a *spiritual* sense. They are ten *representative* men, who are all *outwardly* faithful worshippers of God. The "wise" are *spiritual* worshippers. The worship of the "foolish" is merely external.[1]

"Virgin" is often in spiritual sense (2 Cor. xi. 2; 2 Kings xix. 21; Isa. xxxvii. 22; Jer. xviii. 13, xxxi. 4, 21; Lam. i. 15, ii. 13; Amos v. 2).

Rev. xiv. 4 does not in the slightest degree warrant this dogma of the Church of Rome:—

"It is better and more blessed to remain in virginity or celibacy than to be joined in matrimony" (Council of Trent, session xxiv., A.D. 1563, Canon X.).—PERCEVAL, *Roman Schism*, p. 330.

Follow: as victor-soldiers (xix. 14).

Wherever: in every warfare Christ conducts.

Redeemed from: rescued, delivered, separated from the sinful men, described in ix. 4, 6, 10, 15, 18, 20,—"have not the seal of God in their foreheads."

The first-fruits: only here in the Apocalypse; the beginning of the gathering of souls to Christ. A larger harvest will follow: the first-fruits is the pledge of this increase (1 Cor. xvi. 15; Jas. i. 18). Origin of the term, Exod. xxiii. 19; Lev. xxiii. 10, 11, 14.

---

[1] See "The Ten Virgins in their Spiritual Character," *The Churchman*, Aug. 9, 1884.

5. And in their mouth is found no lie; for they are without fault.

Mouth: for speech; "mouth speaking" (Rev. xiii. 5; Matt. xv. 8, xviii. 16). Distributive singular, *each* mouth.

Is found: by Christ; "I have found" (Rev. iii. 2).

Lie: the lamb-dragon is a deceiver (xiii. 14). The Devil, who inspires him, is a liar (John viii. 44). The redeemed neither deceive nor lie: they are faithful servants of Christ, as they profess to be.

Without fault: blameless. Nothing in them can be blamed: they are "without sin" (Heb. iv. 15). Emphatic; negative for the positive: they are perfect.

SUCCESSION OF ANGELS HERALDING PROPHECIES
(Verses 6–20).

Predictions and fulfilments are in order after the exhibition of the triumphant Church.

The appearance of six heralding angels (verses 6, 8, 9, 15, 17, 18), in *two* groups. First group of three angels, verses 6, 8, 9; second group of three, verses 15, 17, 18.

The numbers are significant.

As *seven* is *absolute completion*, *six* in a group of *seven* is a very full number, — twice three.

There are only *six* angel-trumpeters of woes (viii. 7, 8, 10, 12, ix. 1, 13). The *seventh* trumpets victory (xi. 15).

There are only *six* angel censer-bearers of woes (xvi. 2–4, 8, 10, 12). The *seventh* enacts *completion* (xvi. 17).

As a *full* number, therefore, do the *six* angels present themselves (xiv. 6–20). As *three* is also an *integer*, each angel-group of three is a *full* number.

Moreover, angel is the symbol of *message* in Exod. xiv. 19, 20. In Rev. xiv., the six angel-messengers (verses 6, 8, 9, 15, 17, 18) explain *in detail* the symbolic representation (verse 1) of Christ's victory over all his enemies. There is thus, in chapter xiv., first, *general announcement*, and then more *minute explanations*.

There are, in the New Testament, examples of this twofold form of annunciation.

In Matt. iii. 16, 17, there is, first, the dove, the symbol of a message of peace from God to Jesus Christ; then, the verbal explanation of the actions of the dove, by the voice of the Father.

The same duplex form of divine communication is seen and heard in Acts x. 11–15, 28. First, the symbol of the "great sheet" and its microcosm contents; then, audible words of explanation.

In Rev. xiv. 1-5, the victory of the Lamb over the wild beast from the sea, and over the wild beast from the earth, are most sublimely and impressively celebrated.

In verses 6-20, the several events which *precede and cause* this triumphant victory, and conduct to it, are symbolically enumerated in these *two* forms: first, *predictions* (verses 6-12); then, *fulfilments* (verses 13-20).

FIRST GROUP: PREDICTIONS.

The Publication of the Enduring Good News of God's Coming Judgments (Verses 6, 7).

6. And I saw another angel flying in the eye of the sun, having an eternal message of good news, to publish as good news for them who are abiding upon the earth, even for every people, and tribe, and tongue, and nation.

Saw: see note on viii. 13.

Good news: only here in the Apocalypse. The Greek verb, of which the Greek noun is the root, occurs x. 7, xiv. 6.

Eternal: only here in this book: never elsewhere with this noun. The eternal good news; the good news will endure always.

The "good news" is not here the gospel of Christ, but this eternal good news, namely, that "the hour of his judgment is come" (verse 7).

In the New Testament, the word "gospel" occurs *alone* (without an adjective) thirty-four times; in *every instance with the article*, "*the* gospel." Also when *connected* (with an adjective) the word "gospel" *always* has the article, except once (Rom. i. 1); "gospel" is deprived of the article by the word "God." But in Rev. xiv. 6, "good news" (gospel) is *without* the article. Moreover, the phrases "gospel of God" and "of Christ" *never* have an adjective; but "good news" ("gospel," Rev. xiv. 6) has the adjective "eternal."

These facts of usage utterly forbid our regarding the phrase "eternal good news" (Rev. xiv. 6), as the gospel of Jesus Christ.

To publish: not "preach" (English Version), in the sense of preaching the gospel of Christ, but to publish the good news of God's coming judgment.

For: this is the sense of the Greek preposition with the accusative (Matt. iii. 7); *for* baptism (Luke vii. 44, xv. 4, xxiii. 48; Heb. xii. 10).

People, etc.: xiii. 7.

7. Saying, with a loud voice, Fear God and give him glory, because the hour of his judgment is come; and so worship

the Maker of heaven and earth, and the sea and fountains of waters.

Fear: revere, reverence.
Glory: praise.
Hour: a definite and fixed time.
Judgment: first time in the Apocalypse. In the singular number, only here and xviii. 10, where judgment on Babylon is meant. This, therefore, is the meaning here. "Babylon is fallen, is fallen" (verse 8). The *final* judgment is *not* here intended.
The maker: Exod. xx. 11.
And the sea: Acts iv. 24, xiv. 15.
Fountains of waters: in viii. 10 and xvi. 4, rivers are joined with fountains.

The waters of rivers and fountains are added to the sea to intensify the truth that God is the Creator of all things, without exception. Since the universal Creator, God is to be exclusively worshipped.

This verse embodies these truths: God will destroy all worship of idols; therefore reverence and worship him. Cease from every form of idolatry, both in form and in spirit.

The Announcement of the Fall of Babylon.

8. And another, a second angel follows, saying, Fallen, fallen is Babylon the great, because she makes all nations drink of the wine of the wrath of her fornication.

The second angel follows the first angel. That the second angel follows the first, is certain from this assertion (verse 9): the third angel follows "them;" that is, the third angel follows the *second* angel, and also the *first*. The three angels perform the same actions, and act in the same sphere. But the first angel *flies;* therefore the second and third angels also fly. The first angel flies in the eye of the sun (viii. 13): consequently the second and third angels fly in the eye of the sun. All three angels fly in the eye of the sun, that all the world may see them in their flight, and hear their great messages.

Since these angels are associated *in flight and in place* of announcement, the character of their messages is associated. Each of the three angels delivers substantially the same message. The threefold repetition of the same message, as well as the appearance of three angels, indicates *the certainty* of the destruction awaiting the *apostate* Church of Christ.

In Job i. 14-18, his ruin is announced by a succession of messengers.

"Fallen, fallen is Babylon the great." This is the message the second angel, balancing his wings in the face of the sun, proclaims for every people, tribe, tongue, and nation under heaven.

The verb "fallen" repeated denotes certainty.

Babylon: this is *the very first time* the word occurs in the Apocalypse: mentioned here only to be *prophetically* destined by God to destruction; mentioned afterwards in xvi. 19, where there is *fulfilment* of this prediction.

In xvii. 3-7, 9, 15, 16, 18, Babylon is fully described. xvii. 9, "on *seven* mountains the woman sitteth," identifies Babylon with *Papal* Rome.

In xviii. 2, 10, 21, the fall of Babylon, being accomplished, is commemorated. The idolatrous church is fully destroyed.

Pagan Babylon was the great enemy of the *Jewish* Church. So *papal* Babylon is the great enemy of the *true Church of Christ*.

Fallen, fallen is Babylon: this expression is in Isa. xxi. 9, and is applied to Pagan Babylon on the river Euphrates; also in Jer. l. 23, etc., li. 7, 8.

The word Babylon is derived from the Hebrew *babel*, confusion (Gen. xi. 9).

The great: "Is not this *great* Babylon?" (Dan. iv. 30.)

Of the wine, etc.: this language is taken from Jer. li. 7. Here are two cups: cup of idolatry, and cup of wrath. The wine of idolatry (fornication), Babylon causes the nations of the earth to drink (xvii. 2). The wine of God's wrath, she drinks from his hand (xiv. 10, xvi. 19).

Harlotry is often, in Bible language, the appellation by which to describe faithlessness to God. In its spiritual sense, harlotry is derived from the disobedience of Eve, who, by the act, was faithless to God, and became a spiritual harlot, and thus the model of the spiritual "harlot" Babylon.

The Announcement of God's Judgments upon the Worshippers of the Wild Beast; i.e., upon Idolatrous Christians (Verses 9–11).

9. And another angel, the third, follows them, saying with a loud voice, If any man worship the wild beast, and receive a mark upon his forehead, or upon his hand;

The third angel follows the second and the first, and by flying high in the sky, even in the face of the sun, there, with loud voice, proclaims in the ears of all men the terrific prediction written in verses 9, 10, and 11.

Wild beast: the lamb-dragon, because he affixes the "mark" (xiii. 16, 17).

10. Even he himself shall drink of the wine of the wrath of God, which is mixed pure in the cup of his indignation. And so they shall be tormented in fire and brimstone, in the presence of the holy angels, and in the presence of the Lamb.

Only here in the Apocalypse are angels called holy. In Matt. xxv. 31, the holy angels accompany Christ, when he appears as Judge. Here, also, the holy angels and the Lamb appear together.

11. And the smoke of their torment ascendeth up for ever and ever; and so, no rest day and night have the worshippers of the wild beast and his image, even whoever receives the mark of his name.

The smoke of their torment: the smoke of the fire and brimstone causing their torment; language derived from Isa. xxxiv. 10.
For ever and ever: denotes absolute and unending eternity.
Rest: from torment.
The wild beast: the lamb-dragon, because he affixes the "mark" (xiii. 16, 17).

12. Here is the patience of the saints, who are keeping the commandments of God, and their faith in Jesus.

Trials and sufferings require patience. Unless the saints possess and exercise patience, they will cease to keep the commandments of God, and will abandon their faith in Jesus.
See xiii. 10, where the expression belongs to the *preceding* clause. The same connection must be made here. In both places, patience is explained by Jas. i. 4.
Who are keeping: defines the saints in the clause just before.

SECOND GROUP: FULFILMENTS.

In verses 13–20 are three announcements: (*a*) verse 13, (*b*) 14–16, (*c*) 17–20.

Blessedness of the Dead in the Lord.

13. And I heard a voice from heaven, saying, Write, Blessed are the dead who are dying in the Lord. Henceforth the Spirit saith, Yea, they rest from their labors; for their works do follow them.

"The Order for the Burial of the Dead" repeats these words. To be understood, they must be examined.

(a) The victory symbolized (verses 1-5 of this chapter), (b) the judgment inflicted upon the wild beast (6-11), and (c) the patience of the saints (12), imply *severe conflict*. Conflict implies sufferings and death itself.

The certainty of *violent death* is the occasion of the announcement here (verse 13).

Voice from heaven: may be the voice of God *the Father*, the ultimate arbiter (ix. 13. x. 4, xi. 12, xvi. 1, 17, xviii. 4, xxi. 3, 5).

Who are dying in the Lord: constitute a class existing in every period of the Church.

In the Lord: describes the closest union of the soul with Christ (Rom. xvi. 11; Phil. iv. 1; Philem. 16).

Henceforth: belongs to the verb "saith," not to "dying." It was not "henceforth" that men died in the Lord. There had been previous instances of Christian martyrs: Stephen (Acts vii. 59), James (xii. 2), saints (xxvi. 10), Antipas (Rev. ii. 13).

Yea: "even so," Prayer-Book. The Holy Spirit confirms this voice from heaven; namely, the dying in the Lord are blessed.

Rest: God removes his suffering people, that they may be released from toil and conflict, and enjoy the rest of paradise. Since they are at rest, they are not in purgatory.

Labors: accompanied with beating and groans (ii. 2).

Works: done for Christ in the midst of blows and groans.

Follow: as memorials of the life they lived in his militant Church, and as measures of their heavenly reward (Matt. v. 12).

The First Reaping (Verses 14-16).

The *grain* harvest. The *early summer* harvest in Palestine. There are *two* reapings in this chapter, to denote the *completeness* of the destruction symbolized.

---

14. Also I saw, and behold a white cloud, and upon the cloud one sitting like the Son of man, having on his head a golden crown, and in his hand a sharp sickle.

White cloud: the symbol of punishment. "The Lord *rideth upon a swift cloud*. The Lord shall *smite Egypt*" (Isa. xix. 1, 22). A white cloud, only here. It is not "a *bright* cloud" (Matt. xvii. 5). A white cloud is easily moved by the wind, and becomes "a *swift* cloud."

Sitting: enthroned as *a Judge* (Rev. iv. 2, xix. 4, 11, 19, 21, xx. 11, xxi. 5).

Like: the enthroned Judge represents the Son of man. Likeness, not sameness, identity. Christ in his humanity (i. 13); Christ a *present* reaper.

Golden crown: only here in the New Testament. This crown marks Christ as Victor King.

In his hand a sharp sickle: Christ is Lord of the harvest (Matt. ix. 38). He has authority and power to reap. This is the reaping of the grain-harvest, which in Palestine occurs about Whitsunday (Exod. xxiii. 15, 16).

In the grain-harvest, *the owner of the field himself reaped*. Thus Boaz (Ruth ii. 2, 14); husband of the Shunammite (2 Kings iv. 18).

It is thus in accordance with actual practice, that Christ in symbol does himself use the sickle.

The imagery is here taken from the prophet Jeremiah, "The daughter of Babylon is like a threshing-floor. The time of harvest shall come" (li. 33).

John the Baptist has the same imagery (Matt. iii. 12).

15. And another angel comes out of the temple, crying with a loud voice to him who is sitting on the cloud, Thrust in thy sickle, and harvest; for the hour of harvesting is come, for the harvest is over-ripe.

Another angel: this symbolism may be founded in actual practice. Boaz resided in the city of Bethlehem (Ruth ii. 4). He had a steward who "was over the reapers" (verse 5). He may have personally told Boaz when the reaping must, by the state of the grain, begin.

Temple: the holy of holies, where in the shechinah God symbolically dwelt.

Sickle: symbol of judgment (Jer. l. 16; Joel iii. 13).

Hour: the supreme arbiter, God the Father, determines *the time* of the harvest (Acts i. 7). When he fixes the time, he sends an angel to inform the symbolic judge on the white cloud, and to command him to no longer delay the reaping, but to begin at once.

The harvest: the grain to be harvested.

Over-ripe: in the Greek is "dried up," and the kernels are ready to fall. The iniquity of Babylon is full (Gen. xv. 16).

16. And he who is sitting on the cloud casts his sickle upon the earth, and the earth is harvested.

Upon the earth: upon the breadth of the earth (Rev. xx. 8).
The earth: the grain of the earth.
Harvested: "reaped" by the angel's "sharp sickle."

The Second Reaping (Verses 17-20).

The reaping of the *fruit* harvest, which in Palestine occurs in the autumn. "The harvest is passed, *the summer is ended*" (Jer. viii. 20). The two harvests will utterly divest the broad earth of both grain and fruits. The two symbolic harvests will destroy all the enemies of Christ, whether personal or spiritual.

---

17. And another angel comes out of the holy of holies which is in heaven, having also himself a sharp sickle.

Temple: the holy of holies, the residence of God.

In the second harvest, the owner of the land does not himself use the sickle. The laborers he hires do this kind of harvesting (2 Chron. xxvi. 10; Matt. xx. 1).

This fact excludes the cloud-seated representative of the Son of man (verse 14), the lord of the harvest, from the symbolism of the second reaping. The second reaper, although an angel, represents the steward of the owner. The representative steward is commissioned by God the Father.

(*The Angel of the Fire-Altar.*)

18. And another angel comes out of the altar, who has authority over the fire, and he cries with a loud voice to him who has the sharp sickle, Thrust in thine own sharp sickle, and gather the clusters of each vine of the earth, for its ripe clusters are this instant ripe.

Altar: of burnt sacrifice, under which the martyred saints are praying (vi. 9). Their prayers are now (xiv. 18) being symbolically answered.

Fire: on the great altar of burnt-sacrifice. With the fire, the angel burns the grape-vines. Not only does the angel with the exceedingly sharp sickle cut off the grape-clusters (verse 17), but the angel coming out of the fire-altar utterly burns up all the vines themselves.

Thus destructive and absolute is the completeness of the second reaping. Stripped of their grape-clusters, and incapable of a second bearing, the vines are useless and fit only for the fire. "Withered branches men gather and cast into the fire, and they are burned" (John xv. 6).

St. John derives his symbolism (Rev. xiv. 18) from the prophet Ezekiel. "As the *vine-tree*, among the trees of the forest, which, when meet for no work, I have given to the fire, *so will I give* the inhabitants of Jerusalem" (xv. 5, 6).

19. And so the angel casts his sickle to the earth, and gathers each vine of the earth, and casts it into the great winepress of the wrath of God.

The symbolism of this verse is derived from the prophet Isaiah: "I have *trodden the wine-press* alone. I will tread *the people in mine anger*. Their *blood* shall be sprinkled upon my garments" (lxiii. 3).

The vastness of the images in verse 19 is almost beyond the grasp of the imagination. All the grape-clusters on the surface of the entire earth. A wine-vat large enough to hold all these clusters. The vastness of the imagery symbolizes the *universal* destruction of Christ's enemies, though in numbers they equal the grapes filling the grape-clusters of all the earth.

(The Treading of the Winepress.)

20. And the winepress is trodden outside of every city; and there goes forth blood from the winepress up to the bits of the horses, away a thousand and six hundred furlongs.

Every city: the individualizing singular.

The imagery of a winepress introduces the idea of a city. The owners of vineyards lived in cities. The vineyards were outside the cities. The treading would from necessity take place in the vineyard. The treading described (Rev. xiv. 20) is from the size of the winepress outside all cities.

Blood comes out: blood of the grapes (Gen. xlix. 11), symbolizing the blood of the enemies of Christ. "*Their blood* shall be sprinkled on my garments" (Isa. lxiii. 3).

Bits of the horses: the shed blood of Christ's enemies brings into the scene, by anticipation, the horsemen who slew them (Rev. xix. 14). But soldiers are not horsemen without horses. The depth of the flood of blood from the slain in this anticipated battle is so great that it reaches the bridle-bits of the horses who rush the slaughtering horsemen in their unexampled sword-work of carnage.

A battle was sanguinary, and the blood shed unusual, when it was so deep as to cover the feet of the victors. "The righteous shall wash their feet in the blood of the wicked" (Ps. lviii. 10). But in Rev. xiv. 20, the shed blood is a gory sea in which the horses wade to the height of their bridle-bits.

Away a thousand and six hundred furlongs: in the measure of the great and holy city Jerusalem (Rev. xxi. 13), *away* is evidently *the centre* of the city. From this centre the spectator looks in succession east, north, south, west.

We thus discover, in the measurement *away* a thousand and six hundred furlongs, that *away* is the point *from which* the measuring begins by means of the furlongs. From the centre of the bloody field of slaughter, the furlongs run out in all directions. When *the end* of the measurement is reached by the furlongs, their numerous ends will enclose a circle.

How large is this circle?

The number of furlongs given by St. John is *sixteen hundred*. Ten furlongs are equal to a geographical mile. Sixteen hundred furlongs are *one hundred and sixty* miles. But this distance is only one-half of the diameter of the field of blood measured by St. John. The whole diameter of the field is *three hundred and twenty* miles. The circumference of the field is *nine hundred and sixty* miles.

No such human battle-field is possible. The blood covering the field is too deep, the compass of the field is too large, for reality. St. John here uses *exaggerating* symbols to impress upon the minds and hearts of all men this most weighty truth: Christ's victories over the enemies of his Church will surpass, both in magnitude and in effect, all the achievements of all the military heroes the world has ever already seen, or will ever hereafter see. The symbolized battle-field must be spiritual. The victories Christ achieves are over error, sin, and "the carnal mind."

Why does St. John not record *the burning* of the vines symbolically predicted (verse 18)? The change in the imagery (verse 20) from the blood of grapes to the blood of men excludes further mention of the vines. The fact and the extent of their conflagration, we can easily picture in our imaginations.

CHAPTER XV.

PREPARATION FOR THE OUTPOURING OF THE SEVEN CENSERS.

(*a*) The song of thanksgiving (verses 1–4).
(*b*) The egress of the seven censer-angels (verses 5–8).

THE SONG OF THANKSGIVING (Verses 1–4).

1. And I saw another sign in heaven, great and marvellous: seven angels having the seven last plagues; for in them is ended the wrath of God.

This verse forms the introduction to chapters xv. and xvi.

Sign: a presage of coming events. The seven angels and their censers constitute the sign, the figurative representation of the immediate future.

Great and marvellous: this expression in the New Testament only here and verse 3. Marvellous: fit to excite wonder.

Seven plagues: *full* punishment. "*Sevenfold* into their bosom" (Ps. lxxix. 12).

Last: the seven plagues will end the symbolic drama, in the Apocalypse, of the present world's probationary history.

Is ended: the *exhibition*, in symbol, of God's wrath, will be ended. But the *infliction* of his wrath is not limited by time (xiv. 11, xx. 10).

There is a *second* death (xx. 14).

2. And I saw as it were a sea of glass mingled with fire: also the victors over the wild beast, and over his image and over the number of his name, standing by the sea of glass, having harps for God.

Imperative reasons are there for regarding the impressive scene opened to our sight by this verse as the repetition and amplification of chapter xiv. verses 1–5.

The resemblances between *the persons*, in xiv. 1–5 and xv. 1–4, are these reasons.

1. Both classes are *victors*.

In xiv., (*a*) Father's name in their foreheads (verse 1); (*b*) harping (verse 2); (*c*) redeemed (verses 3, 4).

In xv., (*a*) gotten victory (verse 2); (*b*) harps; (*c*) judgments manifest.

2. Both are victors *over idolatry*, material and spiritual.

In xiv., virgins (verse 4).

In xv., over beast, image, mark, name (verse 2).

3. Both sing songs of victory.

4. Both are harpers.

5. Both stand upon *the same place*.

In xiv., the hundred and forty-four stand (verse 1) "*before the throne*" (verse 3).

In xv., the victors "stand *on the sea of glass.*" But "the sea of glass is before the throne" (iv. 6).

So exact are these fivefold resemblances, that they become *identities*. Persons, character, place, employment, all *the same*. Recapitulation and amplification are here used, because they create impressiveness and denote certainty.

Repetition and amplification characterize other portions of this book, and increase in minuteness, as the drama unfolds itself.

Standing *by* the sea: *ad* mare vitrem (Bengel). "The sea" is the *accusative* in the Greek.

Reasons for preferring *by* to "on," English Version: —

1. *On* the sea is indicated by the Greek preposition with the *genitive* (Rev. x. 5, 8).

2. The same Greek preposition with the *accusative* means *at* or *by*: "*at* the door" (Rev. iii. 20); "*at* the altar" (viii. 3).

3. A sea of glass, *flashing with lightning*, is *not a possible standing-place*.

4. The pavement even of God's throne would not in symbol be represented as large enough to contain the *innumerable* assembly of his redeemed, since the victors (Rev. xv. 2), and the "great multitude which no man could number," form the same worshipping Church.

5. The following instances in the Septuagint, where the Greek word for "sea" is in the accusative with the same Greek preposition as stands in Rev. xv. 2, before the same Greek word for "sea" as is used in these Old-Testament instances, decide most conclusively, that *by*

is the preposition demanded, and that "on" is wholly inadmissible: "at the sea" (Josh. xv. 4, 11, xvi. 8); "by sea" (2 Chron. ii. 16); "by the Red Sea" (Neh. ix. 9).

Sea of glass: appears in Revelation only iv. 6 (see notes) and xv. 2. In both places, the sea is glass pavement before the symbolical throne of God. In iv. 6, the throne is the seat of judgment. The "lightnings and thunderings proceeding out of the throne" (iv. 5), give the throne this character.

In xv. 2, the throne is also the seat of judgment. "The fire" (verse 2) denotes this. "The fire" is the same as the "lightnings" (iv. 5). "Wrath" (xv. 1) decides the character of the throne. God is enthroned to judge and punish the enemies of his Church. "Thy *judgments* are made manifest." (xv. 4).

Mingled with fire: the Greek verb here used is to mix *mechanically*, like sand and kernels of grain. In Rev. xiv. 10 (see notes), the Greek verb is to mix *chemically*, like milk and water. The glass and the fire are not mingled *chemically*, only *mechanically*. The lightning flashes over and along the reflecting surface of the glass. Reflected in the glass, the lightning would appear to the beholder as through it were united with the glass.

The image and the symbolism are signs of terror and of threatened wrath from God. Fire, in Revelation, is often the symbol of punishment (xvi. 8, xvii. 16).

This terrific sea of glass reflecting the lightning-flashes gleaming over it does *not* represent the New Jerusalem (Rev. xxi. 2), the superterrene, heavenly, and permanent abode of Christ's glorified people.

The wild beast: the lamb-dragon, because "the number of his name" (xiii. 17) is here mentioned.

His image: the image of the first beast, the lamb-dragon made in xiii. 14.

Harps for God: for God's praise (verses 3, 4).

3. And they sing the song of Moses the servant of God, even this song to the Lamb, saying, Great and marvellous are thy works, Lord God Almighty: just and true are thy ways, King of nations.

Song of Moses: (Exod. xv. 1-19) is a song of *thanksgiving*. The victors (Rev. xv. 2-4) are singing the same *kind* of song.

The servant of God: Moses was the servant of God (Deut. xxxiv. 5; Josh. i. 1), because appointed by God (Exod. iii. 10). For the same reason, are the one hundred and forty-four thousand "servants of God" (Rev. vii. 3).

Moses, as victor over Pharaoh and the Egyptians, sings his thanksgiving song. Also victors, the redeemed sing in substance the same eucharistic song.

To the Lamb: in Rev. xiv. 1, the Lamb is the leader of the "one hundred and forty-four thousand," because "they follow him" (verse 4).

They are also "the first-fruits unto God and *to* the Lamb," even to the Lamb[1] (verse 4). Since the Lamb is thus their Redeemer, Possessor, and Leader, their "new song" (xiv. 3) may surely be to his praise.

Thus praising the Lamb (xiv. 3), they may (xv. 3, 4) repeat in *express words* the eucharistic hymn they previously sung. The Lamb is the object of praise (v. 12, 13). His praise once given may be repeated, times without number.

Thy works: of mercy to his Church (Ps. cxi. 4).

Just and true are thy ways: works and ways, deeds and methods. Here his ways are judgments (Deut. xxxii. 4; Rev. xv. 4). St. John here quotes Moses.

True: actual, not merely threatened.

Nations: all nations (verse 4). "God is Judge of all the earth" (Gen. xviii. 25).

4. Who shall not fear thee, O Lord, and glorify thy name? For thou only art holy: for all nations shall come and worship before thee, for thy judgments are manifested.

Who shall not fear thee: from Jer. x. 7. Rhetorical question for this assertion: Every one should fear thee.

And glorify thy name: the question in the first clause of the verse is repeated, Who shall not glorify thy name? Every one should.

Glorify: magnify as surpassing all other names.

Name: revealed character (Exod. iii. 14).

Holy: holy and pure. Holy in himself "only." The holiness of angels and men is derived from God.

For (1): makes the perfect holiness of God the motive for fearing and glorifying him.

For (2): makes the actual worship of God by all nations the motive for every individual to fear and worship him.

For (3): makes the actual infliction of God's judgments the motive for this universal worship here predicted.

Judgments: righteous acts, judgments inflicted. In Revelation, only here and xix. 8.

---

[1] Granville Sharp's Rule. Ayre, Introduc., pp. 216, 217.

Are manifested: in Revelation, here and iii. 18, only. Aorist of narration. Also, iii. 18.

The greatest duty of the whole world, at the present time, is submission to Christ, as supreme Teacher and sole Ruler over all souls. This absolute submission, Christ incessantly and everywhere demands. "*All* men should honor the Son, even as they honor the Father" (John v. 23). Christ requires not only all nations, but every individual, to accept his gospel, in its *entirety and exclusiveness*. He does not allow his gospel to be united with any human systems. Sovereign King, Christ admits no rival. He dethrones every associated monarch over human minds and hearts.

The martyrs appear repeatedly in the Apocalypse. They live perpetually in their prayers and thanksgivings. Their prayers and thanksgivings ever live, because God ever holds them in his own perpetual remembrance; and thus they are ever efficient and efficacious.

No effectual prayer, no acceptable thanksgiving, can therefore ever die. The human offerers die and disappear, and their praying voices are silenced and unheard here on earth; but the prayers and thanksgivings Christ's people here offer him do not in their power die with their own death. They live still in their might, because God, being himself ever-living, cannot forget them. They are ever before his eyes, as is the sun in the heavens by day, and as are "the stars and light" (the milky way) (Ps. cxlviii. 3, — Psalter, after the Vulgate, Septuagint, and Hebrew) by night.

THE OPENING OF THE HOLY OF HOLIES, AND THE SEVEN CENSER-ANGELS (Verses 5-8).

These four verses are the bearers of several very important subjects.

The imagery of the passage is largely taken from the sixteenth chapter of Numbers, which must, therefore, in large measure be the interpreter of the passage.

In the sixteenth chapter of Numbers, the following are the great subjects: —

1. A rebellion against the high-priesthood of Aaron. As Aaron was created high priest by God himself, the rebellion was an attempt to destroy an institution of God.

2. The rebels were themselves members of the Jewish Church. The rebellion, consequently, was a Church schism.

3. The form of the rebellion was the attempted exercise of priestly functions, the bearing of censers, and the burning of incense.

4. The vindication by God himself of the Aaronic priesthood.

5. The destruction of the rebels by their own censers, the official instruments they had presumed to assume.

The contents of the sixteenth chapter of Numbers cast strong and illustrative light upon Rev. xv. 5-8.

This illuminating light will exhibit the two passages (Num. xvi. and Rev. xv. 5-8) as parallel in several respects.

1. In Numbers, sixteenth chapter, there is "the tabernacle" (verses 18, 19, 42, 43, 50) with its holy of holies. The same holy of holies appears in Rev. xv. 5, 6, 8.

2. In Num. xvi., is the high priest Aaron (verses 11, 16-18, etc.).

In Rev. xv. 6-8, the seven angels are themselves high priests.

Proofs. — (*a*) The seven angels "come out" of the "holy of holies." Only high priests ever entered the holy of holies (Heb. ix. 7). As a consequence, only high priests come out of the holy of holies. The seven angels are, therefore, high priests.

(*b*) The ornaments on the dress the seven angels wear indicate that they are high priests.

The seven angels are "clothed with pure shining stone" (Rev. xv. 6).

But, according to Ezek. xxviii. 13, "every precious stone" there enumerated are the very same stones as are in the breastplate of the high priest (Exod. xxviii. 17-20).

(*c*) The Aaronic high priests wore golden girdles (Exod. xxviii. 8). The seven angels also wear girdles (Rev. xv. 6).

These are the Bible proofs that the seven angels are symbolic high priests.

Here, we may ask, why are the seven angels (Rev. xv. 6-8) high priests?

They are here as high priests, for the same reasons that Aaron the high priest appears in the case of Korah and his company.

Aaron appears for two reasons: —

I. To vindicate his own high-priesthood (Num. xvi. 5, 17).

II. To destroy "the two hundred and fifty men that offered incense" (Num. xvi. 35) without the appointment of God.

For the very same reasons, are the seven angels high priests in Rev. xv. 6-8.

I. To vindicate *their own high-priesthood.* But what is the high-priesthood of the seven angels?

Their high-priesthood must be the *Christian* high-priesthood.

The present vision relates *to the Church of Christ,* for the victors are singing "the song of *the Lamb*" (xv. 3). The seven angels are, therefore, *Christian* high priests. But as *representative* Christian high priests they must represent *a reality,* and not a shadow; and the reality they repr sent must be *the Christian high-priesthood.*

By means of these exhibitions, St. John discloses to our view, to our recognition, to our belief, this valuable fact, — the existence of the Christian high-priesthood in the Church of Christ *before the close of the first century of the Christian era.*

Nor is it merely the fact which St. John here discloses, that the Christian high-priesthood existed at this early period. St. John also reveals the *nature* of the Christian high-priesthood, as it was in his time.

In its nature, the Christian high-priesthood revealed to us by St. John has these characteristics: —

1. The early Christian high-priesthood is modelled after the high priesthood of Aaron. As high priest, Aaron was the supreme head of the Jewish priesthood.

Because modelled after the Aaronic high-priesthood, the Christian high-priesthood is the supreme head of the Christian priesthood. But the supreme head of the Christian priesthood is not one high priest only.

2. The early Christian high-priesthood, as represented by the seven angelic high priests, is in itself *a parity.*

There are *seven* angelic high priests, *all holding the same offices, and administering the same powers.* No one of the seven is *over* the other six. No one of the seven is *super*-high priest. As high priests, each of the seven angels is *just as high as the other. No one is higher than the rest.*

As seven is a perfect number, the seven angelic high priests represent and include *the entire Christian high-priesthood.* The Christian high priesthood *of parity* is the *only high-priesthood* in the Church of Christ.

No one of these seven angelic high priests is pope. POPERY WAS A NONENTITY IN THE FIRST CENTURY. POPERY WAS A LATER USURPATION AND DOMINATION.

Such is the Christian high-priesthood of the seven representative angels in Rev. xv. 6–8).

How do the seven angels here vindicate their own Christian high-priesthood? By opposing and symbolically destroying the high-priesthood *assumed and represented* by the lamb-dragon, the apt symbol of papal Rome.

II. As in Numbers, sixteenth chapter, Aaron the high priest appears for a second reason, the overthrow of the pretended high-priesthood of the two hundred and fifty usurpers, so the seven Christian high priests appear for the same reason.

They appear for *punitive discipline.* When by the command of God they empty their large censers of their burning contents, the acts of the same angels are symbolic inflictions of punishments.

These judicial acts of the seven angels establish another fact respecting the Christian high-priesthood at the time St. John wrote his Apocalypse. At that time *the Christian high priests were the administrators of Church discipline.* Neither the subordinate priests nor the laity were the ultimate administrators.

The discipline of the early Christian high priests was not the discipline of *death* (this is God's sole prerogative in the brief period of miracles), but their discipline was exclusively the discipline of admonition and excommunication. That this was the nature of the discipline practised by the early Christian high priests, the Scriptures, recording the proceedings of the apostles, amply prove (1 Cor. v. 3-5; 2 Cor. xiii. 2, 10).

There are other obvious and instructive parallels between the sixteenth chapter of Numbers and Rev. xv. 5-8.

1. The shechinah, the visible manifestation of the glory of God, appears in both passages. In Num. xvi. 19, 42, the shechinah is called "the glory of the Lord." In Rev. xv. 8, the shechinah is called "the glory of God."

This twofold appearance of the shechinah is conclusive proof that the imagery in Rev. xv. 5-8 is derived from the sixteenth chapter of Numbers.

2. In both passages, the glory of the Lord appears for the same purpose, — the manifestation of his displeasure.

3. Also, in both passages the censers are changed from instruments of God's mercy into instruments of his wrath. This coincidence is another proof that the imagery in Rev. xv. 5-8 is taken from Numbers, sixteenth chapter.

5. And after this, I saw [in vision]. And the holy of holies of the tabernacle of testimony in heaven is opened.

The holy of holies: the symbolic dwelling-place of God. "Thou dwellest between the cherubim" (Ps. lxxx. 1).

Tabernacle: Heb. ix. 2-5, 9, 11.

Testimony: the ark of the covenant; so called because it contained the two tables of the Decalogue, or Ten Commandments (Heb. ix. 4; Num. ix. 15, xvii. 4, xviii. 2).

The holy of holies is now opened (Rev. xv. 5) to disclose to view the depository of the Ten Commandments, the divine summary of all law and punishment.

Thus, in this symbolic exhibition of judgment, the mercy-seat itself, the top of the ark of testimony, becomes the source of vengeance.

6. And from the holy of holies come out the seven angels who are having the seven plagues, clothed with pure shining stone, and girded around their breasts with golden girdles.

A portion of the contents of this verse has been already sufficiently explained in the introduction to verses 3-8.

Clothed: *self*-clothed.

Girded: the encircling of the body with a girdle was the indication that the wearer was ready for the performance of the work required of him.

"Let your loins be girded about, and ye yourselves like unto men that *wait* for their Lord" (Luke xii. 35, 36).

"Your loins girt about with truth, and your feet shod with *the preparation* of the gospel of peace" (Eph. vi. 14, 15).

7. And one of the four living creatures gives unto the seven angels seven golden censer-basins, full of the wrath of God, who liveth for ever and ever.

One: the four living creatures are the executioners of the judgments of God (Ezek. x. 2, 7). See notes on iv. 6, 7. The seven angels here are their subordinate agents.

Censer-basins: in Bible-Greek, an incense-vessel has *three* names, —

(*a*) Firepan. Exod. xxvii. 3, "firepan" (English Version).

(*b*) "Censer," Num. xvi. 6, 17 (English Version); "censer," Rev. viii. 3, 5 (English Version); and

(*c*) Censer-basin. Exod. xxvii. 3, "basin" (English Version); Rev. v. 8, xv. 7, xvi. 1-4, 8, 10, 12, 17, xvii. 1, xxi. 9, "vial" (English Version).

Had the English Version in Rev. v. 8, etc., used in translating "basin," as in Exod. xxvii. 3, instead of "vial," from the Greek, Bible-readers would not think it is "a small bottle of thin glass."

In use, then, firepan, censer, and censer-basin are identical. They differ only *in size*.

In size, the censer-basin is the Latin *patera*, which held the blood of a bull, — some two gallons.

The censer-basin must have been at least *three times* larger than the firepan, the ordinary censer used by the Levitical priesthood.

St. John (Revelation, chapters xv. and xvi.) places the large censer-basin in the hand of each of the seven incense-angels to indicate the large quantity of fire and incense poured out.

The largeness of the quantity of the fire and incense poured out by the incense-angels symbolizes the largeness and the severity of the punishment inflicted.

Liveth for ever and ever: since God is eternal, his holiness and justice are unchangeable. His eternity also enables him to execute his predicted judgments.

8. And so the holy of holies is filled with smoke from the glory of God, and from his power; and so no one can enter into the holy of holies until the seven plagues of the seven angels are ended.

Glory of God: the *shechinah* in the holy of holies (Exod. xxv. 22; Num. vii. 89; 2 Sam. vi. 6; Heb. ix. 5).

The power of God: kindles the fire in the censer-basins, and imparts efficiency to their pouring out.

No one: so dense is the smoke in the holy of holies, and so bright the flashing glory, that no one can enter.

The reference is here to this record: "When the priests were come out of the holy place, the cloud filled the house of the Lord. The priests could not stand to minister, because of the cloud: for the glory of the Lord had filled the house of the Lord" (1 Kings viii. 10, 11).

Until . . . ended: until the infliction of the seven plagues of the seven angels is ended.

The smoke of the burning incense fills the holy of holies, until the fire and incense in each censer-basin are poured out. In other words, the seven censer-basins are emptied by the time the holy of holies is emptied of its smoke.

How long can the smoke remain in the holy of holies? At the very longest, only for a very few moments. Smoke is the Scripture image of transitoriness (Ps. xxxvii. 20).

The pouring of the seven censer-basins occupies merely a very few moments. The seven angels empty their seven censer-basins almost at the same moment.

Indeed, the seven angels may act *simultaneously*. For impressiveness, *the record* of their actions has *succession*.

The actions themselves may be without succession. The seven angels may pour out the seven censer-basins *at the same instant*.

What does this brevity signify?

1. Long periods of time are not necessary for the final execution of God's purposes and judgments.

Epochs, like the lives of individuals, begin in an instant.

(*a*) During one memorable night, while the Israelites are passing through the opened Red Sea, they are born into independence and national life.

(*b*) Christ, the Messenger of the new covenant (Mal. iii. 1), suddenly appears in his temple in Jerusalem. With his appearance, Judaism, as a ritual institution, disappears, and Christianity, in this decisive instant, becomes its successor forever.

(*c*) The world's *first Easter* begins in a moment. At the transcendent instant of our Lord's resurrection, we all become in him immortal in body, as we were before in soul.

(*d*) The Church of Christ has its *first Pentecost*. Suddenly its one hundred and twenty members are crowned with tongues, and baptized with a new baptism of the Holy Ghost. This sudden baptism animates and moves the Church with a new and enduring spiritual life.

The brevity of time in the outpouring of the seven last censers may symbolize both the sudden disappearance of the evils which afflict the Church, and the sudden arrival of its greatest blessings.

But, whether sudden or gradual, —

2. The departure of the apostate Church from the world is, by the symbolism in chapters xv. and xvi. of the Apocalypse, rendered *most certain*, as well as the survival, prosperity, and perfection of the true Church. Suddenness and brevity are encouraging marks and prophecies of absolute certainty.

CHAPTER XVI.

THE OUTPOURING OF THE SEVEN CENSERS (Verses 1-21).

1. AND I heard a loud voice out of the holy of holies, saying to the seven angels, Go, and scatter the seven censers of the wrath of God upon the earth.

Each censer contains *destructive incense* (Num. xvi. 35, 38), which is a deadly symbol (Rev. viii. 3-5).

The *seven* symbols predict the *total* destruction of the apostate Church, and the errors on which it is founded.

A loud voice out of the holy of holies: the shechinah is in the holy of holies. The loud voice is, therefore, the voice of God the Father. The command uttered by the voice is supreme and absolute. God determines the utter destruction of the apostate Church, and of its cherished errors.

The voice of God comes from the midst of the cloud of burning incense (xv. 8; Exod. xxiv. 16; Ezek. x. 1, 2).

Scatter: when the Greek verb is used with *solids*, as here, fire and incense, it has this meaning.

Earth: the sinful people of the earth; namely, the worshippers of the wild beast (verse 2).

Earth often has this sense in the Scriptures.

"*The earth* was corrupt" (Gen. vi. 11).

"*All flesh* had corrupted his way" (verse 12).

Thus "the earth" and "all flesh," all men, are identical.

Also, Gen. xi. 1, 9; 1 Sam. xvii. 46; 1 Kings x. 24; 1 Chron. xvi. 30; Ps. lxvi. 4.

THE FIRST ANGEL.

2. And the first goes away, and was scattering his censer-basin upon the earth. And there comes a sore, evil and

hurtful, upon the men who have the mark of the wild beast, and who worship his image.

Sore: the Greek word here translated "sore" translates (Exod. ix. 9) the Hebrew word which means leprosy.

Leprosy is an incurable disease. By Ps. li. 7, leprosy is made an emblem of sin.

It is thus made in this way:—

Hyssop is used in *cleansing* the leper (Lev. xiv. 4–6, 52).

The Psalmist, when praying, "*Cleanse* me from my *sin*" (Ps. li. 2), adds, "Purge me with *hyssop*, and I shall be *clean*" (verse 7).

His reference to the *leper-cleansing hyssop* makes leprosy the emblem of sin.

The hyssop, thus cleansing leprosy, is the emblem of *the blood* of Christ. "The blood of Jesus Christ *cleanseth* from all sin" (1 John i. 7).

1. God sometimes sends leprosy as a punishment for sin.

(*a*) Gehazi was made a leper for his eager greed and artful falsehood (2 Kings v. 27).

(*b*) King Uzziah was made a leper for sacerdotal assumption, — for burning incense as a priest (2 Chron. xxvi. 16–21).

2. God sometimes sends *increased sinfulness* to punish previous transgressions.

"As they did not like to retain God in their knowledge, God gave them over to a reprobate mind" (Rom. i. 28).

Judas, at first a pilferer, becomes, in punishment of his thievishness, a traitor and a self-murderer.

"From *hardness of heart, and contempt of thy word and commandment*, good Lord, deliver us." — *Deprecation in Litany*.

We use these facts in explanation of the plague of the first censer.

In Rev. viii. 11, moral stupor, symbolized by "wormwood," is God's infliction for sin.

He may hereafter in the Apocalypse employ a similar infliction in the form of *spiritual leprosy*.

The apostate Church of Rome is characterized by greed, by falsehood, by usurpation. These sins are punished by the infliction of an incurable spiritual leprosy, *self-infallibility*. Infallibility is perfection. Perfection needs no remedy. Perfection admits no cure. An incurable church can only be removed and destroyed.

Lepers were put out of the camp of the Israelites (Num. v. 2).

As an incurable leper, the Church of Rome is, in this chapter xvi., symbolically rejected from the true Church of Christ.

Evil: in itself.

Hurtful: to the sufferers.

With the prophet Isaiah, a diseased body is the emblem of a corrupt and dying Church. In using the phrase, "a sore evil, and hurtful," St. John repeats the instructive and frightful emblem of Isaiah.

Mark of the wild beast: the mark the second wild beast, the lamb-dragon, affixes.

THE SECOND ANGEL.

3. And the second angel was scattering his censer upon the sea, and it becomes blood, as of a dead man; and every soul dies in the sea.

See viii. 8; Exod. vii. 19, etc.

The earth (verse 2) denotes *corrupt* men. "The sea" (verse 3) denotes *wicked* men. "The *wicked* are like the troubled sea" (Isa. lvii. 20).

Wickedness follows corruption.

Like a dead man: like the coagulated blood of a corpse. The figure of a leper is continued.

Every soul: every living man.

Dies: the death is spiritual, occasioned by the spiritual leprosy.

THE THIRD ANGEL.

4. And the third angel was scattering his censer-basin upon the rivers and fountains of waters, and they become blood.

Rivers, etc.: these expressions are defined by this language of xvii. 15. "The waters" *represent* nations, and throngs, and people, and tongues; that is, "the rivers and fountains of waters" represent the masses of men, — all classes of people. The leprosy of sin pervades the common people. The governed as well as the governors, the ignorant as well as the learned, the low as well as the high, the poor as well as the rich, — "all sorts and conditions" of the populace, are stupefied by the prevalent spiritual leprosy.

Becomes blood: becomes leprous blood.

The judgments symbolized by the first three censers are, in their nature, the same spiritual leprosy. The symbols are here presented *three times* to signify *the absolute* certainty of the appalling events symbolized.

That certainty is intended by the threefold repetition of the symbols, we are assured by this language appended to another threefold repetition, "This was done *thrice*" (Acts x. 16). "This was done *three times*" (xi. 10).

In the arithmetic of the Bible, three is an *integer, a full* number (Isa. xix. 24). "Two or *three* witnesses" (Deut. xvii. 6; Matt. xviii. 16). *Three* exhausts the testimony. *Three* renders *the certainty complete.*

The following are the conclusive proofs that *men* are the objects reached by the fire and incense of the first three censers:—

"The earth" (verses 1, 2) is defined by "the men" (verse 2).

In verse 6, the words "have shed," "them," and "worthy," can refer only to persons identical with "the earth" (verse 2), "the sea" (verse 3), and "the rivers and fountains of waters" (verse 4).

That the three censers first scattered are, *in their nature,* one symbolized judgment, is most certain from the *combined* reference of verses 5, 6.

Not till the first three censers are emptied, is there any comment whatever. The comment which then follows (verses 5, 6) evidently regards the actions of these three censers as constituting, *in their character,* but *one judgment.*

The progress of this most figurative book is marked by an increase of repetitions, and by an intensification of metaphors.

The *symbolized prophecies* of the fall of Babylon are *threefold* (xiv. 6-11). The *symbolized fulfilments* of the prophecies are also *threefold* (xvi. 2-7).

The Angel of the Waters (Verses 5, 6).

5. And I heard the angel of the waters say, Righteous art thou, who art and who wast, the Holy, because thou art judging these judgments.

The angel of the waters: the angel having authority over the waters (xiv. 18). The angel of the waters is the third angel himself (v. 4). He has authority over the waters, because he scatters upon them the contents of his censer for their condemnation.

The waters symbolize the common people (xvii. 15). St. John does not here teach that common people have an angel of their own.

Say: in the Apocalypse, the ministers of God's judgments do not usually speak. This angel may be the first and only instance.

The spirit of the drama increases in intensity, and compels one of its actors to utter words (Ps. xxxix. 3).

Righteous: the angel pronounces God just in his punishments. The apostate Church deserves the punishment God inflicts.

Who art, and who wast, the Holy: eternal in his nature, God must be at all times just. While just, he is also holy. His justice cannot destroy his holiness.

These judgments: the judgments inflicted by the three censers.

6. For the blood of saints and prophets are they shedding; and so, thou art giving them blood to drink: most worthy are they.

Blood: their own leprous blood. Like sins, like punishments (Ps. xviii. 26, last clause; Isa. xlix. 26).

The Response of the Altar.

7. And I heard the altar say, Even so, Lord God Almighty, true and righteous are thine acts of judgment.

Heard the altar: heard the persons within the altar. The *metonymy* of the container for the contained. In vi. 9, 10, the souls of the martyrs under the great altar pray for vengeance. In xvi. 6, the prayer of these martyrs is answered. From out of the same great altar, the same martyrs now praise God for the actual vengeance.

True and just: perfect and just (xv. 3).

Acts of judgment: so xiv. 7, xviii. 10, xix. 2.

THE FOURTH ANGEL (Verses 8, 9).

8. And the fourth was scattering his censer-basin upon the sun. And it is given to the sun to scorch the men with fire.

See viii. 12, where similar imagery.

The sun: a literal sense is here inadmissible. Figures in the objects of the preceding censers, "earth, sea, rivers, and fountains of waters," and figures representing *persons*, make the sun in this verse 8, the symbol of a *person*.

But what person? *Christ himself* may be the person symbolized. This very symbolism occurs both in the Old Testament and in the New. In the Old Testament, "The Sun of righteousness with healing in his rays" (Mal. iv. 2).

In the New Testament, our Lord himself uses the same symbolism, "I am the light [the sun] of the world" (John viii. 12).

It is given: authority is implied. Authority is expressed (ix. 3, xiii. 5, 7). In this verse 8, *permission* is given by God to the sun.

To scorch: according to the imagery here employed, the injection of the burning contents of the fourth angel's censer upon the face of the blazing sun causes it to flame out more fiercely and widely, and thus to reach and strike and scorch, with a flashing scorching, the men who deserve the infliction.

The scorching is symbolic. To scorch is here to harm, instead of to "heal;" to blind, instead of to enlighten. Blessings, when abused, God changes into curses (2 Cor. ii. 15, 16).

Christ the emblematic Sun, with light and warmth and healing in his rays, is, by the perverseness and wickedness of errorists, changed in effect into an instrument of punishment and injury.

What a frightful representation of "The *wrath* of the *Lamb!*" (Rev. vi. 16.) While he is a placable Lamb, he "taketh away" our sins. When "his wrath is kindled, yea, but a little, we perish from the right way" (Ps. ii. 12).

The men: who are worshipping the image of the wild beast (verse 2).

9. And so the men are scorched with a great scorching. And yet the men blaspheme the name of God, who has authority over these plagues: and so they repent not to give him glory.

The men: who are idolaters, whether idolatry is material or spiritual.

Are scorched with a great scorching: the scorching is thus intensified. Punishment aggravates and increases their wickedness. They proceed from bad to worse.

Blaspheme God who has authority over the plagues: the wild beast is a blasphemer (xiii. 5, 6). His worshippers imitate him. They blaspheme God by speaking evil of him. They call God unjust and cruel.

By the authority and power God has over the plagues, he can make his chastisements means of blessing. They refuse to see his merciful hand in his inflictions.

They repent not: they cease not either to blaspheme, or to worship the wild beast. Failure in repentance follows persistent blasphemy, idolatry, and moral blindness.

To give him glory: to give God praise; in other words, to worship him by turning from their own blindness to the marvellous light of Christ, the Sun of the soul.

THE FIFTH ANGEL (Verses 10, 11).

10. And the fifth was scattering his censer-basin upon the throne of the wild beast, and his kingdom becomes darkened. And the men gnaw their tongues from the pain.

This wild beast "rises out of the sea" (xiii. 1). He represents the *Pagan* Roman empire, which becomes the *papal* empire of Rome.

His throne is in the city of Rome, and is the symbol of "his power and great authority." "The dragon gave him his power, and his throne, and his great authority" (xiii. 2).

The fifth censer falling upon the throne of this wild beast is a judgment upon the strongest citadel of the papal dominion. In itself, the judgment of *increased spiritual darkness;* an intensification of the previous spiritual leprosy, consuming the life of the usurping papacy.

His kingdom becomes darkened: the throne imparts its own character of darkness to its kingdom.

Becomes darkened. The participle with the substantive verb expresses a state of *continuance.* The papal kingdom is continually becoming darker.

Origin of the figure is Exod. x. 21–23.

The pain: is explained by "pains and sores" (verse 11). As the "sores" are *spiritual* (so "sore," verse 2), "the pain" is also spiritual.

Pain: in New Testament, only Rev. xvi. 10, 11, xxi. 4; hard work, trouble, suffering.

The self-infallible Church of Rome does not renounce its errors. It adds new errors to the old. To the false dogmas of the creed of Pope Pius IV., it subjoins the immaculate conception of the Virgin Mary, and the infallibility of the Pope. The darkness in the Church of Rome deepens.

But the human nature remains unchanged. Every soul of man craves spiritual light. The darker the dungeon, the more pained are the eyes deprived of light. The deeper the ignorance, the more tormenting and unbearable the spiritual hunger and misery. The enslaved and imprisoned *laity* of the Church of Rome will yet break their chains, and burst open their dungeon.

11. And yet they blaspheme the God of heaven, because of their pains and because of their sores; and so they repent not of their deeds.

And yet: contrastive. Sufferings do not yet reform the subjects of the wild beast: they curse God for afflicting them.

God of heaven: God who created the heaven; the *supreme God.* Blasphemy against the *supreme* God is most audacious and sinful.

And so: consecutive. They do not repent and turn from their deeds, from the blasphemies they are habitually uttering.

THE SIXTH ANGEL (Verses 12-16).

These five verses embody a remarkable and unique passage. The sixth angel is the *last*. The plague he ministers is the *very last* plague. The five preceding plagues all relate to *papal* Rome. The subject of Romanism seems exhausted.

The sixth plague may introduce a *different* subject. The sixth plague evidently has a wider application than the preceding plagues. The sixth plague may embrace, not only *all other forms of religious error besides Romanism*, but also *infidelity* in its multiplying phases. The sixth plague may contain all the Asiatic systems, Laou-Tzseism, or Taou-Tzseism, Confucianism, Buddhism, Brahmanism, Parseeism, Mohammedanism, and all the Western denials of divine revelation, infidel science, agnosticism. Romanism is not the only opponent true Christianity encounters. If the Asiatic systems and the Western denials are not included in the sixth plague, it will be hard indeed to find them anywhere in the Book of Revelation.

In examining the portion embraced by verses 12-16 of chapter xvi., we must continually recognize this fact, and be governed by it: *the sixth censer is a plague.*

The consequences flowing from this fact are many: —

1. Since a plague, the sixth censer is *not a blessing*. No blessings whatever are comprehended in the sixth censer.

5. The dried Euphrates (xvi. 12) is *not a blessing*, but is a part of the plague contained in the sixth censer.

3. "The kings [kingdoms] of the east" (verse 12) are also portions of the sixth plague. Thus plagues, "the kingdoms of the east," are *not blessings*. They cannot be *Christian* kingdoms. They are kingdoms, organizations, systems of thought, cherishing and practising deadly hostility to the revelation from heaven by Jesus Christ.

12. And the sixth was scattering his censer-basin upon the great river Euphrates, and its water is dried up, that the way for the kings, who are from the rising of the sun, may be fully prepared.

The great river Euphrates: the same expression (ix. 14) on which see note.

In Isa. viii. 7, 8, the Euphrates is the symbol of *invading armies*.

In Rev. ix. 14, and xvi. 12, the Euphrates is the symbolic barrier against hostile invasion. When the spring floods swell this rapid river, no army can cross it, and Palestine is safe from the attacks and ravages of her Eastern enemies. Thus the symbol of *security*, the

Euphrates, cannot possibly symbolize *papal* Babylon, inasmuch as it continually renders the true Church of Christ *insecure.*

Its water is dried up: there is no reference here to the capture of Babylon by the Medo-Persian king Cyrus (Herodotus ii. 191).

Cyrus did not dry up the Euphrates: he merely turned a portion of the river into a new channel, that his soldiers might be able to ford the main stream.

The reference here is to the fact that the Euphrates is rendered *passable* by the droughts of summer. When the Euphrates is *fordable,* Eastern armies can invade the Holy Land.

The prophet Jeremiah recognizes this fact. "A drought is upon her waters [the waters of Babylon], and they shall be dried up" (Jer. l. 38).

Both Jeremiah and St. John refer to actual occurrences in the river Euphrates.

The way: the road *for* the kings. So "the way, the road *for* the Lord" (Matt. iii. 3).

Kings are kingdoms (Dan. vii. 23).

Kingdoms are the people composing them. "Kingdom [people] divided against itself" (Matt. xii. 25).

Who are from the rising of the sun: distant people of the East, opposed to the gospel of the incarnate Son of God, are intended.

The language of this verse 12 requires a spiritual and enlarged interpretation.

God is pleased to subject his Church to incessant conflicts with error and sin. Here the enemies of the Church are primarily from Eastern countries. As a Jew, St. John derives his images of hostility from Assyria and Babylon, countries east of Judæa, and from countries even more remote. The Eastern countries mentioned in the Bible are Arabia, Babylon, Media, Persia, India (Esth. i. 1, viii. 9), China (Sinim, Isa. xlix. 12). The religious systems of these Eastern countries may therefore be intended by "the kings [kingdoms] of the East;" namely, the systems of Mohammed, Zoroaster, Brahma, Buddha, Confucius, Laou-Tzse.

Infidelity, Western as well as Eastern, whether among Jews, nominal Christians, or heathen, may be included in "the kingdoms of the East," for these reasons: —

1. The word "East" here denotes not so much *locality,* as *opposition* to the Church of Christ.

2. The Jews in the time of St. John, as a nation, were with regard to Christ infidels (Acts xiv. 2), and are infidels now.

3. Our Lord admits the existence of infidelity at every period of the world (Mark xvi. 16).

4. In reference to Christ, all the religious systems of Asia are

to-day infidel. Most of them are also infidel with regard to the existence of God, and the immortality of the human soul.

The sixth and *last* plague must include all the forms of opposition to Christ to be plagued and punished.

Would we, therefore, survey the hostile armies gathering themselves to the battle-field of Armageddon (verse 16), there to exterminate Christianity from the earth, as the prophetic eye of St. John surveys the mustering hosts, we may see there infidelity, both Western and Eastern, whether traditional, scientific, speculative, agnostic, or atheistic.

The Three Unclean Spirits as Frogs (Verses 13, 14).

13. Also I saw [this vision]: out of the mouth of the dragon, and out of the mouth of the wild beast, and out of the mouth of the false prophet, three unclean spirits, as frogs.

In attempting to explain this difficult verse, we shall adhere closely to the language and imagery of the Bible.

1. **Out of the mouth**: is *speech*. Proofs: "That which cometh out of the mouth" (Matt. xv. 11). "Something out of his mouth" (Luke xi. 54). "Out of thine own mouth will I judge thee" (xix. 22). "Communication out of the mouth" (Eph. iv. 29).

2. But speech is *food* in a *figurative* sense.

"I could not *speak* unto you as unto spiritual, but as unto carnal. I have *fed* you with milk, and not with meat" (1 Cor. iii. 1, 2).

Of the dragon, of the wild beast, of the false prophet: in xii. 17 there is the dragon; in xiii. 1, a wild beast from the sea; in xiii. 11, a wild beast from the land.

This threefold enumeration of chapters xii. and xiii. is repeated in xvi. 13. As the same objects are intended in each enumeration, the false prophet of xvi. 13 (first time he is mentioned) is the *second* wild beast of chapter xiii.; that is, the false prophet is the wild beast from the land.

The false prophet: in Revelation, only here and xix. 20, xx. 10.

In Jer. xxviii. 1, the Septuagint calls Hananiah, who lied to Jeremiah, the false prophet. In Rev. xiii. 14, the false prophet *deceives*, and thus is "false." In xix. 20, he is both false and deceiving. He thus deserves the name St. John gives, "the false prophet."

Three unclean spirits: as a symbolic number, three represents an *integer*, or whole number. See notes on vi. 6.

"Israel shall be *the third* [*one* number] with Egypt [*two* numbers] and with Assyria [*three* numbers], a blessing [*one* blessing] in the midst of the land" (Isa. xix. 24, 25).

In practical life, the Jews measured by *thirds*, three being an *integer*. "*A third part* shall be keepers of the king's house; *a third part* at the gate of Sur; *a third part* behind the guard. So [by thirds] shall ye keep *the watch* [the *whole* watch]" (2 Kings xi. 5, 6).

This same arithmetic exists in the Book of Revelation, and in this chapter xvi.

The great city is for three parts (xvi. 19). That is, the great city is three parts. In other words, the great city is, *as a whole*, fallen. No part is reserved from destruction. Otherwise, in Zech. xiii. 8, "*Two* parts shall be cut off, but *the third* shall be left."

Here (Zech. xiii. 8) is the same division by thirds; three forming *the integer*, the whole number.

When, then, St. John says, "I saw *three* spirits," he means to say, "I saw *many* spirits." "Three," in St. John's enumeration, is the equivalent of our Lord's "seven," when describing the action of an *unclean* spirit; "he taketh with him *seven* spirits," that is, *many* spirits (Matt. xii. 45).

Unclean: in what sense? In Revelation, the word is only here, and xvii. 4, xviii. 2, where the word is not explained. In Matt. xii. 45, " unclean " is defined by " wicked," " evil," " hurtful."

St. John, therefore, saw many evil and hurtful spirits issuing from *each* of these three mouths, — the mouth of the dragon, the mouth of the wild beast, and the mouth of the false prophet, the wild beast from the land. Each open mouth, like the open face of the river Nile in the time of Moses, expelling innumerable hordes of invading frogs, sends out an unnumbered host of wicked and hurtful spirits, invading not a single valley, but all portions of the habitable earth.

Does usage elsewhere require the issue of the spirits from *each* mouth? This is the requirement of Bible usage.

"*One witness* shall not rise up against a man for any iniquity: *at the mouth* of *two* witnesses, or *at the mouth* of *three*, shall the matter be established" (Deut. xix. 15).

"Answer in the mouth of these three men" (Job xxxii. 5).

As frogs: not "*like* frogs," English Version.

The word "frog" only here in New Testament. In Septuagint, only Exod. viii. 2, 7; Ps. lxxviii. 45, cv. 30; Wis. of Sol. xix. 10.

The origin of the imagery is this: —

At many points on the Euphrates, there are extensive marshes (*Dict. of the Bible*, article " Euphrates ").

Wherever there are fresh-water marshes, frogs abound. When the marshes dry up, the frogs wander forth to find new marshy grounds having water.

The imagery of the frogs in this verse 13 may be derived from these facts. With the drying-up of the Euphrates, frogs would appear, and sally forth in their uncertain search. Having mentioned the appearance of the river, St. John would very naturally refer to the consequent manifestation of the thirsty frogs.

For a long period were the Euphrates and its accompaniments the source of imagery to the Jews.

For *seventy* years the captive Jews resided on the Euphrates and its tributaries. Familiar, therefore, were they with its different forms of animal life.

Their prophets derive not a few illustrations from the trees and occupants of the great river. "We hanged our silent harps upon its *willows*" (Ps. cxxxvii. 2).

With the prophet Isaiah, the region of the Euphrates is the resort of "dragons and wild beasts" (Isa. xiii. 21, 22), the very same objects St. John introduces into his Apocalypse.

The natural connection of the appearance of the frogs with the failure of the Euphrates by summer droughts admits *the possibility* that the drying of the river suggested frogs to the Hebrew mind of St. John.

His own actual use of the objects "the dragon and the wild beast" (xvi. 13), placed by Isaiah on the Euphrates, creates *the probability*, that, having thus used *a portion* of the objects on the Euphrates, St. John derived the imagery of the frogs from the same locality.

At the present time, frogs swarm in the streams of Palestine (*Dict. of the Bible*, article "Frogs").

Frogs must have been often seen there by St. John. His usage elsewhere, however, shows us that he would take his imagery of the frogs rather from the Old Testament than from personal observation.

In our Lord's account of "unclean spirits," his words agree remarkably with the movements of frogs when deserting marshes deprived of water, "He walketh through *dry places, seeking rest,* and *finding none*" (Matt. xii. 43).

Is it not possible, that among the Jews it was customary, after their captivity in Babylon, to call unclean spirits frogs, and to illustrate the actions of unclean spirits by the uncertain wandering of frogs?

To this question, the following facts are all the answers the Scriptures return; namely, —

1. The action of "the unclean spirit" (Matt. xii. 43) *strongly resembles* the movements of the frog when dislodged by drought.

2. St. John himself (whether or not he follows customary usage, is uncertain) expressly declares that the unclean spirits coming in

swarms from the mouths of the dragon and his two wild beasts were *in appearance* "frogs."

These facts cannot be denied. The possibility and the probability they create may assist us in the interpretation of this figurative and important passage.

1. We have already seen that in this verse "three" denotes a full indefinite number, *many*.

The first time frogs appear in sacred history, they are *in swarms innumerable*. "The frogs came up [from the river Nile], and covered the land of Egypt." So "abundantly" (Exod. viii. 3) did they come, that they entered "the houses, the bed-chambers, the ovens, and the kneading-troughs" (Exod. viii. 6).

The absorbing multitudes of frogs invading Egypt help us understand the imagery indicating countless numbers, when St. John says, "I saw *three* unclean spirits as frogs," — "I saw unclean spirits as innumerable as the frogs in Egypt."

2. The innumerable spirits seen by St. John are "unclean."

By the Mosaic law, the frog was an unclean animal.

"All that have not fins and scales in the seas, and in the rivers, of all that move in the waters, and of every living thing which is in the waters, *they shall be an abomination unto you*" (Lev. xi. 10).

In the spirit of this law, the frog, as food, was not sacred and good, but was profane and hurtful.

In the Wisdom of Solomon (xix. 10), this is the assertion, "the river [Nile] cast up a multitude of frogs *instead of fishes*." The contrast between frogs and fishes proves that the writer here regards frogs as *hurtful food*.

When, then, in Rev. xvi. 13, the frog is the symbol of speech, the speech is bad and anti-Christian.

St. Paul (1 Tim. i. 10, vi. 3; 2 Tim. i. 13, iv. 3; Tit. i. 9, 13, ii. 1, 2, 8) enjoins "sound wholesome doctrine, sound speech;" that is, *healthful* speech.

Frogs, as symbols, are *the exact opposite* of sound doctrine, of *healthful* speech. They represent every religious and moral error which is opposed to the letter and spirit of the gospel of Jesus Christ.

Moreover, in Ps. lxxviii. 45, frogs are said to have "*destroyed*" the Egyptians. Guided, therefore, by this declaration, we are authorized to say, that the frogs without number in Rev. xvi. 13 are symbols not only of unsound doctrine, but of *destructive* doctrine. Error, the opposite and antagonist of truth, so far as error prevails, destroys and annihilates the truth.

14. For they are spirits of devils performing signs, which are going forth upon the kings of the entire habitable world to gather them unto the great day of God Almighty.

For: introduces an explanation of the unclean spirits (verse 13).

Spirits of devils: spirits *proceeding* from devils; spirits *sent forth* by devils.

What is the difference between unclean spirits and devils? In Rev. xviii. 2, devils are *superior* to the unclean spirits. Devil and unclean spirit differ as master and servant differ.

There are *orders* of evil spirits (Eph. vi. 12). Devils are one class; unclean spirits are another class. The two classes cannot be identical. A devil has not a spirit separate from himself: he is himself a spirit.

"Devils" cannot here be the genitive of *possession*, but of *origin*. The spirits *proceed* from devils. Consequently, —

1. Spirits and devils (Rev. xvi. 14) are *two* objects.
2. Spirits are *inferior*. Devils are *superior*.

But the dragon, the wild beast, and the false prophet are themselves devils. From their mouths come the unclean spirits. Accordingly, the devils, from whom the unclean spirits proceed, are the dragon, the wild beast from the sea, and the wild beast from the land.

As devils, the dragon, the wild beast, and the false prophet *are not*, in their inhabitation, influence, and operations, confined to any localities.

"Satan goes to and fro in the earth, and walks up and down in it" (Job i. 7). The Devil is "the prince of the power of the air" (Eph. ii. 2). The air encompasses the whole earth. Wherever, then, there are now "children of disobedience," the Devil is "the spirit now working in them" (Eph. ii. 2). All continents and islands are the wide fields where the Devil exerts his baneful "power" at the present time.

Performing signs: pretended miracles.

The second wild beast professes to perform miracles through the power of the first wild beast (xiii. 12, 13, where see notes). Both wild beasts are servants of the dragon, who is therefore "prince" (Eph. ii. 2) over them. The unclean spirits, the emissaries of the dragon and the wild beasts, also profess to work miracles.

Which (spirits) **are going out** (from the mouths of the dragon and the two wild beasts) **upon the kings**: this sentence is an instance of *constructio prægnans*. The spirits go out from their masters' mouths, and *come upon* the kings to control their minds and lives.

"*Coming upon,*" describes elsewhere the powerful action of the Holy Spirit:—

"Lighting *upon him* " (Matt. iii. 16).

"*Came on them*" (Acts xix. 6).

The coming, therefore, of the unclean spirits, is attended with hurtful power.

The kings: mentioned verse 12, and in the same sense. These kings are kingdoms (Dan. vii. 23). The kingdoms are *the people* composing the kingdoms (Matt. xii. 25), embracing at the present time the vast populations of the Eastern world.

The unclean spirits proceed from the dragon, the wild beast, and the false prophet, the symbolic representatives of the apostate Church of Rome. These spirits, thus originating and thus controlled, in turn create the religious systems of the people of the East, and the infidelity of both East and West.

The principles of this apostate Church, and of these Asiatic and infidel systems, are essentially the same. *Rationalism* is the basis of modern Romanism, as it is the basis of all metaphysical systems and of all infidelity.

The Church of Rome claims perpetual spiritual inspiration. As this claim is *an assumption,* the pretended inspiration can be nothing else than the dictation of *human reason.*

The modern Roman dogma of *transubstantiation* is a series of metaphysical — and, therefore, rationalistic — assumptions. Neither Scripture nor historical tradition knows any thing of the monstrous absurdity.

So far, then, as Rome is false to the teaching of Christ, is this Church rationalistic, and the associate and helper of infidelity.

All the Asiatic systems of religion, and all the forms of infidelity everywhere, are obviously and undeniably *rationalistic.*

In her own modern rationalism, then, Rome identifies herself with every form of religious thought on the Continent of Asia, and likewise with every species of infidelity, whether in the East or in the West.

To gather: the infinitive of design. So, —

"To make war" (xii. 17).

"Battle" (xx. 8).

Day: vi. 17, xi. 8, xii. 6, xviii. 8.

This battle is incessant, at all times, and everywhere (Eph. vi. 12). It prefigures and hastens the final and decisive conflict, when Christ shall prove supreme Victor over all his enemies, — perverted human reason, practical wickedness, and "the carnal mind."

Christ's Warning to His People.

15. Behold, I come as a thief. Blessed is he that watcheth, and keepeth his garments, lest he walk naked, and they see his shame.

Come: the present tense. Christ is now coming all the time.

As a thief: suddenly and unexpectedly (Matt. xxiv. 42–44; 1 Thess. v. 2; 2 Pet. iii. 10). Phrase in Revelation, only here and iii. 3.

Christ comes suddenly to defeat Babylon, and her allies the kings of the East. He exhorts each one of us to be now living and fighting for him.

Watcheth: in Revelation, only here and iii. 3, which see.

Keepeth: holds, retains, keeps white.

Garments: in Revelation, only here and iii. 4, 5, 18, iv. 4, xix. 13, 14. White garments (iii. 4, 5, 18), emblems of holiness of heart (xix. 8).

Walk: live.

Naked: without inward righteousness (iii. 17). In Revelation, only here and iii. 17, xvii. 16.

See: denotes *spiritual* discernment (iii. 18, v. 3, 4). The *subjects* of the verb are the Father, Son, and Holy Ghost, the discerners of the heart (ii. 23).

Shame: in New Testament, only here and Rom. i. 27. Indecency: his shameful want of spiritual holiness.

This, then (verse 15), is Christ's warning and exhortation to every Christian: The world is full of error and sin. Your life of probation may end at any moment. Be watchful over yourself, and against your numerous spiritual enemies. Keep and preserve your inward holiness, lest, when I try your character, I find you destitute of my own holy image in your soul.

Har-Megiddon, the Place of Muster.

16. And so the spirits are gathering the kings unto the place which is called in the Hebrew, Har-Megiddon, the mount of Megiddo.

Gathering: for defeat. The subject of this verb is "the spirits" (verse 14).

"Them" (English Version): that is, the kings, the kingdoms, the people of the kingdoms (verse 14).

Har-Megiddon: Mount Megiddo (Judg. v. 19). The reference is to the victory Barak and Deborah gained over Sisera, the commander of the army of Jabin, king of Canaan.

The defeat of the heathen Sisera was complete. Thus complete will be the defeat of the kings, nations, and religious and metaphysical systems now contending with revealed truth and the Church of Christ.

Not *locality* is intended by Har-Megiddon, but the utter overthrow of all false systems, and the absolute and eternal triumph of Christ's Church on this earth.

THE SEVENTH ANGEL (Verses 17-21).
See xi. 15.

17. And the seventh angel was scattering his censer-basin upon the air; and there comes a loud voice out of the holy of holies from the throne, saying, "It is done."

The air: in Revelation, only here and ix. 2, — the atmosphere.

The reference may be to these words of the Book of Exodus: "The Lord said unto Moses, Stretch forth thy hand *toward heaven*, that there may be *hail* in all the land of Egypt" (ix. 22).

The hand of Moses stretched *toward* heaven brought the plague of hail. The seventh censer cast *upon the air* brings the responses of "voices, thunders, lightnings, a great earthquake, and *great hail out of heaven*" (Rev. xvi. 18, 21).

The atmospheric convulsions at Megiddo are here repeated: "They fought from heaven. The stars in their courses fought against Sisera" (Judg. v. 20).

Comes, etc.: the loud voice from the throne in the holy of holies is the voice of God Almighty, the supreme Judge.

It is done: *prophetically.* The word *anticipates* the great and decisive events of chapters xvii., xviii., xix.

When the final consummation is reached, the same declaration is repeated, "It is done" *actually* (Rev. xxi. 6).

It cannot be undone. All the prophecies of God, both of good and evil, of blessing and curse, will be fully and unalterably accomplished.

18. And so there are lightnings and voices and thunders. Also there is a great earthquake, such as has not been since men were on the earth, so great an earthquake, so very great.

And so: the consequence of the loud voice of God, "It is done."

The unexampled earthquake is a symbolic prediction of the greater changes about to take place among the inhabitants of the earth.

The several comparative expressions magnify the greatness and extent of the earthquake. The greater the earthquake, the greater the divine power exerted; the greater the divine power, the greater the certainty that God's promise, "*It is done*," will be fulfilled.

The Destruction of Babylon and her Allied Cities symbolically predicted (Verses 19-21).

19. And the great city becomes three parts. Also the cities of the heathen fall. And so Babylon the great is remembered before God, to give her the cup of the fierceness of his wrath.

The great city: see xi. 8 and note, xiv. 8 and note, xvii. 18, xviii. 10, 16, 18, 19, 21. These references, and the second clause of this verse 19, prove that the great city is Babylon.

Becomes three parts: see vi. 6, viii. 11, xvi. 13. Three parts are the whole. No part is reserved from destruction. In Zech. xiii. 8, one part is reserved. Both in Isa. xix. 23, 24, and Zech. xiii. 8, three is an *integer*. This usage furnishes an effective key to a portion of the numbers in the Apocalypse.

The cities of the heathen fell: these cities are identical with the kingdoms of the East (verse 12).

Also: additional. The fall of the capital city, Babylon, is accompanied by the fall of its allied cities of the East, partaking of its spirit and character.

Heathen: the Greek word has this sense (xi. 2, and Luke ii. 32).

Here the cities are the capitals of the kingdoms of the East. As a capital, Babylon stands for its kingdom. So also the cities of the East stand for their kingdoms.

Apostate Rome and the heathen systems of religion in the East are alike enemies of the true Church, and are alike destined by God to removal and destruction.

Is remembered: in Revelation, only here; is remembered by God for punishment. Sometimes the remembrance is for blessing (Acts x. 31, compared with verse 4).

Her: Babylon is personified; "*the woman* is the great city" (xvii. 18).

The cup of the wine of the rage of his wrath: the strongest intensification. The cup filled with rage and wrath is most deadly.

A cup containing poison, the ancients sometimes administered to criminals. This practice is the origin of the imagery in Ps. xl. 6, which St. John here repeats.

The Athenians condemned Socrates to drink hemlock.

20. And so every island flees away. Even mountains cannot be found.

The sublimity of verbal brevity.
And so: the unexampled earthquake sinks all islands into the oceans and seas, and levels the highest mountains to uniform plains.
Even: intensive. "*Even* the unclean spirits" (Mark i. 27). "*Even* that which he hath" (iv. 25). "*Even* we ourselves" (Rom. viii. 23).
Mountains: the highest mountains.
Cannot be found: by seeking. "*Seek*, and ye shall find" (Matt. vii. 7). The language is most highly figurative, predicting the greatest religious revolutions and overthrows (vi. 13, note).

Before the geological periods, there were on the surface of the earth no mountains whatever. The great earthquake contemplated by St. John reduces all the present mountain ranges to their original stratified level. Save its utter destruction, the earth cannot experience a greater change than this. Since the symbolical change is thus great without example, the religious revolutions symbolized to occur in the fast-approaching future must in vastness exceed our loftiest imaginations.

21. And great hailstones, each stone as of a talent weight, come down out of heaven upon the men. And yet the men blasphemed God, because of the plague of the hail, for its plague is exceeding great.

Hailstones: Exod. ix. 24. Hailstones symbolize the wrath of God (Josh. x. 11; Ps. xviii. 7, 13; Isa. xxx. 30; Ezek. xiii. 11).
A talent: the Jewish talent, here referred to, weighed more than *one hundred* pounds.
The men: having the mark of the wild beast (verse 2).
Blaspheme: in xi. 13, the survivors repent, but *not here*.

All forms of religious error ultimately resolve themselves into *unbelief and hardness of heart* (Luke xvi. 31). Hardness and impenitence, in turn, accumulate wrath against the day of wrath and revelation of the righteous judgment of God (Rom. ii. 5).

The seven censers (chapter xvi.) are symbolical *predictions*. The subsequent chapters of Part II. — namely, xvii., xviii., xix. — contain the symbolical *fulfilments* of these predictions.

CHAPTER XVII.

THE GREAT ADULTERESS AND HER DOMINION
(Verses 1, 2).

1. AND there comes one of the seven angels, who have the seven censer-basins, and he talks with me, saying, Come hither, I will show thee the judgment of the great adulteress, who is sitting upon many waters.

One of the seven angels: this angel seems to be the seventh. After he empties his censer, Babylon, who is the adulteress, is prophetically destroyed. We may expect the same angel to narrate the causes and antecedents of her destruction.

Will show: will place *before your eyes*. "*I saw* a woman" (verse 3). "*I saw* the woman" (verse 6). "*I saw* her" (verse 6).

The judgment: in Revelation, the word is only here and xviii. 20, xx. 4. In xviii. 20, this noun stands with the verb from which it is derived, thus: from her, God is avenging her judgment *on* you. This verse 20 determines, therefore, the sense of xvii. 1 to be the *infliction* of the judgment *on* the adulteress. "I will place before your eyes the visible infliction of the judgment on the great adulteress."

The judgment on the adulteress is, according to the law of Moses, the loss of life. "The adulteress shall surely be put to death" (Lev. xx. 10).

The great adulteress: the great apostate Church, — great in her size, great in her sin, — by *personification* for her empire.

Through her faithlessness to God, Eve became a spiritual adulteress.

The Old-Testament Church, because unfaithful to God, is called an adulteress. "How is the *faithful* city become a *harlot!*" (Isa. i. 21.) "Thou hast played the *harlot*, yet return unto *me*, saith the Lord" (Jer. iii. 1).

Rev. ii. 14, 20, 21, does not prove that the name "harlot" may describe a *Pagan power*. The Balaamites (Rev. ii. 14) are not Pagan, but are *members of the Church of Pergamos*. Jezebel (Rev. ii. 20, 21) is not Pagan, but is a personification of a *portion of the Church of Thyatira*.

Many waters: the "waters" are symbols of "peoples and multitudes and nations and tongues" (verse 15).

The phrase occurs first in the prophet Jeremiah, where it refers to the historical Babylon: "thou that dwellest upon *many waters*" (li. 13).

St. John repeats the phraseology of this Old-Testament prophet, and applies it to the Babylon on the Tiber.

2. **With whom the kings of the earth are committing fornication, and the inhabitants of the earth are making themselves drunk with the wine of her fornication.**

The Bible connects drunkenness with wantonness, as effect and cause (Dan. v. 23; Rom. xiii. 13). History and personal experience record the same connection. Carnal sins are closely associated. Libertines are often also drunkards.

Fornication is spiritual idolatry. In this verse 2, this idolatry is represented first as a life, and then as an intoxicating draught.

Both rulers and people are guilty of this great sin.

Kings of the earth: worldly rulers, and yet nominally Christian.

Make themselves drunk: John ii. 10. Permit themselves to be made drunk (Rev. xiv. 8).

This is historically illustrated by the state of Europe in the middle ages, when popes controlled kings and kingdoms.

DESCRIPTION OF THE WOMAN (Verses 3–6).

3. **And so he carries me away into the wilderness, by the Spirit. And I see a woman sitting upon a scarlet wild beast, full of names of blasphemy, having seven heads and ten horns.**

The wilderness: the *same* wilderness is here intended as Rev. xii. 6, 14.

In Rev. xii. 6, 14, the wilderness is for *refuge and safety*. In Rev. xvii. 3, the same wilderness is *the resort* of evil spirits and their subordinates (notes on Rev. xii. 6).

Woman: by *personification* for the apostate Church. Identical with the woman of xii. 1–17. The *same* woman in *different* characters, of faithfulness or apostasy.

Our Lord himself predicts apostasy. "When the Son of man cometh, shall he find faith on the earth?" (Luke xviii. 8).

The "harlot city" (Isa. i. 21), even "Judah and Jerusalem" (verse 1), was still "Zion," capable of "restoration and redemption" (verses 25–27). The "harlot Babylon" (Rev. xvii. 5) has the same capability.

Both the women (Rev. xii. 6 and xvii. 3) are *representative* women. Each represents a *Church-condition.* In xii. 6, the woman represents *Church-purity.* In xvii. 3, the woman represents *Church-impurity.*

The *second* representative woman (xvii. 3) is a "harlot." But harlotry implies previous innocence. Harlotry is preceded by purity. No woman is born a harlot. The harlot-woman (Rev. xvii. 3) could not have become such, had she not formerly been a pure woman. The second woman (Rev. xvii. 3) was therefore once a pure woman. The change of the same representative woman from purity to impurity, Jehovah himself recognizes and announces, when he thus exclaims, "How is the *faithful* city *become a harlot!*" (Isa. i. 21.) The same woman is first faithful and pure, and then unfaithful and impure. Eve was holy before she became unholy. Eve was faithful to God before she was unfaithful.

But only in the person of the woman of Rev. xii. 6, does the Apocalypse present any pure woman who could become impure. In this book, therefore, just as in the case of Eve, and as in the Book of Isaiah, the pure woman *precedes* the impure woman. The pure woman of Rev. xii. 6, consequently, becomes the impure woman of Rev. xvii. 3. In other words, the two representative women (Rev. xii. 6 and xvii. 3) are *the same woman* in different characters and conditions.

This, then, is the humiliating and instructive truth represented by the two women (Rev. xii. 6 and xvii. 3): The pure Church of Christ, imitating the degeneracy of Eve and of the Old-Testament Church, degenerates into a Church impure and corrupt, and is changed into a fiend devastating and bloody, fit to saddle and ride a demon arising from the ocean, the *genatrix* of behemoth, leviathan, and sea-serpents; "sitting upon a scarlet-colored wild beast."

Wild beast: the same as in xiii. 1–8. The wild beast out of the sea, the symbol of the *Pagan* Roman Empire (Rev. xiii. 1, 2, notes).

Sitting: not guiding and controlling the wild beast (John xii. 15; Rev. vi. 2), but governed and directed by the wild beast himself.

On account of her bodily weakness, a woman cannot control a wild beast.

The woman on the wild beast is a "queen" (xviii. 7). No queen in the Bible history ever rides in a chariot, on an ass, or on a horse. The image of a woman governing a wild beast is, according to Bible representations, both unnatural and incongruous.

"The woman arrayed in purple and scarlet, sitting upon a scarlet-colored beast," does not guide and govern him: he guides and governs her. As the first wild beast controls and directs the second, so the first wild beast controls and directs the queen sitting upon him. *Pagan* Rome is the foundation of *Papal* Rome.

Papal Rome claims universal empire, both civil and ecclesiastical. The harlot Babylon is the Apocalyptic representative of both these closely associated claims.

Scarlet: *blood*-color, not fire-red (vi. 4, xii. 3).

Bloodshedding is affirmed of the Church of Rome (xvi. 6, xvii. 6, xviii. 24). Her past history verifies the prediction. Both the harlot-woman, and the wild beast she rides and by whom she is directed, are scarlet, because dyed with the blood of the saints which they have already shed, and are, in purpose, continually shedding.

Full: in xiii. 1, only the *heads* of the wild beast display names of blasphemy. Now his *whole body* is covered with these blasphemous names.

In its *Christian* form, the Roman Empire is even more blasphemous than in its Pagan.

"The man of sin opposeth and exalteth himself above all that is called God, or that is worshipped; so that he as God sitteth in the temple of God, showing himself that he is God" (2 Thess. ii. 4).

Seven heads and ten horns: in xiii. 1, this same beast has not only seven heads and ten horns, but ten diadems upon his ten horns. The ten diadems are, therefore, here implied.

4. And the woman was always clothed with purple and scarlet, and gilded with gold and every precious stone, and with pearls, holding in her hand a golden cup full of abominations, even the impurities of her fornication.

Clothed: by others (iii. 5). Her subjects provide her with the most costly luxuries.

Always: not merely on state occasions, but in her every-day life.

Purple: an imperial color (Ecclus. xl. 3, 4; 1 Macc. viii. 14).

Gilded: Exod. xxvi. 32, 37. "Overlaid with gold-leaf."

Gold: gold studs, gems.

Pearls: treasures of the sea, as well as of the land; precious stones, previously mentioned.

Cup: of solid gold; for intoxication (Jer. li. 7). The imagery in the several following places is taken from this chapter of Jeremiah.

Impurities: the "abominations" impart impurity.
Fornication: spiritual idolatry.

5. And upon her forehead a name written: MYSTERY, BABYLON THE GREAT, THE MOTHER OF HARLOTS, AND OF THE ABOMINATIONS OF THE EARTH.

Forehead: "stetisti puella in lupinari . . . nomen tuum pependit in fronte."—SENECA. *Controv.* i.
"Thou hadst a whore's forehead. Thou refusedst to be ashamed" (Jer. iii. 3).
"The whoredom of a woman may be known in her haughty looks and eyelids" (Ecclus. xxvi. 9).
Mystery: the name Babylon, etc., and in a *spiritual* sense. The historical Babylon was the promoter of *literal* idolatry. *Papal* Babylon is the promoter of *spiritual* idolatry.
The mother: the parent-city of other spiritually idolatrous cities.

6. And I saw the woman drunken with the blood of the saints, even with the blood of martyrs of Jesus. And I wondered, thus seeing with great wonder.

Drunken: the woman not only sheds human blood, but she drinks it. She is a cannibal.
Drinking blood is forbidden by God (Gen. ix. 4).
The blood of enemies was sometimes drunken (Num. xxiii. 24; see Rev. xvi. 6).
The martyrs of Jesus: the martyrs *belonging* to Jesus. "*My* martyr" (ii. 13).
Great wonder: St. John is astonished to see the pure woman of xii. 6 changed into an impure monster, gorging herself with human blood. "How is the faithful city become a harlot!" (Isa. i. 21.)

THE MYSTERY OF THE WOMAN AND OF THE BEAST THAT CARRIETH HER (Verses 7–18).

7. And the angel saith to me, Wherefore dost thou wonder? I myself will tell thee the mystery of the woman, and of the wild beast that carrieth her, which has the seven heads and ten horns.

Wherefore: you need not wonder. I will explain.
Mystery: the explanation.
Carrieth: habitually (Luke x. 4; John xii. 6).

EXPLANATION OF THE WILD BEAST (Verses 8-14).

St. John explains the mystery of the wild beast *before* he explains the mystery of the woman.

It is Bible usage to mention the horse *before* mentioning the rider (Exod. xv. 21; Job xxxix. 18; Jer. li. 21; Rev. vi. 2, 4, 5, 8).

8. The wild beast, which thou seest, was, and is not; and yet he is certainly to arise from the bottomless pit, and yet to destruction is certainly to depart; and so the inhabitants of the earth, of whom not a name is written on the book of life from the foundation of the world, shall wonder, because they see the wild beast, that he was, and is not, and yet shall be present.

Wild beast: by *personification*, Rome as a power civil and ecclesiastical.

Was: existed, in past time, in its original secular, imperial, and heathenish form.

Is not: comes to an end in the disappearance of outward heathenism.

And yet he is certainly to arise: spiritual idolatry succeeds the extinction of outward idol-worship.

From the bottomless pit: the abode of the devil, as the following places prove: Rev. ix. 1, 2, 11, xi. 7, xvii. 8, xx. 1, 3, the only instances in Revelation where "the bottomless pit" occurs.

The devil causes the re-appearance of the wild beast in the *Papal* form of the Roman Empire. In the rise and development of the Papal usurpation and domination, the "deadly wound" of the Pagan empire "is apparently healed" (xiii. 3) for a season. The life of the wild beast from the bottomless pit is not immortal.

In chapter xiii. 3, is our explanation of the wound inflicted on the first wild beast, and of its partial and temporary healing. The wound and the healing is a continual process. The gospel is incessantly piercing error with deadly sword-thrusts. The historical facts which follow are illustrations of the vicissitudes of the progressive conflict.

A.D. 476, the German King Odoacer seized the city of Rome, dethroned Romulus Momyllus Augustulus, *the last* of the Roman emperors, and put an end to the Empire of the West (*Revolutions in Europe*, p. 49).

The *spirit* of imperialism, however, survived.

The title of Universal Bishop was first *assumed* by John, bishop of Constantinople, A.D. 587 (JARVIS, *Reply to Milner*, p. 246).

The title of Universal Bishop was *conferred* on Boniface III. by the Roman Emperor Phocas, A.D. 606 (MOSHEIM, *Eccl. Hist.* i. pp. 436, 437).

Thus history confirms the prediction of St. Paul (2 Thess. ii. 6, 7), and the prediction of St. John (Rev. xvii. 8), that extinction of the Roman Empire *Pagan* would be succeeded by the assumption of universal dominion by the Church of Rome.

The supremacy of the Roman Church and pontiff was *proclaimed* by the Lateran Council IV., A.D. 1215 (PERCEVAL, *Roman Schism*, pp. 138, 140, 148).

The Council of Florence *proclaimed* the supremacy of the Pope, A.D. 1438 (PERCEVAL, pp. 153, 358).

The creed of Pius IV., article xi., repeats this decree of the Council of Florence, A.D. 1564 (JARVIS, *Reply to Milner*, p. 123; PERCEVAL, p. xlviii.).

The infallibility of the Pope was *proclaimed* by the Council of Rome, A.D. 1870.

These dates, while they fully confirm St. John's language in Rev. xvii. 8, also prove most conclusively that the Church of Rome, as it now is, is comparatively a novelty, as in her present form and claims she was utterly unknown in the world till the beginning of the *seventh century* of the Christian era. That which is first *is true*. That which is later *is false*. The false, God destines to give place to the true.

And yet to destruction he is certainly to depart: the destruction of the wild beast is contrasted with his re-appearance. As certainly as the wild beast re-appears, so certainly will he disappear. God appoints Popery to destruction. Its life is mortal (2 Thess. ii. 8).

Shall wonder: with superstitious awe.

Present: the Greek verb *always* means *to be present;* never means *to come*.

In the New Testament, the noun derived from this verb *never* means "coming," but *always* means *presence*. The Vulgate *adventus* is not the correct translation of this noun. *Presentia* is the word the Vulgate should have invariably used. "Coming" is mere *arrival*. Presence implies *life, activity, influence*.

In the prediction, "the wild beast shall be present," life, activity, influence, are embodied. The prediction is God's through the declaration of the angel. The prediction reveals the mind and purpose of God respecting the old Roman Empire. In the midst of these external changes, it survives in the mind of God for a season, but is constantly giving place to "the stone cut out of the mountain without hands,". the kingdom of Christ, his true Church, which "shall stand forever" (Dan. ii. 44, 45).

9. Here is the mind which hath wisdom. The seven heads are seven mountains, where the woman sitteth on them.

Here: in the words I am about to speak. In Revelation, the Greek particle translated "here" occurs only in xiii. 18, and xvii. 9; in each place, in a *local* sense.

The mind: that is, the sense, the explanation. In Phil. iv. 7, the same Greek word is translated "understanding." "The peace of God passeth all *understanding;*" that is, all *explanation*.

Wisdom: that is, the meaning intended. Wisdom has this sense in Eph. i. 8: "abounded toward us in all *wisdom, having made known* unto us."

"A patient man will *hide his words* for a time, but the lips of many shall declare his *wisdom,*" the meaning intended (Ecclus. i. 24).

"By speech, wisdom [the meaning intended] shall be known" (iv. 24).

"Every man of understanding knoweth wisdom [the meaning intended]" (xviii. 28).

"Wisdom [the meaning intended] that is hid, what profit?" (xx. 30.)

The explanation of the wisdom — that is, of the meaning intended by wisdom — in Rev. xvii. 9 now follows, in the second part of the verse.

The seven heads are seven mountains: the top of a mountain is sometimes called a "*head*." "*Head* of Lebanon" (Jer. xxii. 6). St. John adopts this usage when he says, "The seven heads [headtops] are seven mountains." The seven headtops constitute, form, seven mountains.

In the Bible, mountains *with numerals* are never used in *a figurative* sense. The seven mountains are *literal, material* mountains.

The seven mountains are the seven material hills, so often mentioned by the Latin classic writers, upon which the ancient city of Rome was built; namely, *Palatine, Quirinal, Aventine, Cœlian, Viminal, Æsquiline, Janiculum.*

The *Latin* writers do not use the word "seven" in the Hebrew sense of many, but in the exact literal sense of seven digits, and *no more.*

St. John, when referring to Rome, as he is in this verse 9, would use the word "seven" in the Latin sense, and not in the Hebrew sense.

The immediate context adds another proof, in the word "where," that the seven mountains are *material.* "*Where* the woman sitteth on them:" on the mountains (verse 9, last clause). "Where" is *local*, and makes the mountains *local and material*. *Eight* times does "*where*" occur in the Apocalypse. In every instance is the particle *local*, and in a *material* sense.

The seven mountains cannot be referred to Babylon on the Euphrates, for this city stood *on a plain*. The city of Jerusalem cannot be the location of the seven mountains. Neither in the Latin nor in the Hebrew sense, had the holy city this number of mountains. Mountains indeed are "*round about* Jerusalem" (Ps. cxxv. 2); but only on *two* mountains, Zion and Moriah, does the Bible locate "the city of the Great King" (Ps. xlviii. 2).

Since the woman represents the city built on seven material mountains, namely, the city which is *Pagan* Rome, on the east bank of the river Tiber, the woman is herself a *twofold* symbol.

We have seen in xiii. 3, that the sea-beast is a *twofold* symbol.

The woman arrayed in scarlet and purple is also a *twofold* symbol. Thus: (*a*) she is a symbol of *Papal* Rome (xvii. 5); (*b*) she is also a symbol of *Pagan* Rome (xvii. 18).

Because this woman is thus a twofold symbol, the imagery of the Apocalypse portraying her downfall describes the destruction of Rome both Pagan and Papal.

The minute details of the prophecies predicting her overthrow apply especially to the fall of *Pagan* Rome. The fall of *Pagan* Rome is the symbol and the assurance of the fall of *Papal* Rome.

The *literal* descriptions are invested with *spiritual* meanings, and, through them, with *destructive power*.

THE SEVEN KINGS.

10. And so represent seven kings. Five are fallen, one is, another has not yet come; and when he comes, for a short time only must he remain.

The Greek of this verse decides that the phrase, "seven kings," forms the predicate of the sentence. The "seven kings" being predicate, the subject of the sentence must be the "seven mountains" of verse 9.

As the subject of the sentence, "the seven mountains" impose upon the words "and are," English Version, this sense.

And so represent: the "and" is *consecutive*, and "are" denotes representation.

The symbolism of the seven heads of the first wild beast is most instructive.

1. The seven heads (since head is a mountain-top) are, in St.

John's exegesis, actually the seven material mountains on which the city of Rome is built.

2. These seven mountains, the *appositive* of the seven heads, *represent* seven kings.

But kings are symbols of *kingdoms*. "The fourth *beast* shall be the fourth *kingdom* ["king," Dan. vii. 17] upon earth, which shall be diverse from all *kingdoms*" (verse 23).

Since kings, in the language of the Bible, are kingdoms, the seven kings (Rev. xvii. 10) cannot possibly denote *different forms* of the Roman Empire under kings, consuls, dictators, decemvirs, military tribunes, emperors, popes.

The seven kingdoms *precede*, in St. John's exhibition, the first wild beast. He comes *after* them (verse 11), and continues their spirit and policy. He now persecutes God's Church. They *before* him persecuted the same Church. This fact reveals who the seven preceding kingdoms are.

Five are fallen: they, therefore, no longer exist. They are five extinct kingdoms; they are five kingdoms that had passed away before the Roman Empire began its life.

In the Apocalypse, the verb "*fall*" describes the extinction of communities (xiv. 8, xvi. 19, xviii. 2. The verb "fall" performs the same office (Rev. xvii. 10).

The Old-Testament history discloses the names of the five extinct kingdoms, — Egypt, Assyria, Babylon, Persia, Greece.

In the Septuagint, the verb "fall" is also the word noting the departure of these five kingdoms. 1. The fall of Egypt (Jer. xlvi. 6); 2. Of Assyria (Isa. xxxi. 8); 3. Of Babylon (Jer. li. 4); 4. Of Persia (Dan. x. 13); 5. Of Greece (Dan. xi. 3).

Each of these five departed kingdoms persecuted the Church of God. Each kingdom is no more. Its own departure prefigures and foretells the extinction of all kingdoms that persecute the Church of God. All earthly kingdoms are Christ's servants, because he ordains them (Rom. xiii. 1). When they persecute his Church, they persecute him (Matt. xxv. 40). Their persecutions of his Church insure their own destruction (Matt. xxi. 41).

One is: the Roman Empire in St. John's day, and for a few centuries afterwards.

Another has not yet come: the nominally *Christian* empire of Rome, beginning with Constantine, in the fourth century, A.D. 324; the union of Church and State.

Short time: as measured by God. With him, "a thousand years are as one day" (Ps. xc. 4).

Must: in the wise purpose of God.

Remain: The Pope of Rome is no longer a *civil* ruler. The battle of Solferino, A.D. 1859, between the Austrians and French and Sardinians, in its results, deprived the Pope of Rome of his *civil* authority, A.D. 1870.

The union of Church and State on the Tiber thus continued for fifteen centuries and a half.

11. And the wild beast which was, and is not, even he himself is the eighth, and so from the seven; and yet to destruction is departing.

Is the eighth: he is in the series of the seven. *Papal* Rome is the eighth kingdom.

Although *without* the article, *eight* is in Greek sense "*the* eighth" (English Version, A.D. 1611), and not "an eighth" (Westminster Revision, A.D. 1881).

This is most certain from these examples, where in each the adjective *eight*, though *without* the article, is necessarily translated "*the* eighth" by the English Version.

"He saved Noah, *the* eighth" (2 Pet. ii. 5).

"In the month Bul, this is *the* eighth month" (1 Kings vi. 38).

The usage of "*this*" (1 Kings vi. 38) so exactly resembles "*he himself*" (Rev. xvii. 11), that since 1 Kings vi. 38 must, in consequence of "this," be translated "this is *the* eighth month," Rev. xvii. 11 must, in consequence of "he himself," also be translated, "he himself is *the* eighth."

The *definite* reference in "this" (1 Kings vi. 38), and in "he himself" (Rev. xvii. 11), *supplies the place* of the article "*the*" before "*eight*" in each verse, but requires the definite article "the" to be *expressed* in the English translation.

And so from the seven: The Papal kingdom of the first wild beast succeeds the seven departed persecuting kingdoms. In spirit and influence the first wild beast still lives in Papal Rome, whatever may be its outward form. Derived from the persecuting kingdoms of the past, Papal Rome is ever ready to execute her printed anathemas against every other form of religion, whenever the favorable opportunity may offer. For the present, the lamb-dragon conceals and denies his teeth.

And to destruction is departing: "shall go into perdition" (verse 8).

God destines Papal Rome to destruction and extinction. Its inherent heathenism and rationalism are constitutional explosives this corrupt Church cannot always restrain.

12. Also, the ten horns which thou sawest are ten kings, who have not yet received a kingdom. But they shall reserve authority as kings, with the wild beast, for one hour.

Ten horns: are *prospective*. The heads of the wild beast are *retrospective* (verse 9).

Ten is a definite number for an indefinite. Bible usage gives indefiniteness to this number.

"The ten horns are ten kings that shall arise, and *another* shall rise *after* them." Thus "ten" by more than ten becomes indefinite.

Ten kings designate, without defining the exact number, the *several* kingdoms which succeed the Roman Empire in its own territory.

As kings: actually reigning. The negative "not yet" requires this sense.

One hour: a short period. The measure is sometimes shorter, "half an hour" (viii. 1).

Perhaps the time measures the duration of each kingdom in its association with the wild beast. He is to be destroyed. Each kingdom may survive his disappearance.

With the wild beast: associated with him in policy and administration.

At the present time the Roman Pope is not a *civil* ruler. His influence with every civil government in the world is constantly diminishing.

13. These have only one purpose; and so their power and authority they are giving to the wild beast.

These: the ten kings.

Purpose: the Greek word is in Revelation here and verse 17, where English Version correctly translates "will." Their purpose is to serve the wild beast.

Power: their own ability.

Authority: the power they delegate to others. They compel their subordinates to minister to the designs of the wild beast. Their subserviency to him is complete and absolute.

14. These shall make war with the Lamb; and yet the Lamb shall overcome them, because he is Lord of lords and King of kings. Also they joined with him (called, and chosen, and faithful) shall overcome.

The Lamb: because repeated, is emphatic. The Lamb himself, by his own power.

Lord of lords: Lord over human lords. The appellation first used by Moses in Deut. x. 17. "Higher than the kings of the earth" (Ps. lxxxix. 27). "Lord of kings" (Dan. ii. 37). Both clauses in 1 Tim. vi. 15; Rev. xvii. 14, xix. 16.

Of kings: over kings.

The Lamb possesses omnipotent power, and is thus superior to all human lords and earthly kings. Thus almighty and supreme, the Lamb should be exclusively enthroned in every human heart.

With him: Christ's human associates and helpers in his perpetual warfare in this world, with sin, the world, and the Devil.

Called: only here in Revelation. Fit to be called by Christ; called by his word and Holy Spirit to be his soldiers.

Chosen: in Revelation only here. Fit to be chosen, selected, and approved, by Christ, for their fidelity to him.

Faithful: unto death, implied in ii. 10, xii. 11.

Overcome: implied from the preceding clause.

No battle for Christ is ever fought in vain. "We are ever triumphant conquerors through him who loves us, and fights with us" (Rom. viii. 37).

15. And he saith to me, The waters which thou sawest, where the harlot sitteth, are indeed nations and multitudes, and peoples and tongues.

Waters: in Isa. viii. 7, waters are emblems of numerous armies. Jer. li. 55: "Babylon, on the Euphrates, dwells upon many waters."

The waters seen (Rev. xvii. 1) are like emblems. By the same imagery, St. John represents the followers of the adulteress Babylon to be so numerous, that he employs *plural* nouns to designate the vast multitudes.

But, in verse 16, the very vastness in numbers of her adherents, God makes the cause and instruments of her total destruction.

Sitteth: upon the seven mountains.

16. And yet, the ten horns which thou sawest, even the wild beast, these shall hate the harlot, and shall make her desolated and naked, and they shall eat her flesh, and they shall burn her in the fire.

And yet: in strong contrast with the condition of the harlot (verse 4).

The greatness of the dominion of the adulteress will prove her ruin. Papal Rome will be destroyed by civil governments. We are already seeing the beginning of the fulfilment of this symbolical prediction. The Pope of Rome no longer possesses temporal power.

Ten: a definite number for an indefinite; namely, many.

Even: the wild beast as manifested in the ten horns, in the numerous and varied forms of his power.

The prediction embraces four specifications: hatred, desolation, consumption, burning.

1. Hatred. They once loved her (verse 2).

They approved and adopted her teachings and practices. They now abhor and reject them all.

Unlawful love is often succeeded by hatred (2 Sam. xiii. 15; Ezek. xvi. 37, xxiii. 22).

2. Desolation and nakedness.

They deprive the usurping queen of her wealth, of her lands and money (xviii. 19), of her kingdoms and subjects (Lam. ii. 21).

They strip her of her royal apparel, and leave her in her nakedness and poverty (verse 4, xviii. 16; Ezek. xxiii. 26).

The present Pope is in part supported by "Peter's pence."

3. Consumption: of her flesh. Once she drank the blood of martyrs (xvii. 6). Now her enemies are not satisfied with drinking her blood; they eat her flesh so voraciously that they are leaving nothing of the dead body, save the bones, picked and dry.

Eating the flesh of another is the mark of the deadliest hostility. "They pluck their flesh from their bones" (Mic. iii. 2).

4. They shall burn her with fire.

By the law of Moses, burning was the punishment of the adulteress (Lev. xx. 14, xxi. 9; Gen. xxxviii. 24).

"The harlot city is to receive its deserved retribution from the *ten kings*, who will grow out of the dismemberment of the Roman Empire." — TERTULLIAN, *De Resurrectione Carnis*, 25.

These prophetical symbols are becoming in this nineteenth century historical facts.

17. For God puts into their hearts to do his will, and to agree, even, to give their kingdom to the wild beast, until the words of God shall be accomplished.

For: introduces an explanation of the mental state of the ten kings before they hated the adulteress.

His will: the will of God respecting the duration of Popery.

The words of God: in chapters xvi. and xvii. Human governments are withdrawing their former allegiance to Popery. The predictions of God foretelling its downfall are beginning to be realized.

The beginning of the desertion prefigures and secures the consummated end.

HIS EXPLANATION RESPECTING THE WOMAN.

18. And the woman whom thou seest is the great city which is holding kingly dominion over the kings of the earth.

Is: represents the great city.
Great city: of the future. *Papal* Rome did not exist when St. John wrote the Apocalypse.
Is holding: in the prophetic present.

CHAPTER XVIII.

THE FALL OF BABYLON (Verses 1-5).

THE revelations of this portion are most impressive. (See Jer. l. 1-46.)

1. Also after these things I saw another angel coming down from heaven, having great authority; and the earth is lightened with his glory.

Another angel: not one of the seven (xvii. 1).
Great authority: from God to destroy Babylon, and to pronounce her fallen.
Lightened: with the light and radiance surrounding him (Ezek. xliii. 2; Luke ii. 9; Acts ix. 3, xii. 7).

2. And he crieth with a strong voice, saying, Babylon the great is fallen, is fallen, and is become the habitation of devils, and the prison of every unclean spirit, and the prison of every unclean and hated bird.

Strong: to indicate the omnipotence of God, who commissions the angel, and gives effect to his repeated proclamation.
Only here in the Apocalypse is "strong" used with "voice."
Is fallen, is fallen: repeated to indicate the unalterable certainty of the prediction. See notes on vi. 8 and xiv. 8.

First Triplet.

The triple curse on Babylon.
The *threefold* curse denotes that cursing is so full, that a fourth curse is impossible.
A triplet denotes *completeness* (Isa. xix. 24). Triplets occur often in the remaining portions of the Apocalypse.

1. First curse, The habitation of devils. "The Church is the habitation of God through the Spirit" (Eph. ii. 22). Babylon (spiritual) herself was once such a habitation, but will become a habitation of devils. Imagery here from Jer. li. 37. See notes on xvi. 14.

In our Lord's parable of the "unclean spirit," "this wicked generation" is the apostate Church of the Jews (Matt. xii. 43-45). The Christian Church, when apostate, resembles the Jewish in character and evil occupation, and destination.

2. Second curse, The prison of every unclean spirit.

Prison is the meaning of the Greek noun in ii. 10, xx. 7. Prison must also be the meaning of the noun in xviii. 2. Even wicked spirits and unclean spirits will regard the accursed place as an unendurable prison. See notes on xvi. 13.

3. Third curse, The prison of every unclean and hated bird. See Isa. xxxiv. 11-15.

Thus inhabited by devils, wicked spirits, and unclean and hated birds, Babylon cannot be inhabited by men. It becomes uninhabitable.

This is the great and admonitory truth presented to our minds and hearts by the triple curse on the great city Babylon. "From generation to generation it shall lie waste; none shall pass through it forever" (Isa. xxxiv. 10).

The nature and extent of God's triple curse, he alone can understand and measure. From its infliction and realization may he ever preserve us through his infinite mercies in Christ Jesus our Lord!

THE CAUSE OF THE FALL OF BABYLON.

3. For, from the wine of the wrath of her fornication all nations are drinking; and the kings of the earth are committing fornication with her; and the merchants of the earth are becoming rich by the power of her luxury.

The cause of the fall of Babylon is her *threefold* bad influence.

Second Triplet.

1. She diffuses spiritual idolatry.
2. She associates with her the kings of the earth, in the practice of spiritual idolatry.

The kings of *the earth* are *godless kings;* "*of the earth, earthly*" (John iii. 31).

3. She encourages worldliness, self-indulgence, and luxury.

These three causes are agencies *completely* sufficient for the fall of Babylon.

THE CALL OF THE SECOND VOICE FROM HEAVEN
(Verses 4-8).

4. And I heard another voice from heaven, saying, Come out of her, my people, lest ye partake of her sins, and lest ye receive a portion of her plagues.

Another: divine voice. In verse 2, the voice is of destruction; here, of warning to the true Church.

My people: only here in the Apocalypse. The term expresses God's affection for his people (Exod. iii. 7).

Come out of her: repeats an exhortation often before made by God (Isa. xlviii. 20, lii. 11; Jer. li. 45; Matt. xxiv. 16).

When the Romans, A.D. 70, besieged the holy city, "the whole body of the Church at Jerusalem [heeded Christ's warning, and] removed from the city, and dwelt at a certain town beyond the Jordan called Pella," in Peræa, on the east side of the Jordan." — EUSEBIUS, *H. E.*, iii. 5, p. 86; *Cruse's Translation.*

Two most pressing reasons for the warning: —

1. Lest ye learn to practise her sins. "Evil communications corrupt good manners" (1 Cor. xv. 33).

2. Lest ye partake of her punishment. Participation in her sins would occasion participation in her retributions.

This voice from heaven fully authorizes separation from the Church of Rome, and fully justifies the reformations of the sixteenth century, and of the present time.

5. For her sins are firmly piled unto heaven; and so God remembers her crimes.

Firmly piled: proudly and defiantly reared, like the Tower of Babel. This language is taken from Jer. li. 9, 53.

"Every high thing that exalteth itself against the knowledge of God" (2 Cor. x. 5).

Remembers: with punishments.

Crimes: acts of injustice.

"The fortress of the high fort of thy walls shall he bring down, lay low, and bring to the ground, even to the dust" (Isa. xxv. 12).

Both the justice and the fidelity of God are pledged, that the apostate Church shall, for her sins "piled unto heaven," and defying the authority and laws of Christ, be annihilated.

6. Give back to her as also she gives, and double to her double according to her works. In the cup which she mixes, mix for her double.

Twofold specification of punishment.

1. **Give back**: "As she hath done, do unto her" (Jer. l. 15). "Happy shall he be, that rewardeth thee as thou hast served us" (Ps. cxxxvii. 8).

2. **Double**: "She hath received double for all her sins" (Isa. xl. 2). Also Jer. xvi. 18, xvii. 18; Zech. ix. 12.

Mix: *chemically*. See note on xiv. 10. Let the punishment be adequate and full.

God himself authorizes these awful denunciations by the "voice from heaven." Peals of thunder filling the whole heavens cannot imitate the purport of the terrors.

7. How much she glorifies herself, and lives luxuriously, so much torment and sorrow give her; for she saith in her heart, I sit a queen, and am no widow, and so I shall in no wise see sorrow.

I sit a queen: I am firmly seated in my throne.
Widow: I am not bereft of my throne (Isa. xlvii. 8).
See: experience, suffer.

Her sins are self-glorification, self-indulgence, and self-confidence. This picture of defiant audacity and supreme rebellion against the sovereignty of God surpasses even the model drawn by the prophet Isaiah (xlvii. 8).

This heart-saying of the proud queen causes the cup of God's punitive indignation to overflow. Cherished sins of the heart always provoke his hottest displeasure.

8. Therefore shall her plagues come in one day, — death, sorrow, and famine; and she shall be utterly burned with fire; for strong is the Lord God who judgeth her.

In one day: suddenly and thoroughly. Brevity is certainty (verses 10, 17).
Shall come: shall arrive, shall certainly come.
Her plagues: her punishments.

Third Triplet.

1. **Death**: instead of escape from widowhood.
2. **Sorrow**: instead of self-indulgence.
3. **Famine**: instead of wealth and luxury. See Deut. xxviii. 48-57.

The order of the words is *anti-climactic*. This order indicates that the inflictions do not come from human sources, but *from the hand of God*.

Eusebius gives us an appalling account of the famine in Jerusalem when besieged by Titus (*Hist. Eccl.*, iii. 6).

Strong: almighty.

Utterly burned with fire: this imagery of burning with fire is derived from the predicted burning of the city of Tyre.

"I will bring forth a fire from the midst of thee: it shall devour thee, and I will bring thee to ashes" (Ezek. xxviii. 18).

Also from the predicted burning of Babylon on the Euphrates (Jer. li. 58).

MOURNING OVER BABYLON (Verses 9-19).

The mourning establishes these facts : —

1. The *actual* destruction of Babylon. Communities never deplore a nonentity.

2. The *extent* of her influence over governments and business.

3. The *completeness* of the destruction of the mystical Babylon.

Under the symbols of queen, kings, merchants of all known traffic, pilots, voyagers, and sailors, the apostate Church and her multiplied and various members, are represented in Rev. xviii. 7-19.

Not only is the queen herself destroyed, but every subordinate king loses his throne, every merchant his business, every seaman his employment.

This utter ruin is the graphic symbol of the complete overthrow of the apostate Church, and of all her adherents.

This being the design of the symbolism, the minuteness of specification in these verses magnifies and intensifies the absoluteness of the universal destruction.

FIRST CLASS OF MOURNERS (Verses 9-10).

9. And the kings of the earth, who committed fornication and lived luxuriously with her, shall weep and cut themselves for her, when they see the smoke of her burning ;

Fourth Triplet.

Three classes of mourners, — kings, verse 9; merchants, verse 11; seamen, verse 17.

Cut themselves: "with knives and lancets, till the blood gushed out upon them," to indicate their intense grief (1 Kings xviii. 28).

These strong expressions of grief prove that the kings of the earth are the most impassioned mourners.

The expressions are much stronger than "weep and mourn" (verse 11), the indications of the grief of the merchants.

Burning: the imagery is taken from a city on fire (Judg. i. 8, xx. 48; Jer. xxxii. 29).

No literal burning is intended. Hopeless destruction is the truth here most emphatically presented.

The destruction of Tyre was deplored in like manner (Ezek. xxvi. 15–xxvii. 36).

10. Standing afar off for the fear of her torment, saying, "Alas, alas! the great city Babylon, the strong city! for in one hour is thy judgment come."

The fear: lest her torment might reach them.

Alas, alas! cries of agony, because of the sudden and hopeless fall of the great and strong city Babylon.

Judgment: condemnation and punishment.

SECOND CLASS OF MOURNERS (Verses 11–16).

11. Also the merchants of the earth are weeping and mourning over her, for no one buyeth their merchandise any more;

The imagery in this verse surpasses in graphic force the imagery portraying the grief of the kings. Their grief is merely *predicted*, "*shall* weep" (verse 10). The grief of the merchants is *enacted*, "*are* weeping." They stand in our presence. We see their tears. We hear their inarticulate cries. Their grief is too deep for definite words. At first they do not with the kings of the earth exclaim, "Alas, alas!" In their silence, St. John is obliged to assign the cause of their speechless distress: "No one buyeth their merchandise any more."

Merchandise: their ships' cargoes. Rome once limited buying and selling (xiii. 17). Now her own commerce totally ceases.

12. Merchandise of gold and of silver, and of every precious stone, and of pearl; also, of fine linen, and of purple, and of silk, and of scarlet; also of every kind of citron-wood, and of every ivory vessel, and every vessel of most costly wood, and of brass, and of iron, and of marble.

These minute specifications, while they magnify the commerce of Rome, exhibit the greatness of the ruin her merchants experience.

The commerce of Tyre (Ezek. xxvii.) furnishes the outline of St. John's details. When he wrote the Apocalypse, Rome in Italy was the centre of the commerce of the known world.

There are records in the New Testament which prove this.

1. Rome was the *political* centre of Western Asia, Europe, and Northern Africa.

"The decrees of Cæsar" (Acts xvii. 7). "Hast thou appealed unto Cæsar? Unto Cæsar shalt thou go" (xxv. 12).

"In Damascus the governor under Aretas the king kept the city" (2 Cor. xi. 32). Both king and governor were appointed at Rome.

"Peter to the strangers scattered throughout Pontus, Galatia, Cappadocia, and Bithynia: Submit yourselves . . . to the king as *supreme*" (1 Pet. i. 1, ii. 13).

"Egypt, Libya" (Acts ii. 10).

2. Rome was the *commercial* centre of these regions (Acts xxvii. 1, 3, 4, 5, 6, xxviii. 11, 16; 2 Tim. i. 16–18).

The articles of merchandise now enumerated (verses 12, 13) are mostly articles of luxury, sumptuous and costly (Rev. xviii. 14).

These luxuries form the following classes (verses 12, 13):—

I. Personal ornaments: gold, silver, precious stones, pearls.
II. Clothing: fine linen, purple, silk, scarlet.
III. Furniture: thyine-wood, ivory, precious wood, brass, iron, marble.
IV. Spices: cinnamon, amomum, incense, ointment, frankincense.
V. Food: wine, oil, fine flour, wheat.
VI. Farm-stock: cattle, sheep.
VII. Travel: horses, chariots.
VIII. Personal service: slaves and souls of men.

Thyine: citron-wood.

13. Also cinnamon and amomum, and incense, and myrrh, and frankincense; also wine and oil, and finest wheat flour and grain; also cattle and sheep; also of horses and chariots; also of captives and of slaves.

Cinnamon: Exod. xxx. 23, probably from Ceylon.
Amomum: a fragrant shrub used in ointments.
Finest wheat flour: Gen. xxx. 14; Ps. lxxii. 16.
Grain: Rev. vi. 6.
Cattle: domestic.
Of horses: cargo implied (verse 12).
Chariots: with four wheels. Roman senators rode in these Gallic chariots.

Captives: were often sold as slaves (Neh. v. 8).

Slaves: in general. "*Souls* of men;" that is, "*persons* of men" (Ezek. xxvii. 13). These slaves may have been girls (Joel iii. 3; Judg. v. 30; Deut. xxi. 10–14), thus constituting the climax of effeminate and sinful luxury in the harlot city.

14. And so, the fruit-harvest causing the desire of thy soul is passing from thee, and all the sumptuous feasts and the splendid garments are perishing from thee, and no more at all shalt thou find them.

The doomed Babylon is now directly addressed.

In this personal address, verse 14 imitates the Old Testament (Isa. i. 5, 7, 10–15; Jer. xxxiv. 3; Ezek. xxi. 3, 4).

In Rev. xviii. 21, Babylon is addressed in the *third* person; but in the next verse 22, in the *second* person. The same change of persons occurs in verses 13 and 14.

And so: the losses mentioned in this verse are the consequences of the universal ruin portrayed in the preceding verses.

These losses are described figuratively and summarily.

(*a*) *Figuratively*. By the fruit-harvest, which is the second and last harvest of the year. "The last harvest is passing from thee. Thy last opportunity of enjoyment is leaving thee. Thou wilt have no more harvest seasons. Thy life is coming to an end."

Causing the desire of thy soul: causing, exciting, but not gratifying. Thy desire for fruit, awakened by the sight of the very last fruits of the year, will not be gratified.

(*b*) *Summarily*. By her feasts and her garments, summarizing all her sensual pleasures.

Feasts: the feast of Belshazzar (Dan. v. 1–4) did not exceed in sumptuousness the feasts of the Roman emperors.

Garments: "They that wear soft clothing are in kings' houses" (Matt. xi. 8).

Not find: by searching (xvi. 20). Finding absolutely impossible.

15. The merchants of these articles, who are becoming rich by her, shall stand afar off, for their fear of her torment; thus weeping and wailing.

The weeping and wailing of the merchants is repeated from verse 11, for impressive effect. We see their tears, and we hear their wails a second time; and thus our convictions of their desolation and wretchedness are profoundly deepened.

16. Saying, Alas, alas! the great city, which is clothed in fine linen and purple and scarlet, and gilded with gold and every precious stone, and pearls; for in one hour is so great wealth made a desolation.

Alas, alas! the merchants, at first silent through their excessive grief, at length recover their voices, and with the afflicted kings utter the same exclamations of wretchedness.

Fifth Triplet.
Fine linen, purple, scarlet.

Sixth Triplet.
Gold, precious stones, pearls.

In one hour: one single hour. With God, great changes are often instantaneous. "In the twinkling of an eye, at the last trump" (1 Cor. xv. 52).

THIRD CLASS OF MOURNERS: THE WORKING CLASS ON THE SEA
(Verses 17-19).

Three, in Bible enumeration, is a *full* number. The three classes of mourners, therefore, include and represent all classes. The mourning of the subjects of the harlot-queen is universal.

17. Also every helmsman, and every passenger, and sailors, even all who follow the sea, are standing afar off.

Helmsman: Acts xxvii. 11.
Passenger: literally, he who is sailing for some place.
Sailors: Acts xxvii. 27, 30.
Follow the sea: as their business. Literally, work the sea, ply the sea. "Do business in great waters" (Ps. cvii. 23).

These indefinite phrases are here used to express comprehensive enumeration, by which to denote all classes of seafaring people.

18. And were crying, because seeing the smoke of her burning, thus saying, What city like the great city?

What city like: literally, What like? the word "city" being implied, but not expressed. "City" is suppressed by the strong emotion of the suffering speakers.

The great city: the previous question creates this exaggeration in the mouths of the seamen reduced to poverty by the fall of Babylon, — the *greatest* city!

The greatness of Babylon, in the vastness of its commerce and the facilities of its business, aggravates the loss these seamen are suffering, as well as their consequent misery.

19. And they cast dust on their heads, and are crying, weeping and wailing, saying, Alas, alas! the great city, by which all are made rich who have ships in the sea, out of her costliness; for in one hour is she made desolate.

The grief deepens as the mention of the ruined classes proceeds.
Cast dust: in token of grief (Josh. vii. 6).
The seafaring people are more demonstrative in their grief than either the kings or the merchants.
The great city: the greatest city. It is the nature of deep grief, to dwell upon its losses, and to repeat its exclamations expressive of its misery.
"O my son Absalom, my son Absalom! O Absalom, my son, my son!" (2 Sam. xviii. 33.)

EXULTATION IN HEAVEN COMMANDED BY THE ANGEL.

20. Rejoice over her, thou heaven, even ye saints, and ye apostles, and ye prophets; for from her God avenges her judgment on you.

The exultation commanded by the angel is in contrast with the lamentation in verses 9-18. The classes of exultants are *three*, — saints, apostles, prophets, — the same in number as the mourners. The rejoicing is as universal as is the sorrow.
Thou heaven heaven for its inhabitants (Deut. iv. 26; Ps. lxix. 34; Isa. xlix. 13, "Sing, O heavens"). "*The heaven* and earth sing for Babylon" (Jer. li. 48).

Seventh Triplet.

1. **Ye saints**: under the altar (vi. 9, 10); martyred saints (xviii. 24).
2. **Ye apostles**: in the largest sense, — messengers (Rev. ii. 2). The messengers Christ sends to preach his gospel.
3. **Ye prophets**: martyred prophets (xviii. 24). The New-Testament prophets both predict and instruct.
Is avenging: is inflicting judgment, punishment (vi. 10).
From her: God exacts from Babylon the judgment she inflicted upon the Christian martyrs (verse 6).

On you: the same form of expression as this, the judgment *on* the harlot (xvii. 1).

This command of the angel is promptly obeyed in the quadrupled Alleluia (xix. 1–8).

SYMBOLIC CONFIRMATION OF GOD'S JUDGMENTS UPON BABYLON.

21. And a strong angel takes up a stone, like a great millstone, and casts it into the sea, saying, Thus with violence shall Babylon, the very great city, be cast [out of sight], so that in no wise shall she be found hereafter.

The destruction of Pharaoh and his host illustrates the imagery in this verse. "Pharaoh's chariots and his host hath the Lord cast into the sea; his chosen captains also are drowned in the Red Sea. The depths have covered them: they sank into the bottom *as a stone*" (Exod. xv. 4, 5).

"The persecutors of our fathers in Egypt, thou threwest into the deeps, *as a stone* into the *mighty waters*" (Neh. ix. 11).

The sea: in St. John's vision, the Mediterranean, surrounding the island of Patmos.

Seraiah, the servant of Jeremiah, casts a stone into the Euphrates to symbolize the utter destruction of its city Babylon (Jer. li. 63, 64).

AMPLIFICATION BY THE STRONG ANGEL OF GOD'S JUDGMENTS UPON BABYLON (Verses 22, 23).

Universal silence is the inclusive judgment.

1. The sounds heard both in peace and war are all silent.
   (*a*) In peace: harpers, singers, pipers.
   (*b*) In war: trumpeters.
2. Human occupations silent. Every artisan of every art.
3. Family life ceases: millstone, lamp.
4. The family, the source of human life, ceases: bridegroom, bride.

22. And the voice of harpers, and singers, and pipers, and trumpeters, shall in no wise be heard in thee any more; and every artisan of every art shall in no wise be found

in thee any more; and the sound of a millstone shall in no wise be heard in thee any more.

Harpers: rejoicing (Job xxi. 12; Isa. xxiv. 8).

Singers: the harp was accompanied by the voice (Ps. lxxi. 22; Ezek. xxvi. 13).

Pipers: blowing *reed* instruments (Matt. xi. 17), not "flute-players" (Westminster Revision).

Every artisan: the Bible list of artisans is large: bakers (Jer. xxxvii. 21), barbers (Ezek. v. 1), blacksmiths (Isa. xliv. 12), carpenters (Isa. xliv. 13), coppersmiths (2 Tim. iv. 14), engravers (Deut. xxvii. 15), fullers (Mark ix. 3), glass-blowers (Rev. iv. 6, xv. 2), goldsmiths (1 Chron. xxix. 5), masons (2 Kings xii. 12), moulders (Deut. xxvii. 15), painters (Jer. xxii. 14), potters (Jer. xviii. 2), ropemakers (Acts xxvii. 32), sailmakers (Isa. xxxiii. 23), shipbuilders (1 Kings ix. 26), shoemakers (Isa. v. 27), silversmiths (1 Chron. xxix. 5), spinners (Exod. xxxv. 25), tanners (Acts ix. 43), weavers (Exod. xxxv. 35).

What silence follows the cessation of these numerous pursuits!

Millstone: same language in Jer. xxv. 10. Usually turned by women (Matt. xxiv. 41).

In Babylon no millstone is turned. The women are all dead and motionless. Every house is silent.

23. Also the light of a lamp shall in no wise shine in thee any more; and the voice of a bridegroom and of a bride shall in no wise be heard in thee any more.

Lamp: language taken from Jer. xxv. 10. No lamp is lighted anywhere; no breath to kindle the flame; no hand to set the light on the lampstand. Every house is dark: the darkness of death reigns in every dwelling.

Bridegroom and bride: language taken from Jer. vii. 34, xvi. 9, xxv. 10.

Bridegroom, bride: the source of human life fails. No more bridegrooms, no more brides, no more children, no more families. Man, as a race, is ended. The primal command, "Be fruitful, and multiply, and replenish the earth, and subdue it" (Gen. i. 8), is forever revoked. With his life, the presence and dominion of man cease. Wild beasts will now roam and ravage. Wild birds will henceforth scream and revel.

In horrific certainty nothing can surpass these depopulating specifications of consummated and changeless desolation.

The present desert site of Babylon on the Euphrates is the visible counterpart of this symbolic silence and death.

CAUSES OF THE UNIVERSAL DESTRUCTION.

24. For thy merchants were the great men of the earth; for all nations are deceived by thy sorcery. Also in her the blood of prophets and saints is found, and of all the slain upon the earth.

Eighth Triplet.

These causes are *three*. The *threefold* enumeration, denoting *completeness*, is continued.

In the presentation of the first and second causes, the personified city of Babylon is still addressed.

1. *First cause.* The wickedness of the Roman merchants.

Thy merchants are *the great men of the earth.*

(a) The designation, *of the earth,* places the great men in the class of the worldly and wicked. See notes on xvi. 1.

(b) The Greek term translated "great men" occurs in the New Testament only three times,— in this verse, and Mark vi. 21, and Rev. vi. 15.

In Mark vi. 21, the great men ("his lords") are among the drinking companions of Herod Antipas, who demanded the unjust death of John the Baptist. "*For their sakes which sat with him,* the king sent an executioner, and commanded John's head to be brought" (verses 26, 27).

In Rev. vi. 15, "the great men" are conspicuously among the unrepenting enemies of Christ.

Since in these two places "the great men" denote the worldly and the wicked, "the great men" must also denote the worldly and the wicked in Rev. xviii. 24, the only other place where the word occurs in the New Testament.

Each Roman merchant was the counterpart of the prophet Hosea's merchant: "the balances of deceit are in his hand: he loveth to oppress" (Hos. xii. 7).

God destroyed Pagan Rome for the same reason that he destroyed the city of Tyre.

"By the multitude of thy merchandise they have filled thee with violence. Thou hast defiled thy sanctuaries *by the iniquity of thy traffic;* therefore will I bring forth a fire from the midst of thee; it shall devour thee, and I will bring thee to ashes" (Ezek. xxviii. 16, 18).

For its iniquitous traffic, God burned ancient Tyre. For their own iniquitous traffic in Pagan Rome, her oppressive merchants behold the city they had doomed burning before their eyes.

2. *Second cause* of the destruction of Babylon. *Her sorcery.*

Are deceived by thy sorcery: what is sorcery?

(1) According to the immediate context, sorcery is a deceit, a deception, a pretence. Sorcery claims to be something which it is not.

(2) In itself sorcery is, —

(*a*) Divination; assumed superhuman foresight (Acts xiii. 6).

(*b*) The pretended exercise of superhuman power.

The people of Samaria called Simon the sorcerer "the power of God" (Acts viii. 10).

Thus sorcery is both divination and magic. In each of these forms: —

3. Sorcery becomes *idolatry*, by attributing to created persons and things foresight and power possessed exclusively by God.

Sorcery may include the pretended miracles of Papal Rome.

Idolatry in the heart excites the displeasure of God not less than material idolatry (Ezek. xiv. 7, 8).

Pagan Rome was largely infidel. Infidelity always degenerates into superstition. Superstition is the inventress and administratrix of sorcery in all its modifications.

3. *Third cause* of the destruction of the harlot city. *The murder of prophets, saints, and martyrs.*

Eusebius, the Church historian, shows the fulfilment of these predictions respecting the bloodshed of Christian prophets, and saints, and martyrs, by the emperors of *Pagan* Rome (*Ecclesiastical History*, book viii., and *Book of Martyrs*, pp. 317-375).

The history of St. Bartholomew's Day shows us not only the murders of Protestants, *Papal* Rome then committed, but also the approval by the Pope and his cardinals of the savage outrage, and their frantic exultation over it.

THE APOCALYPSE HISTORICAL.

We can now, perhaps, answer this question: How far is the Book of Revelation *historical?* When the fulfilment of an Apocalyptic prophecy can be verified by history, secular or church, then the event becomes historical.

By the application of this safe test, the prophetic fall in the Apocalypse, both of the Pagan city of Rome, and of its Pagan empire, are established as historical verities.

Pagan Rome, on the east bank of the Tiber, has for centuries been an absolute desolation. Before the close of the fifth century, the empire of Pagan Rome was annihilated by the invasions of savage hordes from the East and North.

The fall of Pagan Rome is prophetic of the fall of Papal Rome.

The majestic symbols of defeat and victory, of destruction and revival, St. John here places before our eyes, are too vast for human foresight even feebly to trace and measure. As prophecies, these symbols predict two certain events in the coming future: (a) The overthrow and disappearance of every institution, social, civil, and religious, which is *anti-Christian;* and (b) the incessant growth and universal dominion of Christ's subverting kingdom of righteousness, holiness, and peace. As God's reconstructing hand is present in all existing changes, so will it be present in all future revolutions.

"I will overturn, overturn, overturn [completely overturn] it [every false thing]: and it shall be no more, until he come whose right it is; and I will give it" *to Christ* (Ezek. xxi. 27).

CHAPTER XIX.

THANKSGIVINGS IN HEAVEN FOR THE FALL OF BABYLON, FOR THE MARRIAGE OF THE LAMB, AND FOR HIS VICTORIES.

CHAPTERS xix.-xxii. resemble Ezek. xxxvi.-xxxix.

THE ALLELUIAS (Verses 1-6).

These are *four* (verses 1, 3, 4, 6). Each alleluia contains a *triplet*,—salvation, glory, power (verse 1). The worshippers also form a *triplet*. (*a*) "Much people" (verse 1); (*b*) The elders and the living creatures (verse 4); and (*c*) "All God's servants, small and great" (verse 5).

As *three* is a complete number, the *fourth* alleluia has entered upon a *second* triplet, one number only of which is uttered, to indicate that the second triplet *will never be completed*.

Alleluias will be *perpetual*, even *eternal*. Throughout eternity, God will be praised for the downfall and annihilation of the apostate Church, for the union of Christ and his true Church, and for his triumph over sin, death, and Satan.

First Alleluia.

1. After these visions, I hear a sound of words, as the great voice of much people, saying in heaven, Alleluia; All salvation, and all glory, and all power are our God's:

Hear: hearing now takes the place of seeing (xviii. 1).
Much people: the true Church of Christ.

Ninth Triplet.

Much people; elders and living creatures; all God's servants.

Alleluia: in the New Testament, only in this chapter. Its meaning in the Hebrew is, Praise ye Jehovah. "Praise ye the Lord" (Ps. civ. 35).

Tenth Triplet.

All salvation, all glory, all power. "To the Lord are *all* things; to whom be *all* glory" (Rom. xi. 36).

He alone has the *power* to give his people *salvation*. To him alone belongs the *glory*.

2. For true and righteous are his judgments; for he is judging the great harlot, who was corrupting the earth with her fornication, and is avenging the blood of his servants at her hand.

True: see xv. 3.

Corrupting: "I am against thee, Babylon, O *destroying* mountain, which *destroyed* [art corrupting] all the earth" (Jer. li. 25), ever corrupting both the religion and morals of the world.

The earth: that is, mankind (Gen. vi. 11; Rev. vi. 8).

Avenging: exacting in vengeance (2 Kings ix. 7).

At her hand: by demanding payment from her hand.

Second Alleluia.

3. And a second time they say, Alleluia. And her smoke rises up for ever and ever.

Second time: for two reasons: (*a*) For emphasis; (*b*) To denote *extension of time.*

The second alleluia is prolonged in its performance. This prolongation is indicated by the Greek accusative of the time.

Rises up: the perpetual ascent of the smoke of the harlot-city's burning causes the extension (see xiv. 11; Isa. xxxiv. 10).

The smoke of the burning city arises forever as an eternal memorial of the justice of God in destroying the apostate Church. The alleluia arises forever as an eternal memorial of the mercy of God in delivering his true Church and the world from the hurtful example and persecuting ravages of the spiritual adulteress.

The Response of the Elders and the Living Creatures. — Third Alleluia.

4. And the twenty-four elders and the four living beings

fall down and worship God, who sitteth upon the throne, saying, Amen; Alleluia.

Elders, etc.: iv. 4–6. The judges and the executioners also exclaim, Alleluia.

Throne: of judgment (iv. 2).

Amen: so be it. Emphatic repetition of alleluia.

Alleluia is thus repeated *the third time*.

The praises now given God for his judgments and mercies are in themselves complete, because proclaimed *three* times, — a *full* number.

The Voice from the Throne.

5. And a voice comes out of the throne, saying, Praise our God, all ye his servants, all ye that fear him, all ye small and great.

A fourth alleluia (praise our God) commanded.

Eleventh Triplet.

(*a*) Servants; (*b*) That fear God; (*c*) Small and great.

(*a*) **His servants**: faithful members of Christ's Church (Rev. vii. 3).

(*b*) **That fear God**: they that *in every nation* fear him (Acts x. 35). St. Paul distinguishes between the "men of Israel" and "ye that fear God" (Acts xiii. 16; Rom. ii. 14). The saved of the heathen.

(*c*) **Small and great**: young and old, children and adults (Matt. xxi. 15, 16).

Answer of the Three Classes to the Voice from the Throne. — Fourth Alleluia.

6. Also I hear an answer, as the voice of a great multitude, and as the voice of many waters, and as the voice of mighty thunders, saying, Alleluia; for the Lord our God, the Omnipotent, reigneth.

Twelfth Triplet.

(*a*) Great multitude; (*b*) Many waters; (*c*) Mighty thunders.

1. **Voice of a great multitude**: as the united voices of a vast crowd.

The imagery may be derived from the vocal worship of the great multitudes assembled at Jerusalem on the three annual festivals, when the attendance was national and enormous.

"The singers went before, the players on instruments followed after: among them were the damsels playing with timbrels" (Ps. lxviii. 25).

"*All Israel* sounded, by *lifting up the voice* with joy; *with shouting*, and with the sound of the cornet, and with trumpets, and with cymbals, making a noise with psalteries and harps" (1 Chron. xv. 16, 28).

"*All the people* said Amen, and praised the Lord" (1 Chron. xvi. 36).

2. **Many waters**: as the unceasing roar of the swelling waves of the tossing sea (see i. 15).

3. **Mighty thunders**: as the echoing peals of the deafening lightning-strokes.

The simultaneous alleluia of the innumerable assembly of immortal voices of small and great, of children and adults, not only more than equals, but immeasurably surpasses, the commingled harmony of the shouting masses, of the resounding ocean, and of the all-pervading thunders. No earthly sounds can adequately represent the majesty and sublimity of the response the hosts of heaven return to the voice from the throne commanding the response.

The alleluia anthem, St. John's ear alone hears, is A SUPERMUNDANE MAGNIFICAT.

Reigneth: the Greek verb is the aorist, which the English Version correctly here translates as a present tense. God has defeated Babylon, and all his enemies, and is reigning omnipotent on his throne of judgment, and in his Christian kingdom.

The vision of the quadrupled alleluia anthem of the Church universal ends with verse 6.

The Design of the Alleluias.

Would we perceive the design of the four alleluias, we must recall to our notice the symbolical character of the Apocalypse. In the alleluias, as in every portion of the book, there are these fundamental portions:—

1. The *actuality* from which the symbolism is derived. In the alleluias, the choirs of King David constitute the actuality (1 Chron. xiii. 8).

2. The alleluias themselves constitute the *symbolism*. They symbolize some object outside of themselves.

3. The alleluias symbolize the *universal joy* created by the triumphs of Christ, and the defeat of his foes. Music is itself the symbol of gladness (Luke xv. 25, 32).

When "*all* the ends of the earth shall see the salvation of God, they shall break forth into joy [*such as is here symbolized*]: with the voice *together shall they sing*" (Isa. lii. 8-10).

To this symbolized joy, every human soul, renewed in the image of Christ, is at the present time contributing a note by his own unceasing heart-song.

St. Paul recognizes this undying music of the renewed soul, "making melody *in your heart* to the Lord" (Eph. v. 19).

The strings of this inner harp, God creates in sanctified hearts, nothing outward can break and silence. The heavenly strings are always vibrating, and always diffusing gladness; in darkness as well as in sunlight; in affliction and sorrow as well as in external prosperity and comfort.

These incessant heart-songs, though heard by no human ear save the consciousness of each happy possessor, form over the surface of the earth, wherever the gospel and the Spirit of Christ inspire the cheering and abiding music, *a united anthem*, which is ever loud and welcome in "the ears of the Lord of Sabaoth," and are in part the fulfilment and the realization of the prophetic alleluias St. John heard in heaven.

The preservation and perpetuation of Christian heart-songs in this sinful world is the ground of hope, both for the salvation of individuals, and for the extension and prevalence of the joyous and gladdening gospel of Christ unto even the ends of the habitable earth.

THE MARRIAGE OF THE LAMB (Verses 7-9).

7. Let us rejoice and be exceeding glad, and give him glory; for the marriage festival of the Lamb is come, and his wife is making herself ready.

Thirteenth Triplet.

Rejoice, be glad, give glory.

The marriage of the king follows, as a usual sequence, after his firm establishment in his throne (1 Kings ii. 46, iii. 1; 2 Chron. xxi. 5, 6).

Naturally, the expression of joy *succeeds* the occasion of the joy.

"When they saw the star, they rejoiced" (Matt. ii. 10).

"The friend of the bridegroom rejoiceth, because of the bridegroom's voice" (John iii. 29).

But here (Rev. xix. 7) the joy *precedes* the occasion of the joy.

It is the joy of *certain faith*. Faith believes the event foretold will occur, because predicted by God, and therefore rejoices *in anticipation and by faith*.

The same reversed order appears in xviii. 20, xix. 1, 3, 6, and for the same reason.

Thus previous usage explains why in this verse 7 there is the expression of joy before the cause of the joy is mentioned.

Let us rejoice, etc.: these exulting words (verses 7, 8, 9) are *not* from the throne (verse 5). The angelic speaker reveals himself (verse 10).

Exceeding glad: exult.

Give glory: that is, praise him.

Marriage-festival: "marriage-supper" (verse 9; see Matt. xxv. 1–10).

His wife: his Church. "Thy Maker is thy husband" (Isa. liv. 5).

"The husband is the head of the wife, even as Christ is the head of the Church" (Eph. v. 23).

Christ and his Church are now, in spiritual union and oneness, husband and wife. Their future reign over the world is, in Rev. xix. 7–9, represented as the occasion of such joy as marks a marriage festival.

Is making herself ready: is preparing for the festival. The preparation is described in the next verse (verse 8) "array in fine linen, the righteousness [acts] of saints." The preparation is, therefore, *a righteous life*, inspired and perfected by *internal* righteousness (Matt. v. 6); is *holiness of heart and life*.

This is Christ's present and incessant command to every Christian, "Son, go *work* to-day in my vineyard" (Matt. xxi. 28). Only the *actual and habitual doer* of this work, which he requires of each one of us who bears his name, "is making himself ready" for Christ's final welcome. "Come unto the marriage" (Matt. xxii. 4).

WORK, not mere spirituality, IS THE PREPARATION.

8. And it is given her to be clothed in fine linen, white and clean, for the fine linen is the righteousness of the saints.

Is given: God permits the Church to be clothed with Christian graces. He permits her to be saved. He saves her by his mercy (Tit. iii. 5).

We cannot save ourselves. "Without me ye can do nothing" (John xv. 5).

Fine linen: a simple dress, although ornamented, "adorned" (xxi. 2). In strong contrast with the gaudy attire of the harlot (xvii. 4).

Righteousness: righteous acts (xv. 4; Rom. v. 18). The acts of the saints are made righteous by the blood of the Lamb (Rev. vii. 14).

Is: represents. This is the meaning of "is" (Matt. xxvi. 26).

The saints: compose the Church, the Lamb's wife.

9. And he saith to me, Write, Blessed are they who are called to the marriage-supper of the Lamb. Also he saith to me, These sayings are the true sayings of God.

He saith: an angel (verse 10). The interpreting angel of i. 1.
Write: on account of the supreme importance of the declaration I now utter (i. 11, xiv. 13).
Blessed: see i. 3. No blessing greater than this call.
Called: not only invited (Matt. xxv. 3), but accepted as guests (verse 10).
These sayings: the sayings included in xvii. 1–xix. 9.
True: the sayings God himself utters, and therefore unalterable and most credible.

ANGEL-WORSHIP FORBIDDEN.

10. And I fall before his feet to worship him. And he saith to me, See thou do it not. I am thy fellow-servant and of thy brethren, who have the testimony respecting Jesus. Worship God alone: for the testimony [the testifier] respecting Jesus is the Spirit inspiring prophecy.

I fall before his feet: St. John seems not to distinguish between the voice from the throne (verse 5), and the voice of the angel (verses 7 and 8). Perhaps the angel, when he began to speak, was invisible.
Worship him: as divine. Worship, in the highest sense. This verb always has this sense in the Apocalypse.
See thou do it not: do not give divine honor to an angel; he is only a created being.
St. Paul pronounces the worship of angels a delusion (Col. ii. 18). It is not merely a delusion. It is idolatry, because it is worship given a creature.
Thy fellow-servant: my service is the same as thy service. I am thy official equal.
Respecting Jesus: see 1 John v. 9.
Alone: the contrast between the worship given to an angel and the worship given to God creates this emphatic sense.
For: introduces the reason for the official equality of the angel with St. John and his Christian brethren. This is the reason. They are all inspired by the same Spirit of prophecy. They are all made to drink of one Spirit (1 Cor. xii. 13). They are all moved by the Holy Ghost (2 Pet. i. 21).
But the Holy Spirit in them is the Spirit of Christ (1 Pet. i. 11).

His Spirit is, therefore, the Spirit of prophecy who inspires them. This common inspiration creates official equality. Thus inspiring them, the Spirit of the prophecy is himself the testimony (the author of the testimony), the testifier, respecting Jesus. He testifies respecting Jesus, as well as the angel, St. John, and his brethren.

There are thus two sufficient reasons against St. John's worshipping the angel.

1. His official equality with St. John.

2. The Spirit of prophecy, and not the angel, is the author of the testimony respecting Jesus.

This is the teaching of the angel himself.

1. I am thy fellow-servant. I am nothing more than a servant in giving my testimony respecting Jesus, and not its author. For, —

2. The testimony, the author of the testimony, the testifier, is the Spirit of prophecy. So fully and exclusively is he its author, that he himself is the Spirit *inspiring* prophecy. "All Scripture [testimony, prophetic or otherwise] is given *by inspiration of God*" (2 Tim. iii. 16).

THE TRIUMPHS OF THE LAMB (Chapters xix. 11, xx. 1-6).

The Consummation of all the Preceding Symbols.

11. And I saw the heaven opened. And behold a white horse, and his rider called Faithful and True, and in justice doth he judge and make war.

Heaven opened: the opening of heaven is the initiation of great events (iv. 1, xi. 19, xv. 5).

White horse: this expression in the Apocalypse, only here and vi. 2.

White is the emblem of victory (see vi. 2, note).

Horse: kings rode on horses (Esth. vi. 8).

His rider: this rider is a symbol of Christ, the Word of God (xix. 13).

The rider (vi. 2) is a symbol of the same person. The other horses and riders of vi. 4-8, having served their *symbolic* purposes, have disappeared.

The symbol of Christ returns (xix. 11) to show the result of these accomplished purposes.

Faithful and True: see iii. 14. The attributes by which he triumphs. The possession of the same attributes will cause his followers to triumph.

In justice: the Greek word is in Revelation only here and xxii. 11, where, because contrasted with "unjust," must signify *justice*.

This sense (Acts xvii. 31; Rom. ix. 28; Heb. xi. 33), "The Word of God," here fulfils Isaiah's prophetic description of Christ (Isa. xi. 3–5).

Doth he judge and make war: the *present tense* of the verbs "judge" and "war" teaches us that Christ is a *present* judge and a *present* warrior; that he is now at the *present hour* judging both his Church and the world, and also continually fighting for his Church and making it victorious, and continually fighting against its enemies and causing their defeat.

12. Also his eyes are a flame of fire; and on his head are many diadems; having a name written which no one knows save he himself.

The first clause of this verse is, as a description, parenthetic.

His eyes: see i. 14. The eyes of fire symbolize the punishment the Supreme Victor will now inflict.

Diadems: in the Apocalypse only here and xii. 3, and xiii. 1.

The difference between crown and diadem is noticed (xii. 3, note). The single crown (vi. 2) has become, in his successive victories, many diadems.

Having: is a *modal* participle, belongs to "judges and makes war" (verse 11), and thus is ready to describe *the manner* of the judging and of the warring.

Name written: unknown to all, save to Christ himself.

In the Greek and Latin, the word "name," since derived from verbs which signify "to know," is the means by which something is made known.

Were the name here an explanation, it would describe the *manner* of Christ's judging and warring. But since the name is unknown save to Christ, it is not an explanation, and consequently Christ does not here disclose his manner of judging and warring. This manner he reserves for the exercise of his own unrevealed wisdom.

The rider wearing many diadems has already *three* names, "Faithful and True" (verse 11), "The Word of God" (verse 13), and "King of kings and Lord of lords" (verse 16).

These names constitute

The Fourteenth Triplet

in this part of the Apocalypse.

The three names are *personal* names, because describing his *personal* character. As *personal* appellations, the *threefold* symbolism indicates that these three *complete* the present description of his *personal character*.

What can a *fourth* name, known in its meaning only to the victor rider, denote?

From the fact that the name is known only to the bearer, it must denote *secrecy*.

"The angel of the Lord said unto Manoah, Why askest thou after my name, seeing it is *secret?*" (Judg. xiii. 18.)

A name of God is the disclosure he makes in it of his nature and character (Exod. iii. 13, 14).

In Rev. xix. 11, 13, 16, Christ in three names reveals himself as (*a*) "faithful and true" to fulfil all his promises to his true Church, and all his judgments upon his apostate Church; as (*b*) able to do all this, because as "the Word of God" he is in his nature divine, and therefore sure to prove himself in this world (*c*) "King of kings and Lord of lords."

More knowledge of himself than the truths contained in these three names, he does not here reveal. He holds exclusively in his own infinite knowledge both *the time* when he will actually become Supreme Ruler on earth, and also *the methods* of his justice (verse 11) by which he will achieve his triumphs and impose his punishments.

Since a divine name is God's special disclosure of himself, and since Christ does not disclose either the time or the methods of his actual supremacy, his reserved knowledge, in contrast with the disclosures in the three names of the context, becomes in effect *a secret name* (Acts i. 7).

Importance of these Four Names.

These four names in Rev. xix. constitute *the instructive and definite explanation the Apocalypse itself gives of its own character and design.*

Throughout the entire book, Christ is the same kind of Revelator he is in the four names. Everywhere is he "Faithful and True." Everywhere is he the eternal and almighty "Word of God." Everywhere is he supreme "King" and universal "Lord." But nowhere are *the times* of the events predicted fixed and definite. Nowhere does he exhibit *the exact instruments* he employs to revolutionize the world, and to extend and establish his Church till the full knowledge of himself shall cover the whole earth as the waters now cover the seas.

The explanation the Apocalypse, *by means of the four names*, gives of itself, is *the true and authoritative explanation.* It is useless to seek any other.

13. And clothed with a mantle dyed with blood: and his name is called The Word of God.

Mantle: the upper garment.

Dyed with blood: the blood of his conquered enemies. In depth their blood must have reached his horse's bridle (xiv. 20) to have dyed his mantle.

The Word of God: John i. 1; 1 John i. 1. The Eternal and Almighty Word of God incarnate.

14. And on white horses, the armies, which are in heaven, clothed in fine linen, white, clean, follow him.

Armies: are angels. *When inflicting judgments*, as Christ is here, he is attended by angels (Matt. xiii. 41, xxv. 31, xxvi. 53; 2 Thess. i. 7). The saints are not judges till Rev. xx. 4, and are never executioners.

White: with impartial justice will the angels act as executioners.

Follow: Christ leads. The armies of angels follow. "My Father gives me more than twelve legions of angels" (Matt. xxvi. 53).

"O Everlasting God, mercifully grant, that by thy appointment thy holy angels may *succor and defend us on earth;* through Jesus Christ our Lord" (*St. Michael and All Angels*).

15. And out of his mouth goeth a sharp two-edged sword, that with it he may smite the nations; and he himself shall rule them with an iron sceptre: and so he himself treadeth the winepress of the wine of the fierceness of the wrath of God Almighty.

Out of his mouth: the sharp sword is therefore "the sword of the Spirit, which is the word of God" (Eph. vi. 17).

Sword: a broad-sword. In vi. 2, Christ in symbol begins the battle *with arrows*. In Rev. xix. 15, Christ in symbol finishes the battle with the heaviest and sharpest sword ever wielded by a horseman.

Smite: slay, destroy.

Nations: classes of unbelievers.

Iron: irresistible, not oppressive.

Wine-press: in Revelation, only xiv. 19, 20, and xix. 15. Imagery from Isa. lxiii. 3.

Wine: grape juice, like blood in its color. Words are here multiplied to show the severity and completeness of Christ's punishments.

16. And he hath on the mantle and upon his thigh the name written, KING OF KINGS, AND LORD OF LORDS.

The thigh: the place of the girdle, in which is the sword (Ps. xlv. 3; 1 Sam. xxv. 13).

The name may be on the sword. The victories achieved by his sword are virtually marked on it by his triumphant name, "King of kings, and Lord of lords."

King of kings: King over kings.

Lord of lords: Lord over lords. Thus is Christ UNIVERSAL SOVEREIGN (Matt. xxviii. 18; see Rev. xv. 4).

SYMBOLIC PREDICTION OF CHRIST'S VICTORY OVER THE BEAST AND THE FALSE PROPHET (Verses 17, 18).

See Ezek. xxxix. 17, 22.

17. And I saw an angel standing in the sun, and he cries with a loud voice, saying to all the eagles that fly in the face of the sun, Hither, gather yourselves unto the great supper of God.

The call to the birds of prey, repeated from 1 Sam. xvii. 46; Isa. xviii. 6; Jer. vii. 33, xii. 9; Matt. xxiv. 28.

Eagles: "wheresoever the carcass is, there will *the eagles* be gathdred together" (Matt. xxiv. 28).

In the face of the sun: the Greek word is in Revelation only viii. 13 (see notes), xiv. 6, xix. 17.

Feast of God: feast prepared by God, the carcasses of the slain at Armageddon (xvi. 16).

The number of eagles hasting on swiftest wing to the immeasurable battle-field is far beyond all human count. The summoning angel utters his call from the face of the sun. Each shooting ray of the bright luminary shining in all directions is a messenger bearing the loud command to the ear of every listening and waiting eagle. When we can count the sun's rays, then can we number the flocks of eagles started from their perches, scenting from afar the piled corpse-ground, and speeding with most rapid flight to the coveted carnival.

18. That ye may eat the flesh of kings, and the flesh of captains, and the flesh of strong men, and the flesh of horses and their riders, and the flesh of all [the slain] both freemen and slaves, both small and great.

Fifteenth Triplet.

Kings, captains, strong men.

A most frightful representation of utter defeat and universal slaughter. Riders and horses and footmen "in one red burial blent."— BYRON, *Battle of Waterloo*.

Flesh: repeated *five* times to magnify the numbers of the slain prepared for the hungry and thronging eagles.

Kings: the armies are so large that many kings are needed to lead the different national forces.

Captains: captains of thousands, *chiliarchs*, the officers of the armies. Great armies have great divisions. No division here smaller than a thousand men.

Strong men: the soldiers, the rank and file. The prophet Isaiah explains how these soldiers are strong. "None shall be weary nor stumble among them" (v. 27).

All: the slain (xviii. 24).

Freemen and slaves, small and great: a most desperate battle. The enemies of Christ summon into the field all their forces, not only freemen, but slaves; not only adults, but youths and boys.

But numbers, however large, cannot save the hosts fighting against Christ from repulse and slaughter. All are "dead corpses" (Isa. xxxvii. 36), and flocks of screaming eagles are hovering over the countless dead to tear their flesh from their bones.

THE FULFILMENT OF THE SYMBOLIC PREDICTION OF DEFEAT AND VICTORY (Verses 19-21).

19. And so I saw the wild beast and the kings of the earth and their armies gathered together to make the war with him who sitteth upon the horse, and with his army.

I saw: no mortal eye ever before or since saw such a gathering. On the exciting day when the President of the United States of North America is elected, fifty millions of people are in purpose gathered together. But these numbers covering a continent are but one man compared with the wild beast's gathered armies covering all continents.

Wild beast: introduced xiii. 1. He heads and leads the numerous armies gathered against Christ.

Kings of the earth: wicked kings (vi. 15, xvii. 2, 18, xviii. 3, 9).

The war: predicted (xvii. 14).

Sitteth: is sitting. Not "sat," English Version.

The Capture of the Wild Beast and the False Prophet: their Punishment.

20. And the wild beast is taken, and with him the false prophet, who doeth signs before him, by which he deceives them that receive the mark of the wild beast, and them that

worship his image. Although alive, the two are cast into the lake of fire, which is burning with brimstone.

He who affixes "the mark" **is taken**: the capture of the leader of an army is its hopeless defeat (Josh. xii. 9-24). When Napoleon III. surrendered at the battle of Sedan, Sept. 2, 1870, the French cause was lost.

False prophet: in xiii. 11-17, the actions of the second wild beast are identical with the actions of the false prophet mentioned in this verse 20. The second wild beast and the false prophet are thus proved to be the same person.

His image: the image of the first beast, the lamb-dragon causes to be made (xiii. 14).

The lake: the first time in Revelation. Afterwards, xx. 10, 14, 15, xxi. 8; Dan. vii. 11. There may be allusion to Gen. xix. 24 and Dan. iii. 19-21. Thus confined, the two wild beasts are powerless and harmless. They no more afflict the world of mankind.

Destruction of the Army.

21. And the rest are slain with the sword of him who sitteth upon the horse, which sword goeth out of his mouth. And so all the eagles are satiated with their flesh.

The rest: the numerous kings and their numberless armies (verse 19).

The victory of King David over the Syrians may have suggested the imagery in this clause (2 Sam. x. 18).

The horse: archers begin the battle (Rev. vi. 2; 1 Sam. xxxi. 3). Horsemen with their swords finish the battle (2 Sam. i. 6).

All the eagles: although innumerable, they could not devour all the slain.

No real army ever equalled this representative host of slain. No literal defeat is here predicted. Both victory and defeat are spiritual. The battle is between Christ's truth and human error. Christ will, with his truth, yet displace all human errors.

When, A.D. 451, Aetius the Roman general, with Theodoric king of the Visigoths, defeated Attila king of the Huns, in the battle of Chalons, on the Marne, France, the battlefield was strewn by one hundred and sixty-two thousand corpses, — the most destructive battle ever fought. — MILLOT, *Elements Hist.*, ii. 406.

Infinitely greater is the slaughter symbolically predicted by St. John in Rev. xix. 21.

But all the descriptions (Rev. xix. 11-21) are figurative and spiritual. The *presence* of Christ to destroy Jerusalem (Matt. xxiv. 27) was *invisible*. He will also be *invisible* in Rev. xix. 11-21. Both the conflict and the victory are *spiritual*, because *out of his mouth* proceedeth the sharp two edged sword (verse 15). "The sword of the Spirit is the Word of God" (Eph. vi. 17). By his revealed word and his Spirit, Christ wars and contends with *the minds and souls* of men. The struggle and conflict now dividing and enlisting mankind for so many weary centuries are between truth and error, between holiness and sin, between happiness and misery; between the fallen and sinful Adam, and Christ the second Adam, the incarnate Lord from heaven.

Each one of us is a soldier on this present battlefield, and is making his own place and destiny in it. There is no neutral position. He that is not for Christ is against Christ. In this spiritual battle, which no one can shun, victory is won only by "manful and continual fighting against sin, the world, and the Devil." Continual fighting triumphs by this habitual prayer: "Merciful God, grant that the old Adam in me may be so buried, that the new man may be raised up in me. Grant that all sinful affections may die in me, and all things belonging to the Spirit may live and grow in me. Grant that I may have power and strength to have victory, and to triumph against the devil, the world, and the flesh" (*Public Baptism of Infants*).

Each one of us shall die on this battle-ground, either a *coward defeated*, or A BRAVE AND A VICTOR.

CHAPTER XX.

THE SEIZURE AND CONFINEMENT OF THE DRAGON
(Verses 1–3).

1. AND I saw an angel coming down out of heaven, holding the key of the bottomless pit, and a great chain on his hand.

An angel: a symbol of Christ's power in this world (Luke xi. 20). When on earth Christ cast out devils, and thus has power over them at the present time.
Bottomless pit: in Rev. ix. 1, 2, 11, xi. 7, xvii. 8, xx. 1, 3.
Prisons were sometimes subterranean. Such was Jeremiah's (Jer. xxxviii. 6).
Key: ix. 1. The holder of the key of the prison is its keeper.
Chain: "This chain" (Acts xxviii. 20). The chaining of the prisoner made his confinement more sure (Acts xii. 6).
All this representation is figurative, and yet describes a present reality (Luke x. 18, "the power of the enemy").

2. And he lays hold on the dragon, the old serpent, who is the Devil and Satan, and binds him for a thousand years.

Lays hold on: Mark xiv. 51, "seizes."
Dragon: xii. 3, note.
Serpent: xii. 9, note.
Devil and Satan: xii. 9, note.
Binds: with the chain.
The wild beast and the false prophet are already cast out of this world (xix. 20). Now Satan himself is bound.
Absence of evil is the negative side of this world's condition. The prevalence of the gospel, and the blessings and happiness it confers, is the positive side of this world's bliss.

A thousand years: first time in Revelation. Afterwards only verses 3, 4, 5, 6, 7. Definite time for indefinite. This is indisputable Bible usage (Deut. i. 11, vii. 9; Judg. ix. 49; 1 Chron. xvi. 15; Ps. xc. 4; Eccles. vi. 6; Wis. xii. 22; Eccles. vi. 6, xvi. 3, xviii. 10, xxxix. 11, xli. 4, 12; 1 Macc. ii. 38; 2 Pet. iii. 8).

Since the thousand years in Rev. xx. 2 is thus proved by Bible usage to be an *indefinite number*, therefore it cannot be *a definite millennium, a definite* period of a thousand years. A millennium, in this sense, has always been, and always will be, a chimera.

Christ is stronger than Satan (Luke xi. 22). Already has the power of Christ silenced, in large portions of this world, heathen oracles, dethroned material idols, and demolished their sacrificial altars. God is incessantly fulfilling his promises to his incarnate Son (Ps. ii. 8; Ezek. xxi. 27). Past victories are certain pledges of future triumphs. Haste is often a characteristic of God's *mercy* (Isa. lx. 22). May he, in his mercy, hasten the utter overthrow of Satan in this wicked and suffering world!

3. And casts him into the bottomless pit, and shuts it up, and sets a seal over him, that he may no more deceive the nations, until the thousand years are ended. After these years, he must be loosed for a short season.

Sixteenth Triplet.

Casts, shuts, seals. The imprisonment of Satan is complete.
Casts: throws (Job xxx. 19).
Shuts: its mouth (Ps. lxix. 15).
Sets a seal: of clay (Job xxxviii. 14; Bel and Dragon, verses 11, 14; Matt. xxvii. 66).
Must: by God's purpose (Matt. xxiv. 6).
A very short: so the emphatic Greek.

At the end of the thousand years, Satan is still Satan. Imprisonment does not improve him. Punishment with him is not reformatory. "Like people, like priest" (Hos. iv. 9).

How Satan is bound and loosed, we will consider when we examine Rev. xx. 7–9.

VINDICATION AND REWARD OF THE SUFFERING CHURCH OF CHRIST (Verses 4–6).

The passage included in verses 4–6 is one of the most important in the Book of Revelation. The passage exhibits *the consummation of the great drama of this world's history.*

The drama begins with chapter iv. The drama ends with verse 6 of chapter xx.

In chapter vi., verses 9–11, the martyr saints pray the Lord to vindicate their deaths, and to reward them for the injuries they have received.

Their importunate prayer is in part immediately answered; for their investment in white robes constitutes them victors, and also candidates for higher honors when the full number of their fellow-martyrs shall be completed.

In chapter xx., verses 4–6, there is the most graphic and impressive exhibition of the *full vindication* of these very praying saints, and of their associate martyrs, and also of the *exalted dignity* with which they are all now rewarded.

In vi. 9, these Christian martyrs are under the great altar of burnt sacrifice, and prostrate in their flowing blood.

In xx. 4, the bloody altar, and their prostrate bodies covered with gore, have disappeared. The scene of violence gives place to an occasion of joy and honor. The white-robed martyrs are the occupants of thrones, are in the possession and enjoyment of a kingly life, and are reigning with Christ himself, King of kings, and Lord of lords.

Enthronement is the consummation of dignity and bliss, by the promise and appointment of the Captain of our salvation. "To him that overcometh will I grant *to sit with me in my throne*, even as I also overcame and am set down with my Father in his throne" (Rev. iii. 21).

This dignified and blissful consummation is the great reward still promised all the martyrs of Jesus.

See notes on v. 10, and vi. 11.

---

4. And I saw thrones (and persons are sitting upon them, and so vengeance is granted the enthroned), also [I saw] the souls of the beheaded, because of the testimony for Jesus, even because of the word of God; even I saw the souls who did not worship the wild beast, not even his image, and did

not receive the mark upon their forehead, and upon their hand; and so they are living, and are reigning with Christ a thousand years.

I saw: in vision. This word "saw" introduces a *new* vision (xiii. 1, 11, xiv. 1, 6, 14, xv. 1, 2, 5, xviii. 1, xix. 11, 17, 19, xx. 1).

Thrones: the plural in Revelation only here and iv. 4, xi. 16, where the twenty-four elders are the occupants. *Thrones*, then, in Revelation, are occupied by *human* beings, and therefore are thus occupied in xx. 4.

The throne is a symbol of conquest and exaltation. So our Lord teaches (iii. 21).

Are sitting: in this verse are *four* Greek narrative aorists, which are to be translated as present tenses; namely, "are sitting," "is given," "are living," "are reigning."

Are sitting: in Revelation, the Greek verb is only here and iii. 21, where the verb describes enthronement. So also here. Persons are sitting upon them; that is, are sitting upon *the thrones* (iv. 2).

I. The souls of the beheaded here occupy the thrones. They are reigning with Christ (verse 4) at the end. But they must occupy thrones *before* they can reign.

II. The occupants of the thrones are not only the souls of the beheaded, but their *fellow-martyrs* (vi. 9) are also occupants.

That "the souls of the beheaded" and the souls in vi. 9 constitute *one body*, we are forced to believe by these stringent facts: —

1. Both classes are martyrs: "slain," vi. 9; "beheaded," xx. 4.

2. St. John (vi. 11) pronounces both classes *one brotherhood*: "their brethren." The "beheaded" (xx. 4) are the "brethren" of the "slain" (vi. 9).

3. If the "beheaded" (xx. 4) are not the "brethren" predicted (vi. 11), then this prediction (vi. 11) *has no fulfilment* in the Book of Revelation. If there is no fulfilment, then we are left without proof that the prayers of martyred saints are ever answered. Without this proof, the Book of Revelation would be incomplete. All other predictions in this book have, *in the book itself*, records of their fulfilment. The predictions in vi. 11 cannot be an exception.

4. If the full answer to the prayers of the "slain" (vi. 9-11) is not embodied in xx. 4, etc., this Book of Revelation contains no answer whatever to their impatient entreaties.

5. Identity in the cause of their suffering foreshadows for both classes of sufferers — the "slain" and the "beheaded" — identity of reward.

Both were martyred for the same reasons: "For the word of God and for the testimony which they held" (vi. 9). "For the witness of Jesus, and for the word of God" (xx. 4).

6. God (vi. 11) expressly promises the "slain" (v. 9) that they and their martyred "brethren" shall be avenged and rewarded *together*. Their brethren are avenged; "vengeance is granted them" (xx. 4). Consequently, the "slain" themselves are also here (xx. 4) avenged and rewarded. Both classes occupy thrones. Both classes are living kingly lives. Both classes are reigning with Christ.

Vengeance is granted: *The true sense of the Greek word krima*, we will now ascertain.

In Rev. vi. 10, this is the prayer of the "slain:" "How long, O Lord, dost thou not *judge (krineis)* and *avenge (ekdikeis)* our blood?"

These are the constraining reasons for regarding the words, "Vengeance is granted" (xx. 4), *as the recorded answer to this prayer.*

1. (vi. 10) "judge" and "avenge" are so closely connected in sense, that "judge" includes "avenge," and thus also includes the meaning of *vengeance*.

2. In Rev. xix. 2, "judged" is expressly defined by "avenged." But "judged" is the very verb from which the Greek noun *krima* is derived. Consequently, St. John himself gives to this noun the meaning of *vengeance*.

3. *Krima* itself has in Revelation the meaning of *vengeance*.

In Revelation, *krima*, "judgment," occurs only *three* times (xvii. 1, xviii. 20, and xx. 4). The meaning of *krima*, in xvii. 1, and xviii. 20, must, therefore, be the meaning of *krima* in xx. 4.

In xvii. 1, *krima* is the *judgment* of the great whore. But *krima* here is defined by "judged" and "avenged" (xix. 2); and since "avenged" imparts its meaning to "judged," vengeance is the meaning of "judgment," in xvii. 1.

In Rev. xviii. 20, *krima* also means "vengeance." It derives this meaning from the verb "judged," in this verse, which means "avenged," and thus requires this translation for the verse, "God avenges on her her vengeance on you."

This is the proof, from Revelation itself, that *krima*, in Rev. xvii. 1, and xviii. 20, means *vengeance*. *These two places* give that sense of *krima* to *krima* in xx. 4. In xx. 4, *krima* cannot escape from the meaning of *vengeance*. We must define *krima*, in Rev. xx. 4, *by its meaning in the Book of Revelation.* We must not look to other portions of the New Testament for the meaning of *krima* in Rev. xx. 4.

Krima (Rev. xx. 4) does not constitute the martyrs *judges*. They are suppliants for *vengeance* ("avenge," vi. 10), and "vengeance," *krima* (xx. 4), is granted them. They are here seated, not on thrones of *judgment*, but on thrones of *conquest and exaltation*.

I saw the souls of the beheaded: *with the article*, as here, souls, in the New Testament, means either in the body (Rev. xii. 11) or disembodied (1 John iii. 16; Rev. vi. 9, xx. 4).

When *without* the article, "souls" means *persons* (Acts ii. 41, vii. 14, xxvii. 37; 1 Pet. i. 9, iii. 20; 2 Pet. ii. 14; Rev. xviii. 13).

Beheaded: the Greek participle is derived from a noun which means *an axe;* beheaded *by an axe.*

Here only in the New Testament. In the Septuagint, only 1 Kings v. 18, for the Hebrew *satal,* to cut ("hew," English Version).

Thus, as stones may be hewn by a chisel, the Hebrew verb does not necessarily include *an axe,* as does the Greek participle in Rev. xx. 4. Literally, then, the Greek participle means beheaded by *an axe,* which was a *Roman* instrument of beheading. Howson (Conybeare and Howson) thinks St. Paul suffered death in this way. If literally beheaded by the axe, the martyrs (Rev. xx. 4) were under the *Pagan* Roman Empire. See ii. 13.

But the "beheaded," as well as the "slain" (vi. 9), are *representative* martyrs, and, as such, include in symbol *all actual martyrs in all ages,* whatever may be the instrument of execution. The beheading here need not be understood as *literal.* The word may be used *figuratively,* to describe the *severity and bloody character* of the martyrdom.

Because of the testimony for Jesus: depicts the *positive* virtues of the beheaded.

Who did not worship, etc.: exhibits their *negative* virtues (xiii. 15, 16).

Before "who did not worship," supply "souls," and translate. "even the souls who did not worship."

The wild beast: the lamb-dragon.

His image: the image he causes to be made (xiii. 14).

Mark: he affixes (xiii. 16, 17).

Are living: the Greek verb is in Revelation only, i. 18, ii. 8, iii. 1, iv. 9, 10, vii. 2, x. 6, xiii. 14, xv. 7, xix. 20, xx. 4, 5.

In these senses, see ii. 8. Note: —

1. To have *bodily* life, i. 18, ii. 8, xiii. 14, xix. 20.
2. To have *moral* life, iii. 1.
3. To live *eternally,* iv. 9, 10, vii. 2, x. 6, xv. 7.

These three divisions of meaning exhaust the list of places where the Greek verb, "to live," is found in Revelation; except xx. 4, 5, after whose signification we are now inquiring.

1. "To live," in Rev. xx. 4, 5, cannot mean, the martyrs have *bodily* life. They are *disembodied* souls, and therefore destitute of material bodies and of *bodily* life.

To say they have *resurrection* bodies, because partakers of "the first resurrection" (verse 5), is *an assumption;* since it can never be *proved* that "the first resurrection" is a *bodily* resurrection.

2. "To live," cannot mean, the martyrs have *moral* life. The pos-

session of moral life made them martyrs. Moral life cannot be *the consequence* of their martyrdom.

3. "'To live," cannot mean, the martyrs have *endless* life. Endless life is the *inherent* possession of every human soul. The martyrs were *always* immortal. It cannot be proved that they became immortal in consequence of their martyrdom, or of any other event in their history.

We have thus exhausted the explanations of "to live," furnished by the Book of Revelation itself. Its definitions fail to define "are living" (xx. 4, 5).

Our next resort for an explanation of "are living" must be to *the context*. In the context, "are living" *is contrasted* with "beheaded." But beheading implies both *degradation and misery*. The opposite of degradation and misery is *exaltation and happiness*. "Are living" may, then, mean, the martyrs are *exalted and happy*. *They are living an exalted and happy life*.

Bible usage elsewhere gives "to live" this very meaning, and thus confirms the contextual meaning.

1. Exaltation : "Oh that Ishmael might *live* before thee! I will make him a *great nation*" (Gen. xvii. 18, 20).

2. Happiness: " *We live*, if ye stand fast in the Lord" (1 Thess. iii. 8.

The explanation of "are living" (Rev. xx. 4, 5), which the context demands, and Bible usage confirms, we are not at liberty to reject, but are bound by the laws of language to accept, hold, proclaim, maintain.

Are reigning with Christ: are reigning: are kings in dignity. "Makes us a kingdom" (Rev. i. 6). Makes us Christians kings in present exaltation and blessings.

With Christ: on the earth. "Makes them to our God a kingdom, even priests, and they shall reign *on the earth*" (Rev. v. 10).

St. Paul also describes Christians as reigning in the present life with Christ; as having a present *spiritual* enthronement. His words embody truths which the English Version does not fully exhibit.

"When we were dead in sins, God quickens us *with Christ* (by grace *are* ye saved) [the quickening, then, is a *present* act], and raises us *with* Christ [gives us, with the raised Christ, a *spiritual* resurrection], and makes us sit [as reigning kings] with Christ, in heavenly blessings in Christ Jesus [in him by spiritual union] (Eph. ii. 5, 6).

"Even now we sit there in him" (Bishop LANCELOT ANDREWS, vol. i. *Serm.* vii. p. 115; Bishop JOSEPH HALL, *Christ Mystical*, chapter v. 1).

The explanation that St. John, in Rev. xx. 4, may describe the present spiritual enthronement of Christians with Christ, does not conflict with this language of his in the passage, "The souls of the beheaded are reigning with Christ;" because, —

1. These beheaded souls have neither *present existence*, nor *present* locality. They are not *actually* living and rejoicing, either on earth, in paradise, or in heaven. The souls of the beheaded are nothing else and nothing more than *symbolical representatives* of Christ's suffering Church in this world, from generation to generation, until Christ shall return to end its momentous and protracted probation.

2. These symbolical representatives of Christ's suffering Church, in all ages, and of ultimate victory and triumph over all opposition, appear, in symbol, *as souls*, because they could not be exhibited as Christians enduring *death*, the completion and perfection of all bodily suffering, unless they are shown in the model drama *as souls disembodied*. The character of disembodied souls, when once imposed by the nature of the symbolism they are presenting, must be continued whenever they exhibit themselves. Because, for the perfection of suffering, they are at first souls under the altar, they must continue to be souls, even when sitting on thrones, when living exalted lives, and when reigning with Christ on earth.

This whole exhibition is nothing but *symbolic representation*. When we forget the fact, then difficulties arise in our minds, and perplex us. When we remember and hold the fact, the perplexing difficulties vanish.

A thousand years: this indefinite period of time belongs not to the souls *erroneously supposed* to have actual existence and definite locality, but to the great object represented by the present symbolism, — *the true Church of Christ in this world, in its prolonged history;* suffering, enduring, victorious, triumphing, exulting, enthroned with Christ for a blissful period, the end of which he holds in his own measureless and inaccessible knowledge.

THE REST OF THE DEAD: THE FIRST RESURRECTION.

5. The rest of the dead live not, until the thousand years are ended. This is the first resurrection.

The rest: are *in contrast* with the souls of the beheaded (verse 4), and therefore constitute a *different* class of souls, and possess a *different* character. They are not holy souls, but are wicked souls.

The contrast is created by the declaration "live not."

Since they are *wicked* souls, they cannot be awaiting the resurrection unto eternal life. The life they have not, cannot be a *bodily-resurrection* life.

In two other instances in Revelation, does "the rest" indicate contrast (ii. 24, xi. 13).

Of the dead: "the rest," because in contrast with the souls of the beheaded, are themselves souls. They are called "dead," because they are souls *disembodied*. Their bodies are dead, and give *to their supposed personality* this appellation, "dead." The rest of the *dead*, and the rest of the *souls*, are in meaning identical. But though "the rest" are souls, they are not souls *in reality*, but only *in symbol*. They are *representative* souls. They represent an object, the *direct opposite* of the object the souls of the beheaded represent. The souls of the beheaded represent the true Church of Christ. The wicked souls represent his apostate Church, and all its members in this world.

They live not: the wicked souls, as symbols, "live not," in a sense the exact opposite of the life the souls of the beheaded are enjoying. As representatives of the apostate Church, and all its members in this world, the wicked souls are not occupying thrones; they are not living exalted and happy lives; they are not reigning with Christ on earth. In their symbolism, "the rest of the dead" are in appalling contrast with this enthronement, with this happiness, with this union and living with Christ. They are degraded. They are wretched. They possess not either the image, the character, or the fellowship of Christ. They represent unrenewed, unsanctified, unholy souls. They represent the unbelieving, prayerless, godless, wicked, self-indulgent class, which always forms so large a portion of every generation of mankind.

Until the thousand years are ended: since a thousand years is in itself an *indefinite* period, it cannot have *a definite and complete* end.

The thousand years can never be *literally* ended. They can be ended only *figuratively*.

Do periods of time ever, in the language of the Bible, have *figurative* endings?

The Bible itself answers this question in the affirmative.

"Samuel came no more to see Saul *until the day of his death*" (1 Sam. xv. 35).

"Michal had no child *unto the day of her death*" (2 Sam. vi. 23).

In these passages, there are two periods of time: (*a*) "came no more," and (*b*) "had no child." *Simple prose* endings to these periods would be, in the one case, *at all*, (*a*) "came no more *at all ;*" in the other case, *ever*, (*b*) "had no child *ever*."

But, instead of these simple terms of emphasis, there is, in the quotations from the Books of Samuel, the strong *figure of hyperbole:* in the first instance, (*a*) "until the day of his death;" in the second, (*b*) "unto the day of her death."

By this usage of *figurative* endings of negative assertions, this language, "until the thousand years are ended," must be explained. This *hyperbole* St. John uses instead of the simple emphasis, *ever:* The rest of the dead live not *ever*. Enthronement, an exalted and happy life, and dominion and union with Christ, are *never* theirs.

We are obliged to accept and use this *figurative* explanation of the first clause of Rev. xx. 5, simply because there is no other explanation, either biblical or possible. The *indefinite* period of a thousand years cannot admit a *literal* explanation.

The Underlying Basis of the Symbolism in Rev. xx. 4, 5.

According to St. John's symbolical statements in the passage, the souls of the beheaded are rewarded by being enthroned with Christ, and the rest of the dead are punished by being left in their degradation and wretchedness *immediately after death*.

This symbolical truth presupposes other truths: —

1. With the termination of each human life, its probation ends utterly.

2. There is no probation after death. There is no second probation.

3. The state after death proceeds as it begins. As the happiness of the saved never ends, so the misery of lost souls never ends.

4. Punishment in the world of the dead is not reformatory. The present life is the only period God gives us for repentance and reformation.

5. There is no purgatory.

6. The state of departed souls is unalterable.

7. Prayers for the impenitent dead are useless.

8. Prayers for the blessed dead presuppose their imperfection. On the contrary, the Scriptures teach their perfection. "The spirits of just men *made perfect*" (Heb. xii. 23).

9. All the truths in the Book of Revelation respecting the true Church and the apostate Church apply to the *individual members* of these churches, as churches are *composed of individuals*. We are neither saved nor lost as *corporations*, but only as *individual souls*.

The First Resurrection.

This is the first resurrection: the demonstrative pronoun "this" refers "the first resurrection" to the state of the souls of the beheaded, described in verse 4. This state is *figurative and spiritual*. The consequence of this fact can be neither denied nor ignored. Since the state of the souls of the beheaded is a *figurative and spiritual* state, "the first resurrection" is also *figurative and spiritual*. "The first resurrection," since identical with the figurative and spiritual state of the souls beheaded, *cannot be material and bodily*.

St. John calls the state of the beheaded souls a resurrection, just as the prophet Ezekiel calls the revived and improved state of the Jews a resurrection. Of their former wretched and hopeless state as a nation, "the dry bones" Ezekiel sees in vision are a just emblem. These dry bones clothed with flesh, and animated with new life, are the emblem of their improved condition, and thus are, to the Israelites as a people, a resurrection.

St. John, in Rev. xx. 4, 5, repeats Ezekiel's imagery and language. When in the Book of Revelation we see the Church of Christ for the first time, her slain saints are *entombed* under the altar (vi. 9). In Rev. xx. 4, 5, the Church has left her tomb; and her new condition of enthronement and dominion is to her, *figuratively*, a "*resurrection*" from death.

Nor is St. John the only New-Testament writer to whom the prophet Ezekiel suggests resurrection imagery. St. Paul, in his Epistle to the Romans, predicts with exultation the universal conversion of the Jews to Christ. As this enraptured Hebrew of the Hebrews contemplates the Church in its Jewish enlargement, he exclaims, "What is it but *life from dead?*" (Rom. xi. 15.)

The *first* resurrection. The expression is only here, and in verse 6.

This *first* resurrection is a *spiritual* resurrection.

1. The prophet Ezekiel mentions two resurrections, — material, xxxvii. 10; spiritual, verse 11.

2. Our Lord himself describes two resurrections, — material, John v. 28, 29; spiritual, verses 25, 26.

3. St. Paul also teaches two resurrections, — material, 1 Cor. xv. 52; spiritual, Rom. vi. 5; Col. ii. 12, 13.

Reasons why St. John's First Resurrection (Rev. xx. 5, 6) is a Spiritual Resurrection.

1. The *symbolic* character of the Book of Revelation *requires* the *figurative* and spiritual sense of the expression, unless the context forbids this sense.

2. In the Book of Revelation, St. John has *two deaths*, — one *bodily*, "there shall be no more death" (xxi. 4); the other spiritual, "thou art dead" (iii. 1), "the *second* death" (ii. 11, xx. 6, xxi. 8).

St. John, then, only repeats *his own usage*, when he also has *two resurrections*, — the opposites of the two deaths, — one *bodily* (Rev. xx. 12, 13); the other *spiritual*, made so by this usage of St. John himself.

In no place does St. John use *the exact* phrases, the *second* resurrection and the *first* death; but the *second* death, thus *undefined*, is figurative and spiritual. The same is true of the *first* resurrection; because *undefined*, the *first* resurrection is also figurative and spiritual.

3. In Rev. xx. 6 is this assertion: "Upon him that hath part in the first resurrection, the second death hath no power."

But the second death is a *spiritual* state (verses 14, 15, ii. 11, xxi. 8); *a state of spiritual death.*

Here mark the assertion of St. John, as thus explained by himself. This is his own explanation. The subject of the first resurrection *cannot experience the spiritual state* called the second death. He cannot experience this spiritual state, *because he is in a different spiritual state.* He cannot experience spiritual death, because he is in the *opposite* state, *the state of spiritual life.* He cannot die the spiritual death, because his soul *has been raised* from the death of sin unto the life of righteousness. Thus does St. John's own assertion, "Upon him that hath part in the first resurrection, the second death hath no power," prove that "the first resurrection" is a *spiritual resurrection.*

4. The adjective "first," attached to "resurrection," proves the resurrection to be *spiritual.*

The proof presents itself in these forms: —

(*a*) "First" is an adjective of enumeration. Its noun, "resurrection," existed *before* it was enumerated. "Resurrection" existed *before* "first" was attached to it. "The resurrection" existed *before* it is mentioned (Rev. xx. 5).

But we have already proved that "the resurrection" (Rev. xx. 5) is a *spiritual* resurrection. The consequence cannot be resisted, namely, "the resurrection" (Rev. xx. 5) existed as a *spiritual* resurrection, *before* it is mentioned in the Book of Revelation.

(*b*) This previously existing spiritual resurrection of Rev. xx 5. is identical with the spiritual resurrection taught by our Lord in these words: "The Son *quickeneth* whom he will. He that believeth on him that sent me *hath everlasting life,* and is passed *from death unto life.* The hour is coming, and *now is* [in this present life] when the dead shall hear the voice of the Son of God; and they that hear *shall live.* For as the Father hath life in himself; so hath he given to the Son to have *life in himself*" (John v. 21, 24–26).

The spiritual resurrection of Rev. xx. 5 is identical with the spiritual resurrection our Lord confers (John v.), for the following reasons: —

(1) The spiritual resurrection conferred by our Lord is itself "the *first* resurrection," because, —

(*a*) It is *first* taught by our Lord. No previous revelator ever mentions, *in express phrase*, a spiritual resurrection.

(*b*) The spiritual resurrection taught by our Lord is also "first," because he himself connects it with a *second* resurrection. Thus: "The hour is coming, in the which *all that are in the graves* shall hear the voice of the Son of man, and *shall come forth;* they that have done good, unto the resurrection of life; and they that have done evil, unto the resurrection of damnation" (John v. 29).

(*c*) The spiritual resurrection taught by our Lord (John v. 21-26) is likewise *first*, on account of its absolute necessity. The spiritual resurrection must *precede* the second, or the second will be "the resurrection unto damnation" (John v. 29).

St. Paul presents the two resurrections in this very order; the spiritual first, as essential to the happiness of the second. "That I may know *the power of his resurrection*, being made *conformable unto his death;* if by any means I might attain *unto the resurrection of the dead*" (Phil. iii. 10, 11).

(2) We have shown that "first" demands for "resurrection" identification with some *previous* spiritual resurrection. This requisite identification is set forth *fully and completely* with the spiritual resurrection of John v. 21-26. Identification of the resurrection (Rev. xx. 5) with any other resurrection than that taught by our Lord *is impossible*. We are therefore bound by the impossibility to receive and maintain *this sole identification*.

"This is the first resurrection," *as consummated* in St. John's vision (Rev. xx. 4, 5).

"The first resurrection" has two consummations.

It is consummated *symbolically* in Christ's triumphing Church (Rev. xx. 4). It will be consummated *actually*, when "life from the dead" (Rom. xi. 15) shall fully come, not only to all Jews, but to all Gentiles.

6. Blessed and holy is he who hath part in the first resurrection. Over these [blessed and holy ones] the second death hath no authority. On the contrary, they shall be priests serving God, even Christ, and they shall reign with him a thousand years.

Holy: the blessedness will consist largely of holiness.

He who hath part: he who partakes of his portion. In the New Testament, this expression only here and John xiii. 8.

The second death: only in Revelation, and there only here and ii. 11, xx. 14, xxi. 8.

The second death implies sinfulness, "fearful, unbelieving," etc. (xxi. 8).

No authority: sinfulness hath no authority over the holy. "Jesus Christ hath perfected forever them that are sanctified" (Heb. x. 14).
Priests: i. 6, v. 10.
Even Christ: Granville Sharp's Rule, Ayre. Introduction, pp. 216, 217.
A thousand years: for this indefinite period will there be in this world a succession, in increasing numbers, of holy souls serving Christ "in spirit and in truth" (John iv. 24).
This service is worship (Rev. iv. 8–11) and obedience (John xv. 14).
So long as we worship and serve Christ, we are a portion of the growing succession, and of the increasing holy Church.

THE LOOSING AND THE DEFEAT OF SATAN (Verses 7–10).

These subjects seem, at first sight, to embody difficulties which are insuperable. But apparent difficulties are not always real difficulties.

The Book of Revelation itself creates apparent difficulties. The book is a symbolical drama. Because it is a drama, its visions seem to present themselves in chronological order. This *dramatic chronology* makes the loosing of Satan *subsequent* to the enthronement of the saints and the consummation of the triumphs of the Christian Church.

Then, in the Apocalyptic drama, the enthronement of the saints, and the binding and loosing of Satan, are apparently acts done in a very few moments.

But drama is only a *series* of symbols, and its *continuous* chronology is only in appearance. The exaltation of the saints and the treatment of Satan may, when realized, be events both *gradual and contemporaneous*.

All these great events symbolized may actually occur, not only *at the same time*, but *at different times*. The acts, whatever they may be, prefigured by the binding and loosing of Satan, may transpire not merely simultaneously, but at periods both past and present.

The important truths signified by the opposite conditions of Satan are, that he is both a *weakened* and an *existing* power in the world. Though chained, he is not yet dead.

Were he dead, this life of ours would cease to be a life of probation. When Satan disappears in the lake of fire and brimstone, after his final defeat with Gog and Magog, this earth itself will also disappear, by being burned up. Then will all human probation cease; for the day of judgment with its unalterable decisions will immediately follow.

The *progressive* character and the *simultaneousness* of the events indicated by the binding and loosing of Satan remove from Rev. xx. 7–10 a portion of the difficulties which at first sight present themselves to our minds.

So long as this earth continues, it will be infested with evil. Satan will not be an enemy absolutely conquered, till this present world terminates, and he is banished to eternal and hopeless punishment.

In its dramatic character, the Book of Revelation exhibits *results*, not their *processes*. When the angel exclaims, "Babylon is fallen" (Rev. xviii. 2), he prophetically announces a *finished result*. But the *process* by which this result will be reached is not yet finished, but is still transpiring. This being the case, the inhabitants of this earth may have been in the midst of these processes during centuries now past, and may be in the midst of these processes at the present time.

The former destructive hostility to pure Christianity, waged by civil governments and false systems of the gospel, though not extinct, is certainly for the present at least restrained and modified.

In countries nominally Christian, and in all heathen communities, *infidelity* is the modern form of opposition to the revealed religion of Jesus Christ.

Since Satan is still a living power in the world, he may be in this nineteenth century gathering his forces for his most deadly assault upon the Christian revelation, and we Christians of the passing hour may be living in the midst of the stirring muster.

This surely may be our situation. If so, Gog and Magog

do not belong solely to the remote future. If we will listen, we may now hear the blast of their trumpets. If we will open our eyes, we may now see the flights of their arrows and the thrusts of their spears.

---

7. And when the thousand years are ended, Satan shall be loosed from his prison.

The thousand years: of his binding. This began when Christ was on earth (Matt. iv. 1–10; Luke x. 18). The thousand years, indefinite in extent, was in its beginning contemporaneous with the beginning of the gospel, which in its indefinite duration is also measured by a thousand years, since during this uncertain period of time the saints are reigning with Christ on earth (Rev. v. 10). The saints began thus to reign so soon as there were Christian believers (Eph. ii. 6). Satan's binding and the saints' reign with Christ thus began together. They continue together through the same indefinite duration, and they will end together.

The loosing is a process, as well as a final result, portrayed by the graphic symbol of his *going out* of his prison "to deceive the nations" (Rev. xx. 8).

The process of Satan's loosing is contemporaneous with the process of his binding. The two processes in point of time run parallel with each other. During the Christian era, Satan is a conquered and restrained and yet an active enemy.

Through Christ's help, we can always overcome Satan. Still he is always ready to tempt us to sin, and always able to ruin us, unless standing in Christ's greater might we "resist the devil," and then he flees from us (Jas. iv. 7).

At the close of the Christian era, Satan will attempt to consummate the destruction of the second Adam, which he is now continually plotting. But his own defeat will be signal and complete, and his own ruin beyond recovery. Satan will never leave the "lake of fire and brimstone" (Rev. xx. 10).

Symbols.

An Apocalyptic symbol exhibits a complete and immediate occurrence. Because *complete* in its nature, a symbol cannot describe a comparison. Comparisons are defined only by language either spoken or written. There can be no degrees in symbols. In them, however, degrees may be implied. This implication must be always recognized in all symbolic representations. In their outward character merely, symbols, although graphic and impressive, are inadequate substitutes for language.

A symbol is, in its nature, not only full and complete, but is also *immediate*. A symbol knows, in itself, nothing of *time*. A symbol is a *present* vision, and not the picture of a process.

Thus, both complete and timeless, a symbol must be always estimated according to its actual design and capability. A symbol is not definite language, and must never be interpreted as such. When regarded as the adequate substitutes of explicit language, symbols convey false and erroneous impressions.

These obvious differences between symbols and words will greatly help us rightly understand the binding and loosing of Satan (Rev. xx. 1-3, 7-10).

In symbol, the binding is apparently total and timeless. But when regarded in its exhibition as symbolic, the binding is invested with degrees and temporal progression.

The loosing of Satan is to be interpreted by his binding, and becomes gradual, and is incorporated into the lapse of centuries.

The great and decisive battle between the Word of God, and Satan and his two wild beasts (Rev. xix. 11-xx. 1-3, 7-10), is symbolically described as *one* battle fought at *one* time. Yet actually this battle is *continuous*, and is waged *at all times*.

This unceasing perpetuation of the battle is explicitly proved by the following account of our Lord's incessant employment in this present world: He goes forth *conquering* and to *conquer* (Rev. vi. 2).

Thus Christ is a perpetual victor. But victory requires conflict: conflict requires enemies. The habitual and ever-fighting enemies of Christ are no other opponents than Satan and his two wild beasts. Their hot battle against him is continual and never-ending.

This representation of the battle constantly prosecuted between the Word of God, and Satan and his two wild beasts, explains the binding and loosing of Satan. They are symbolized as *different* events, occurring at *different* times. Yet, like the battle between Christ and his spiritual foes, the binding and the loosing may be *simultaneous* events.

Indeed, the binding and the loosing are, in the visions St. John saw, *a part and continuation* of the great and unremitted battle itself, between Christ and his chief adversary the Devil.

In this stern and protracted conflict, the Word of God is *ultimately* victorious and triumphant. In the process and in the details of the awful warfare, Satan sometimes recovers himself for a season after a defeat. At such times he is symbolically "loosed." Whenever he is worsted, he is then symbolically "bound" and restrained.

Can the subjoined words of St. John be so explained as to accord with the explanation just given?

"Satan should deceive the nations no more till the thousand years should be fulfilled; and after that he must be loosed a little season" (Rev. xx. 3).

"When the thousand years are expired, Satan shall be loosed out of prison, and shall go out to deceive the nations which are in the four quarters of the earth" (verses 7 and 8).

All these strong and positive assertions are derived from the accompanying symbols of binding and loosing, with their inability to express comparisons and portray degrees, and are conformed to these symbolic conditions.

1. This is pre-eminently the case with the unrestricted negation, "No more." The symbolism demands the phrase. The Devil, "bound with a great chain, cast into the bottomless pit, shut up" in it, and its door sealed over him, could "no more deceive the nations." The symbolism renders his deception impossible. The truth underlying the symbolism is the comforting fact that through Christ's overmastering power, the influence of Satan in this world is diminished, and is diminishing. "No more" is itself symbolic, and not to be understood in its full restriction.

2. The loosing of Satan is the exact counterpart of his binding. His confinement denotes partial loss of power. His loosing is not unlimited, but has its degrees of restraint.

3. The rigid symbolism of the passage also provides sufficient explanation of the meaning of "the thousand years."

When in Rev. xx. 4, it is said, "The souls lived and reigned with Christ a thousand years," the time is *indefinite* according to frequent usage in both Testaments of the Bible. The indefinite period cannot, therefore, be limited in its duration. When, consequently, it is written, "an angel bound Satan a thousand years" (Rev. xx. 2), "the thousand years should be fulfilled" (verse 3), "the thousand years are expired" (verse 7), the limitations are wholly symbolic. They are occasioned by the pervading symbolism. The binding and the loosing of Satan, although actually simultaneous, are in symbol necessarily pictured as occurring in succession. Symbolically the loosing must by the change succeed the binding. But the succession is solely in appearance, created by the symbols. The period of "the thousand years" is, both with the binding and the loosing, not definite in time, but is indefinite. Throughout the entire indefinite duration of this world's existence, the increasing defeats and partial successes of Satan will ever run parallel not only to each other, but also to the accompanying victories and triumphs of the Word of God and of his saints, who, in unbroken perpetuity, are here on earth reigning with their omnipotent Lord, ever by his gospel and his Spirit subduing and recovering to himself the precious souls of men he purchased by his atoning blood, as his present right and his indisputable possession.

8. And he shall go forth to deceive the nations which are in the four corners of the earth, Gog and Magog, to gather them for the war: whose number is as the sand of the sea.

To deceive: xii. 9. Satan's aggressive armor is always deception (John viii. 44). His greatest deception is the denial of his own existence.

Four corners: every portion (vii. 1; 1 Sam. xiv. 38), Hebrew.

Gog and Magog: Gog is the name of the king. Magog is the name of his people. His kingdom was in "the north part" (Ezek. xxxviii. 15), in the region north of the Black and Caspian seas, the land of *Scythia*, the most barbarous and savage country of ancient times.

"Barbarian, Scythian" (Col. iii. 11).

"Those poor men, if they had told their cause, yea, before the *Scythians*, should have been judged innocent" (2 Macc. iv. 47).

"The Scythians are a people who rejoice in murders, and scarcely differ from wild beasts" (Josephus against Appian, ii. 37).

In Ezek. xxxviii. and xxxix., Gog and Magog prophetically invade the land of Israel, and are defeated.

The prophet Jeremiah, i. 14, iv. 6, vi. 22-24, predicts the invasion of the land of Israel *from the north*, and by the north must mean Scythia, as he does not mention Babylon till chapter xx. 4 of his book.

Scythopolis, city of *Scythians*, was six hundred furlongs, seventy-five miles, from Jerusalem (2 Macc. xii. 29). By 1 Macc. v. 52, Scythopolis is identified with Bethsan, the modern *Beisan*, in the Jordan valley, twelve miles south of the Sea of Galilee, and four miles west of the Jordan.

Bethsan was a strong military position (1 Sam. xxxi. 10; 1 Macc. v. 52, xii. 40, 41). Its name *Scythopolis* proves its possession by a body of Scythians, who may have invaded Palestine, according to the predictions of Jeremiah and Ezekiel, and according to the history of Herodotus, B.C. 600 (i. 103-105).

We may therefore conclude, that both Ezekiel and St. John, when referring to Gog and Magog, derive their prophetic imagery from an *actual* invasion of the Holy Land by the barbarous Scythians.

We thus discover not only the origin of St. John's imagery in Rev. xx. 8, but also his design in referring to the Scythians. By this reference he predicts the most violent and deadly assault on the part of large numbers of mankind upon the Church of Christ, and their utter defeat.

As the sand of the sea: that is, "innumerable" (Heb. xi. 12).

9. And they come up upon the breadth of the earth, and compass the fortress of the saints, even the city which is beloved. And yet, there comes down fire out of heaven from God, and utterly devours them.

Come up: implies attack. "Go up against" (Judg. i. 1).

Breadth: the whole extent (Gen. xiii. 17; Job xxxviii. 18; Isa. viii. 8; Hab. i. 6).

The armies of Gog and Magog occupy the entire surface of the earth.

Compass: in Luke xxi. 20, this verb describes the desolating siege of Jerusalem. The armies of Gog and Magog are *besieging* "the beloved city." St. John may derive his imagery from the sieges of Jerusalem by the Babylonians (2 Kings xxv. 1, 2) and by the Romans (Luke xxi. 20, 28).

The language of St. John indicates the desperate peril to which "the beloved city," now in a state of close and assaulting siege, is exposed.

The fortress: in the New Testament, the English Version translates the Greek noun (*a*) "army" (Heb. xi. 34); (*b*) "camp" (Heb. xiii. 11, 13); (*c*) "castle" (Acts xxi. 34, 37, xxii. 24, xxiii. 10, 16, 32).

The context of Rev. xx. 9 requires "castle," *fortress*, as the meaning of the Greek noun in this verse. The saints are evidently reduced to the last extremity. They do not risk a battle in the open field. They retire to their only fortress left them, their "beloved city."

The beleaguered saints may be suffering the consequences of a long and hopeless siege, "famine and pestilence" (Deut. xxviii. 52-57; 2 Kings xxv. 3; Jer. xxxii. 24).[1]

The horrors of starvation and pining death seize the decimated defenders of the last stronghold of revealed religion in this world.

This is St. John's startling exhibition of the final struggle between infidelity, and loyalty to Christ.

The Tower of Antonia, called by St. Luke "the castle" (Acts xxi. 34, 37), St. John had often seen. He may have taken his imagery (Rev. xx. 9) from this castle, as he uses the same Greek word which is translated "castle" by St. Luke.[2]

The capture of the Tower of Antonia by Titus, the Roman general, was the total destruction of the Jews as a nation.[3] The annihilating

---

[1] Eusebius describes the famine in Jerusalem, when besieged by the Romans, *E. H.*, iii. 6, pp. 87, etc.

[2] *Dict. Bible*, i. p. 816.   [3] *Id.*, ii. p. 1307.

event must have left an indelible impression upon the mind of St. John.

According to our Lord's own prediction (Luke xxi. 28), the destruction of Jerusalem was succeeded by the prosperity and extension of his Church.

"So long as the shadows of the Levitical law, along with city and temple, were standing, the kingdom of God, or *the free exercise of the Christian religion*, did not as yet enjoy unrestricted-scope." — BENGEL on Luke xxi. 28.

"When ye see all these things that I have foretold you, begin to come to pass, then take comfort, and expect with confidence that the time of your deliverance and of *the firm and universal establishment of my church* draweth nigh." — DR. SAMUEL CLARKE on Luke xxi. 28.

The siege of Jerusalem by the Romans may have suggested to St. John the imagery in Rev. xx. 9. But how different the results of the two sieges! At Jerusalem the Roman besiegers are victors, and the besieged Jews are destroyed. On the contrary, in Rev. xx. 9, the besiegers, Gog and Magog, are totally destroyed, while the besieged, the Church of Christ, is triumphant and perpetual victor, and sole possessor of the liberated and Christianized earth.

Even: defining the nature of the fortress the saints are holding; namely, "the beloved city."

The city: iii. 12, on which see notes.

Beloved: by Christ (i. 5, iii. 9). Over Jerusalem, on Mount Zion, Christ shed tears of love (Luke xix. 41). Christ's love illumines the last scene in the history of his Church in this world. The very last word in this history is CHRIST'S LOVE. When the besieged and imperilled, diminishing Church cannot save itself, CHRIST'S LOVE SAVES IT (Rom. viii. 37).

Fire comes down: (Gen. xix. 24; Ezek. xxxviii. 22, xxxix. 6). Every portion of the circumambient atmosphere over the entire earth flashes with falling lightning. The destruction of Gog and Magog is sudden and utter, and is from God (Matt. xxiv. 27).

Utterly devours: their destruction is complete. "God makes an utter end" (Nah. i. 9). Second strokes of lightning do not fall.

The impressive symbols of a vast besieging army, and of a closely besieged castle, terminate with the absolute destruction of the investing army, and with the rescue and triumph of the desperate fortress.

These overwhelming symbols are too huge and impossible to be interpreted *literally*. They must be understood *spiritually*.

The imperishable truths taught by the shining symbols St. John saw pictured on the sky encircling Patmos, are for our present encouragement, and for our persistent endurance in the service of Christ.

1. Infidelity will yet cease in this world.
2. Faith in Christ will be universal.
3. The Church of Christ preserves the faith.
4. His Church will triumph over every form of opposition.
5. Though not *in person*, yet by his truth, by his Church and ministry, and by his Spirit, Christ will be UNIVERSAL KING on this earth in its present material state.
6. The complete conversion of the world to Christ will be his *greatest miracle*. "My word shall not pass away" (Matt. xxiv. 35).

"Therefore, my beloved brethen, be ye stedfast, unmovable, always abounding in the work of the Lord, forasmuch as ye know that your labour is not in vain in the Lord" (1 Cor. xv. 58).

10. And the devil, who deceiveth them, is cast into the lake of fire and brimstone, where are the wild beast and the false prophet; and they shall be tormented day and night, for ever and ever.

Deceiveth: the devil deceives infidels by the hope that they will destroy the Church, and be masters of the world. Their hopes end in remediless disappointment.

They: the wild beast, the false prophet, and the devil.

Day and night: incessantly.

For ever and ever: in the Greek, unto the eternities of the eternities; that is, eternally.

The devil has a *moral* nature. His nature is eternal. His moral and eternal nature is his eternal torment. The torment of the Devil is, in part, *self-accusation*. This is the torment of all *moral* beings in this world and in the world to which all souls are hastening.

Thus, with the exception of xxii. 6–20, ends the *second part* of the Apocalypse of St. John. With it also ends his symbolical exhibition of the probationary history of the Church of Christ and of the human race. Our Lord's own words form its most appropriate summary and final exhortation: "Enter ye in at the strait gate; for wide is the gate, and broad is the way, that leadeth to destruction, and many there be which go in thereat; because strait is the gate, and narrow is the way, which leadeth unto life, and few there be that find it" (Matt. vii. 13, 14). "It is finished" (John xix. 30). "The master of the house is risen up, and hath shut to the door" (Luke xiii. 25).

RETROSPECT.

We have now beheld the series of visions Jesus Christ showed unto his servant John, and through him also shows to every human being who will read the Book of Revelation.

These numerous visions display in prophetic symbols the history of the Church of Christ, from its beginning in Palestine, nineteen centuries since, to its end in the remote future.

Next to seeing objects with our natural eyes, symbolic vision is the most convincing form of proof in our possession. Vision brings its representations into the present moment, and causes them to appear as present realities.

It is a fact worthy of special notice, that the word *hope* has no place in the Apocalypse. There is no room for hope. Hope enters the future, and there finds the objects on which it rests. Vision has no future: it lives only in the present. As proof, vision does not depend upon reasonings and demonstrations and conclusions. Vision merely displays its object; and its exhibition is to the mind of the beholder a present reality, bringing with it its own truth, and impressing it indelibly upon his conviction and judgment. Vision is a kind of proof which can reach every human heart. All minds cannot weigh demonstrative evidence; but all eyes can see, and all hearts can believe, the visions they behold.

The visions of the Apocalypse show its design. Christ designs the book for all eyes and all hearts. When the book is more generally read, Christianity will be more generally believed and obeyed.

The Book of Revelation most clearly and most positively foretells and contemplates *the universal prevalence and dominion of the Gospel of Jesus Christ in this present world.*

Confirmations of the prophetic declarations of the Apocalypse abound, both in the book itself, and in the past history of the Christian Church, and in the present condition of the Church and the world.

I. The instrumentalities Christ himself provides, in the Book of Revelation, for the conversion of the whole world to himself, strongly confirm the symbolic predictions he there exhibits.

1. In the very first vision Christ grants us in the Apoca-

lypse, he manifests himself as "THE SON OF MAN" (Rev. i. 13).

As "the Son of man," Christ is *God incarnate.* He himself, though God, *partakes of our human nature.* In our nature, he now ever lives, and ever will live. Christ's incarnation creates in the human family universal brotherhood. Christ's incarnation is the pledge and the power insuring the realization both of the universal brotherhood of mankind, and of their universal restoration from the slavery of sin to the liberty of holiness.

2. In the Apocalypse, the Son of man "hath the seven Spirits of God" (iii. 1). By this possession and control, the Son of man provides for his own incessant presence in his Church and the world, and also for the renovating and transforming power of all the agencies he appoints for the instruction, improvement, and salvation of men, — his ministry, his Bible, his sacraments, his worship, his Church.

Both Christ incarnate and the Holy Spirit are omnipotent and omnipresent. Thus almighty and everywhere present, they are fully equal to the complete accomplishment of the superhuman work the Apocalyptic symbols so positively and so repeatedly predict, — the universal extension and sovereign rule in all lands of the gospel of the incarnate Son of the merciful Father of all human spirits.

II. The past history of the Church of Christ largely confirms the prophetic symbols of the Apocalypse, respecting the universal reign of his gospel.

In the centuries gone by, the gospel has not been a dead letter in the world. The gospel has abolished human slavery in all Christian countries. The gospel converted the Northern hordes which overturned the Roman Empire, from heathenism to Christianity, and out of this Christianized barbarism constructed Christian Europe.

The Christian civilization which now cheers and blesses all Christian lands is the work of the power of God in the Gospel of Jesus Christ.

Before the coming of Christ, women were, in all heathen communities, slaves. Of their present freedom, culture, and refinement, the gospel of Christ is the sole author.

These are some of the mighty achievements and blessings of the gospel during the period we so justly call *the Christian era*. The past insures the future.

III. The present spirit of the Church, and of the world, still more amply confirms the hopeful predictions of the Apocalypse respecting the future universality of the Gospel.

1. Never since apostolic days, has the Church of Christ been so extensively and powerfully pervaded and controlled by the *missionary spirit*, as at the present. This spirit of Christian benevolence and effort characterizes all names and bodies of Christians. If separated from each other on other grounds, they are all united as one man in the burning and impellent purpose of obeying Christ's undying command, "Preach the gospel to every creature."

Nor is the missionary spirit simply the common purpose of all Christ's people. All continents and islands are vocal witnesses to the most encouraging fact, that, " wherever the foot of man treads," Christian missions are *accomplished blessings*.

2. *Care for the poor*, to an extent before unknown in the history of the world, inspires and controls innumerable multitudes of Christian hearts. Wherever *care for the poor* is practical and efficient, it is the realization of Christ's universal brotherhood; and the old and desolating evils of ignorance, intemperance, licentiousness, brutality, starvation, misery, and premature death, depart like the possessing demons of old at the resistless command of Christ.

The gospel enjoins *the spirit of peace*. The observance of this injunction by modern nations has, without doubt, recently increased.

(*a*) The causes of national hostility have diminished. The neglect of legitimacy in the kingly succession is no longer the occasion of a declaration of war, and the invasion of the offending kingdom.

(*b*) In national differences, there is a growing disposition to settle the conflicts by arbitration.

Both the diminution of the occasions of war, and the preference of peaceful arbitration over resort to settlement by armies, are cheering indications that the gospel of peace is erecting not only an abiding throne in the palaces of kings, but also a permanent seat in all halls of legislation.

The past and present victories of the gospel of Christ are pledges and securities of its future triumphs. The gospel is a stream which acquires width and depth and strength, the farther it progresses. The power of the gospel will be vastly greater in the next generation than it is in the present. Its inherent force will constantly increase. Its human agents will be immeasurably multiplied. The inspiring breath of the Holy Spirit will be the new life of souls beyond all count. The Son of man, embraced because of his own surpassing love for his own brotherhood, will yet be welcomed, beloved, adored, and served by all hearts.

This remarkable structural peculiarity of the Apocalypse prefigures both the coming history of the gospel, and its final triumphant glory. As the visions of the book are multiplied, *their vividness becomes brighter and brighter*. This glowing splendor is the foreshow of the radiance from the rising sun, diffusing the full realization of the ecstatic bliss the gospel will confer when sin and misery will be on this happy earth only historical remembrances; and holiness, and the pure image of Christ, will be the possession and joy of all the Christian brethren and Christian sisters, redeemed and cleansed by his blood, and saved and prepared for his second advent by the grace and power of the Holy Ghost.

THIRD DIVISION (Chapters xx. 11–xxii. 1–5).

CHAPTER XX. (*continued*).

THE UNIVERSAL JUDGMENT AND ITS DECISIONS
(Verses 11–15).

11. And I saw a great white throne, and him who sitteth upon it; from whose presence the earth and the heavens flee away, and no place is found for them.

Great white throne: "I saw the Lord sitting upon a throne, high and lifted up" (Isa. vi. 1). The occupant of this throne is the Son of God (John xii. 41).

The occupant of the great white throne of final judgment is God the Son (Matt. xxv. 31–46; John v. 22).

In Isa. vi. 9, the Son of God on his throne sends forth the prophet Isaiah, one of the precursors of the gospel ministry.

From his great white throne (Rev. xx. 11), he summons all nations of men before him to account for the reception they have given this ministry.

The universal resurrection *precedes* the universal judgment (John v. 27–29).

This resurrection is *material*, because our Lord in the context (verses 25, 26) distinguishes it from the *spiritual* resurrection. Since the universal resurrection is, therefore, literal and visible, the universal judgment will also be literal and visible.

"Before him shall be gathered all nations" (Matt. xxv. 31, 32).

Great: compared with the "thrones" of the saints (Rev. xx. 4), and all other thrones.

White: with "throne" nowhere else in Bible Greek.

The garment of the enthroned Judge, "the Ancient of days," is white (Dan. vii. 9). White is the emblem of *purity;* "made their robes *white* in the blood of the Lamb" (Rev. vii. 14). Applied to a judgment-throne, white denotes *impartial and absolute justice.*

The earth and the heavens: the present earth and its present heaven, or atmosphere. "The heavens and the earth which are *now*" (2 Pet. iii. 7).

Place is not found for them: the present earth and its heaven totally disappear. They are to be entirely and forever destroyed. "The heavens and the earth, *which are now,* are reserved *unto fire. The heavens shall pass away*, and the elements shall melt with fervent heat; *the earth also shall be burned up*" (2 Pet. iii. 7, 10).

Since the present earth and its heaven are thus to be utterly destroyed, they are not to be renovated for the residence of Christ's people after the universal judgment.

The repeopling of the earth after Noah's flood does not foreshadow and predict any such renovation. The only *shadow* of this prediction is the misunderstanding of these words of St. Peter, "The world that then was, being overflowed with water, perished" (2 Pet. iii. 6).

"The world" in this verse 6 is *not* the material earth, but is "the world *of the ungodly*" (2 Pet. ii. 5).

This is St. Peter's own explanation. "God spared not *the old world*, bringing in the flood upon *the world of the ungodly*" (2 Pet. ii. 5).

According to St. Peter, therefore, "the old world" is not *the old earth*, but is solely "the world of *the ungodly.*"

As the world, in 2 Pet. ii. 5, is the world of the ungodly, so, in 2 Pet. iii. 6, the world is not the old earth, but is exclusively the world of ungodly men. When, then, in 2 Pet. iii. 6, St. Peter saith, "The world perished," he does not say *the earth perished*, but this is his *only* declaration: The world *of the ungodly* perished.

As the earth did not perish in the days of Noah, it was not *afterwards* renovated. By Noah's flood, the *material* world did not perish, only the *ungodly* world, the *ungodly* people, perished. Since the *material* world did not then perish, it was *not then renovated* to be the pledge and the model of its renovation and inhabitation at Christ's second coming.

12. And I saw the dead, great and small, standing before the throne; and books are opened: and another book is opened, which is the book of life: and from the records in the books, the dead are judged, according to their works.

The dead: are all men who have died. That the expression, "the dead," designates all who have died, is certain from the receptacles out of which these dead come. These receptacles are the "sea, death, and Hades" (verse 13). Each of these receptacles delivers all its contents. There are no reserves. But death and Hades hold *all* the dead. "Death passed upon *all* men" (Rom. v. 12).

St. John himself thus, by the receptacles of the dead, affirms that "the dead" include all men who have died.

All these dead are no longer dead. They are all alive. "Delivered up" by the sea and death and hades, they are all "risen from the dead" (1 Cor. xv. 20).

Risen from the dead, all are clothed with immortal bodies. "The dead shall be raised incorruptible" (1 Cor. xv. 52). Each "is raised a spiritual body" (verse 44).

Great and small: all ages of men, all mankind who reached the age of personal responsibility before they died.

Standing before the throne: standing for trial. "I stand at Cæsar's judgment-seat" (Acts xxv. 10).

This present earth and its heaven having disappeared, the place of Christ's great white throne and the standing-place of the risen dead may be the limitless space now enclosed by the earth in its annual circuit. Christ's omnipotence will provide a judgment-hall of sufficient amplitude.

Books are opened: containing accusations (Dan. vii. 10; Ps. lvi. 8; Isa. lxv. 6).

The symbolism of books represents, —

I. Conscience (Rom. ii. 15). The consciences even of the wicked will approve the decisions of Christ.

II. The moral law under which men were living, and still at the judgment-seat retained in their memories.

III. The omniscience of the Judge (John v. 45).

The book of life (Exod. xxxii. 32; Ps. lxix. 28; Dan. xii. 1; Mal. iii. 16; Phil. iv. 3; Rev. xiii. 8, xvii. 8, xxi. 27): symbolizes the omniscience and love of Christ (Matt. xxv. 33, 34).

In the books: in the several books.

According to their works: in this world (2 Cor. v. 10).

So impartial and just will Christ's final sentences be, that neither angel nor human soul will dissent either in word or in conviction.

Every mouth will be stopped (Rom. iii. 19).

Every heart will hide the bitterness it knoweth (Prov. xiv. 10).

13. And the sea gives up the dead that are in it; and death and Hades give up the dead that are in them; and they are judged, each one, according to their works.

The sea: designates all oceans and seas — all waters, as distinguished from the dry land.

The *material* sea is meant. In the Apocalypse, the word "sea" occurs twenty-four times. The "sea of *glass*" *three* times (iv. 6, xv. 2 twice) is figurative. In every other instance the sea is contrasted with the *material* earth, and is therefore itself *material*. Usage, not conjecture, decides the sense in which "sea" is to be understood in Rev. xx. 13.

Our Lord predicts the resurrection of all the dead buried *on the land*: "All that are in the graves [tombs] shall come forth" (John v. 28, 29).

This prediction St. John enlarges, by foretelling the resurrection of *all the drowned*. This class of the dead includes vast multitudes.

(*a*) The antediluvians who perished in Noah's flood.

(*b*) The Egyptians who were drowned in the Red Sea.

(*c*) The combatants who were killed in naval engagements.

(*d*) The mariners and travellers, who, during the many centuries of navigation, have disappeared in the ingulfing waves of the sea.

To our apprehension, the resurrection of the buried in the sea seems more difficult than the resurrection of the buried on the land. In our minds, the lost at sea have no locality: on the contrary, we know the very places where the precious dust of the sleepers in graves is awaiting its return to life.

Perhaps St. John addresses this apprehension of ours, when he assures us that even the sea, through the omnipotence of Christ, shall at the universal resurrection recall to life the unknown myriads now sleeping in the silent depths of all seas.

How the sea can surrender its dead, when, according to Rev. xx. 11, the earth, and with it the sea, has passed away, is not a real difficulty. Rev. xx. 11 describes the *consummation* of the last judgment; Rev. xx. 13 describes *the process* of the last judgment before its absolute completion.

Death: in the language of the Bible, death is a king (Rom. v. 14), "reigning from Adam to Moses," and from Moses to the end of the world, over the *bodily* life of every human being. From the dominion of this king, no one escapes: "It is appointed unto men to die" (Heb. ix. 27).

But Christ has conquered death (1 Cor. xv. 57). At the universal resurrection, Christ compels death to surrender *the bodies* of all men, on which Christ himself then confers animal life.

Hades: the invisible world; "the place of departed spirits" (Apostles' Creed, Book of Common Prayer). Hades thus holds at the present time *the souls* of all the disembodied children of Adam.

The duration of the disembodied state, though long, is temporary. Hades, when Christ comes to judgment, will deliver all souls into his hands. The re-union, through Christ's resistless power, of all the bodies and all the souls of mankind, will constitute the *universal resurrection*, the great preparation for the *universal and final judgment*.

Judged each one according to their works: *works*,—not thoughts, not feelings, not words, not profession, either merely or mainly; but *works*. Work is thought, feeling, speech, profession, *acted*. Action is consummation. Action includes all its predecessors. Action expresses character. Most justly do our works decide our eternal destiny. What depth of emphasis do these facts create in this exhortation of St. Paul, "Be careful to maintain good works" (Tit. iii. 8).

14. And death and Hades are cast into the lake of fire. This second death is the lake of fire.

Cast into the lake of fire: and there burned up; that is, death and Hades cease to exist. Men's bodies die no more. Men's souls are no more separated from their bodies. The place of departed spirits is annihilated.

This second death is the lake of fire: this second death *is caused* by the lake of fire. When the subject is *capable of cessation*, extinction follows immersion in the lake of fire. When the subject is inherently deathless, endless suffering follows.

The fact, though most appalling, is most undeniable. It is St. John's *divine* teaching, and so must be true and unalterable. "Whosoever was not found written in the book of life was cast into the lake of fire" (Rev. xx. 15).

Death and Hades are capable of cessation: every human soul is eternal. "These shall go away into *everlasting* punishment" (Matt. xxv. 46). The eternity of the punishment proves the eternity, in their nature, of the punished. Thus eternal in its own nature, every human soul is incapable of cessation. Whatever, then, is represented by the lake of fire, be it an accusing conscience, or infliction from God, or both, the misery of lost souls, as portrayed by St. John, is hopeless. "Who shall dwell with everlasting burnings?" (Isa. xxxiii. 14.) Who can consent to make himself incapable of regeneration, and to fit himself solely for the companionship of the devil and all unholy souls?

15. And if any one is not found written in the book of life, he is cast into the lake of fire.

Is not found: omission from the book of life involves not only the loss of heaven, but also the actual infliction of the second death (verse 14, note).

The non-appearance of one's name in the book of life must therefore be *his own fault and his own sin*. "I have no pleasure in the death of him that dieth, saith the Lord God; wherefore, turn yourselves, and live ye" (Ezek. xviii. 32), WHILE YE CAN.

Our Saviour gives the true reason of the sinner's spiritual death and endless misery: "*Ye will not* come unto me, that ye may have life" (John v. 40). "Who can understand his errors? Cleanse thou me from my *secret* faults" (Ps. xix. 12). "*Create in me a clean heart*, O God, and *renew a right spirit within me*" (Ps. li. 10).

CHAPTER XXI.

THE NEW JERUSALEM.

INTRODUCTION.

In attempting to understand St. John's description of the New Jerusalem, two rules are essential: —

1. Rejection of all astronomical facts disclosed to us by modern science.
2. Adoption of St. John's imagery derived from the Old Testament.

I. St. John knew nothing of the actual connection between the earth and the sun and moon. He did not know that the earth revolves about the sun, and the moon about the earth. With him the earth was not essentially dependent upon the sun and moon. He could, therefore, construct a world without either sun or moon.

He knew nothing of the origin of rain by the process of evaporation of water from the ocean; nothing of the formation of clouds, and the precipitation of their contents to the earth. He could, in consequence, make an earth without an ocean, and without a concave atmosphere.

St. John's ignorance in these respects we must constantly recognize, in our attempts to understand him when drawing pictures of the New Jerusalem.

II. In constructing the New Jerusalem, St. John would, as a Jew, familiar and filled with the ideas of the Old Testament, freely employ its peculiar imagery.

The Old Testament exhibits the heavenly state of God's people in two forms, — *a country* and *a city*.

1. The picture of heaven as *a country* is derived from the earthly Canaan.

Instances of this representation we find both in the Old and New Testaments.

Among these instances, the following are most instructive: —

(*a*) " Thine eye shall behold *the land that is very far off* " (Isa. xxxiii. 17).

" I believed to see the goodness of the Lord *in the land of life* " (Ps. xxvii. 13).

Also Ps. cxvi. 9, cxlii. 5.

(*b*) This very imagery our Lord uses in one of his beatitudes : —

" Blessed are the meek, for they shall inherit *the land* [of life] " (Matt. v. 5).

2. The picture of heaven as *a city* is derived from Jerusalem on Mount Zion.

St. Paul declares the city Jerusalem to have both a literal and a spiritual signification : —

(*a*) " Jerusalem *which now is* " (Gal. iv. 25).

(*b*) " Jerusalem *which is above* " (verse 26).

" Ye are come unto *Mount Zion*, and unto *the city* of the living God, *the heavenly Jerusalem* " (Heb. xii. 22).

" Abraham looked for *the city* having *the foundations* " (xi. 10).

With these Bible representations of heaven, both as *a country* and as *a city*, in his mind, St. John, when in Rev. xxi. 1 he sees " a new heaven and a new earth," the future residence of the risen and glorified saints, describes the new world both as *a country* and as *a city*.

At first sight, the new heaven and the new earth appear to be *a city*. But when we learn the symbolic dimensions of the " New Jerusalem," and recall the vast size of the typical Jerusalem of the prophet Ezekiel (xlviii. 30–35), a model which St. John himself follows (chapters xxi., xxii., of his Apocalypse), we perceive that the city of Jerusalem is, in its enlarged extent, *a country.* As a city, the New Jerusalem fills the *entire land* of the heavenly Canaan. Country and city are, in their dimensions, *but one and the same.*

The fact of local identity will help explain portions of St. John's language in his delineations of the New Jerusalem, "the new heaven and the new earth."

REPETITIONS IN CHAPTERS XXI. AND XXII.

In all the preceding sections of the Apocalypse, *recapitulation* is an obvious and instructive characteristic of the book. The same peculiarity pervades the last two chapters. The design of the repetitions is *impressiveness and certainty* (Gen. xli. 32).

There are two exhibitions and descriptions of "the New Jerusalem."

The *first* exhibition and description occupy xxi. 2-7.

The *second* exhibition and description occupy xxi. 9-xxii. 15.

The *second* portion contains repetitions and amplifications of the first portion.

1. The city itself; xxi. 2 is amplified by xxi. 9-xxii. 5.

2. Its blessings; xxi. 3, 4, 5, are amplified by xxi. 22-26, xxii. 2-5.

3. Its citizens; xxi. 6, 7, are amplified by xxi. 24, 27, last clause, and xxii. 3-5, 7, 11, 14.

4. Its outcasts; xxi. 8 is amplified by xxi. 27 and xxii. 11, 15.

5. Its security, namely, Christ's eternity; xxi. 6 is amplified by xxii. 13, "the Beginning and the End."

---

1. And I saw a new heaven and a new earth; for the first heaven and the first earth are passed away. And so there is no more sea.

A new heaven and a new earth: in the Bible, "heaven and earth" sometimes mean *this material world.*

"*Thy heaven* that is *over thy head,* and the earth that is *under thee*" (Deut. xxviii. 23).

"*Heaven and earth* shall pass away" (Matt. xxiv. 35).

"*The world* passeth away" (1 John ii. 17).

When, therefore, St. John sees a new heaven and a new earth, he sees *a new world.* The heaven and earth St. John sees are "new," because they *differ* from the old heaven and earth. The old heaven and earth were *material.* The new heaven and the new earth are, consequently, *immaterial and spiritual.*

Are passed away: the departure and destruction of the old material earth and its heaven (its atmosphere) make necessary the creation and appearance of a spiritual world for the residence of the saints with spiritual bodies.

The new world is not the old world *spiritualized,* but is *a different and better creation* than the old world of matter.

No more sea: for the omission of the sea in the new world, there is this obvious reason: a material sea cannot exist in a spiritual world. The absence of the sea proves, therefore, the spirituality of the new world. A world without an ocean, and consequently without evaporation, without rain, rivers, vegetation, and animal life, must be spiritual.

2. **Even the holy city, the New Jerusalem, I saw coming down out of heaven from God, prepared as a bride adorned for her husband.**

The holy city, the New Jerusalem, is identical with the new heaven and the new earth. The new heaven and the new earth is the new world for the residence of the saints; and this new world is the New Jerusalem, the holy city.

Coming down: the descent of the New Jerusalem cannot be *to this present earth.* In St. John's vision, this present earth, "the first earth," *has forever passed away* (verse 1).

In Rev. iii. 12, the New Jerusalem is described as the city "which *is coming down* out of heaven." According to this description, in *the present* tense, this city is *incessantly coming down.* This *incessant descent* of the New Jerusalem is its great characteristic, pertaining to it continually and perpetually.

The descents, then, which St. John sees (Rev. xxi. 2, 10) are by no means *the first descents* of the holy city of God.

The *first* descent (Rev. iii. 12) is a symbol of *the divine origin of the Church.*

The other recorded descents (Rev. xxi. 2, 10) are also symbols of *the same kind of origin.*

That descent denotes *divine original,* this following narrative proves:—

Peter saw "*heaven opened,* and a certain vessel *descending* unto him" (Acts x. 11).

"I saw a certain vessel *descend,* let down *from heaven*" (Acts xi. 5).

The great truth of the divine origin of the Church, thus symbolized, is also expressed in these plain words of the enthroned Alpha and Omega: "Behold, *new* am I making all things" (Rev. xxi. 5, 6).

The *descent,* therefore, of the New Jerusalem does not teach that its *location* will be on this earth. This earth is to be *utterly* destroyed (verse 1, note).

The descent of the New Jerusalem is the creation of the new heaven and the new earth, the new world, for the eternal home of the risen and glorified people of God.

Prepared: not the city, but its inhabitants. This is Bible usage. "When he was come into *Jerusalem, all the city* was moved" (Matt. xxi. 10).

As a bride: xix. 7.

Adorned: the bride's adornment, the Bible thus specifies: (*a*) attire (Jer. ii. 32), "fine linen" (Rev. xix. 8); (*b*) jewels (Isa. lxi. 10; Rev. xxi. 19).

THE TABERNACLE OF GOD (Verses 3-8).

3. And I heard a great voice from the throne, saying, Behold the tabernacle of God with men, and he shall dwell with them, and they themselves shall be his people, and he himself, God with them, shall be their God.

From the throne: from the enthroned King (xix. 5).

The tabernacle of God with men: "tabernacle" in Revelation only here and xiii. 6, xv. 5. See Lev. xxvi. 11, 12, from which the language of this verse is derived.

By the *shechinah,* God dwelt in the tabernacle in the wilderness. The prophet Ezekiel repeats this language (xxxvii. 27).

Men: as a class of beings (Jas. iii. 9).

Seventeenth Triplet.

(*a*) Dwell with them, (*b*) his people, (*c*) their God.

1. **Dwell**: in New Testament, only John i. 14; Rev. vii. 15, xii. 12 xiii. 6, xxi. 3; implies recognition and love on the part of God.

2. **People**: Greek, peoples. The Church includes "all sorts and conditions of men" (Ps. cxvii. 1; Rom. xv. 11).
God with them: "Immanuel, God with us" (Matt. i. 23).
3. **Their God**: his presence with his glorified saints completely fulfils these ancient promises of God's continual presence with his people, and watchful care over them (Exod. xxix. 45; Lev. xxvi. 11, 12; Ezek. xxxvii. 27).

4. And God shall wipe away every tear from their eyes; and there shall be no more death, nor sorrow, nor crying, nor pain; for the first things are passed away.

Wipe away every tear: repeated from Isa. xxv. 8.
Death: xx. 14, first clause.
Nor, etc.: negative specifications of the causes and accompaniments of death.
First things: sin, death, and their consequences (Matt. xii. 45; 2 Pet. ii. 20).

5. And he that sitteth on the throne saith, Behold, I am making all things new. Also he saith to me, Write: for these words are faithful and true.

Sitteth: God the Son. "The Alpha and Omega" (verse 6, i. 8, xx. 11; Matt. xxv. 31).
New: different.
Write: my words just spoken.
Faithful and true: most certainly am I making a new and better world, with new and better relations and conditions.

6. Also he saith to me, They are done. I myself am the Alpha and the Omega, the beginning and the end. I myself to him that is athirst will give of the fountain of the water of life freely.

They are done: my words (verse 5) are fulfilled, accomplished, done.
Alpha, etc.: I am the same in my nature always. I cannot change. Having promised, I shall perform.
Give: to drink, "give to eat" (ii. 7).
Fountain: vii. 17; John iv. 10, vii. 38; Ps. xxxvi. 9; Isa. lv. 1; Jer. ii. 13, xvii. 13.
Freely: gratuitously. In Revelation, only here and xxii. 17. No payment is required. "*By grace* are ye saved" (Eph. ii. 8).

7. He that overcometh shall possess these things. And I will be his God, and he shall be my son.

Possess: have and enjoy (1 Kings xxi. 16).
These things: these blessings.
I will be, etc.: 2 Sam. vii. 14. The promise of God to Christ, the seed of David. This promise Christ extends to every Christian conqueror.
His God: to keep, and bless him.
My son: to love and serve me.
The reciprocal affection of an earthly father and son is the reference and illustration here used.

THE SUBJECTS OF THE SECOND DEATH.

8. But the fearful, and unbelieving, and abominable, and murderers, and adulterers, and sorcerers, and idolaters, and all liars, shall have their part in the lake burning with fire and brimstone: which is the second death.

But: creates contrast between "God's people" (verse 3) and the subjects of the second death, who refuse to take Christ as their king.

Eight Classes.

1. **The fearful**: the cowardly, in contrast with the courage of the conqueror (verse 7), who "stands" firmly (Eph. vi. 13); who "fights" (1 Tim. vi. 12); who "earnestly contends" (Jude 3).
"Fearful:" the Greek word in the New Testament only here and Matt. viii. 26; Mark iv. 40. The fearful lack faith in God (Mark iv. 40), and are afraid of other men (Prov. xxix. 25; Heb. xiii. 6).

2. **The unbelieving**: only here in Revelation, in contrast with "faithful unto death" (ii. 10).

3. **The abominable**: in the New Testament only here and Rom. ii. 22. Abhorred by God; abominable, because "working abomination" (Rev. xxi. 27); "abominations and filthiness" (xvii. 4); the impurities and cruelties of idol-worship (1 Kings xi. 5; 2 Kings xvi. 3); the worshippers of the dragon and the wild beast (Rev. xiii. 4), in contrast with the worshippers of God and the Lamb (v. 14).

4. **The murderers**: both (*a*) actual, a numerous class in every period of the world; and (*b*) in the sense given by our Lord (Matt. v. 22), murderers in disposition and purpose. In contrast with the followers of this exhortation of St. John, "Let us love one another" (1 John iv. 7), and in contrast with all Good Samaritans.

5. **The adulterers**: the transgressors of the seventh commandment of the Decalogue, in its letter (1 Cor. vi. 18) and in its spirit

(Matt. v. 28). In contrast with the observers of "all purity" (1 Tim. v. 2), and with "the pure in heart" (Matt. v. 8).

6. **The sorcerers** (see xviii. 23, note): in contrast with the obedient to these rules: "Believe in God" (John xiv. 1), and "In all thy ways acknowledge him" (Prov. iii. 6).

7. **The idolaters**: the worshippers of material idols (Hos. viii. 4), and of any object whatever, more than God (Matt. vi. 24). In contrast with God's true worshippers (John iv. 23).

8. **The liars**: false swearers, liars, and deceivers; the opposite of him "that speaketh the truth in his heart" (Ps. xv. 2). "Create in me a clean heart, O God; and renew a right spirit within me" (Ps. li. 10).

Christ's Own Amplified Description of the Broad and the Narrow Ways.

Rev. xxi. verses 6, 7, 8, are Christ's *own words*.

I. *They are his amplified description of the broad way* (Matt. vii. 13).

Every human soul has, by his creation in the image of God, *moral light*; "the light that is in thee" (Matt. vi. 23).

From this natural possession the broad way has these eight descending steps just described; each in succession a more aggravated refusal to obey the moral light, with which Christ endows every human being.

1. Cowardice.
2. Unbelief.
3. Acceptance of false religion.
4. Indulgence of malignant passions.
5. Indulgence of animal appetites.
5. Superstition.
7. Mental blindness; inability to distinguish between spiritual and material objects (Isa. xliv. 9–20).
8. Moral blindness. Unable to discern between truth and falsehood, the lost soul cannot speak the truth; having become, in his incessant degradation, a helpless liar.

The lost soul is, in these eight processes, the author of his own ruin.

II. *Christ's Amplified Description of the Narrow Way* (Matt. vii. 14).

1. Courage to follow moral light.
2. Belief of divine revelation.
3. Rejection of religious errors.
4. Restraint of malignant passions.
5. Government of the animal appetites.
6. Recognition of God's providences.

7. Mental illumination by the study of the Holy Scriptures (2 Pet. iii. 18).

8. Moral illumination by the Holy Spirit (Prov. iv. 18; John vii. 17, xvi. 13; 1 John ii. 20).

The Broad Way leads to the "without" (Rev. xxii. 15).

The narrow way leads the soul to Christ and to the New Jerusalem.

A MORE DISTINCT VISION AND DEFINITE DESCRIPTION OF THE NEW JERUSALEM (xxi. 9–xxii. 5).

9. And there comes one of the seven angels, who have the seven censers, which are full of the seven last plagues; and he talks with me, saying, Come hither, and I will show thee the bride, the Lamb's wife.

Show: In xvii. 1, the angel shows the *apostate* Church. Here the angel shows, in contrast, the *faithful* Church. We may regard these showing angels as different persons.

Bride: see verse 2.

Wife: see xix. 7. The betrothed virgin was called wife (Matt. i. 20; Deut. xx. 7).

The Church of Christ is, in this world, only the betrothed wife. In the New Jerusalem, the Church will be the married wife.

10. And he carries me away by the Spirit, and sets me on a great and high mountain, and shows me the holy city Jerusalem descending out of heaven from God.

The Spirit: the Holy Spirit, who places St. John's mind in a state of trance (i. 10, note).

Mountain: elevation secures extensive views. From the top of Pisgah, Moses views the land of Canaan (Deut. iii. 27, xxxiv. 1–4); God sets the prophet Ezekiel "upon a very high mountain," to show him the prophetic temple, city and country (xl. 2, etc.); our Lord taketh Peter, James, and John into a high mountain, when he shows them the vision of his transfiguration (Matt. xvii. 1, 2; Mark ix. 2). The angel, carrying St. John to a high mountain to show him the New Jerusalem, follows these examples.

11. Having the glory of God. The light from it is like the most precious stone, as the crystal jasper-stone.

Glory of God: *the shechinah*, the glorious presence of God himself (verse 23, xv. 8). "The glory of the Lord filled the tabernacle"

(Exod. xl. 34). "The cloud, the glory of the Lord, filled the house of the Lord" (1 Kings viii. 10, 11).

The light from it: the glory shining from it. The light coming from the *shechinah* becomes the light-giver, the illuminator, the luminary. In the New Testament, the Greek word is only here and Phil. ii. 15. In the Septuagint (Gen. i. 14, 16; Wis. xiii. 2) the Greek noun is the name of the sun and moon.

The crystal jasper-stone: the ice-clear jasper; of clear white color, the emblem of purity and holiness.

12. Having a wall great and high, with twelve gateways, and at the gateways twelve angels, and on the gateways names written, which are the names of the twelve tribes of the children of Israel.

Having: the city having (verse 10).
Wall: the old Jerusalem had a wall (2 Kings xviii. 26; Neh. iv. 6).
Great and high: strong and lofty, for security.
Twelve gateways: three gateways on each side-wall (verse 13).
Twelve angels: cherubim guarded the Garden of Eden. To this fact there may be here allusion. If so, the twelve angels may here be cherubim. "The angel of the Lord encampeth about them that fear him" (Ps. xxxiv. 7).

Angels are needed at the gateways to enforce the prohibition (verse 27).

Written: engraven.
Twelve tribes: represent the whole Church of God, Christian as well as Jewish (Matt. xix. 28).

13. At the east, three gateways; and at the north, three gateways; and at the south, three gateways; and at the west, three gateways.

These constructions are derived from the encampment of the Israelites in the wilderness. "On the east side toward the rising of the sun, Judah, Issachar, Zebulon. On the south side, Reuben, Simeon, Gad. On the west side, Ephraim, Manasseh, Benjamin. On the north side, Dan, Asher, Naphtali" (Num. ii. 3, 5, 7, 10, 12, 14, 18, 20, 22, 25, 27, 29.

I. The order here follows the course of the sun, — east, south, west, north.

II. Ezekiel gives a different order and a different classification: *north*, Reuben, Judah, Levi; *east*, Joseph, Benjamin, Dan; *south*,

Simeon, Issachar, Benjamin; *west*, Gad, Asher, Naphtali (xlviii. 31–34).

III. St. John's order differs from each of the other orders: East, north, south, west.

The changes by Ezekiel and St. John may be to denote the *unearthly* nature of the cities and of their citizens.

14. And he shows me the wall of the city having twelve foundation-stones, and upon them are the twelve names of the apostles of the Lamb.

The strength and stability of the wall depend upon the strength and stability of the foundation-stones (Matt. vii. 24–27).

Foundation-stones: between the twelve gateways. Each foundation-stone must be of great length and size (1 Kings v. 17; Ezra vi. 3). At Baalbek there are now foundation-stones sixty feet long, seventeen feet broad, fourteen feet thick.

Upon them: upon the foundation-stones. The names of all the apostles are upon *each* foundation-stone. "The *foundation* [not foundations] of the apostles" (Eph. ii. 20). All the apostles are here *equal* in position and authority. This heavenly symbolism is an exact copy of the apostleship existing in the Christian Church when St. John wrote the Apocalypse. On the foundation-stones of the New Jerusalem, the *perfect equality* of the apostles in their office is engraven *twelve* times (there is ample spare room), that it might never be changed in the Church on earth. There is no supremacy of the Pope in the Church triumphant. The time will come when there will be no supremacy of the Pope in the Church militant.

St. John sees his own name engraven *twelve* times on the foundation-stones of the Church in glory. The sight may have inspired him to write afterwards, "We *know*, that when Christ shall appear, *we shall be like him*" (1 John iii. 2).

The Number Twelve in Verses 12, 13, 14.

Twelve (*a*) gateways, (*b*) angels, (*c*) tribes, (*d*) foundation-stones, (*e*) apostles.

1. The twelve tribes (verse 12) are the *representatives* of all the members of God's Church, Jews and Christians (Matt. xix. 28). Twelve is therefore here a *definite* number for an *indefinite*. The twelve tribes in Rev. xxi. 12 represent "*all* the tribes of the earth" (Matt. xxiv. 30).

2, The twelve apostles (verse 14). There were more than twelve apostles of the Lamb: Paul was an apostle (Rom. i. 1); Barnabas was an apostle (Acts xiv. 14). Since there were more apostles than twelve, the number twelve in Rev. xxi. 14 is *representative*, and consequently is a *definite* number for an *indefinite*.

3. The character of the number twelve, when defining tribes and apostles, determines its character when defining gateways, angels, and foundation-stones. In each of these instances, twelve is a *definite* number for an *indefinite*. The holy city has more than twelve gateways; more than twelve angels stand at these numerous gateways. The foundation-stones are not merely twelve, but are many.

These facts respecting the numbers in Rev. xxi. 12, 13, 14, will greatly assist us when we meet with other numbers in this third part of the Apocalypse.

THE MEASUREMENT OF THE HOLY CITY (Verses 15-17).

15. And the angel talking with me was holding a measure, a golden reed, that he might measure the city, and its gateways, and its wall.

A measure: why this measurement?
1. To give to St. John, and through him to others, an exact and impressive description of the holy city.

Ezekiel witnessed a similar measurement, the design of which was *definite impression and distinct narration* (xl. 2-5).

"The man said unto me, *Behold with thine eyes, and set thy heart upon all that I shall show thee; declare all that thou seest to the house of Israel*" (verse 4).

2. To denote the perpetuity of the city (Zech. ii. 1-5).

"Measure Jerusalem. For I, saith the Lord, will be unto her a wall of fire round about" (verse 5).

16. And the city lieth foursquare, and its length is as great as the breadth; and he measures the city with the reed twelve thousand furlongs. Its length and breadth, even on its top, are equal.

Four-square: the Greek word means four *equal* corners. The four corners are all *right* angles; not *acute*, not *obtuse*, not *curvilinear*. This is the explanation of Ezekiel: "The altar twelve cubits long, twelve broad, *square* in the four squares [parts; Greek, "sides"] thereof" (xliii. 16).

Twelve thousand furlongs: fifteen hundred miles. Each side of the city measured three hundred and seventy-five miles. These numbers are definite for indefinite. This city is too large for this present earth. Its vastness indicates its unearthly nature.

Its length and breadth, even on its top, are equal: this translation can be fully justified by Bible usage.

1. A city with a wall three hundred and seventy-five miles high cannot be symbolized by any earthly city; but all Bible symbolism is derived from some earthly reality. No such earthly reality of a city ever existed. A symbolical city with its height as great as its length and breadth is an impossibility and an absurdity. We are not obliged to suppose any such monstrous and impossible symbolism. "Height" is here capable of a consistent explanation, and of a practicable sense.

2. Height, in the Greek word it here represents, sometimes means *top*, the *top-surface* of the wall.

"He walked *upon the top* [Greek, *epi kupsos*] of the earth." Literal translation of Ecclus. xlvi. 9.

3. A wall was measured *on its top*.

"The Lord stood *upon a wall* with *a plumb-line* in his hand" (Amos vii. 7).

"The man *went up the stairs and measured*; he measured *from the roof* of one chamber *to the roof* of another" (Ezek. xl. 6, 13).

That is, on each flat roof he measured the tops of the walls of the several chambers.

4. With the words "length," "breadth," "top," the word "measure" is implied. "With what *measure* ye measure" (Matt. vii. 2). "He measured the wall, *a hundred forty-four cubits*, the *measure* of a man" (Rev. xxi. 17).

Usage, therefore, warrants this translation of Rev. xxi. 16, last clause: "The measures of the length and of the breadth, even on the top, are equal."

In its own series, the Greek conjunction *kai*, represented by *and*, is often in its last mention explanatory; namely, *even*.

5. The explanation given above of the word "height" is not only warranted by Bible usage, but is demanded by verse 17, which gives the height of the walls of the city as *two hundred and sixteen feet* instead of *three hundred and seventy-five miles.*

In *literal* measures, the holy city is 140,625 square miles. This extent exceeds in size all New England and the States of New York and New Jersey. The measures of the holy city cannot, then, be taken *literally*.

In *indefinite* measures, the measures St. John intends us to take, the bounds of the holy city are limitless, its extent inconceivable, the designation of its locality impossible. The holy city cannot be built on this earth. The holy city can be constructed only in the boundless heavens.

The Height of the Wall.

17. And he measures its wall, one hundred and forty-four cubits; man's measure, that is, of the angel.

One hundred and forty-four cubits: 216 feet, 72 yards. A wall 216 feet high would require proportionate thickness; perhaps 30 feet.

In Rev. vii. 4, and xiv. 1, the definite number one hundred and forty-four is used for an indefinite. Indefiniteness is also the character of a hundred and forty-four in Rev. xxi. 17. The height of the wall is indefinitely lofty.

Man's measure: the angel used the common human measure. In our explanations of the passage, we must measure by his standard.

THE MATERIAL OF THE HOLY CITY (Verses 18-21).

18. And the building of the wall is jasper; and the city is pure gold, like clear glass.

The building: the structure.
Jasper: the material of the wall, its body compacted.
The city: in its area of streets (verse 21).
Pure gold: gold translucent (verse 21).
Clear: as water, translucent.

19. And the foundations of the wall of the city are adorned with every kind of precious stone; the first foundation, jasper; the second, sapphire; the third, chalcedony; the fourth, emerald.

The wall of the city is itself jasper. The foundations (material, not mentioned because covered and invisible by the ornamentation) of the wall are ornamented by twelve kinds of precious stones.

King Solomon ornamented "with precious stones" the temple he built in Jerusalem (2 Chron. iii. 6; 1 Chron. xxix. 2). These precious stones were ornaments on the surface of the foundation-stones.

"I will lay thy stones *with fair colors*, and lay thy *foundations* with *sapphires*" (Isa. liv. 11).

This form of ornamentation explains St. John's description of the structure of the holy city.[1]

The Twelve Precious Stones.

1. **Jasper:** crystal hue.
2. **Sapphire:** blue.

---

[1] *Dict. Bible*, iv. p. 484; *Dict. Gr. and Rom. Antiq.*, p. 771, a ¶2.

3. **Chalcedony.**
4. **Emerald:** green.

20. The fifth, sardonyx; the sixth, sardine; the seventh, chrysolite; the eighth, beryl; the ninth, topaz; the tenth, chrysoprase; the eleventh, jacinth; the twelfth, amethyst.

5. **Sardonyx:** pale rose and white.
6. **Sardine:** red.
7. **Chrysolite:** goldstone, chrysolith, chrysolite, pale green.
8. **Beryl:** sea-green.
9. **Topaz:** yellowish tint.
10. **Chrysoprase:** gold-leek, greenish golden color.
11. **Jacinth:** dark blue.
12. **Amethyst:** violet.

The great variety of the contrasted colors increases the beauty and splendor of the appearance.

THE GATEWAYS OF THE HOLY CITY.

21. And the twelve gateways are twelve pearls. Separately each one of the gateways is of one single pearl. And the broad street of the city is pure gold, as brightly translucent glass.

The gateways: the two doors of each gateway. Each door is a single pearl.

The broad street: in the city of *Shushan*, there was an avenue, bearing this pre-eminent name, the broad street of the city (Esth. vi. 9).

Other ancient cities had similar avenues.

In the city of Damascus, "the street called Straight" (Acts ix. 11) was *one hundred feet wide* (*Dict. Bible*, art. "Streets").

Pure gold: paved with pure gold. The streets of ancient cities were sometimes paved. Herod the Great paved one of the streets of Jerusalem.

With Tobit, a costly pavement is essential to the perfection of his ideal Jerusalem.

"The streets of Jerusalem shall be paved with beryl and carbuncle and stones of Ophir" (xiii. 17).

Brightly translucent: while permitting the light to pass through it, the translucent gold radiates the light, causing it to shoot forth rays. The Greek embodies all this meaning.

THE TEMPLE OF THE HOLY CITY.

22. And yet I did not see a temple in the city; for the Lord God Almighty, even the Lamb, is its temple.

In the Greek, holy of holies, a part of the temple, is used for the whole.

Is its temple: the Lord God Almighty, even the Lamb, is worshipped *without a temple.*

Heaven realized and spiritual, and the worshippers themselves, spirits in spiritual bodies, cannot admit a temple, either symbolical or material.

THE LIGHT OF THE HOLY CITY.

23. Also the city hath no need of the sun, nor of the moon to shine in it; for the glory of God doth lighten it, and the Lamb is its light.

The sun: Isa. lx. 19.
Light: John viii. 12; Isa. lx. 20; Mark ix. 3.

"*Sun of my soul,* thou Saviour dear." — JOHN KEBLE.

THE CITIZENS OF THE HOLY CITY.

24. And the nations shall walk by means of its light, and the kings of the earth are bringing their glory into it.

This is the fulfilment of Isaiah's prophecy, "The Gentiles shall come to thy light, and kings to the brightness of thy rising" (lx. 3).

Nations: "all nations shall serve him" (Ps. lxxii. 11).

Walk: shall live and have their happiness in the light of the city, even in the Lamb. They enter into his joy (Matt. xxv. 21).

Kings: the kings in the holy city were once "of the earth" earthy, and sinful. They are so no longer. They are not only "brought" themselves (Isa. lx. 11), but they are bringing into the city their own subjects, and are thus becoming "nursing fathers" (xlix. 23).

It is quite possible that "their glory" may mean *their subjects.*

"He delivered *his strength* [his strong men] *into captivity,* and *his glory* [his glorious victors] into *the enemy's hand.* He gave *his people* over unto the sword, and was wroth with *his inheritance*" (Ps. lxxviii. 61, 62).

Here "strength, glory, people, inheritance," are all identical. A king's "people" are his *subjects.* It is thus possible for "glory" (Rev. xxi. 24) to mean *subjects.* It is St. John's practice to use words in *figurative* senses. If "glory" (Rev. xxi. 24) may mean subjects, the passage accords with this prophecy of Isaiah, "Kings shall be thy nursing fathers" (xlix. 23).

THE SECURITY OF THE HOLY CITY.

25. And its gateways are not shut at all by day; for no night shall be there.

By day: as there is no night in heaven, "by day" is the only time the gateways can be shut. But as there are no enemies to enter the city, it is secure with open gateways. Since the day is perpetual, the gateways are never shut. They are perpetually open. They are perpetually secure.

"Thy gates shall be open continually; they shall not be shut day nor night" (Isa. lx. 11).

No night: the presence of the Lamb creates perpetual day.

The glorified saints are never weary. They do not need the rest of night.

There is here no reference to our present earth. It exists no longer. Its diurnal revolutions have forever ceased.

THE RICHES OF THE HOLY CITY.

26. And they shall bring the glory and the honor of the nations into it.

They shall bring: men shall bring.

The glory and the honor: as this verse repeats Isa. lx. 11, "men may bring unto thee the *wealth* of the Gentiles," glory and honor may signify wealth. Thus the glory and the honor may be the wealth the nations possess.

But material wealth cannot have place in the New Jerusalem.

Apart from figures, St. John declares that the regenerated nations brought into the holy city will increase its spiritual riches. Souls saved and glorified are Christ's most precious treasures.

With this verse 26 ends St. John's description of the holy city. The description begins with verse 11, and consists of these *seven* specifications, thus rendering the description *complete*, namely: —

1. Shechinah (verse 11).
2. Wall (verses 12–21, 25).
3. Street (verse 21).
4. Temple (verse 22).
5. Light (verse 23).
6. Citizens (verse 24).
7. Wealth. Human souls saved and glorified (verse 26).

EXCLUSIONS.

27. And in no wise shall enter into it any unholy person, and any one practising abomination and falsehood.

Eighteenth Triplet.

(*a*) defileth, (*b*) abomination, (*c*) lie.

1. First exclusion. Every unclean thing. Every thing unholy (Acts x. 14, xi. 8). The neuter for comprehensiveness. Every unholy person.

2. Second exclusion. Any one working abomination; that is, practising idolatrous abominations (see verse 8).

3. Third exclusion. Any one practising falsehood. Every one that "maketh a lie" (xxii. 15).

Written: approved by Christ. "Well done" (Matt. xxv. 21; Rev. xx. 15). Approval follows the record. "Thy people shall be delivered, every one that shall be found written in the Book" (Dan. xii. 1).

Modern astronomers, finding the sun unlike any earthly substance, do not venture even a sketch of this self-evolving and self-involving luminary.

Since the centre of our material system cannot be described, much less can the present abode of the Sun of righteousness, and the future home of his glorified saints. No human mind can add any thing to the vision St. John had of the New Jerusalem.

"Imagination's utmost stretch
In wonder dies away!"
MRS. ANNE STEELE.

CHAPTER XXII.

DESCRIPTION OF THE HOLY CITY (*Continued*).

THE RIVER OF LIFE.

1. Also he shows me a river of water of life, bright as crystal, proceeding out of the throne of God, even the Lamb.

River: this river mentioned in Revelation, only verses 1 and 2; Gen. ii. 10; Jer. ii. 13; Ezek. xlvii. 1–5; John iv. 6, 14; Rev. vii. 17, xxi. 6.

The river symbolizes the spiritual life of which Christ is the Author, and which he continually imparts to his people (John xiv. 19; 1 Cor. x. 4).

Bright: verse 16.
Proceeding: Ezek. xlvii. 1–5.
Throne: symbol of God himself (Matt. xxiii. 22).
Even: Granville Sharp's rule (Ayre, Introduct., pp. 216, 217).

THE TREE OF LIFE.

2. Between the broad street of the city and the river is the tree of life, on each side of the river, bearing twelve kinds of fruit, yielding its fruit each month: even the leaves of the tree are for the health of the nations.

Between: in the space between.
The tree of life: as a class of trees. There are many separate trees of this class on each side of the river of life (Gen. ii. 9; Rev. ii. 7). The tree *giving* life (Gen. iii. 22).

Water and fruit were the means God provided for preserving the lives of Adam and Eve in the Garden of Eden (Gen. ii. 10, 16). Their appetites of thirst and hunger were thus satisfied.

Of these animal appetites our Lord makes a spiritual application. "Blessed are they which do hunger and thirst after righteousness, for they shall be filled" (Matt. v. 6). St. John, in Rev. xxii. 2, employs the same imagery to indicate the perfect provision God prepares for the spiritual wants of the citizens of the New Jerusalem.

On each side of the river: "at the bank of the river were very many trees on the one side and on the other" (Ezek. xlvii. 7).

Bearing twelve kinds of fruit: "all trees shall bring forth new fruit" (Ezek. xlvii. 12).

Each month yielding its fruit: the productiveness is unearthly. "Solomon had twelve officers over all Israel, which provided victuals for the king and his household: each man *his month* in a year made provision" (1 Kings iv. 7).

The victuals thus furnished at short and regular intervals would be abundant. There would be no deficiency.

The spiritual provisions in the Holy City are, through Christ's life, constant and most ample.

The Numeral Twelve.

In this verse 2, the numeral "twelve" occurs the *seventh* time in St. John's description of the New Jerusalem. In his employment of numbers, chance is not the guide. System and intention are apparent everywhere.

There is significance in each of the numbers twelve and seven.

The number twelve has an instructive history, from which we can gather its significance when used by St. John.

1. "The sons of Jacob were twelve" (Gen. xxxv. 22).

2. "All these [twelve] are [represent] the twelve tribes of Israel" (xlix. 28).

The twelve sons of Jacob, thus representing the twelve tribes of Israel, represent the Church of God as it was then constituted; as Israel is the true Church of God (Gal. vi. 16).

3. "Moses built twelve pillars, *according to the twelve tribes of Israel*" (Exod. xxiv. 4). Because there were twelve tribes, Moses made twelve pillars: the number of the tribes determined the number of the pillars. The fact is instructive and explanatory.

4. Aaron bore on his breastplate, and "on his heart," the twelve names of the tribes of Israel, "for a memorial" of God's love of his Church (Exod. xxviii. 12, 30).

5. There were twelve loaves of shewbread; symbols of spiritual blessings in Christ (Lev. xxiv. 5).

6. There were twelve princes of Israel (Num. i. 44).

7. The animals and the utensils connected with the service of the tabernacle of the Israelites were twelve in number (Num. vii. 84–87).

8. Aaron's rod was one of twelve rods (xvii. 6).

9. Twelve spies visited Canaan (Deut. i. 23). Each tribe was thus represented.

10. At the crossing of the Jordan, the twelve memorial stones were placed by twelve men (Josh. iv. 2-8). Another instance of tribal representation.

Other instances follow: —

11. The molten sea stood on twelve oxen (1 Kings vii. 25).

12. Twelve lions skirted Solomon's throne (x. 20).

13. Twelve stones were in Elijah's altar, "according to *the number of the tribes* of the sons of Jacob, unto whom the word of the Lord came, saying, Israel [prevailer with God] shall be thy name" (xviii. 31; Gen. xxxii. 28).

14. Our Lord makes the twelve tribes of Israel representatives of his own Church (Matt. xix. 28).

This Bible history of the number twelve discloses its significance in its sevenfold application by St. John to the New Jerusalem. The name "twelve" designates in every instance the holy city *as the beloved Church of Christ.*

The number *seven* indicates fulness, completeness. When used symbolically, as it is here by St. John, it is another form of St. Paul's declaration, "The love of Christ *passeth knowledge*" (Eph. iii. 19).

Other indications of Christ's love cluster around St. John's exhibition of the golden city.

1. All its surpassing excellences are marks of Christ's surpassing love.

2. Its inconceivable costliness is perhaps the most impressive emblem of Christ's inconceivable love. His love for us cost him his life, — his priceless blood.

Visible to the eye of faith is this inscription on every portion of the Jerusalem above: "Eye hath not seen, nor ear heard, neither have entered into the heart of man, the things which God hath prepared for them that love him" (1 Cor. ii. 9).

The leaves of the tree are for the health of the nations: this imagery, like much of the preceding, is from the prophet Ezekiel. "The fruit of the tree shall be for food, and the leaf of the tree for medicine" (xlvii. 12).

As the occupants of the New Jerusalem cannot need food, so they cannot need medicine. This language must therefore have a spiritual explanation.

Nowhere in the Bible are the leaves of fruit-trees said to be medicinal. To suppose them medicinal, as is the case with Ezekiel and St. John, is to suppose them possessed of extraordinary power. This exceptional possession by leaves we can express by saying, *even* the leaves are for medicine. This may be the sense intended by both

Ezekiel and St. John. If so, then we may understand them as speaking *figuratively*, and as declaring this fact respecting the garniture of the heavenly city. Every thing, however insignificant in itself and usually worthless, even a leaf, shall contribute something to the comfort and bliss of Christ's beloved people who "walk the golden streets" (Rev. xxi. 21; ISAAC WATTS, *Hymnal*, 462).

PERFECTION OF THE HOLY CITY (Verses 3-5).

3. And no longer shall there be any accursed person; and so the throne of God, even of the Lamb, shall be in the city, and his servants shall serve him.

Accursed person: this is the meaning of the Greek noun. "I could wish that I myself were *accursed*" (Rom. ix. 3). "Calleth Jesus *accursed*" (1 Cor. xii. 3). "Let him be *accursed*" (Gal. i. 8).

A "curse" coming from God is, in Greek, a different word from that translated "accursed." "Under the *curse*" (Gal. iii. 10). "Redeemed us from the *curse*" (13).

No accursed person: the underwritten prophecy may have suggested the expression, "There shall be no more *the Canaanite* in the house of the Lord of hosts" (Zech. xiv. 21). Canaan was cursed (Gen. ix. 25), and so was an *accursed person*.

Achan, who coveted and took for his own, portions of the spoils of the city of Jericho when captured by Joshua, defines the kind of accursed person who is no longer in the holy city (Josh. vii. 1-25).

The sinful dispositions Achan exhibits are, (*a*) *covetousness*, "I coveted the goodly Babylonish garment, and two hundred shekels of silver, and a wedge of gold of fifty shekels" (verse 21); (*b*) *selfishness*, "I took them and hid them in the earth, in the midst of my tent;" and (*c*) *disregard* of the welfare of the whole body of the Israelites, and of the lives of his own sons and daughters (verses 15, 24).

Achan is a primary Judas, and the representative of this class of selfish people described by our Lord, who always seek their own advantage, and care not for others. "I was an hungred, and ye gave me no meat; I was thirsty, and ye gave me no drink; I was a stranger, and ye took me not in; naked, and ye clothed me not; sick, and in prison, and ye visited me not" (Matt. xxv. 42, 43).

When, therefore, St. John writes, "There is no longer any accursed person in the holy city," his record embodies a twofold declaration.

1. Negative. No Achan, no Judas, no Demas, who loves this present world (2 Tim. iv. 10), "no covetous man who is an idolater," (Eph. v. 5), no person living solely to himself, no soul not loving

others as he loves himself, and loving Christ more than he loves any other being, "hath any inheritance in the kingdom of Christ" (Eph. v. 5).

2. Positive. St. John's negative sentence here emphasizes its opposite.

The citizens of the New Jerusalem not only bear Christ's test when he judges them in the last day, but they forever possess and cherish the loving dispositions by which he then tries and approves them (Matt. xxv. 35, 36). They love Christ supremely; and, because they thus love him, they "love one another with a pure heart fervently" (1 Pet. i. 22).

St. John's negative sentence in Rev. xxii. 3 is the completion of his portraiture of the perfection "of the saints in light." Their highest perfection is not external glory, but is their love for Christ and their mutual love fully consummated.

This consummation is the principal design and work of the gospel of Christ from its foundation to its top-stone. Its proposed transformation of human hearts into living temples of love incarnates the Word of God, brings the Holy Spirit from heaven, prepares there new mansions of bliss, inspires new alleluias, fills the new world with glorified spirits innumerable, all perfect in love for each other because all are perfect in Christ who is himself "LOVE" (1 John iv. 16).

St. John's outline of the perfection of the New Jerusalem most instructively and impressively illustrates St. Paul's "excellent way" to its full possession. "Now abideth faith, hope, charity, these three, but the greatest of these is *charity*" (1 Cor. xiii. 13).

It is up this great ladder of St. Paul's that ascending angels carry the spirits of the just to the wall of the holy city; but it is only their own "charity" that opens the gates of pearl, admits the glorified to the golden streets, and thus consummates the perfection of the saints, bearing the image and possessing the holiness of Jesus. *The loving brotherhood of mankind, the great object of the incarnation of the Son of God, is realized.*

The throne: not of judgment (xx. 11), but of mercy (Heb. iv. 16).
Shall serve him: in adoration, love, and praise (vii. 15, 10).
They serve Christ "with a perfect heart, and with a willing mind" (1 Chron. xxviii. 9).

4. *And they shall see his face, and his name shall be on their foreheads.*

See his face: "stand continually before him" (1 Kings x. 8); shall be in his presence, and enjoy his favor.

On their foreheads: God marks them his own servants and friends, and cheers them with his exhaustless love.

5. And no night shall be there; and so they need no light of a lamp, nor the light of the sun; for the Lord gives them light; and they shall reign for ever and ever.

No night: see xxi. 23.
Lamp: xxi. 23.
Sun: Isa. lx. 19.
Shall reign: shall be kings. The saints have two reigns:—
1. On earth (Eph. ii. 6; Rev. v. 10, xx. 4, 6).
2. In the New Jerusalem, for ever and ever (Rev. xxii. 5).

RESUMPTION OF THE SECOND DIVISION (Verses 6-21).

The second division of the Apocalypse, chapters iv.-xx. 1-10, contains the symbolical history of the Church of Christ *in this world*, the long and unknown period between his two advents, — his incarnation, and his second coming to raise all the dead and to judge all mankind.

The third division, xx. 11-xxii. 1-5, describes the universal resurrection and judgment, and the opposite places to which he assigns the righteous and the wicked.

At chapter xxii., verse 6 to the end of the book, there is *a resumption of the second division*, with this most important subject closely connected with the universal judgment at his second advent: *the present judgments of Christ in this world.*

In the second division itself, the symbolical Judge is *God the Father.* In the resumption of the second division, Christ himself. enthroned with his Father (iii. 22), is the present Judge of mankind; continually and incessantly judging all nations and all individuals, and determining their relations to him, and their different conditions, according to their moral characters and their actual lives.

The *present judgment* of Christ is thus described by himself: —

"The Father *judgeth* no man, but hath committed all judgment unto the Son. The Father gives the Son authority to execute judgment, because he is the Son of man. My judgment *is* just" (John v. 22, 27, 30).

"I have many things *to judge of you*" (viii. 26).

"He that rejecteth me, and receiveth not my words, *hath* one that *judgeth* him; *the word* that *I speak*, that shall judge him in the last day" (xii. 48).

Christ's final judgment will confirm his present judgment. "For *judgment* I am come into this world, that *they which see not might see*, and that *they which see might be made blind*" (ix. 39).

"*Now* is the judgment of this world" (xii. 31).

In the very first chapter of the Apocalypse, Christ appears as Judge, moving for the administration of his judgments in the midst of the seven churches.

Whenever he appears afterwards in the book, he is the same kind of judge, ever present with his Church, and ever present in the world, to reward the righteous, and to punish the wicked.

Thus Christ himself is the author of the startling truths, that he himself is the PRESENT JUDGE of the hearts of all men, and that the guide to his perpetual decisions is the relation they themselves create between his Spirit and their own souls.

THE TRUTHFULNESS OF THE BOOK.

6. Also he saith to me, These words are faithful and true: and the Lord God of the spirits of the prophets sent his angel to show to his servants the events which must quickly be accomplished.

The speaker is the angel mentioned in i. 1, xxi. 9.

These words: the entire Book of the Apocalypse: "the words of the prophecy of this book" (xxii. 18).

Faithful and true: iii. 14, xix. 11, xxi. 5.

The spirits: Num. xvi. 22, xxvii. 16.

The prophets: of the New Testament, Rev. x. 7, xxii. 9.

The God who made the spirits of the prophets, and revealed to the spirits of the prophets the truths they declared to his Church.

His angel: i. 1, xxi. 9.

His servants: on earth, i. 1.
Must: by God's determination (Acts xv. 18).
Quickly: as soon as the events are predicted, they begin to be accomplished.

7. Behold, I come quickly. Blessed is he that keepeth the words of the prophecy of this book.

I come: I am coming already.
Quickly: without delay. Christ here speaks in place of his angel.
Keepeth: observes and obeys, i. 3, note.
Prophecy: the *prophetic* character of the Apocalypse is here re-asserted.
(Elsewhere, i. 3, xxii. 10, 18, 19.)

ATTEMPTED IDOLATRY OF ST. JOHN.

8. And I John myself am the hearer and eye-witness of the prophetic visions. And when I heard and saw, I fell down to worship before the feet of the angel who is showing me these things.

I John myself, etc.: a strong affirmation of the truth of the Apocalyptic prophecies.
Fell down: xix. 10. The appearance of the angel must have been most majestic and glorious, to cause St. John to repeat his attempt to worship a created being. Christ, although present to inspire and guide the angel, is himself invisible.

ANGEL-WORSHIP FORBIDDEN.

9. And he saith to me, Take heed, do it not. I am thy fellow-servant and of thy brethren the prophets, and of them that keep the words of this book.

While the angel *refuses* worship, Christ *accepts* it (xxi. 22). Both here and xix. 10, the language equalizes the prophetic office. The angel is the *fellow*-servant of St. John and of his brethren the New-Testament prophets, and so not their official superior.

The scene of St. John's attempted worship of the angel is repeated from xix. 10. By this repetition, the prohibition of all angel-worship is also repeated, and thus most strongly emphasized, and made absolutely and forever obligatory.

THE PROPHECIES OF THE APOCALYPSE TO BE PUBLISHED.

10. And he saith to me, Seal not the words of the prophecy of this book; for the time is near.

Seal not: that is, publish widely. To seal is not to publish. Not to seal is, therefore, to publish. The emphatic negative, Seal not; for the positive, Publish widely.

The time: when the prophecy will begin to be fulfilled, is approaching.

The command of Christ, enjoining the unlimited publication of the Apocalypse, enjoins at the same time the universal reading, study, adoption, use, and acceptance of the book, as divine and authoritative.

MORAL LIBERTY PERMITTED.

11. Let the wrong-doer be doing wrong still; let the filthy man make himself filthy still; let the righteous man be doing righteousness still; let the holy man make himself holy still.

The prescience of God does not change the free-will of mankind. The prophecies of the Apocalypse do not diminish human liberty. The wicked can still be wicked. The righteous must still practise righteousness, in order to perfect holiness and secure the possession of heaven.

The two clauses of verse 11 form an emphatic parallelism.

In the first and third sentences, the "*doing*" is *to others*. In the second and fourth sentences, the action of each man *upon himself* is described. Our translation of the clauses of this verse is fully justified by Bible usage.

CHRIST THE IMPARTIAL JUDGE.

12. Behold, I come quickly; and my reward is with me, to repay every man as his work is.

I come quickly: to fulfil the preceding prophecies I have published, by symbols and by word of mouth. Christ is at the present time judging both the righteous and wicked, by his providences, and by his spiritual influences on their hearts. Christ is not merely the *future* Judge of the world: from his ascension to this very hour, he has been its Judge, and will be its Judge until his second advent. By his judgments in this world, Christ is always shaping and forming the eventful and momentous history of the human race.

My reward is with me: the reward Christ repays all men without exception is twofold.

ST. JOHN THE DIVINE. 383

(a) The "righteous man's reward." Matt. x. 41.
(b) "The reward of iniquity." Acts i. 18 ; 2 Pet. ii. 13.
Repay: in kind; good for good; evil for evil; every man as his work is.
(a) When it is righteous. Ps. xviii. 25; Rom. ii. 7.
(b) When it is evil. Ps. xviii. 6; Rom. ii. 8, 9.

THE ETERNITY OF CHRIST ENABLES HIM TO REWARD AND PUNISH.

13. I myself am the Alpha and Omega, the first and the last, the beginning and the end.

Nineteenth Triplet.

(a) Alpha, etc.; (b) first, etc.; (c) beginning, etc.

His eternity is complete and absolute. Nothing before Me, nothing after Me: "Jesus Christ, the same yesterday, and to-day, and forever" (Heb. xiii. 8); unchangeable in his nature, and at all times, past, present, and future, administering impartial justice to all mankind, both as nations and as individuals.

Alpha: i. 8, xxi. 6.
First: i. 11.
Beginning: xxi. 6.

NATURE OF HIS REWARDS AND PUNISHMENTS (Verses 14, 15).

Rewards.

14. Blessed are they who wash their robes; for their authority shall be over the tree of life, and by the gateways may they enter into the city.

Twentieth Triplet.

Three forms of blessedness: (a) washing, (b) tree of life, (c) entrance into the holy city.

1. **Wash their robes**: the Greek verb translated "wash" is remarkable for the instruction it embodies. It implies *the personal activity* of the agent. He washes *himself*. The fountain in which to wash is the blood of Christ (vii. 14).

Washing the robes includes, therefore, (a) trust in the efficacy of Christ's blood for pardon (Eph. i. 7), and (b) personal activity and diligence in saving one's own soul (Phil. ii. 12).

2. **Tree of life**: Rev. ii. 7, xxii. 2.
The blessing the tree of life symbolizes is in this world, as well as

in the holy city (1 Cor. x. 4; John vi. 35; 1 Cor. x. 16), *Christ's life in our souls.*

3. There is a gate and pathway in this life, which, when entered and followed, not only leads to the holy city, but is a present reward in the moral strength and inward peace which self-denial, self-government, and obedience to Christ always confer (Prov. iii. 17; Rom. xv. 13).

The Place and Subjects of Christ's Punishments.

15. Without are the dogs, and the sorcerers, and the fornicators, and the murderers, and the idolaters, and every one loving and making a lie.

Without: is the place where Christ inflicts his punishments. Without, as often represented in the New Testament, is a place of misery, and this for several distressing reasons.

1. It is a place of *privation.*

It is outside of the Church of Christ (1 Cor. v. 12). Thus separated from the Church, the outside place is deprived of all the blessings the Church possesses; the Bible, the ministry, the sacraments, the example and help of Christian people, the presence of Christ, and the influences of the Holy Spirit.

Every human soul deprived of these Church blessings is miserable. He cannot be happy, and his self-imposed misery is his unceasing punishment.

2. Outside the Church of Christ is also a place of *bad and most hurtful influences.* It is the abiding place of the seven spiritual monsters enumerated by St. John in this verse 15, whose society is the transforming mould of all wickedness, and whose consuming influence is kindled by the fires of hell.

3. Union in the society of these spiritual monsters, and subjection to their burning influence, is to be *one of their number, to be one of them,* both in spirit and character, and, therefore, is participation in their own inherent and growing fourfold wretchedness; namely, —

(*a*) The possession of malignant passions: they "hate one another" (Tit. iii. 3).

(*b*) "Hateful" in themselves, they hate themselves, and often through self-disgust commit suicide.

(*c*) Their sense of loss distresses them; the loss of opportunities, the loss of holiness, the loss of the fellowship of the good, the loss of the approval and the presence of Christ.

(*d*) Their heaviest misery and their severest punishment are the reproaches of an accusing conscience, which because within them, and inconsumable, is more tormenting than a lake of fire.

It is both painful and disgusting to notice the revelations of criminal courts, and to read the confessions of murderers and suicides. But there is an instructive reason why we should observe these revelations, and peruse these confessions. They are exhibitions of the methods Christ now employs to punish the wicked by allowing them to make themselves self-destructionists, self-accusers, and self-murderers. These exhibitions cannot indeed benefit the dead, but they warn the living. Even a bird shuns a net (Prov. i. 17). The instinct of a bird ought not to be stronger than reason and conscience and the fear of God, on the part of human souls.

There are in this verse *seven* classes of outcasts from the true Church in this world, and from the holy city in heaven. By this sevenfold classification, St. John indicates that the enumeration is complete. All classes of outcasts are included in it.

1. **The dogs**, etc.: the dogs, etc., previously mentioned (chapter xxi.). The dogs. The impure (Deut. xxiii. 17, 18).

2. **The sorcerers** (xxi. 8).

3. **The fornicators** (xxi. 8).

4. **The murderers** (xxi. 8), including *self*-murderers, Saul (1 Sam. xxxi. 4), Judas (Matt. xxvii. 5).

5. **The idolaters** (xxi. 8).

6. The lover of lies.

7. The maker of lies.

The worst class of outcasts are liars.

Also mentioned last (xxi. 27), because they constitute the worst and most hopeless class.

JESUS THE AUTHOR OF THE APOCALYPSE, AND THE KING OF ALL WORLDS.

16. I Jesus sent my angel to testify to you these revelations concerning the churches. I myself am the root, even the offspring of David, the bright morning star.

Twenty-first Triplet.

(*a*) root, (*b*) offspring, (*c*) star.

You: St. John and his readers.

1. **The root:** "a root out of the stem of Jesse" (Isa. xi. 1); "a root of Jesse" (verse 10). The root of David is, therefore, a shoot from the root of David.

2. **The offspring of David:** since David's offspring, Christ is *King* (Luke i. 32).

3. **Star:** ii. 28. A star is the symbol of royalty (Num. xxiv. 17; Isa. xiv. 12).

The morning star is the brightest of all stars, consequently "the bright morning star" designates Christ as *Universal King*.

"King of kings, and Lord of lords" (Rev. xix. 16).

"*All* power is given unto me, *in heaven and in earth*" (Matt. xxviii. 18).

THE GOSPEL INVITATIONS, CONDITIONS, AND DUTIES.

17. And the Spirit and the bride say, Come. And let him that heareth say, Come. And let him that is athirst come. And whosoever will, let him take the water of life freely.

Twenty-second Triplet.

Three invitations: come, come, come.

1. The Spirit invites, namely, the Holy Spirit. Everywhere in the New Testament, *the* Spirit is the Holy Spirit, unless *the context* forbids, as in 2 Cor. iii. 17.

2. The bride, the Church (Rev. xxi. 2, 9, 10; Eph. v. 23, 32), invites.

3. The hearer of the Gospel himself invites. Every one who hears the Gospel is thus *by Christ himself* made a herald and a teacher of his "unsearchable riches" (Eph. iii. 8).

Twenty-third Triplet.

Three conditions.

1. *Desire* to have the gospel is the first condition. Every human soul *thirsting* for the water of life may come and drink.

2. *Determination* to come and drink is the second condition. "Whosoever *will*, let him take the water of life." Simple desire is not sufficient to bring to us the water of life. *The will must resolve* to take and drink, and this continually, daily, hourly, every moment.

3. The *freeness* of the gospel is the third condition. This most precious gift of God cannot be bought with money (Acts viii. 20). Neither works nor merits can obtain the gift of salvation. "According to *his mercy*, God saves us" (Tit. iii. 5).

Twenty-fourth Triplet.

Three duties. Each duty is *to come to Christ*. When we habitually come to him, our duty is *completely* done. Three is a full number, and here denotes *duty completed*.

This verse 17 is Christ's *message of love* to every human soul. In its *love* this message repeats the loving declaration with which Christ ends his messages to the seven churches. "Behold, I stand at the door, and knock: if *any man hear my voice, and open the door*, I will come in to him, and will sup with him, and *he with me*" (iii. 20).

Here his message of love *precedes* his warnings. Even when threatening, Christ is still our *loving* Saviour.

ADDITIONS AND REMOVALS FORBIDDEN (Verses 18, 19).

Additions.

18. I, even myself, testify to every man who heareth the words of the prophecy of this book: If any man shall add unto them, God shall add unto him the plagues which are written in this book.

God shall add: Deut. vii. 15.

The additions forbidden are unwritten traditions, apocryphal books, erroneous comments intentionally made.

Removals.

19. And if any man shall take away the words of the book of this prophecy, God shall take his part from the tree of life and out of the holy city, which are described in this book.

Take away the words: this removal can be done in two ways:—

(*a*) Omissions from the sacred text itself.

(*b*) Intentional changes and perversions of the grammatical sense.

His part: every human being has *potentially* and *conditionally* a part in the tree of life and in the holy city as they exist, both in this world and in the new world Christ is now creating for his people.

Described: the tree of life and the holy city are minutely and most attractively portrayed. Every man may therefore see the nature and extent of the forfeiture he hazards in case he attempts to alter and misrepresent the precious contents of the Apocalypse.

FINAL ATTESTATION OF THE TRUTH OF THIS PROPHETICAL BOOK.

20. The Testifier saith, Yea, I come quickly. Amen. Come, Lord Jesus.

The Testifier: is the Lord Jesus. "I testify" (verse 18). "Come, Lord Jesus" (last clause of verse 20).

Saith yea: the Greek *nai*, translated "yea" by the English Version (Rev. xiv. 13), confirms *previous words* (i. 7, xiv. 13, xvi. 7), and therefore also xxii. 20, as these four places are the only places in the Apocalypse where *nai* occurs. In sense, "yea" here equals the assertion: This book is most true.

I come: I am coming to execute judgment *in this world.* This is the meaning of "I come" (verse 12), where Christ immediately adds, "my reward *is* with me, to give every man according as his work *is.*" "In righteousness he *doth judge*" (xix. 11).

"All power is given me *in earth*" (Matt. xxviii. 18). "*I am with you alway, even unto the end of the world*" (verse 20).

Amen: St. John's assent to the Lord's declaration, "I come quickly."

Come: in the same sense as "I come," in the preceding clause. St. John thus prays with the Psalmist, "Arise, thou Judge of the world, and reward the proud after their deserving" (Ps. xciv. 2). "Save thy people, and bless thine inheritance" (Ps. xxviii. 9).

Lord Jesus: nowhere else does St. John use this expression. As "Lord," he is able to judge and save. As "the *man* Jesus" (1 Tim. ii. 5), he loves his people, and will love them "unto the end"(John xiii. 1).

THE BENEDICTION.

21. The grace of the Lord Jesus be with the saints.

The whole book is for the saints. Its final benediction ever accompanies them. "Grace to help in time of need" (Heb. iv. 16); grace to bear their trials ; grace to love each other, and all mankind ; grace to love, serve, and please Christ.

"Thou art the King of glory, O Christ. We believe that thou shalt come to be our Judge. We therefore pray thee, help thy servants whom thou hast redeemed with thy precious blood. Make them to be *numbered with thy saints in glory everlasting.*" AMEN.

www.ingramcontent.com/pod-product-compliance
Lightning Source LLC
Chambersburg PA
CBHW030425300426
44112CB00009B/860